GOVERNING LAW RISKS IN INTERNATIONAL BUSINESS TRANSACTIONS

GOVERNING LAW RISKS IN INTERNATIONAL BUSINESS TRANSACTIONS

PHILIP R. WOOD CBE, KC HON

OXFORD
UNIVERSITY PRESS

Great Clarendon Street, Oxford, OX2 6DP,
United Kingdom

Oxford University Press is a department of the University of Oxford.
It furthers the University's objective of excellence in research, scholarship,
and education by publishing worldwide. Oxford is a registered trade mark of
Oxford University Press in the UK and in certain other countries

© Oxford University Press 2022

The moral rights of the author have been asserted

First Edition published in 2022

Impression: 1

All rights reserved. No part of this publication may be reproduced, stored in
a retrieval system, or transmitted, in any form or by any means, without the
prior permission in writing of Oxford University Press, or as expressly permitted
by law, by licence or under terms agreed with the appropriate reprographics
rights organization. Enquiries concerning reproduction outside the scope of the
above should be sent to the Rights Department, Oxford University Press, at the
address above

You must not circulate this work in any other form
and you must impose this same condition on any acquirer

Public sector information reproduced under Open Government Licence v3.0
(http://www.nationalarchives.gov.uk/doc/open-government-licence/open-government-licence.htm)

Published in the United States of America by Oxford University Press
198 Madison Avenue, New York, NY 10016, United States of America

British Library Cataloguing in Publication Data
Data available

Library of Congress Control Number: 2022946089

ISBN 978–0–19–288864–8

DOI: 10.1093/law/9780192888648.001.0001

Printed and bound in the UK by
TJ Books Limited

Links to third party websites are provided by Oxford in good faith and
for information only. Oxford disclaims any responsibility for the materials
contained in any third party website referenced in this work.

For my wife Marie-Elisabeth

CONTENTS–SUMMARY

Preface	xxiii
Acknowledgements	xxv
The Author	xxvii
List of Abbreviations	xxix
1. What this book is about	1
2. Role of law	16
3. Scope of contracts	33
4. Governing law and choice of courts	58
5. Predictability	74
6. Insulation of contract from foreign laws	97
7. Business orientation	109
8. Freedom of contract	119
9. Exclusion clauses	135
10. Insolvency law indicators and risks	156
11. Insolvency set-off	174
12. Security interests	188
13. Commercial trusts	207
14. Corporate law indicators and risks	220
15. Regulatory law indicators and risks	244
16. Courts, litigation, and arbitration	251
17. Non-legal indicators and risks	262
18. Comparison of jurisdictions of the world	268
19. Protecting a governing law	294
20. History and the future	299
21. Conclusion	306
Sources and References	309
Index	317

CONTENTS

Preface — xxiii
Acknowledgements — xxv
The Author — xxvii
List of Abbreviations — xxix

1. WHAT THIS BOOK IS ABOUT — 1
    Introduction — 1
        In one sentence — 1
        Ubiquity of governing law — 1
        Freedom of choice of contract law and courts — 1
        Jurisdictions of the world — 2
        Risks of governing law and courts — 2
        English and New York law — 3
    Families of Law — 3
        Summaries of families of law — 3
        Jurisdictions specially covered — 5
    Methodology and Scope — 5
        Key indicators — 5
        Number of key indicators — 6
        Internationally mobile transactions — 6
        Business transactions — 7
        Morality and justice of legal policies — 8
        Focus on contracts — 8
        Amounts involved — 9
        Assumptions as to the drafting of documents — 10
        Citation — 10
    Summary of Main Governing Law Risks — 11
        Outline of main areas of risk — 11
        Mnemonic of the main issues — 12
        What is being measured overall? — 12
        Narrowing of scope of governing law — 13
    Summary of Conclusions — 13
        The 1357 ranking — 13
    Conclusion — 14

2. ROLE OF LAW — 16
    Law as Ideology and Moral Code — 16
        Law as ideology — 16
        Societies without law — 16
        Moral basis of law — 17
        Law as a utility — 18
        Law as a means of survival — 18

The role of law and governing law	19
Limits on the role of law	20
Law and religion	21
Economic Value of Law	21
Economic value of a governing law	21
Methods of valuation	22
The costs of law	23
Governing Law as a Monopoly	23
Dominant governing laws as conferring hard and soft power	23
Fulfilment of vital need	24
Advantages of dominant position to users	25
Multiplier effects	25
Abuse of a dominant position?	26
Competitor imitation	26
Importance of protection of value	27
Economic value of physical clustering	27
Hard power—the US dollar	27
Hard power—English law	28
Soft power and hard economic value	28
Impact of the Growth of Law	29
Background to the growth of law since 1830	29
Reasons for growth of law	30
The law and money, banks, and corporations	31
Conclusion	32
3. SCOPE OF CONTRACTS	33
Contracts Based on Assets	33
Grouping of contracts	33
Asset-related contracts	33
Classes of asset	34
Intangible assets	34
Goods	35
Land	35
Financial, Corporate, and Commercial Transactions	36
Functional division of contracts into classes	36
Financial transactions generally	36
Loan transactions	37
Guarantees	38
Restructuring agreements	38
Title finance	38
Derivatives	39
Securitisations and other receivables transfers	40
Foreign exchange contracts	41
Exchanges and central counterparties	41
Funds	43
Other financial contracts	43
Significant corporate transactions generally	44
Sale of corporate shares	44
Raising of equity capital	45

Sale or merger of a business	45
Joint venture agreements	46
Typical commercial agreements	46
Real property agreements	47
Comparison of General Risk Characteristics of Contracts	47
Risk factors	47
Banks and bondholders versus corporate management	47
Interdependence of banks/bondholders and corporations	48
Lenders versus shareholders	49
Other financial contracts	49
Commercial transactions	49
Significance of chains of contracts for predictability	50
Interdependence of contracts	51
Multiple mutual contracts	51
Standard forms	52
Transfers of Property on Sale	52
Contract and property	52
The doctrine of false wealth	53
Meaning of the best public title	53
Best public title for receivables	54
Objections to the doctrine of false wealth	54
Comparative survey of false wealth for sales	54
Priorities; security interests	55
Conclusion on false wealth	55
Digital Contracts; Green Transactions	56
Cryptocurrencies, decentralised finance, and smart contracts	56
Green transactions	56
4. GOVERNING LAW AND CHOICE OF COURTS	**58**
Introduction	58
Purpose of this chapter	58
Principles well-established internationally	58
Governing Law of Contracts	58
Free choice of governing law	58
Governing law in the absence of express choice	59
Matters decided by the governing law	60
Matters Not Decided by the Governing Law	60
Narrowing of scope of governing law	60
Criminal law	60
Corporate law	61
Court procedure	61
Consumer law	61
International conventions	62
Contract law	62
Transfers of property	62
Regulatory law	62
Insolvency law	63
Tort law	63
Mnemonic for overriding laws	63
Choice of law clause	64

Governing Law of Non-contractual Claims	64
Less freedom than contracts	64
Examples of non-contractual liabilities	64
Codes on governing law of non-contractual liabilities	65
Free choice of governing law	65
Scope of the governing law	66
Choice of Courts	66
Factors influencing choice of courts	66
Jurisdiction clauses	67
Summary of long-arm jurisdiction	68
EU Judgments Regulation 2012	70
Jurisdiction over torts	70
Hague Convention on Choice of Court Agreements 2005	71
Arbitration	72
Insolvency override of jurisdiction and arbitration clauses	72
5. PREDICTABILITY	**74**
Purpose of Predictability and Summary	74
Predictability as a legal value	74
Summary of key indicators	75
Codification and Binding Judicial Precedent	76
Codification	76
Doctrine of judicial precedent	77
Stability of the law	78
Doctrine of Good Faith in Contract	78
Good faith doctrine generally	78
Good faith generally in England	79
Good faith generally in France	79
Examples of good faith laws	79
Good faith generally in the United States	81
English right to choose good faith voluntarily	82
Universal basic contract standards	82
Contract Terminations	83
Typical termination clauses	83
Symbolic case of *The Laconia*	84
Policies of upholding immediate termination clauses	84
Other English examples of terminations	85
Terminations under French law	87
French legal interventionism elsewhere	88
Terminations under German law	89
Termination clauses on insolvency	89
Mandates and Heads of Terms	89
Market practice	89
International summary	90
Pre-contract Disclosure	92
Background	92
English law on pre-contract disclosure	93
French law on pre-contract disclosure	93
Pre-contract disclosure elsewhere	93

Other Good Faith Situations	94
Consents and discretions	94
Agreements to negotiate in good faith	94
Duties to cooperate	94
Hardship clauses	95
Other cases	96

6. INSULATION OF CONTRACT FROM FOREIGN LAWS 97

Summary	97
Unilateral changes of contract	97
Article VIII 2b of the IMF agreement	97
Insulation as a key indicator	98
Background history of destabilising laws	98
Latin American republics in the 1970s	98
Greek bankruptcy in 2012	99
Insulation by External Governing Law	99
Insulation under English law	99
Insulation under US law	101
Stabilisation clauses	103
Article VIII 2b of the IMF Agreement	103
Text of article VIII 2b	103
Subsequent exchange controls	103
'Exchange contracts'	104
Exchange control regulations	105
Conclusion on article VIII 2b	106
Other Aspects of Insulation	106
No external assets; local insolvency proceedings	106
Illegality at place of performance	107
English protection of contracts on insolvency	108

7. BUSINESS ORIENTATION 109

Introduction	109
Promoting economic development	109
Measurement of business orientation	110
Historical examples of business orientation	110
Compulsory Notice of the Assignment of Receivables	111
Reasons for notice of assignment	111
International position on compulsory notice of debt assignments	112
Criticism of compulsory notice of debt assignments	113
Conflict of laws on compulsory notice of debt assignments	114
Deprivation of the Assets of a Bankrupt Corporation	115
Joint ventures	115
'Flip clauses' as a deprivation	116
Turnover subordinations	117
Post-commencement proceeds of security	117
Other Indicators of Business Orientation	118

8. FREEDOM OF CONTRACT 119

Freedom as a Value	119
Freedom generally	119

xiv CONTENTS

A theory of law based on liberty versus restriction	119
Freedom to choose predictability without court intervention	120
Key indicators of freedom of contract	120
Free Choice of Governing Law and Courts	121
Free choice of governing law	121
Non-symmetrical jurisdiction clauses	123
Conclusion on governing law and choice of courts	125
Prohibitions on Clauses Restricting the Assignment of Receivables	126
Restricting bans on assignments	126
Historical background to the marketability of property	126
Reasons for restricting the marketability of receivables	127
Set-off and netting are prejudiced by assignments	128
English law mainly allows restrictions on assignments	129
Other jurisdictions allowing non-assignment clauses	129
Jurisdictions prohibiting non-assignment clauses in financing transactions	130
Other jurisdictions nullifying non-assignment clauses	131
Conclusion on bans on non-assignment clauses	131
Bondholder Democracies	132
Collective action by bondholder voting	132
English law on bondholder collective action	132
US law on bondholder collective action	133
Bondholder collective action clauses elsewhere	134
Relevance of this key indicator	134
9. EXCLUSION CLAUSES	**135**
Background to Exclusion Clauses	135
Exclusion clauses generally	135
Summary of key indicators	135
General Review of Exclusion Clauses Internationally	136
English law on exclusion clauses	136
Exclusion clauses in civil code countries	138
Exclusion clauses in France	139
Exclusion Clauses in Unregulated Offering Documents	140
Syndicated bank credits	140
International bond issues	140
Unregulated disclosure documents	140
Issuer liability	141
No exclusion for fraud	141
Sources of law	141
Big pocket liability of arrangers and underwriters	141
Corporations as black bags	142
Liability of an arranging bank for a syndication offering memorandum	142
Liabilities of arranging banks in England	142
Liability of arranging banks in the US	143
Underwriter liability for unregulated bond prospectuses generally	144
Underwriter liability in England for an unregulated prospectus	144
US underwriter liability for an unregulated prospectus	144
Universal liability for fraud	145
Liability of underwriters on an unregulated prospectus elsewhere	146

Underwriter Liability on Regulated Prospectuses Generally	147
Intensification of liability	147
Underwriter liability for a regulated prospectus	147
US regulated prospectuses	148
English law on regulated prospectuses	150
Regulated prospectuses elsewhere	150
Derivatives Liability	151
Typical forms of disclaimer	151
English law	152
US law	153
German law	154
Conclusion	155
10. INSOLVENCY LAW INDICATORS AND RISKS	**156**
Why Insolvency Law is Relevant	156
Importance of insolvency law	156
Insolvency rules are mandatory	156
Understanding Insolvency Law	157
Essential elements of bankruptcy	157
Impact of the bankruptcy of corporations on legal systems	158
Summary of methods of insolvency risk mitigation	158
Three methods of handling insolvencies	159
Work-outs and judicial rescue plans	160
Creditors involved in work-out and judicial rescue plans	161
International diversity of insolvency approaches	161
Harmonised International Insolvency Laws	161
EU Insolvency Regulation and UNCITRAL Model Law	161
Summary of the EU Insolvency Regulation 2015	162
Exceptions to opening state applicable law	163
Summary of the UNCITRAL Model Law on Cross-border Insolvency	164
Insolvency jurisdiction and applicable law outside treaties	165
Insolvency of corporations, banks, and sovereign states compared	165
Key Indicators of Insolvency Law	166
Triple super-priority insolvency claims	166
General attitude of the legal families to the three super-priority claimants	167
The triple super-priorities satisfy the eligibility tests for key indicators	167
Role of the contract governing law in achieving super-priority	168
Central counterparties and the triple super-priority claimants	168
Bankruptcy ladder of priorities	169
Contract and lease terminations on insolvency	170
Other insolvency key indicators	171
Conclusion	172
11. INSOLVENCY SET-OFF	**174**
Essentials of Insolvency Set-off and Netting	174
Insolvency set-off and netting as a key indicator	174
What is insolvency set-off?	174
What is netting?	175
Two-way payments	175
Policies of insolvency set-off and netting	175

Carve-out statutes	176
Jurisdictions having carve-out statutes	176
Excessive intricacy of carve-out statutes	177
Protection of Insolvency Set-off by Governing Law	178
Free contract choice of insolvency set-off	178
Other EU protections	179
Comparative Survey	180
Armour-plated protections in English set-off	180
EU Restructuring Directive 2019	181
Insolvency set-off in the US	181
Set-off in the English common law jurisdictions	182
Insolvency set-off in the Napoleonic jurisdictions	183
Insolvency set-off in the Roman-Germanic jurisdictions	184
Insolvency set-off in the Mixed civil/common law jurisdictions	184
Set-off mutuality	185
Avoidance of build-ups of set-offs	185
Set-off against assignees and other intervenors	186
Conclusion	187
12. SECURITY INTERESTS	**188**
What are Security Interests and their Key Indicators?	188
What is a security interest?	188
Security interests are a protection against insolvency	189
Key indicators of security interests	189
International summary	190
Use and Importance of Security Interests	192
Importance test of key indicators	192
Home loans	192
Special purpose companies	192
Small and medium-sized companies	193
Publicly listed companies	193
Sovereign states	193
Trade finance	194
Financial markets	194
Title finance	195
Conclusion	195
Comparative Law of Security Interests	195
Pros and cons of security interests	195
Security interests according to the families of jurisdictions	196
American and English security interests	198
Financial Collateral Directive 2002 and Settlement Finality Directive 1998	200
Aircraft and ships	201
Governing Law and Security Interests	201
Role of the governing law of security interests generally	201
Governing law of contract for security agreement	202
Scope of security interests	203
Scope of collateral and publicity	203
Recharacterisation of title finance as a security interest	204
Trustees of security	204
Permissible secured debt	205
Transfers of secured debt	205

Enforcement remedies	205
Bankruptcy	205
Corporate structures to minimise risks	206
Conclusion	206

13. COMMERCIAL TRUSTS — 207

Background to Commercial Trusts — 207
   Non-recognition as unjust enrichment — 207
   What is a trust? — 207
   What are trusts used for? — 208
   Breakdown of key indicators — 210

International Survey of Trust Recognition — 210
   Common law jurisdictions — 210
   Civil law trust statutes — 211
   Napoleonic group — 211
   Other family groups — 211

Objections to the Trust — 212
   Background — 212
   False wealth — 212
   Priority risks — 212
   Other objections — 213
   Doctrine of specificity — 213
   Impact on the tracing of illegal proceeds — 213
   Short history of the rejection of the trust — 214
   Impact on legal systems outside Western Europe — 214

Maximisation of Trust Recognition and Risk Mitigation — 215
   Objectives — 215
   Governing law of the trust contract — 215
   Hague Trust Convention 1985: governing law of the trust — 215
   Location of trust assets under EU Insolvency Regulation — 216
   Location of trust assets at domicile of trustee — 217
   Recognition of trusts under a foreign governing law — 218

Conclusion — 219

14. CORPORATE LAW INDICATORS AND RISKS — 220

Governing Law and Corporate Transactions — 220
   Shares compared to bonds — 220
   Main corporate transactions — 222
   Structural methods of avoiding local corporate law — 223
   Conflict of laws in corporate transactions — 223

Key Indicators of Corporate Law — 224
   Main and ancillary indicators — 224
   Role of companies in modern societies — 225
   Families of law and corporate law — 225
   Why corporate law differs from financial law: the straight line and the triangle — 226
   Objectives of corporate creditors, shareholders, and management generally — 227
   Objectives of creditors — 227
   Objectives of shareholders — 228
   Objectives of management — 228
   Other constituencies — 228

Financial Assistance to Buy Own Shares	228
What is financial assistance?	228
England	230
European Union	230
France	231
Germany	231
United States	231
Elsewhere	232
Conclusion	232
Director Personal Liability	233
Introduction	233
Conflict of laws and director liability	233
Universal heads of liability	233
Fraudulent trading	233
Wrongful or negligent trading	234
Duties to file on insolvency	234
Liability for negligent management	235
Conclusion	236
Other Key Indicators of Corporate Law	236
Introduction	236
Availability of the corporate form	236
Limited liability and the veil of incorporation generally	237
Single purpose companies	237
Central banks	238
Shareholders as de facto directors	238
Bankruptcy consolidation	238
Subordination of shareholder loans	239
Maintenance of capital	239
Shareholder equality and minority protections	239
Corporate governance	239
Enforcement penalties	240
Takeovers	240
Corporate guarantees	241
Conclusion	242
Economic and fairness justifications	242
Comparative conclusions	242
15. REGULATORY LAW INDICATORS AND RISKS	**244**
Introduction	244
Pervasiveness of regulation	244
Main fields of regulation	244
Why regulation is different from the ordinary law	245
Financial Regulation	246
Essentials of financial regulation	246
Financial regulators	246
Financial codes of conduct	247
Prospectuses	247
Frauds	247
Managing regulatory risk	247
Key Indicators of Financial Regulation	248
Key indicators generally	248

Differences in enforcement	249
Differences in protectionism	249
Intensity of investor protection	250
Degree of freedom	250
Conclusion	250

16. COURTS, LITIGATION, AND ARBITRATION — 251

Judiciary	251
Politicisation	251
Business orientation	251
Judicial consensus building	252
Choice of Courts and Risk Generally	252
Reasons for choice of courts and indicators	252
Role of the law of the courts	253
Trauma of litigation	254
Key Indicators of Litigation	254
US litigation	254
Class actions	256
Discovery of documents	257
Non-conflicting Indicators	257
Reason for exclusion	257
Pre-judgment freezes	257
Enforcement of foreign judgments	258
Sovereign immunity	259
Arbitration	259
Introduction	259
Advantages and disadvantages of arbitration	260
Use of arbitration in financial and corporate transactions	260
Conclusions	261

17. NON-LEGAL INDICATORS AND RISKS — 262

Introduction	262
Familiarity of Governing Law	262
Brand recognition of a legal system	262
Market reaction to legal gaffes	263
Language	264
English as the language of international business	264
Reflections on English as a language	264
Financial Centres	265
Attributes of a financial centre	265
Financial centres and the legal system	266
Legal Infrastructure	266
Political and rule of law risks	266
Conclusion on legal infrastructure	267

18. COMPARISON OF JURISDICTIONS OF THE WORLD — 268

Identifying the Families of Jurisdictions	268
Importance of identifying families of jurisdictions	268
Themes and key indicators	268
The triple polarisation of law	269
Development of Legal Indicators for Comparative Law	270
Herstatt 1974	270

British Eagle 1975   270
Iran 1979   270
Sovereign bankruptcies in the 1980s   271
The conundrum of insolvency set-off   271
General Features of the Families of Law   273
    Export of legal systems   273
    Limited overlap between families of religion and law   274
    Diversity of cultures within the legal families   274
    Rejection of a foreign ideology?   274
    Use of world maps   275
    What is a jurisdiction?   275
    Which laws are family of law and which laws are not?   276
    Main competing legal systems   277
American Common Law Jurisdictions   277
    Members of the group   277
    Historical background   278
    Legal culture and key indicators   278
Conclusion   279
English Common Law Jurisdictions   279
    Members of the group   279
    Historical background   280
    Legal culture and key indicators   281
Conclusion   282
Napoleonic Jurisdictions   282
    Members of the group   282
    Napoleonic sub-groups   283
    Historical background   284
    Legal culture and key indicators   284
Conclusion   285
Roman-Germanic Jurisdictions   286
    Members of the group   286
    Sub-groups of Roman-Germanic jurisdictions   286
    Historical background   286
    Legal culture and the key indicators   287
Conclusion   288
Mixed Civil/Common Law Jurisdictions   288
    Members of the group   288
Conclusion   289
Islamic Jurisdictions   289
    Members of the group   289
Conclusion   290
New or Transition Jurisdictions   291
    Members of the group   291
Conclusion   291
Unallocated Jurisdictions   291
    Members of the group   291
    High seas and space   292
Statistics on the Families of Law   292
Conclusion on the Families of Law   292

19. PROTECTING A GOVERNING LAW	294
The Need for Protection	294
Responsibility	294
International examples of law monitoring bodies	295
Achievements and weaknesses	296
A body to protect English law	297
Conclusions	298
20. HISTORY AND THE FUTURE	299
A Reconsideration of Legal History	299
Different timing of the Industrial Revolution	299
Indelibility of existing law	301
Cultural Revolution of 1968	301
Brexit	303
Roman law and the present	304
The future	305
21. CONCLUSION	306
Weighting of the Main Themes	306
Methods of weighting	306
The Nature of Freedom	307
Choices of Governing Law	307
Sources and References	309
Index	317

PREFACE

This is a new kind of law book.

It is designed to bring new life into comparative law. It does this by focusing on the hard issues robustly, by dealing with a wider range of issues, by covering the whole world, by proposing a proper methodology, and, most of all, by promoting the law as a foundational ideology. It sets out the policies of the law so that the law is not just a flat recitation of law data, like a train timetable.

It is intended to be read from cover to cover like a non-fiction book.

My hope is that it will be accessible to those who know little about the law, and also by people who are well-informed experts. If both groups can conclude that they have learned something which they did not know before, then I will be proud.

One consequence of the above is that the book has to be fairly short.

In terms of technique, there are no footnotes. My supporting citation is either in the text itself or dismissed to notes concealed at the end. At least the reader does not have to read the book in two places at once.

Another consequence is that I might occasionally depart from the dry classical style of the official legal opinion.

I write as someone who has been both a practitioner and an academic for many decades: a healthy balance. I have studied the law in books and also seen the law in action, the law in flight.

In the course of my life in the law, I have visited all the jurisdictions of the world via a study of their laws and a great many of them in person. I only wish that I had visited all of them physically so that I could speak with the people there. For all of them seem to believe in the law in principle, even though they may differ on the particular expression of the laws. Otherwise they would have abolished them. So at least the world is united on the fundamental need for its greatest ideology, the work of a prodigious number of centuries by a prodigious multitude of people, to whom I pay my respects by this book.

Philip Wood
Knowle Grange Gardens
Shere, Surrey, England
1 June 2022

ACKNOWLEDGEMENTS

I pay tribute to the huge number of people who have contributed to my thinking and work over the years on the subjects contained in this book, to my colleagues at my former firm Allen & Overy, and to the universities I have taught at, to the hundreds of lawyers in the many countries of the world I have spoken, to my students, to the many friends who have been prepared to listen to me and guide me, to all of those who helped me in producing my works on which this book is based, including my personal assistants, librarians, and those who produced and printed the documents, and to the publishers of my works and articles.

I pay special tribute to the leading lawyers who advised me on aspects of this book in roundtables organised by Stephen Denyer and Carly Hollingsworth at the Law Society of England and Wales, to those who aided me subsequently on the laws of their jurisdictions, to the senior lawyers who read drafts of chapters of this work, namely Elizabeth Gloster, Helen Dodds, Guy Beringer, Barney Reynolds, and Yannis Manuelides, and to Jeff Golden and Carl Baudenach for their contributions.

I am grateful to Rachel Mullaly at Oxford University Press for her support of the publication of this book and to those at OUP, including Rebecca Lewis, who brought this book to fruition.

None of the above is responsible for the opinions in this book or for its errors and shortcomings.

Finally, as always, I owe a debt above all to my wife Marie-Elisabeth and to my family who have been such a joy to me.

THE AUTHOR

Philip Wood was born in Livingstone near the Victoria Falls in the then Northern Rhodesia, now Zambia. He has a general humanities degree from the University of Cape Town, an MA in English literature from the University of Oxford, and an honorary doctorate from the University of Lund in Sweden. He took first class honours and was a triple prize-winner in the Law Society's qualifying professional examinations in England.

He was a partner in the international law firm of Allen & Overy for many years. He was head of the firm's banking department and subsequently the head of the firm's Global Law Intelligence Unit.

He was formerly Visiting Professor in International Financial Law at the University of Oxford, Yorke Distinguished Visiting Fellow at the University of Cambridge, and Visiting Professor at Queen Mary University, London, and at the London School of Economics and Political Science. He has lectured at more than seventy-five universities worldwide and has written more than twenty books.

In 2010, he was appointed honorary Queen's Counsel. In 2015, he was awarded a CBE in the Queen's Honours List.

LIST OF ABBREVIATIONS

AGBG	German Act on Standard Terms 1976
BA	Bankruptcy Act
BGB	German Civil Code
BGH	Bundesgerichtshof *(German Federal Supreme Court)*
BL	Bankruptcy Law
CA	Court of Appeal
CA 2006	Companies Act 2006 (UK)
CC	Civil Code
CCP	Code of Civil Procedure
CHAPS	Clearing House Automated Payments System (UK)
CHIPS	Clearing House Interbank Payments System (US)
ComC	Commercial Code
CPR	Civil Procedure Rules
CUP	Cambridge University Press
DTC	Depository Trust Company
ECJ	European Court of Justice
ECtHR	European Court of Human Rights
EEA	European Economic Area
EU	European Union
EU Insolvency Regulation	Regulation (EU) 2015/848 on insolvency proceedings (recast)
EU Judgments Regulation	Regulation (EU) 1215/2012 on jurisdiction and the recognition and enforcement of judgments in civil and commercial matters (recast)
EU Restructuring Directive	Directive (EU) 2019/1023 on preventive restructuring frameworks
Financial Collateral Directive	Directive 2002/47/EC on financial collateral arrangements
GDP	gross domestic product
GmbH	*Gesellschaft mit beschränkter Haftung* (company with limited liability)
HL	House of Lords
IA 1986	Insolvency Act 1986 (UK)
IMF	International Monetary Fund
IR 1986	Insolvency Rules 1986
ISDA	International Swaps and Derivatives Association, Inc
LMA	Loan Market Association
OUP	Oxford University Press
PC	Privy Council
PD	Practice Direction
QB	Queen's Bench
Restatement	Restatement of the Law by the American Law Institute

Rome I	Regulation (EC) No 593/2008 on the law applicable to contractual obligations
Rome II	Regulation (EC) No 864/2007 under law applicable to non-contractual obligations
SC	Supreme Court
Settlements Finality Directive	Directive 98/26/EC of 19 May 1998 on settlement finality in payment and securities settlement systems
UCC	Uniform Commercial Code (US)
UCP	Uniform Customs and Practice
UK	United Kingdom
UNCITRAL	United Nations Commission on International Trade Law
UNIDROIT	International Institute for the Unification of Private Law
US	United States
WTO	World Trade Organization
ZPO	Zivilprozessordnung *(German: Judicial Code)*

1
WHAT THIS BOOK IS ABOUT

Introduction

In one sentence

1.1 This book is about the advantages and the risks involved in the choice of law governing an international contract or other transaction, plus the accompanying choice of courts, in the fields of wholesale (non-consumer) financial, corporate, commercial, and insolvency law—broadly business law—on a comparative basis.

Ubiquity of governing law

1.2 Every contract, every sale, every aspect of every legal transaction, must be governed by the law of one of the world's jurisdictions. A legal transaction cannot exist on its own in a legal vacuum or be its own law. Each aspect must belong to a legal system of a territory, called a jurisdiction, it must have a home, a root which feeds it, a set of laws of a place which tells us what the transaction means and what its effect is.

1.3 In addition, all legal transactions, even if initially arbitrated, are ultimately subject to the courts or other authority of a jurisdiction which can determine whether the transaction is legally valid, how it is to be interpreted, and how it is to be enforced.

Freedom of choice of contract law and courts

1.4 In many cases, particularly with contracts, the parties are free to choose the governing law of the contract and then that chosen law applies to most, but not all aspects, of the transaction. The law generally also gives the parties a somewhat lesser freedom to choose the courts which can hear disputes about the contract or other transaction and enforce it. The parties can also often choose private arbitration but even this is supervised by a court somewhere. If the parties do not choose the governing law, the courts will choose for them, usually on the basis of centre of gravity tests.

1.5 In some cases the parties cannot choose the governing law of their transaction or the law which would govern all the issues in respect of the transaction, or the courts. The governing law is mandatory, compulsory, forced upon parties by the iron will of the law.

1.6 Hence, one of the themes in this book is the scope of freedom. This question invites an assessment of whether the law should restrict us only so as to liberate us, or whether other principles command compulsory obedience.

Jurisdictions of the world

1.7 There are about 320 legal jurisdictions in the world, assuming we leave out space and the seas. A legal jurisdiction is a territory which has a legal system which is different from that of other territories. A legal jurisdiction is different from a sovereign state, and indeed many sovereign states, of which there are nearly 200, have embedded within them numerous separate jurisdictions. For example, on the one hand the UK technically has about seven different legal jurisdictions, the main ones being England (which for this purpose includes Wales), Scotland, and Northern Ireland. The US has fifty jurisdictions, or fifty-one if you include the District of Columbia. On the other hand, France is a unitary state, although even there most lawyers would treat Monaco as a separate jurisdiction.

1.8 One test of whether a jurisdiction qualifies as a jurisdiction is the formal test of whether you have to be officially qualified to practise law there. Another more subjective test is whether a transactor would think it desirable to consult local lawyers as to the validity of the transaction.

1.9 Theoretically, parties could choose any one of these 320 jurisdictions to govern their contract, but in practice the parties choose the law and courts of a jurisdiction which they are familiar with or which they consider to be suitable for the transaction.

Risks of governing law and courts

1.10 As each legal system has its own laws, the governing law involves different risks, some of which can involve an unsuspected ambush, an unexpected liability or a contract which is different from what a party expected. The law is quite a minefield. One of the main purposes of a choice of governing law is to reduce the legal risks. Risk control is a major task of corporate management and government administration. Corporate law and applicable regulatory law, such as financial regulation, specifically and whatever form of words is chosen, impose duties on corporate management to use due diligence in their management decisions. Credit rating agencies take legal risks into account. Risks are typically specified in offering circulars for securities. Choices of governing law are crucial to mitigating risks. This is all the more so because of the colossal amounts involved in the fields of commercial and financial law, because of the large number of countries now embracing market economics, because of the momentous changes we are experiencing, and because of the sheer complexity of the international sphere.

1.11 Note that this book is concerned with the mitigation of risk by a choice of governing law and courts. I am not discussing the mitigation of legal risk by other methods, such as by taking out insurance or buying a derivative or obtaining a guarantee. All of these involve a cost.

1.12 This book is therefore primarily about the factors which parties should take into account when they choose the governing law and the courts for a transaction, and in particular the legal risks which they take. The book also identifies main areas where the parties have a choice and describes the impact that these mandatory areas can have on the contract and how to mitigate those risks where possible.

1.13 This discussion is particularly relevant in view of the fact that most practising lawyers are trained in the laws of only one jurisdiction, but nevertheless frequently have to advise on international transactions. For example, lawyers commonly have to advise on the basic issue of choice of law impartially and objectively and for that purpose they would need to have command of the risks and advantages of a great many potential legal systems. This book is specifically intended to deal with that problem as best I can without you having to spend many years studying the comparative literature. I aim to describe the key points you should bear in mind as concisely and clearly as I can.

English and New York law

1.14 The task is eased by the fact that English law and New York law are the two most widely legal systems used to govern large transactions between business firms. These transactions include, for example, syndicated bank credit agreements, international bond issues, derivatives, joint venture agreements, large commodity sale agreements, aircraft and ship charterparties, construction projects, and intellectual property licences.

1.15 Those two legal systems are therefore international public utilities. They are widely used by parties who have nothing to do with England or New York and have no connections or links with England or New York. They believe that they can safely choose one of these governing laws because the fact that large numbers of other firms also choose the system reassures them that the legal system is suitable, or else there would have been market objections. The fact that the use of these systems is so widespread also means that the respective legal systems no longer belong just to England or New York. The law-makers and courts in those territories just look after the legal system for the rest of the world. They are custodians.

1.16 It is not unusual for an ideology to be taken up and used to govern the mores and conventions of an alien society. Religions are in the same bracket. Roman law itself became separated from Rome at the time of the fall of the Roman Empire. It was then semi-codified and organised in Constantinople in the 530s under Emperor Justinian. After a dark silence of several centuries, Roman law reawoke in Europe from about 1100 onwards, where it still forms the foundation of the laws in Europe and hence much of the rest of the world—a stunning achievement for the ancient classical population of one smallish but beautiful peninsula in western Europe. The legacies of Rome to the rest of the world are its laws and its religion, two ideologies overlapping in their intent.

Families of Law

Summaries of families of law

1.17 Another method of simplifying the task of understanding is that it is possible to divide the 320 legal systems into family groups which share similar features. Historically, the laws of most of world's 320 jurisdictions are based on that of a few countries. These jurisdictions may be broadly classified into four main groups:

- the *American common law group*, comprising the states of the US and about ten other territories, mainly islands;
- the *English common law group*, originally championed by England and comprising about eighty-five jurisdictions scattered all over the world. This group includes England, Ireland, Hong Kong, Australian jurisdictions, all Canadian jurisdictions except Quebec, Singapore, India, Pakistan, Bangladesh, Malaysia, Kenya, Nigeria, Ghana, and some significant island jurisdictions, such as Bermuda and the Cayman Islands;
- the *Napoleonic group*, championed originally mainly by France and comprising about eighty-six jurisdictions. This group includes Belgium, Italy, Luxembourg, and Spain, almost the whole of Latin America, most north African territories, such as Egypt, Tunisia, and Morocco, as well as numerous sub-Saharan territories from the Ivory Coast to Angola and Mozambique, via the two Congos;
- the *Roman-Germanic*, championed originally by *Germany*, with contributions from the Netherlands and Switzerland. There are about thirty-four jurisdictions in this group, including Turkey, as well as Austria, Poland, the Scandinavian countries, the Baltic countries, South Korea, and Indonesia.

1.18 The balance of the jurisdictions is made up of:

- *mixed common/civil jurisdictions*, such as China, Japan, South Africa, and Panama, as well as the Channel Islands—about eighteen jurisdictions in all;
- *Islamic jurisdictions*, such as Saudi Arabia. Countries such as Iraq, Iran, and Libya are Napoleonic but with an Islamic override, typically stating that the code is subject to Islamic law, as in Iran. They total about eleven jurisdictions.
- *new or transition jurisdictions*, numbering about eighteen, such as Russia, Ukraine, Belarus, the central Asian 'stans', and Vietnam;
- *unallocated* jurisdictions, about six, such as Antarctica, North Korea, and Cuba.

1.19 In very crude terms, a ranking of 40 per cent common law, 30 per cent Napoleonic, 20 per cent Roman-Germanic, and 10 per cent the rest would not be too far out. This is what I describe as the triple polarisation of jurisdictions in the nineteenth century, followed by the breakaway of the US into a separate group. The four main groups account for more than 85 per cent of the jurisdictions of the world. There is a detailed analysis of all jurisdictions in Chapter 18, plus some statistics. The statistics show that nearly all of the law in the world was borrowed from or significantly influenced by a Western model. It is still possible to detect underlying features which are common to each of the groups and which enable us to take huge steps forward in understanding the jurisdictions of the world simply by understanding each one of the 'big four' legal jurisdictions.

1.20 I sometimes refer to the members the Napoleonic and Roman-Germanic jurisdictions and their variants as civil or civil code jurisdictions, as opposed to the common law jurisdictions.

1.21 A possible mnemonic for these eight groups is to imagine four persons, one from each of England, the US, France, and Germany, sitting on a bench traditionally attired, and add MINU (*M*ixed, *I*slamic, *N*ew, *U*nallocated) = BIG FOUR plus MINU.

Jurisdictions specially covered

1.22 This book will deal with the question of why English and New York law enjoy a dominant position in the transactions I am concerned with in this work. Apart from the big four (England, France, Germany, and New York), I will also refer to a number of other jurisdictions which might become competitors. These include, amongst others, Singapore, Hong Kong, and Ireland in the English common law group, Japan and China in the mixed group, Sweden, Switzerland, and the Netherlands in the Roman-Germanic group, as well as Belgium, Spain, and Italy in the Napoleonic group. There are also possible future regional centres, such as South Africa, Kenya, and Nigeria. Mauritius is also worth a special note, as are tax haven jurisdictions like Cayman and Jersey.

1.23 But I will pre-eminently be concerned with the attributes of the big four jurisdictions. The reason for this is that these jurisdictions have played the most important role in the formation of legal systems around the world and therefore may be taken as reasonably representative as yardsticks or templates for many others. However, although traditional jurisdictions in the English group and in the traditional Napoleonic group still exhibit striking family likenesses in their group, there has been much splintering and fragmentation of individual members of other groups, particularly advanced countries, such as Belgium and the Netherlands.

1.24 Quite a few important jurisdictions do not seem to have publicly announced ambitions to serve as the governing law of international contracts, possibly such as Japan, Italy, Denmark, and Spain. It may be that they prefer to be neutral and indeed it is true that, when the international business community relies on your law, then you might tend to incur a responsibility to the international community to ensure that their preferred norms are taken into account in law-making. The result is that foreigners would then have a kind of restraining 'vote' in domestic law-making and judicial decisions. That may, however, not be such a bad thing.

1.25 Nevertheless, this book is about all of the jurisdictions of the world and I intend that they will all get a mention. I do not see why we should leave anyone out. After all, everyone has a chance if they want it, and who knows what the future holds, or who will leap up to grasp the crown.

Methodology and Scope

Key indicators

1.26 In measuring legal systems, I use specific key indicators to exhibit the general position or approach of the legal system. There are so many cases, statutes, scholarly writings, commentaries, dissertations, articles, and other outpourings on the law that it is just not feasible to cite even a tiny fraction of them, not even 0.00001 per cent.

1.27 For this method to work, the key indicators must ideally satisfy four conditions.

1.28 The first is that they should be measurable, just like litmus paper, or the red shift in astronomy. Inevitably, some tests will be qualitative, not quantitative, but it must be our aim not to measure by criteria which are matters of general style or culture without some hard evidence. It is usually not possible to measure with absolute statistical precision some concepts which are at the heart of the law, such as justice or fairness or a sense of morality, or qualitative ideas, such as freedom of contract or business orientation or creditor or debtor friendliness. My indicators therefore are highly specific and often technical so as to improve accuracy and focus.

1.29 Secondly, the key indicators should involve transactions which are important and economically significant. They should be significant and commonly used in the type of transactions we are talking about, in the central thrust of the stream, not just the eccentric tributaries or side streams. An economically important and frequent transaction has a greater weight in terms of risk assessment.

1.30 Thirdly, the key indicators should be symbolic or allegoric or representative so as to reflect or illustrate the norm or the mean of the attitude of the jurisdiction to the test, or a general tendency.

1.31 Fourthly, they should involve principles which clash, which are in severe conflict between jurisdictions, which are contrasting, ie where there is diversity, not harmony. It is not necessary to discuss the vast areas of commonality between jurisdictions, such as offer and acceptance in contract. I do not measure the flat and equal plains, but only the ridges and the ravines. It is on the ridges and in the ravines that we encounter the unexpected and the ambush, and therefore the dangerous.

1.32 The indicators should be reasonably limited in number so that the overall picture is not confused by thickets of detail, so that we can see the whole rising field and not just the blades of grass, the whole sea, not just the gush of surf and foam.

1.33 I therefore *measure the important symbolic clashes*. The mnemonic is MISC—*M*easure the *I*mportant *S*ymbolic *C*lashes.

Number of key indicators

1.34 This book mentions about seventy key indicators, to demonstrate the thirteen main themes listed below in paragraph 1.62. However, it would be impracticable in a short work to analyse all of these across even just the four main jurisdictions. I therefore focus on a much smaller number of main indicators—nearly thirty of them—to give those main indicators a decent airing. The others are mentioned in order to indicate whether the chosen main key indicators produce a result which is consistent with other key indicators and also to suggest avenues for further research by comparative lawyers.

Internationally mobile transactions

1.35 I deal only with international transactions, not with those which are purely domestic. The reason is that purely domestic transactions will usually in any event be governed by local law and in some of the main codes, such as the codification of choice of law in the EU (also applying also in the UK), local domestic law will often be mandatory. The internationally mobile transactions are those where the parties can choose the governing law so that the contract is portable between legal systems. The term 'internationally mobile transactions' was used by Oxera Consulting in its report of October 2021, 'Economic value of English law'.

A transaction can be internationally mobile in that sense even though all of the elements of the contract are domestic. One may also add that it is almost always the case that the chosen governing law does not govern everything and indeed an important test of a jurisdiction's credentials on freedom of contract is the extent to which it narrows or restricts or chokes the otherwise ample power and width of the governing law. **1.36**

An internationally mobile transaction is therefore one which you can carry around in your suitcase as you travel the world, its lakes and rivers and seas, its fragrant gardens of flowers and trees, and its sandy deserts. **1.37**

Business transactions

I limit myself to business transactions and exclude consumer transactions. In almost all jurisdictions there is a great divide between the attitude of the law to people who are sophisticated enough to run a business and who can afford to pay for legal advice on their major transactions, as opposed to the attitude of the law towards the protection of consumers and other individuals not acting in the course of their business. The law is layered or tiered. The boundary or perimeter between these groups is often blurred or shifting in the haze and dust. For example, the consumer protections may be extended to small family businesses, who are really individuals wearing the armour of the corporate form. The boundary curtain may be lifted even further up into medium-sized businesses. **1.38**

The reader may assume in this work that the parties involved are able to look after themselves and that, even if they do not have comparable bargaining power, they at least can obtain professional advice and can decide whether or not they will proceed with that particular counterparty on the other side. While the law often does distinguish between business and non-business parties, often by intricate definitions of sophisticated or professional parties as against the rest (depending on the area of law), the law does not generally require complete equality of bargaining power. This must obviously be the case since the degree of bargaining power varies from transaction to transaction according to the circumstances and it would not be feasible for the law to fashion its remedies according to these shifting weights on the scale. The law generally also does not investigate whether persons, who satisfy a business test indicating sophistication, are in fact sophisticated or actually apply that sophistication to the case in hand or simply don't care or are impulsive. **1.39**

It will usually be the case that the transactions in question will involve significant amounts and that in aggregate they are important to individual economies. **1.40**

The business arena is totally dominant in modern developed societies. Apart from civil servants, only an insignificant number of people work for themselves on the land and the **1.41** contribution of agriculture, which is itself a business, is less than 2 per cent of GDP in most developed economies. Almost all of the population for most of their lives, except for childhood and old age, work in a business, particularly corporations, and a very large proportion of companies are indeed family or small businesses.

1.42 In addition, London is one of the world's two largest financial centres and hosts vast volumes of business and markets, including markets for securities, foreign exchange, syndicated bank credits, international bond issues, and the like. A financial centre is underpinned by a legal system which must be suited to this type of business: markets must have a single legal platform in order to operate. Participants prefer a legal system which has a high degree of freedom and openness to business, which is predictable and which is not anti-business or disproportionately pro-debtor. If we did not have these markets, there would be nothing on the plate for breakfast.

Morality and justice of legal policies

1.43 In the case of nearly all the differences between legal systems which I note in this book, it would not be right to describe the opposing views as either morally offensive on the one side or virtuous on the other, the one good, the other bad. Most of the issues involve the balancing of controversial policies where the resulting choice is well within the range of reasonable debate and rational choice.

1.44 Lawyers have a duty to their clients to advise them impartially and objectively. There is no room for legal nationalism, legal chauvinism, or legal jingoism in the advice which they give. Yet it goes without saying that it is not easy to be impartial about one's own legal system.

1.45 My own legal system is English law and that is the one which I know best. I hope to represent other legal systems fairly but it is not feasible to be always accurate about one's own legal system, let alone everyone else's. There will doubtless be errors and omissions in my analysis which I hope readers will pardon.

1.46 It should be remembered throughout that the main four legal systems discussed in this book have been spectacularly successful and, although we may cavil about or dispute this or that aspect, one must always have a sense of proportion and recognise the extraordinary contribution and the extraordinary achievement of these legal systems and of others in their groups.

Focus on contracts

1.47 Contract is the fundamental legal transaction considered in this book. A contract is an agreement between parties which it is intended to have legal effect, that is, to be enforceable by the courts. It does not include an agreement to go out to dinner, but it does include an agreement to sell something for a price.

1.48 There are other related transactions, such as the transfer or delivery of assets on sale, or the grant of a security interest over an asset, such as a mortgage, charge or pledge, or a trust of an asset, such as the custodianship of securities by a bank holding in trust for the real or beneficial owner. But usually all of these transactions are enveloped in a contract, such as an agreement to sell, or an agreement to grant security.

Other legal areas are relevant, such as non-contractual wrongs (torts in common law jurisdictions, called delicts in other jurisdictions), such as negligence or liability for misrepresentation. But in the main contract is everywhere, contract is king. So many contracts are made every day that they shimmer like the evening sun on the ripples of a vast lake. The idea that the state will enforce promises was a huge and bold step in the formation of law, and an essential one too. **1.49**

My main focus is on what is called private law, not the traditional criminal law, such as murder or theft which involve public controls, or family or inheritance law, or constitutional law, or tax law, or accounting law, or public international law, which is the law between sovereign states. **1.50**

This book is for all of those enter into international contracts or who have to study or advise on them. There are over 7.7 billion people in the world producing around 87,000,000 million dollars (that is, US$87 trillion) of GDP every year, either directly themselves or through many millions of artificial people, called corporations. One would imagine that at least half of these make one contract every day, such as a contract to buy a loaf of bread. Most of these contracts will be neither international nor wholesale, but the number of international business contracts made every day must run into many millions. Multiply by 250 working days a year to get an annual figure. One can only guess what that annual figure might be, but I would speculate that the number is huge. **1.51**

Amounts involved

The amounts involved in the transactions which are the subject of this book are large. In order to have a pictorial measure of the numbers with so many zeros, imagine a piece of graph paper which is a metre square and therefore representing a million. A billion is the same metre of graph paper but stretched a kilometre to the side—just over half a mile. A trillion is the same metre square of graph paper but stretched a kilometre to the side and also a kilometre upwards. Thus, a billion is much bigger than a million and a trillion is much, much bigger than a billion. **1.52**

A useful—although vague—measurement of very large monetary amounts is the gross domestic product (GDP) of a country—sometimes called 'grossly deceptive product', but nevertheless a reasonably workable measure of how big an economy is, even if crude. The world GDP in 2019 was probably around US$87 trillion, although a different way of measuring would produce more. **1.53**

Foreign exchange turnover on the major exchanges is probably over US$500 trillion per year. That is US$500,000 billion, or US$500,000,000 million or US$500,000,000,000,000. One day's trading probably equals the official foreign reserves of all countries combined. **1.54**

1.55 The turnover of payment systems is over US$1,500 trillion per year. These systems get through world GDP every fortnight or so.

1.56 Flows of financial assets are much larger than flows of trade goods—maybe 100 times as much.

1.57 Syndicated bank credits, which are loans made by several banks under the same agreement, are probably six or seven times larger than bond issues, which are loans split up into pieces, called bonds or notes, which can be sold on a market. Bond issues are in turn are much larger than issues of equity shares every year. Some syndicated credits exceeded US$50 billion.

1.58 The corporate assets of the world's biggest bankruptcy was about US$530 billion (Lehmans in 2008). This overtopped the US$100 billion of WorldCom (in July 2002) and the assets of Enron (US$60 billion in 2002). Argentina's insolvency in 2002 (the world's then largest) involved over eighty bond issues totalling perhaps US$132 billion. The Greek bankruptcy in 2012 involved over €530 billion in bonds and official loans.

Assumptions as to the drafting of documents

1.59 In most of the transactions I discuss, I assume that the parties have drafted their contracts correctly and fully, for example, that they have made an express choice of governing law and choice of courts, that the contract adheres to market practice, and is not a contract informally drawn up and full of gaps, and that any disclaimers or exclusions of liability the parties need are properly prepared. This book does not discuss fall-back situations, such as discovering what the governing law is in the absence of an express choice or trying to find out what the parties meant. The reason for this is that an attempt to deal with this gap-filling would make it impossible to deal with the matters which I intend to deal with in a way which is as simple and as brief as is possible.

Citation

1.60 This book is intended to be readable, as opposed to a forgotten reference work on a dusty shelf. I have therefore limited the amount of citation in the text and banished all footnotes to the Sources and References at the end of the book for those who wish to follow up on statements in the text. The object is to make it unnecessary for the eye to be constantly flickering fitfully up and down in case something should be missed and to avoid the intrusive chatter from the bottom of the page.

1.61 Some of my statements are not derived from the books, but from half a century of discussions with lawyers around the world and with many thousands of students and academics, discussions which were often informal. Others are derived from conducting international transactions and in particular from internal memos and the internal resources which a large international firm accumulates over the years. If I made even a minimal attempt to record some of these sources, neither the reader nor I would ever go home.

Summary of Main Governing Law Risks

Outline of main areas of risk

The following is an outline of the main themes which I will be investigating in detail in order to describe some of the main distinctive characteristics of legal systems which impact on the risks a governing law. There are thirteen of them. **1.62**

- *Predictability* of the contract or transactional terms, ie legal certainty, the role of case law as binding precedent, and the scope of judicial intervention via 'good faith' or similar doctrines which can introduce uncertainty into contracts. Predictability and certainty of the agreed terms, such as events of default and contract termination rights can be fundamentally important in transactions involving very large amounts or carried out with great rapidity in markets.
- *Insulation* of the contract from interfering foreign laws, such as moratoriums and exchange controls, including the impact of the IMF Agreement. If the contract cannot be insulated, then it would be possible for the country of a debtor, say, unilaterally to change or nullify the contract by passing a moratorium law or exchange controls, or passing a law converting the currency of the debt into a worthless local currency.
- *Business orientation* of the legal system, with a discussion of what is meant by business orientation and how it affects the attitude of the law to business transactions.
- *Freedom of contract*, that is, the extent to which the parties are free to determine the contractual terms as opposed to the degree of restriction imposed by the law. Freedom and liberty are important values in the law, as they are in life.
- *Exclusion clauses and mis-selling liability* are examined both generally, and then specifically in relation to private offering circulars and derivative transactions. Some main questions are whether arrangers of transactions can exclude their liability for information provided by a borrower of bank loans or an issuer of bonds—it is not their information.
- *Insolvency law* indicators and risks, the impact of insolvency law on transactions and the extent to which insolvency law destroys previous freedoms. Insolvency law is a major indicator of the approach of a jurisdiction generally by reason of the passions aroused by the losses incurred on an insolvency. Next, there are separate chapters on the triple super-priority claimants on insolvency, namely, insolvency set-off, security interests, and commercial trusts, such as custodianship of securities, each of which is systemic in financial and other markets. The triple super-priority claims are major mitigants of insolvency risk.
- *Insolvency set-off*. This issue arises where a creditor who is owed a debt by an insolvent corporation, also owes a debt to the insolvent corporation so that there are reciprocal claims. If the creditor can set them off, the creditor is in effect paid to the extent of the set-off and hence escapes an insolvency loss. Two of the family groups are mainly hostile to insolvency set-off, a hostility which substantially increases risk exposures on insolvency. The amounts involved in financial markets eligible for set-off exceed world GDP many times.

- *Security interests.* These are such items as mortgages, charges, and pledges. Secured creditors escape the insolvency to the extent of their security and therefore they reduce their risks. The scope and validity of security interests on insolvency vary widely. Again, the amounts involved are colossal, especially collateral in financial markets.
- *Trusts.* A trust arises where one person has the public title to an asset which it holds for the benefit and the property of someone else, such as a bank acting as a custodian of a customer's investments. The trustee holds for the benefit of the beneficiary. This trust must be effective on the insolvency of the trustee and immune from the private creditors of the trustee so that the beneficiaries get their assets back in full, free of the insolvency. More than half the jurisdictions of the world do not recognise the trust for all assets, although there are many carve-outs. I deal only with commercial trusts and not family trusts or trusts under the will of a deceased individual. Commercial trusts far exceed family uses.
- *Corporate law indicators and risks.* These include director personal liability, the prohibition on a company giving financial assistance to buy its own shares, takeovers and share acquisitions, the raising of equity capital, and the compulsory subordination of debt (shifting the priority of debt down a rung in the bankruptcy ladder of priorities, usually resulting in the fact that the debt does not get paid). This chapter discusses in addition why most core corporate transactions are less sensitive to governing law risks than financial transactions.
- *Courts, litigation, and arbitration.* This chapter also covers the judiciary, notably their impartiality, independence, integrity, experience, and non-politicisation. Litigation policies and risks include class actions, contingent fees, disclosure of documents, proportionality, worldwide freezes, and the enforcement of foreign judgments.
- *Regulatory law.* Regulatory law indicators and risks, including proportionality.
- *General non-legal features,* such as market familiarity, language, legal expertise, and legal infrastructure risks, such as rule of law and political risks.

Mnemonic of the main issues

1.63 This list of thirteen issues results in the rather ungainly mnemonic of:

Predictability, Insulation, Business orientation, Freedom of contract, Exclusion clauses, Insolvency, Set-off, Security interests, Trusts, Corporations, Regulation, Courts, Other, that is, PIB–FEISST–CoRCO.

1.64 No doubt it would be possible the reshuffle the letters to produce something more memorable, although at the expense of an orderly progression.

What is being measured overall?

1.65 The generic values that are being measured are broadly values which are sympathetic to enterprise and business, which are creditor-friendly, and which favour freedom in the areas concerned.

The opposite values are a greater hostility to or distrust of business, an attitude that freedom is mainly abused by the strong to oppress the weak, and a strong belief in the regulated state to curb the excesses of business. **1.66**

At the extreme ends, these values are a sunny belief in economic progress and liberty, as against a severe anti-capitalistic despotism. **1.67**

There is no precise match between the specific indicators and the above values. Indeed, the more generic the value, the weaker is the potency of a key indicator to measure that value. **1.68**

Narrowing of scope of governing law

Although the parties to a contract may freely choose the governing law, the scope of that governing law in deciding whose law applies to the risk issues involved in that contract differs very substantially between jurisdictions. In some jurisdictions, some areas of law are unexpectedly treated as mandatory and override the governing law if you end up in the courts in the country imposing the compulsory rule. They narrow down the scope of the governing law and sometimes smash it in crucial areas. **1.69**

I summarise these mainly menacing dominant laws, which restrict freedoms, in the mnemonic 6C–TRITO, which is explained at paragraph 4.29 in Chapter 4 on the topic of matters not decided by the governing law. There is quite some overlap with the main themes already described, such as adverse mandatory contract laws introducing unpredictability or destroying the insulation of a contract against exchange controls, or insolvency, regulatory, or litigation rules which override the governing law in the courts concerned. The object of the discussion about the elements of law which narrow the windpipe, sometimes almost to strangulation point, is to view not only the fortress of the governing law, but the assailants on the governing law. **1.70**

Just for the sake of the record at this point, the elements of 6C–TRITO which restrict the ample scope of the governing law and therefore limit risk control via the governing law are the criminal law, corporate law, court law, consumer law, conventions, contract law, transfers of property, regulatory law, insolvency law, tort law, and others. **1.71**

Summary of Conclusions

The 1357 ranking

In general, a risk ranking of the four jurisdictions on the basis of an averaging of the thirteen risk factors described in this book would seem to indicate a very broad spread as follows: **1.72**

- 1 England   Blue
- 3 New York   Green
- 5 Germany   Yellow
- 7 France   Red

1.73 This ranking is to some degree qualitative since the subject does not allow mathematical precision. The ranking is a rough rule of thumb. It is an order of rank between the jurisdictions, not a statistic or fixed notches on a ruler. The interval between the rungs varies according to the deal and the legal rule which is measured.

1.74 An alternative is to ascribe a colour range of blue, green, yellow, and red. The colour bands are broader and do not give a false impression of statistical accuracy.

1.75 I do not attempt to state whether the 1357 ranking is out of ten points or twelve points or twenty points, since this would involve an assessment of overall impact on the society which would be too speculative to be of any real use. Again, the length of the scale varies between the themes and depends on the deal.

1.76 We have to live with the imprecision of generalisations. Some things are as difficult to measure as the location and speed of electrons at the same time. It is not just the law which defies accuracy. Nature does as well.

1.77 However, the ranking does seem to reflect a pattern which I experienced as a practitioner and which, I suspect, reflects market experience, accounting for the dominance of English and New York governing law internationally.

1.78 The ranking is considered to be consistent with the index of elements which restrict the scope of that law and which are contained in the mnemonic 6C–TRITO.

1.79 Both New York and English law share common attitudes to most of the issues under discussion. The difference in ranking is attributable to the vagaries of jury trials, the higher degree of politicisation of New York state courts as opposed to the federal courts in New York, to an insolvency regime which is more pro-debtor than the English regime, and to the greater aggressiveness of litigation and regulatory enforcement in the US compared to the other three jurisdictions.

1.80 The intriguing question is the extent to which the 1357 rule applies to members of the family groups. Although there are many exceptions and qualifications, it would seem that there is a high degree of correlation within the family groups on the main risk factors. But the correlation is weaker in the case of highly developed members of the family groups concerned, many of whom have been active in reforming their laws individually in one direction or another.

Conclusion

1.81 The legal systems concerned have been built up over centuries and represent the accumulated reflections of history. It is considered unlikely that they are a snapshot of current attitudes or the culture and opinions of the majority of people in the countries in the jurisdiction concerned. Political and cultural views tend to be evanescent and fleeting and it is right that the law should not make any attempt to imitate the swiftly changing shades of dark and light or the ephemerality of opinion or the temperature of mood from hot to cold and back. The statute book has to endure as a solid sculpted rock at the centre of flowing society.

1.82 We also have to ask ourselves why these legal systems should be so different when, notwithstanding all the superstition and stereotypes, the peoples are so similar and indeed when all the peoples of the world are so similar. That is a topic which I shall not completely leave aside.

1.83 We shall commence our discussion of the key indicators in Chapter 5, but first in the next three chapters to come we must deal with some foundational matters to set the scene.

2
ROLE OF LAW

Law as Ideology and Moral Code

Law as ideology

2.1 Before we turn to governing law, our first topic must be the role of law in modern societies and also its economic value. This is an essential subject for understanding the context of what follows later in this book and why a legal system as a national asset deserves to be protected and sustained.

2.2 A legal system is an ideology. It embodies the ethics, the norms, the morality, the accepted modes of a society. It would not be possible to run a modern society without having any laws in the hope of relying solely on forbearance, innate morality, and the need for mutual protection.

2.3 Laws do not only cover murder, rape, robbery, fraud, and other serious crimes or our constitutional laws, or our family laws. They also cover taxation, bankruptcy, the laws of money, banks, and corporations.

Societies without law

2.4 How would you have an economy at all if there were no law of contract or of sale? How could anyone rely on the voluntary promise of somebody to pay for goods or securities or foreign exchange or land if there were no courts to enforce the promise and award compulsory compensation if the promise is broken? A society would not survive if a person could lie about his credit or injure you or your property or if it were left to a perpetrator to decide how much compensation to pay, if any. It would not be possible for a government to tax individuals or corporations if the taxpayer had no obligation to pay, enforceable by the courts, and could decide for themselves how much they would pay, if anything. There could be no kind of society at all if murder went unpunished or a robbery attracted no retribution or there were no rules preventing arbitrary arrest or expropriation, or anybody could move into your house with their family and drive around in your car and crash it, just for fun, where there was no constitution enabling voting for parties, and no proper method of peacefully electing leaders. How would we be able to deal with complicated disputes on contracts involving different legal systems unless we had rules on how you decided those disputes and what the rules should be? How could we have any kind of regulation about the safety of buildings, or safety standards for vehicles, or the supervision of the capital of banks, or for orderly bankruptcies or insolvency rescues, or for corporate takeovers or for enforcing competition between businesses and preventing monopolies? We could not have any kind of basic international relations without treaties and some sort of supranational tribunals, however weak, to enforce them. We could not have any orderly succession to assets when a family member dies unless we had safe rules about the validity of wills and about succession if there is no will. How could we insure our assets or our health without legally binding insurance policies if the insurance company could just pay out whatever it liked or nothing at all?

In our context, how could we have any means whereby the money of the people accumulated in banks could be lent out to finance the purchase of homes or the building of bridges or hospitals or the manufacture of vehicles or for any other business purpose unless we had laws about the grant of mortgages and enforceable rules as to the repayment of loans, together with interest? How could we have any basic financial system without the operation of clearing and settlement systems, which involve colossal amounts, unless we had bulletproof rules to validate their functions? **2.5**

It is therefore a platitude that the laws are the foundation of a society and necessary for our survival. They are our scriptures. If we did not have laws, then gangs would roam the streets, smashing and robbing, and predatory ruffians would seize the reins of power and set the military upon the people, until the people cried out, 'We must put a stop to this, we must have laws, we must have the rule of law'. In large modern societies where most of the population lives in cities, often with millions of people, it would not be realistic to rely on shaming or ostracism or the need for reciprocity or the desire for approval or social pressures. We only have to look at failed states, or kleptocratic despotic governments, to see what happens when central authority collapses or abandons the rule of law, and to see the economic destitution of the people as a result. We only have to view the terrible finds in archaeological excavations of axes, knives, and mass graves of people who have been tortured and exterminated to see what really happened in ancient societies without the rule of law. We have only to see the massive fortifications around ancient cities to divine what people were really worried about. **2.6**

The need for law is not based on a judgment that most people are wicked. On the one hand, there is no doubt there are some people who are wicked most of the time and a lot more people who can be forced into wickedness by reason of an unusual fear or threat. It seems fair to say that most of the population are normally good, or would like to be good. On the other hand, it would not be at all unusual that, if there were no laws, large sections of the population would not pay taxes voluntarily, and would often seek to reduce the compensation for a breach of contract, or for a negligent injury which they caused, or would resist a sale of their home if they fail to repay a mortgage loan. **2.7**

Moral basis of law

The fact that legal systems are our ideologies is underlined by the fact that most of the laws are not just utilitarian or functional. They are drenched and saturated with a sense of morality, of ethics, and of justice. It is not just murder, rape, and robbery which engage the moral sense. Even taxation poses moral issues as to the extent to which individuals in many countries should part with more than half of their income towards paying for the education, health, and pensions of others, as well as defence and law and order. Most taxation **2.8** nowadays is compulsory charity. Even the bankruptcy ladder of priorities, whereby some creditors are paid in priority to others, is based upon a view of justice as to who should be paid, the victor and the victim.

2.9 Practically everything in the law is controversial, involves a clash of views, and a collision of interests, all inextricably knotted into contrary views about justice or fairness. Even in the case of the law of contract, which has been around for centuries, there are still major unsettled issues between jurisdictions as to whether contracts should be enforced as written, or whether the courts can intervene to change contracts which they think are unfair, ie whether the outcome of a contract should be predictable. There are dramatic gaps between jurisdictions on such systemic issues whether on insolvency a creditor should be allowed to exercise a set-off in order to get paid, on the extent to which the creditor should be entitled to receive and enforce a mortgage or other security interest, and whether a custodianship by way of trust of securities is valid. It has proved impossible to get jurisdictions to agree on these and other issues over centuries.

2.10 The laws of the country are an embedded morality which represents their credentials, their confidence and self-esteem, the result of trial and error since ancient times, the result of an age-old yearning for justice and fairness, the canons and rules by which they live through their lives.

Law as a utility

2.11 It is true that some legal rules are utilitarian. For example, it does not really matter whether the law requires us to drive on the right or the left of the road, so long as one side is chosen. Because many laws are seen as purely functional without issues of morality or justice, legal systems have often been compared to platforms or transport networks or communications networks. These metaphors are in many respects apt representations of what legal systems do in the sense that legal systems enable activities which could not otherwise take place. I myself describe English and New York law as international public utilities, in the sense that they are used as platforms or infrastructure which enable transactions to go ahead on the basis of rules which enjoy the trust and confidence of the parties.

2.12 We do not have to decide which metaphor is best as between the functional and the philosophic or spiritual. The laws together are the largest, the most comprehensive, the most exhaustive of all the moral systems which we have in the modern world. The great religions never came anywhere near the extent of the secular laws. For example, when the Emperor Justinian had Roman law compiled around 535 AD, that compilation at the time far exceeded the collections of law in the Jewish and Christian bibles and far exceeded the legal content of the Koran which appeared about a century later. Now there are no other ideologies for life which remotely contest the size and scope of the laws.

Law as a means of survival

2.13 The laws are often seen as a means to promote economic welfare and to maximise human happiness, and indeed these are worthy objectives of the law.

There is another crucial point here. This can be illustrated by two symbolic historical events. **2.14**

On 2 July 1816, at 3.00 pm, the French frigate *Medusa* struck a sandbank sixty miles off the coast of west Africa. The terrified crew and passengers built a raft out of planks of the ship and 147 people got on the raft. The captain and the crew climbed into the six ship's boats to row to the shore 'to get help'. After twelve days rolling around rudderless on the sea, only fifteen were left alive on the raft when it was rescued by another French ship the *Argus*. Nearly all the rest were killed in the fighting for the brandy and the biscuits. The raft is portrayed in a stupendous and justly famous canvas by Gericault which hangs in the Louvre in Paris. **2.15**

On 5 August 2010 at around lunchtime, thirty-three miners in a mine in Chile heard a thunderous crack and rumbling of rock above them. They were trapped more than 2,000 feet down. Yet they all escaped after sixty-nine days. So what was the difference compared to the raft? **2.16**

One difference was that the Chilean miners elected a leader who then made rules rationing food and water and sharing what they had. Thus, they had a constitutional law and a rudimentary legal system. But on the raft the captain left the ship and they had no rules about food and drink. They had no laws, just anarchy. The Chileans survived but those on the raft did not. They were lifted from the cavernous dark into warm yellow light. **2.17**

So that is the answer. We have laws to survive. **2.18**

The role of law and governing law

The reason that I make the above assertions about the general role of law in a book about the governing law of business transactions are several. Firstly, parties do not choose a governing law of a transaction just because legal systems insist that every transaction must have a governing law. They choose the governing law because a set of enforceable rules is necessary for the transaction to take place at all, except in trivial or informal cases. **2.19**

Second, since legal ideologies differ as widely as religious or philosophical ideologies, the ideology which parties choose to govern their transactions must express their beliefs about the rules of justice and morality governing their transaction. **2.20**

Thirdly, because legal systems have a utilitarian or functional impact, the governing law involves a choice about suitability, efficiency and cost. **2.21**

Fourthly, in choosing a governing law and the accompanying courts, the parties are choosing a different set of risks. The assessment of risk is a crucial aspect of the management of any business. **2.22**

Fifthly, the parties are choosing an ideology which best suits their interests, eg the predictability of the contract which they have written and agreed, whether the contractual regime gives them freedom or imposes restrictions on liberty, whether the law chosen is debtor-friendly or creditor-friendly, whether the legal regime has a tendency to support transactions as opposed to destroying them or annihilating them for some metaphysical legalistic **2.23** reason grounded in ancient and obsolete doctrine, whether the courts of the country are impartial, incorruptible, and independent without a local bias, and whether the country concerned adheres to the rule of law.

2.24   Finally, parties choose a legal system which can develop the law so as to meet changing market requirements and new transactions. Thus, over the last fifty years or so English law as the legal backbone the London financial centre had to accommodate bank loan syndications, the rapid development of the international bond market, the arrival of derivatives and securitisations and very large increases in the amounts involved, the volatility of markets and increases in legal risks. In that way economies thrive, rather than wither and die.

2.25   In Gericault's painting of *The Raft of the Medusa* painted between 1818 and 1819, there is a figure of a man in the centre foreground lying on his front with one hand over a beam. You cannot see his face. The model for that figure was Delacroix who, when he saw the painting, was reported to have run down the street screaming out of terror and ecstasy. Delacroix in 1830 painted the allegorical *Liberty Leading the People* which hangs in the same salon at the Louvre as *The Raft of the Medusa*. The whole of society is represented in this picture, infused with some passionate ideal. A young boy brandishes two pistols. Liberty herself clutches in her left hand a long rifle with the bayonet out.

2.26   This tumultuous scene represents the struggle for political liberty. But in our context it also represents another liberty, the liberty which people have to choose the law which governs there transactions, to choose their courts freely to hear disputes on their transaction, and to choose the terms on which they agree to regulate their relationship. All of these freedoms are part of the greater and most precious freedoms in our societies. If the law restricts us, as it must, it does so only in order to liberate us.

Limits on the role of law

2.27   Some limits on the role of law must be mentioned.

2.28   The most obvious is that, despite the moral foundations of law, there are many bad laws. If a people want to know why they have bad laws, they should just look in the mirror. That is so at least in those countries in which the people have a say in their laws. Or could have a say if they organised themselves sufficiently and did not support dictatorships or authoritarian rulers. A free choice of governing law enables parties to mitigate the problem of bad laws.

2.29   It is also obvious that in many territories the law is not enforced or is enforced weakly. Again, a choice of governing law can mitigate this risk.

2.30   A further limitation is that the law does not cover all moral questions. Private morality is below the radar of law. Private morality covers things like anger, rants, rage, bullying, humiliation, nastiness, opportunism, contempt, meanness—things which can make life unpleasant or sometimes intolerable. Outside some erosion in employment law and in a few other areas, these things are not punished by the law and do not attract legal compensation, lest we all end up in prison. Nor does the law generally enforce virtues, such as fortitude or hard work. The boundary between enforceable morality and unenforceable morality is contested in most systems, such as the role of the doctrine of good faith in contract law.

The location of the boundary between the law and private morality is also controllable by a choice of governing law. Clearly, dishonesty, fraud, and lies which cause loss are everywhere within the ambit of the law and not merely a matter of private morality.

Law and religion

I mentioned above that our laws are our new scriptures. There are obviously many differences between law and religion. Law does not offer a supernatural being who looks after us and measures us, nor does it contemplate individual immortality, both of which are at the heart of religions. The law does, however, offer survival as its main object, but does not defy individual death. **2.31**

The law does not provide moving rituals, or the same consolations, or the choirs. It does, however, give us better control over our lives. It does not seek to find out the meaning of life, but rather to keep us alive long enough to find out. The object of the law is not to pardon or forgive people but rather to impose a penalty or payment of damages for a breach of contract. But then the matter is over, not added up after death. **2.32**

Both law and religions arouse passions and sometimes fanaticism, because they are moral codes. Both aim to suppress savagery and to promote peace and liberty. You do not have to be initiated into the law; it applies to you anyway. As with religions, the law has epic heroes, most of them forgotten. The law does not insist on onerous rituals as a sign of commitment and seriousness, such as worshipping at temples, fasting, or walking in processions singing. **2.33**

Both have their specialised priests or ministers or rabbis or imams to interpret the ideology. Lawyers too have to be qualified, as do judges, but their jobs are unlike those of priests. Religions have rules and regulations and they have a system of rewards and punishments. **2.34**

The range of the codes of religions are tiny compared to the laws. For example, the laws have detailed codes about democracy, the rule of law, corporations, money, insurance, bankruptcy, and intellectual property. Religions do not have anything like the sophisticated laws which the legal system has about serious crimes or the protection of the accused. As mentioned, religions cover private morality, which is below the threshold of the law, including such matters as feeling internal rage, revenge, and evil thoughts. On the one hand, the religious codes are very ancient and have tended to ossify and petrify. The law, on the other hand, advances relatively quickly as circumstances and opinions change. Indeed, it often moves too quickly when there ought to be more stability and reflection. **2.35**

Economic Value of Law

Economic value of a governing law

What is the economic value to a country if its law is widely used as the governing law of contracts? This is a question posed by Oxera Consulting of Oxford in a report of October 2021 prepared for LegalUK on 'Economic value of English law'. Their research led them to the **2.36** conclusion that the value of English law to the UK is enormous and went far beyond benefits to the legal sector for English law. It underpins hundreds of trillions of dollars of annual business activity domestically and internationally. It is a national asset.

Methods of valuation

2.37 You can attempt to value a legal system which serves as a governing law by adding up earnings, such as these earned by law firms and arbitrators, plus the generation of jobs in the legal system, by the direct income from insurance premiums or other contributions to GDP, by calculating the tax take, or the net value of exports, or the percentage of employment, or tabulating the gross amount involved in transactions, including the huge amounts involved in, say, the foreign exchange and derivatives market, running (in the UK) to many trillions.

2.38 A valuation often relies on network effects, such as the increase in relevant case law and expertise, the reduction in transaction costs flowing from familiarity, and hence a lesser need for an expensive investigation. Then there is the cumulative impact of popularity, ie the more people who use the system, the more are the other people who are drawn to it, because of the reassurance of numbers. Crowds breed more crowds, unkindly called the herding effect.

2.39 The abundant literature on the wealth and poverty of nations and development, and indeed on economic history, relentlessly emphasises the importance of what economists call 'contract and property rights', 'institutions', and 'the rule of law'. The mainstream consensus of this literature overwhelmingly values the law as one of the main foundations of economic value and prosperity. This is also the conclusion of many institutions which rate political risk, legal infrastructure, and the like, such as the World Bank Doing Business Survey (now abandoned), the Heritage Foundation, the World Economic Forum, the World Justice Project, Transparency International, and many other institutions engaged in rating political and similar risks. If you code the tables of the combined results of these bodies, the colours show a dramatic and consistent correlation between legal infrastructure, such as the rule of law, against GDP. Red on law, red on poverty. Blue on law, blue on wealth. This conclusion seems to point to more than an incidental correlation.

2.40 It is not easy to quantify with precise metrics the value of wealth, plenty, and health against misery, starvation, and sickness, or to measure happiness versus tyranny and fear. This does not deter statisticians from estimating the value of a life (eg by calculating the cost of medicines and care), or the reduced road congestion if there is a rail network, or the improved quality of life due to natural capital, such as open land, lakes, rivers, and forests. These valuations often depend on wobbly and subjective data where it is difficult to distinguish and disentangle what value comes from the activity concerned and what from other inputs. If we can measure biodiversity and develop the methods to do so, then we can also develop methods to measure legal factors and how they contribute to economic welfare and also to psychological welfare and our sense of justice.

2.41 All that one can say is that, if you did fix a price on the value of a much-used governing law, it would be very large.

The costs of law

But then, of course, there are the costs of a legal system such as the costs of courts, of parliaments, of consultations, of the composers of laws, of ministries of justice, and generally of the huge apparatus of making laws, maintaining the laws, and providing tribunals to enforce the laws, together a significant slice of the annual budget of commercial states. It is not a surprise therefore that a legal system cannot be created overnight. The experience of transition countries which moved from communism to market economics over the last fifty years seems to suggest that it takes at least fifty years to create a new private law legal system, even when ample precedents are available to copy from. **2.42**

The achievement of legal maturity could well take these countries at least another fifty years before they have developed laws which match their expectations and which their courts can administer with confidence. It is apparent for example that these new or transition legal systems have not yet decided on some of the basic issues which I include in my main indicators, including key questions about predictability of contract, freedom of contract, insolvency set-off, the scope of security interests, and the commercial trust, as well as significant areas of corporate law. It takes time to decide; much, much longer than people think. Indeed, some of these issues have still not been decided in Europe after a thousand years or so. **2.43**

There is also the issue that foreigners have a shadow 'vote' on the legal system since, in order to maintain the popularity of the legal system internationally, the domestic legislators and courts must take into account the wishes of foreign residents who did not qualify for a formal vote. **2.44**

The costs of the law, coupled with international pressures, plus the difficulty of weighing the fiercely competing policies and getting it right, all underline the importance of ensuring that there is some institution whose sole job it is to monitor the law according to specific criteria on an independent basis, lest all the effort and expense be wasted. This is a subject to which I return towards the end of this book. **2.45**

Governing Law as a Monopoly

Dominant governing laws as conferring hard and soft power

There are arguments that the dominant use of a governing law internationally confers both hard and soft power on the jurisdiction which produces the legal system. This proposition can be explored by examining the following semi-monopolies: **2.46**

- The *US dollar*—which is the world's leading reserve currency.
- The jurisdiction *Delaware* in which most of the New York-listed corporations are incorporated—some of the most valuable corporations in the world.
- The *ISDA master agreement* for derivatives, which covers individual derivative transactions without having to write out the whole agreement each time, and the *Uniform Customs and Practices for Documentary Credits*, which are standard forms for trade credits. Both of these are almost universal in their acceptance throughout the world.

- *SWIFT*—the messaging system for banks, based in Belgium, which is used by virtually all international banks. It is purely a messaging system between banks detailing payments to be made from one bank to another. It does not make the transfers itself.
- *CLS Bank* based in New York but mainly operating in London, which handles the settlement netting of most wholesale bank foreign exchange payments in the major traded currencies (many hundreds of trillions annually). In substance, the bank makes sure that the payment and delivery of the two foreign currencies are simultaneous so that neither party has to take the risk that it has paid its currency but the counterparty becomes insolvent before payment of its currency. If you sell your car, you need to make sure that you are paid before you deliver the car to the buyer. CLS stands for continuous linked settlement. CLS has accounts at the major central banks.
- Three securities clearing corporations, *Depository Trust Company* in New York, which clears nearly all US listed securities, and *Euroclear* in Belgium and *Clearstream* in Luxembourg, which between them clear practically all listed international bonds. There are other clearing systems which enjoy dominant positions. A clearing system keeps accounts of investments such as bonds and shares, owned by its participants, just as a bank keeps accounts of your money. The transfers are made from account to account so that there is no necessity to get on your bike to deliver physical securities against physical cash in another part of town. It is all done on an electronic account.
- *English law*, which, together with New York law, enjoys a near duopoly as the chosen governing law of major international and trading contracts.

2.47 These cases are a diverse set including a national currency, a jurisdiction which is not a sovereign state, two private master contracts, several private institutions, and a legal ideology from a territory which is not a sovereign state (there are at least seven separate legal jurisdictions in the British Isles).

2.48 We can instantly recognise two features they do share:

- they are all semi-monopolies in that they hold a dominant share of the market in their fields; and
- they deal with stupendous amounts and are therefore absolutely central to the world economy.

2.49 What are some of the lessons we can derive from these examples which might enable us to draw general conclusions about the creation of the economic value of a governing law and what the jurisdiction would have to do to preserve that value? They include those set out below.

Fulfilment of vital need

2.50 All the cases fulfil a vital need. The fulfilment of that need has an economic value. Thus, every contract must be governed by the law of a jurisdiction and cannot exist in a legal vacuum. The value lies in the advantages conferred by one rule-set over the other, eg how they reduce risks and transaction costs in relation to the transaction concerned. The world needs a currency for international trade which does not involve extra transaction costs. The world needs the standard form of ISDA and the UCP. The world needs clearing systems to handle the volume of transactions cheaply and efficiently.

Advantages of dominant positions to users

In most of the cases, the users are content with only one option, and usually not more than three. In the case of Delaware, US corporate founders have fifty states to choose from—far too many to consider each time. In the case of governing law, contractors have about 320 jurisdictions to choose from—again more confusion. In practice, the two most common choices for large international contracts are English and New York law. The more those legal systems are used, the more the ISDA and UCP forms are used, the more they attract case law and expertise. The more that corporations in the US use Delaware as the domicile of incorporation, the more the Chancery Court in Delaware favours one of the parties in the corporate triangle of management, shareholders, and creditors (Delaware favours management). One reason for that is herd behaviour or tipping into popularity, ie the more users there are, the more attractive the institution becomes. **2.51**

Another underlying reason is that it is much easier and less expensive in terms of investigation and security to choose the same one each time and to choose what everyone else chooses (so it must be acceptable). The process is automatic. The safety and confidence bred by familiarity breeds more familiarity. Accountants describe this as goodwill. There is no question that the goodwill enjoyed by a brand can have huge economic value. Another effect is that incumbents can rely on the inertia of the users who would otherwise have to have to make a leap into the unknown. **2.52**

Multiplier effects

Increasing use also has an agglomeration effect, eg the increase results in greater experience and knowledge which in turn improves the service, ie it is another multiplier of value. This is obviously the case with Delaware, SWIFT, the ISDA master agreement, the UCP in trade finance, the clearers, and CLS Bank. In the case of a governing law, like English law or New York law, the increase in expertise and the advantages flow from wider experience of economically valuable transactions, eg greater predictability and the coverage of more situations by precedents. The width of the experience of transactions also increases the capacity to develop general principles from a multitude of particular cases (lowering transaction costs) and to promote sophisticated innovation where these are an extension of existing transactions, such as, for example, insurance to derivatives (whereby you can 'insure' your interest rates and the value of your investments or currencies), and debt factoring to securitisations (which are a sophisticated form of the sale of commercial receivables in order to raise money). The success of the legal brand encourages the judiciary and the authorities to foster the policies which make the brand successful. All the benefits are available to all users, even though they do not directly contribute. **2.53**

Abuse of a dominant position?

2.54 The disadvantages of a dominant position have been well established for centuries and controlled in the business sphere by competition or antitrust laws. The abusive conduct typically includes the maintenance of higher prices, the exclusion of other businesses from entering the field, and excessive power, for example, in relation to lobbying governments.

2.55 In relation to most of the institutions under discussion, it would seem that either there is no abuse of position or users can easily choose another a competitor. Why would anybody break up SWIFT or the clearers or CLS Bank if there is no abuse of their dominant position?

2.56 There are other advantages to the singularities, eg the authorities only have to deal with and regulate one institution, and users do not have to look into the matter each time, or to change their documents, or investigate different risk factors, or retrain their staff, or devote extra management time to all these factors—so long as the provider performs at reasonable cost.

2.57 It would seem odd to castigate the monopoly of the ISDA master agreement or the UCP as abusive of a dominant position. If they did fail their users, they would soon lose favour in the market, and indeed in both cases the institutions concerned go to great lengths to consult their customers. In the case of legal systems, such as Delaware law or English or New York law, users can at any time switch their allegiance to any of the other legal systems, more than 300 of them.

2.58 Further, the law is an ideology and no-one ever thought to outlaw an legitimate ideology for monopoly reasons. Democracy is an ideology and we cannot have too much of it. Religions are an ideology and, if dominance were a danger, then Christianity and Islam, which are the two mega religions in the world today, would have to be broken up and their proselytisers fined. We do not reject a language because it is dominant.

Competitor imitation

2.59 The fact that potential competitors strenuously seek to break into some of these institutions demonstrates that they think it has substantial economic value. One only need point to the many challenges to the power of the US dollar—not only from sovereign states, but also from populist cyrptocurrencies. As to the law, at the time of Brexit several EU countries announced plans to set up courts using the English language and applying English law. The EU Commission sought to weaken the attractiveness of English law, eg opining against UK accession to the Lugano Judgments Convention, and the promotion of requirements for certain euro-clearings to be located in the EU.

2.60 Gulf countries (Dubai, Abu Dhabi, and Qatar) introduced enclave financial centres based on English law. Singapore appears to base its ambitions of becoming a major financial centre by tracking the merits of English law. Mauritius, aiming to become a kind of Luxembourg for Africa and India, switched decidedly to English law private law in its crucial insolvency regime, thereby overriding the Napoleonic heritage. China installed essentially English law approaches into its private and commercial law, such as the trust and insolvency set-off, partly via Hong Kong and Singapore, which are both English-based jurisdictions.

All these instances testify to the high estimation placed on the economic value of English law by potential competitors. **2.61**

Importance of protection of value

At the same time, the goodwill attached to an institution can be dramatically and suddenly damaged if it fails its users. The damage is magnified by the number of users. A series of bad judicial decisions or adverse statutes could quickly weaken the goodwill of a legal system, just as a scandal can seriously damage the goodwill of a corporation and sometimes lead to its downfall. The events can cause consternation in markets, even though apparently technical, such as an English case in the late 1980s declaring that derivatives entered into by local authorities were outside their powers, and a more recent New York case during the 2010s on the pari passu clause in Argentinian bonds, until then considered to be harmless boilerplate. See Chapter 19. This factor underlines the investment and planned effort needed to maintain the brand. **2.62**

Economic value of physical clustering

The location of the favoured institution attracts economic value in the form of additional businesses and people establishing themselves in that location. They cluster because of the advantages of physical proximity. The clustering of the core specialists in turn attracts other businesses and people to serve the core, whether other professionals or restaurants. These clusters produce jobs, economically valuable transactions, wealth, and an increased tax take. This seems still to be the case, even in an age of virtual communication. **2.63**

In the case of the law, apart from lawyers themselves, the clustering effect attracts markets and any business to the location where the character of the local law is a material factor. It also attracts students and high level researchers to local universities. The contribution of education to local GDP is large in the case of the UK and the US. **2.64**

Hard power—the US dollar

The status of the institution often confers hard power which is valuable economically. The leading example is the US dollar. The US dollar enjoys 'exorbitant privileges'. These include the hard power derived from the ability to sanction foreign states and their banking systems because in practice they have to use the US dollar payment system located in New York (mainly CHIPS). This police power can be and is used to promote US foreign policy interests at the macro level against menacing sovereigns and **2.65** terrorists and to enforce its regulatory powers, eg to control money laundering and market abuse (insider dealing, market manipulation, even tax collection). Another economically vast privilege is the ability of the US to finance itself cheaply by foreign borrowings and under its own law. Most business and sovereign states need US dollars because of the fact that commodities, bonds, and the like are commonly priced in dollars. The US can therefore in addition inflate its currency to pay its debts. The value of the economic power that the US has over the rest of the world and the economic value of its borrowing and other privileges derived from the status of the US dollar are so colossal that quantification seems pedantry.

Hard power—English law

2.66 Just as the dominance of the US dollar confers hard power and therefore huge economic value, so also does English law, although to a different extent. For example, if the UK government can issue bonds abroad which are subject to English law because it is trusted, then English law has a market value in reducing the price and encouraging investors because of confidence in the legal system. If the US and the UK together decided to introduce a state bankruptcy regime for bonds (which laws usually cover most of the eligible debt of bankrupt sovereigns—there is no such regime at the moment), they could do so by inserting the appropriate clauses in New York and English bonds which would cover most of the international foreign bonds. Again it is thought most unlikely that both sovereigns would exercise those powers, but the ability to do so in as yet unthought-of cases could translate into substantial economic value. The result of these examples is that the governing law confers hard power, just as the US dollar confers (a different) hard power. Power can have substantial economic value.

Soft power and hard economic value

2.67 The status of the legal system of a jurisdiction might have a major effect on the perception and reputation of that state and its economy. A legal system expresses the codified values of a society—its standards, its norms, its freedoms, its ethics and morality, its sense of justice. If these values are shared by others or aspired to or admired by others, the affinity or admiration or confidence thereby engendered might often affect the willingness of the other, whether governmental of private, to enter into alliances and treaties, to cooperate in defence and security, to cooperate in the suppression of international criminality, to share sensitive information, to make investments, to provide finance, and to engage in trade.

2.68 In view of these advantages, it is not surprising that the use of a jurisdiction's law as an international governing law is not just a matter of patriotic honour or pride: it has significant results in terms of economic gain and hard power. It is also clear that a governing law could quickly lose its position if it fails its users. There is nothing wrong with competition. At least the international business community has a choice.

Impact of the Growth of Law

Background to the growth of law since 1830

2.69 The dominance of just two legal systems in international business transactions shows a trend to simplicity because of the sheer size of legal systems and their laws. It is a quite a feat to understand even one legal system to the extent necessary to choose it as a governing law. It is worth recounting very briefly a history of the growth of law that took place over the last two centuries or so since 1830 when the population of the of the world first reached one billion. It is now more than seven times as large at about 7.8 billion. That is, for every one person in 1830 walking alongside you on the pavement, there are now eight people.

2.70 Over the same period world GDP per capita grew from US$700 billion to US$87,000 billion, and the GDP per person grew from about US$700 (two dollars a day) to about US$7,700, more than ten times as much. The current figures should be adjusted downward somewhat to reflect 2000 values but the degree of magnitude is clear.

2.71 How much has the law grown since then? This is extraordinarily difficult to measure but I suggest that the growth of written law in the books in the entire world since 1830 has been not just 1,000, not just 10,000 times, but much much more, maybe more than 100,000 times. In the UK alone it has been calculated that there were more than 200,000 statutory instruments (that is, delegated subordinate legislation, excluding case law and proper statutes), since 1950. It probably does not really matter that we cannot be precise, since it is evident that there was a huge surge upwards from the early nineteenth century onwards.

2.72 Back in 500 BC, the content of law, at least written law, seemed rather small. Hammurabi's code of more than 1,000 years earlier in 1772 BC, which is contained on the 2.25 metre (7.4 feet) stele now in the Louvre in Paris, contains 282 rules of law. Hammurabi was a Babylonian king. The early Romans were reputed to have had Twelve Tables dated about 450 BC. The laws in Leviticus, in the biblical Old Testament, amount to a few hundred articles—tiny compared to modern legislation.

2.73 We can work out the length of the codes of Justinian codifying Roman law around 533 AD and we can measure the barbarian codes of following centuries in the Dark Ages. When a collection of all current laws in Castile was printed at the king's command in 1569, it filled only two volumes, albeit there were 4,000 laws. In the next 100 years or so there was a proliferation of local codes in Europe. We can also measure the size of the codes in the early codification movement, starting in France in 1804. We can measure the size of US tax law in the nineteenth century as against the size of US tax law now. We know that prior to the nineteenth century, company law hardly existed and there was no such thing as securities or financial regulation, let alone the other fields of regulation which now are leviathans and behemoths on the legal landscape. So it does not seem too unreasonable to estimate that the growth of world law is well in excess of 100,000 times larger since the early nineteenth century and could in fact be much larger.

Reasons for growth of law

2.74 Although one must be careful about establishing cause and effect relationships when there is only a correlation, what seems to have happened around 1830 is that, when the population of the world reached the first billion and subsequently accelerated, the increased number of people produced more wealth. Compared to a million people, a billion people think of more things, invent more things, make more things. The result of this prodigious multitude of effort by such a vast number of people produces wealth which is measured by GDP. The money went into banks and capital markets. This wealth in turn was funnelled into corporations by way of investment by share capital, bank loans, and bonds. Banks made loans out of the cash deposited with them to finance new businesses. Insurance companies and banks invested in equity share capital and bonds for the new industries of the industrial revolution. Modern corporate law was invented. Previously business was conducted through partnerships where the partners were each liable for all the debts of the firms, a risk which was inconceivable for investors in the new businesses who had no day-to-day control over the management of the business.

2.75 The rapid expansion of business led to a demand for credit which in turn led to bankruptcies and losses. The reaction of law-makers then as now was to wave the legal wand and rush in new laws to mitigate the devastation wrought by large corporate bankruptcies, including the bankruptcy of banks. Hence the advent in due course of financial and corporate regulation, corporate governance, financial statements, and generally a massive increase in the amount and sophistication of law, including basic subjects such as the law of contract and the law of sale. The inventiveness of science was accompanied by the exhilarating ingenuity of the law.

2.76 If we were also to plot the amount of the growth of the corpus of all the scientific subjects, from medicine to physics, we would see a growth probably greater than the growth of law by a large margin.

2.77 Over recent decades legal risks have now intensified around the world. The volume of law is now out of control and is unmanageable. What is needed is a flame-thrower. The following are the main reasons:

- While one can discern broad trends, harmonisation of law at the detailed level in our fields has not happened. Instead, the law has splintered and fissured into fragments like a stone hitting a windscreen.
- A large part of this increase results from the intensification of regulatory regimes, notably in the West.
- Almost all of the 320 jurisdictions are now part of the world economy in the sense that they have businesses, banks, and corporations which do business with other countries. Few countries are hermetically sealed off. Even Cambodia has a stock exchange, even Chad and Kyrgyzstan are interested in advancing their economies. Only a few countries stand loftily apart, either resentfully, such as North Korea, or because they are not really interested, eg Bhutan or Turkmenistan.
- The law is much more volatile than it has ever been and changes rapidly, sometimes with no apparent reason, arbitrarily, just because somebody wants to 'reform' the law or has a flash of anger.

- In developed countries, domestic and financial and corporate law has broken up into tiers or layers internally, with different protections for different sectors of the population, usually politically driven. Thus, in England there are eight tiers for security interests and nearly thirty different bankruptcy regimes.
- Many countries give extra-territorial effect to their laws especially in the case of money-laundering, data protection, market abuse (such as insider dealing), and anti-trust (competition) law. Hence, practitioners have to pay regard not only to their own laws but to those of many other countries as well.
- There is great diversity around the world as to how the law is actually applied and the sophistication, or lack of it, in the legal infrastructure. For example, the basic law in Burundi and Belgium derives from the same roots, but the application is very different. One therefore has to cope with yet another layer—the written law or the law on the books, and then whether or not it is applied.

The law and money, banks, and corporations

2.78 I said above that legal systems are profoundly moral in that scope and effect. They express profound concepts of justice. Yet the choices between one legal policy and another are usually hard to make since the competing claims are frequently both compelling and almost evenly balanced. The law has to choose. For example, this problem appears in the law relating to money, banks, and corporations, which together have been the engines of growth and huge improvements in economic welfare and material well-being since 1830. At that time, almost all the people in the world lived in miserable poverty and destitution but that is far from the case now.

2.79 At one time people, particularly in agricultural societies, thought that money was an evil. Yet it is clear now that money was one of greatest inventions of the human mind. It would have been impossible to have prosperity without these tokens. You could not buy a loaf of bread by handing over some socks you had knitted the night before. We have to have a means of exchange in precise units. Further, money represents the work and labour of the people. It expresses the value of their efforts and their talents. It connects us to other peoples because we could not have trade without using tokens. Also, money is a source of value and it is that money, when converted into investments many of which are near money-like government bonds, which connects us to our future and preserves us in the future. It is plain that money can be the source of financial oppression in the hands of imprudent central banks who permit inflation. Money now compared to what it was a century ago is practically worthless. Hence, money is a proper object of morality but the idea that money of itself is wicked or a source of greed and oppression has little credibility.

2.80 A second example concerns banks. Once money was in invented it was necessary to have somewhere to put it. Hence the invention of banks who look after the people's money. They also supply credit in the sense that these pools of money are intended to be used like rainwater to irrigate the land. Hence, when you switch on the light, the light comes on. It comes on because the (hopefully renewables) power station has been built out of bank money. But in substance, if you strip away all the corporate forms, which are nothing more than marks in a registrar's book, it is not the bank's money which builds the power station. It is the money of the people, ultimately the citizen. It is the citizens, with the products of their work and labour, who switch on the light. Of course, a great deal of money is wasted through mismanagement or credulity or misfortune. But then a lot of people waste their lives and that is not unreasonable.

2.81 Hence, the legal protection of banks is in substance a protection of the citizen. It is not that simple, of course, because the intermediary is also subject to a moral law in its task of representing the people. Nevertheless, this example shows that a simplistic approach needs to take into account a complicated set of issues of justice and fairness.

2.82 The extraordinary rise of prosperity and production after 1830 was in the main carried out through corporations with money credit from banks and shareholders. This prosperity is expressed in the measure GDP, which is in substance a measure of work and labour, talent, and effort, and the means of our survival. Money, corporations, and banks are creatures created by the law. Each is insubstantial, a non-being, not even a shadow of a shadow. Each is a creation of the human imagination, an idea.

Conclusion

2.83 There is no question that the law is of inestimable value to modern societies. Laws which are used as a governing law internationally are of even greater value and are a national asset. A national asset of such prodigious value requires prodigious efforts and discipline to maintain it and to protect it. Protecting the law requires a profound understanding of what it is for and what the ideology represents.

3
SCOPE OF CONTRACTS

Contracts Based on Assets

Grouping of contracts

3.1 This chapter describes the main groups of contracts which we are concerned with in this book. The aim is to consider whether they are internationally mobile contracts in the sense that they can be subject to a choice of governing law, and to establish the degree of risks relating to such matters as predictability, freedom of contract, business orientation, and the minimalisation of insolvency and other risks by the choice of a governing law and courts. I group the enormous scope and variety of modern business contracts into general classes which are functional rather than the somewhat theoretical divisions you might get in the law books. One of the objectives of this survey is to draw attention to the huge quantities and diversity of assets as an antidote to the limited view of transactions you sometimes find elsewhere.

Asset-related contracts

3.2 A major super-set of contracts of comprises contracts related to assets or property. One is struck by the sheer variety of assets and also by the range of contracts which are concerned with assets, quite apart from the diversity of those relating to services, or work, or raising capital.

3.3 You can sell an asset, or grant security over an asset, such as by mortgage or pledge or charge, or lease or charter or hire out the asset or let someone else use it. You can hire capacity on a satellite or space rocket, or you can hire a work station in an office block. You can lend investments under a stock lending agreement, or sell an asset with an option to repurchase—a repo. The latter is a transaction conducted in large volumes every day in financial markets as a security substitute. You can have a contract to manage or maintain or operate or look after the asset by way of custody, or a contract to manufacture or produce or construct the asset, or a contract to advise about the asset. Those are no less than twelve things you can do with an asset and there are probably more. You multiply the categories of assets—many hundreds—by at least twelve to count the basic classes of contract. The stupendous variety of these asset-based contracts stems from the stupendous variety of assets and the large variety of things you can do to them.

3.4 For example, one of the leading codifications of the law of security interests—Article 9 of the US Uniform Commercial Code—lists more than forty different classes of assets which the code considers merit special treatment. The number of legal issues to consider in putting together a security package is also somewhere around forty, one of which (priorities) may involve more than a couple of dozen different priority questions. If you multiply the combinations, you arrive at a staggeringly huge number of issues.

Classes of asset

3.5 An asset is property which is defined as something which can be specifically identified, and which the holder can freely and exclusively use and enjoy, sell, exchange, or destroy. Many assets do not qualify for this absolute and exclusive freedom and are hemmed in with restrictions, such as regulatory restrictions on who the asset can be sold to, such as the exclusion of retail buyers of investments without a public prospectus.

3.6 Practically everything is property. One can think of only a few exceptions, such as a bolt of lightning, the spray of an ocean wave, an ephemeral mist in the early dawn, or an unexpressed idea.

3.7 We may now classify assets according to the conventional legal taxonomy of property into intangible assets, tangible assets, and land.

Intangible assets

3.8 These are sometimes called intangible movables and are an extremely important class in modern economies, probably the largest class in developed countries. They are exceptionally mobile internationally in the sense that many of them can be subject to a choice of governing law. The main exceptions are shares in a company which are invariably governed by the law of the constitution of the company. Many of them are invisible, once they are stripped of their documentary clothing, such as shares or bonds. But we should not delude ourselves into thinking that they do not exist and are just an ephemeral nothing or emptiness. That is because, apart perhaps from intellectual property, they need at least two people (including legal people like sovereign states and corporations) to make them, even if embodied in a blockchain. These two people are, for example, a lender and borrower, a shareholder and a company, a car owner and an insurance company. It is true that you cannot have a picnic on an intangible asset or race it down the motorway, but intangible assets proliferate prodigiously and are essential in modern economies.

3.9 This teeming class includes investment property, such as shares, bonds, participations in mutual funds, derivatives, book-entry securities held in securities settlement systems, and digital assets such as cryptocurrencies represented by a piece of code. The class also covers compensation claims, litigation claims, and governmental compensation for compulsory acquisition. A very large set is formed by the half a dozen categories of intellectual property, such as patents, trademarks, and software rights, plus human knowledge and research, software, and goodwill.

3.10 The class includes the intangible asset of contracts which themselves can be sold, such as the benefit of receivables, of commercial contracts for the sale of assets, or for the leases of those assets, licences of intellectual property or syndicated credits, or bank accounts, or insurance claims, or guarantees, or performance bonds. Some may be secured on assets.

Included technically in this class of invisibles are treaties, which are really just contracts between sovereign states, and government concessions, eg to build and operate a power station or a licence to operate a bank.

Goods

3.11 Goods or chattels often come under the legal heading of tangible movables, which is an apt description. The contracts of sale or security which cover these assets are also exceptionally internationally mobile, again in the sense that they can be subject to a choice of governing law from any jurisdiction. They show human ingenuity and productivity at its most appealing and attractive, although not always. Some are ugly or dangerous or just rubbish. The class includes wheat and vegetables, minerals, plastics, chemicals, foodstuffs, animals, plants, large equipment and machinery, toys, white goods, transportation chattels (including ships, barges, aircraft, drones, satellites, cars, and large diggers), mobile homes, mobile phones and computers, railway rolling stock and locomotives, and containers.

3.12 Some of these are registered in an asset title register in the same way as land, notably ships and aircraft.

3.13 We have artistic chattels such as paintings and jewellery, also bullion and human parts such as blood plasma and kidneys. You could say that the class includes electricity.

Land

3.14 The last and most venerable category of asset is realty or land, categorised by jurists as immovables. You can divide up land into separate classes, such as residential homes, office premises, industrial property, and agricultural property. Land includes crops and timber, so long as uncut. It includes minerals, stone, oil, and gas, so long as unextracted. It includes lakes and rivers. The contracts can be leases of land or rights of way. It covers things attached to the land such as roads, railways, tunnels, bridges, mines, masts, electric or fibre optic cables, or pipelines, depending on the degree to which the asset is fixed or embedded in the land.

3.15 You cannot choose the governing law over a land title nor, usually, a tenancy of land, even though this is a kind of contract and is characterised as such in many jurisdictions. Land is immovable, so a contract relating to land is often not in practice internationally mobile from the governing law point of view. But it could be. One can have a contract for the sale of land or of tenancies of land which can have a governing law different from the fixed location of the land. One can also have agreements to grant security over land, although very often these sales and mortgages must comply with local form to be registered.

3.16 There are about 148 million square kilometres of land in the world. The whole surface of the planet is about 510 square kilometres. Some of this is neither land nor sea, such as the North Pole, which is just an enormous floating iceberg. The sea is the commons. Space is also the commons, but both can be the subject of contracts, such as a contract to fling a satellite into orbit.

Financial, Corporate, and Commercial Transactions

Functional division of contracts into classes

3.17 A useful way to analyse how the key indicators apply to business transactions is to classify the contracts into categories which bring out the intensity of the relevance of the key indicators to that category. This taxonomy is different from the classification usually used in books on contract law or in codes of law, classifications which often do not reflect what is actually going on in the real world nowadays.

3.18 I propose three very broad heads which have numerous subsets and in that way we find some quite remarkable results. It is not necessary to be definitionally pure and precise; nor is the list by any means exhaustive. The aim is to discover a common core in the group without necessarily identifying all of the little fluttering electrons spinning round the atomic nucleus further and further away into the fringes beyond the powerful positivity at the centre.

3.19 The three broad heads are:

- financial transactions
- corporate transactions
- commercial transactions.

3.20 Each set of transactions commonly includes a large array of ancillary contracts around a main central contract.

Financial transactions generally

3.21 I divide the broad head of financial transactions into eight main subsets. I explain these transactions in more detail than corporate and commercial transactions because it is possibly the case that some financial transactions are less well understood than routine corporate and commercial transactions.

3.22 Virtually all of the thirteen main risk areas are crucial to these contracts because of the size of the transactions and a peculiarity of the risks which are inherent to the transactions. These risk areas include predictability so that the terms which have been agreed are upheld by the courts, insulation against foreign adverse laws in the debtor's country, such as exchange controls and moratoriums, business orientation so that they are not trumped by some obsolete legal rules out-of-touch with the market, freedom of contract so that the parties can meet new circumstances and special risks, exclusion clauses so that the parties can define the risks they have towards each other and therefore measure them for capital adequacy and other purposes, protection against insolvency risks, such as mitigation of risks by insolvency set-off and netting, by security interests and by commercial trusts, freedom from disproportionate regulation or disproportionate litigation, and impartial non-politicised standards from enforcing courts.

Loan transactions

3.23 Syndicated bank credits and international bond issues are economically of very large importance in the world. They are both loans. One class is loans made by multiple banks under the terms of a single credit agreement in favour of a borrower. The other class is loans made by numerous investors who subscribe for little pieces of the loan in the form of bonds. Bonds are often listed on a stock exchange to improve the range of investors who can invest in these bonds, although they are normally traded between institutions privately off the exchange. In the case of bonds, the borrower is called the issuer. The bonds are bought by institutions such as banks, insurance companies, and mutual funds. The bonds are very easily transferable and the holders record them in a clearing system which keeps accounts for holders. By contrast, the sale of participations in loan agreements is complicated, although there are standard forms and standardised procedures.

3.24 Both syndicated credits and bonds set out the financial terms, such as repayments and the calculation of interest, covenants of the issuer or borrower, eg not to encumber its assets, events of default upon which the lenders can accelerate the loans so that they become immediately due and payable, and lender democracies to make decisions, especially if the borrower is in financial difficulties. They invariably contain a choice of governing law and courts and, if relevant, a waiver of sovereign immunity. Bond issues are surrounded by other documents such as subscription agreements, paying agency agreements, trust deeds, and the like.

3.25 A syndicated bank credit agreement in the standard form of the Loan Market Association can run to more than 100 pages, all in poised Augustan classical prose, exquisitely clipped. US forms lurch towards a more luxuriant gothic style with provisos upon provisos. By contrast, the highly standardised terms of bond issues used to be crammed into one single page on the back of a bond, printed with all the intricacy of a currency note, now replaced by a bland typed version held by the global custodian for the clearing system. The bonds themselves have vanished into electronic notation on an illuminated screen.

3.26 Bond issues are often documented under programme documents which set out common terms for incorporation according to each issue to save writing it out again each time. A syndicated loan and bond issue are launched with the help of an information memorandum (syndications) or offering circular (bonds) prepared by the borrower with the help of the arrangers. The arrangers are commercial or investment banks.

3.27 Most bond issues are made to sophisticated investors and are usually exempt from public prospectus requirements. The greatest volume are denominated in US dollars. The proportion of issuers of international bonds is usually around one-third sovereign states, another third banks, and the remaining third corporates.

3.28 The loans or bonds may be guaranteed, typically by group companies, and may also be secured on the borrower's assets in which case there will be security agreements. If the loans are tiered in priority, there will be inter-creditor agreements between the classes of creditors to subordinate the junior lenders.

3.29 Corporate bonds may be convertible into shares of the borrower or will have warrants attached to buy shares of the borrower.

3.30 Syndicated loan agreements and bond issues are the archetypal international mobile transactions governed by a legal system external to that of the borrower or issuer, often English or New York law.

Guarantees

3.31 Many financial transactions are guaranteed. The guarantee is a separate internationally mobile transaction, although it is often governed by the same law as the obligation guaranteed. Guarantees come in many forms, such as conventional bank guarantees, first demand guarantees, standby letters of credit, and credit default swaps.

Restructuring agreements

3.32 If a debtor hovers on the edge of insolvency, then a private agreement with its banks and bondholders may be necessary. This is called a 'work-out'. The financial agreements are internationally mobile, as with the original syndicated credits and bond issues.

3.33 In practice, in big cases the original bank loan agreements and bonds to be restructured are governed by English or New York law and it follows that English or New York law will be adopted to restructure them. The security documents will be accompanied by local security documents for local assets.

3.34 The restructuring of the debt of sovereigns is generally accomplished by an exchange offer whereby the sovereign agrees to exchange the old defaulted bonds for new bonds which are rescheduled. The exchange offer in the case of sovereigns is typically governed by New York or English law, one which again is usually the governing law of the original bonds.

Title finance

3.35 To complete the picture on what are in substance secured loans or similar, there is a large class of transactions which are essentially entered into for the purpose of raising money, using a security substitute called title finance. Examples are finance leases of aircraft, ships, satellites, or other equipment, and a sale and repurchase of securities (repo). Other variants are hire purchase, factoring of receivables, and sale and leaseback (usually of land). In this class, one might include stock lending whereby dealers can borrow a stock from another dealer in order to satisfy a sale of the stock which the dealer does not own. When the time comes for the borrowing dealer to repay equivalent stock, the price of the stock may have dropped in value so the dealer makes a profit. This transaction comes under the generic description of 'shorting'.

3.36 To take the example of a repo, a counterparty which wishes to raise finance could sell bonds to the financing party, such as a commercial bank or a central bank. The financing party pays the counterparty the current price for the bonds. Under the terms of the contract, the financing party can, at the end of the term, eg overnight or measured in months, call upon the counterparty to buy back the bonds at a price equal to the original purchase price plus an amount equal to interest on the original price over the period of the financing. The counterparty also has this option. The transaction could simply be framed as the counterparty borrowing a loan from the financing party and charging the bonds to the financing party to secure the loan. But a secured loan would get involved in all the fuss and restriction in the law relating to security interests which has no relevance to this vast market between institutions. In addition, under a repo the financing party acquires the full ownership of the bonds and can therefore use them for collateral or for securities lending. So the bonds are put to good use, which in turn reduces the transaction costs. An additional difference is that the financing party owns the bonds and so if the financing party becomes insolvent before the repurchase, the counterparty has lost the bonds which would not be the case with a pledge or charge.

3.37 Similarly, an airline could borrow money from banks to buy an aircraft and then mortgage the aircraft to the banks to secure the loan. A similar result can be achieved by a financial lease, which is the usual way in which aircraft are financed. A company owned by the lending banks buy the aircraft from the manufacturer, register it with this company which then leases the aircraft to the airline. The lease payments would be the capital price of the aircraft plus an amount equal to interest. This arrangement in some jurisdictions again avoids the fuss of security interest law and also has tax advantages, which are encouraged by tax authorities to facilitate the purchase of aircraft.

3.38 Repos and stock lending are carried out under standard form agreements settled by various market associations.

3.39 Compared to the above title finance transactions, the amounts involved in the retention of title to goods, which is another form of title finance, are tiny, but receive disproportionate attention in the law books on contract.

3.40 Whether these title finance transactions are recharacterised as security interests and made subject to the regulation of security interests, like a bird shut up in a cage, receives differing treatment. The jurisdictions of the world are split on this issue.

3.41 The documentation for the main title finance transactions almost invariably make an express choice of governing law and courts and so are internationally mobile.

Derivatives

3.42 Just as you can ensure your car against a crash or your home against a fire, you can also insure against the risk that the interest rates you pay go up or the investments or the currencies or commodities you hold go down in value The transactions are variously called interest swaps (the most common), forwards, or options. Some derivatives, called credit default swaps, are effectively guarantees of bonds (usually). They are entered into almost entirely between large institutions who can quantify and tolerate the risks. Regulation generally excludes retail investors.

3.43 A much-used transaction is an interest rate swap under which a borrower of a bank loan or the issuer of a bond, where the interest floats up and down, agrees for a fee to pay a bank or other dealer interest at a fixed rate, in return for which the dealer pays the borrower the floating rate so that the borrower can pay this floating rate to the lending banks or bondholders. The effect is that the borrower only pays fixed interest. These transactions are usually documented under a master agreement of ISDA. The master agreement is an umbrella agreement containing provisions such as events of default and termination clauses and other important clauses allowing a non-defaulting party to terminate all transactions against a defaulting party, to calculate the losses and gains on each of them and then to set them off. This results in a massive reduction in exposures. Each specific transaction is documented by a confirmation between the parties which absorbs the master agreement and then briefly sets out the terms of the particular deal based on shorthand definitions published by ISDA.

3.44 The ISDA master agreement is around twenty-four pages long, including the schedule, and reads almost like a standard term loan agreement with the financial terms gutted out. Every word is pored over by derivatives lawyers. However, the books of definitions which can be incorporated in confirmations for each deal are bulky and bristling with technicality.

3.45 The transactions are not technically insurance or guarantees and are typically called 'hedging', as opposed to insurance.

3.46 The nominal amounts of derivatives outstanding at any one time runs into hundreds of trillions of US dollars, although the actual daily exposures on termination are very much less.

3.47 Derivatives are also internationally mobile transactions and again most are governed by English or New York law. One result is the accumulation of case law in those jurisdictions and the relative dearth elsewhere. There are French and German forms which are used for domestic transactions. The French form is also used in Francophone Africa.

3.48 Regulation in the US, UK, and continental Europe, as well as elsewhere, requires simple derivatives to be cleared through a clearing house.

Securitisations and other receivables transfers

3.49 Under a securitisation a bank, say, sells home mortgage loans it has made to homeowners to a specially formed company. This special company issues bonds, usually to sophisticated investors, to raise the purchase price for these home loans to be paid to the bank seller. The company then charges the benefits of all the home loans to a trustee for the bondholders. Typically, there is more than one tier of loans, and sometimes as many as three tiers with senior, mezzanine, and junior bonds.

3.50 The usual main motive for these transactions is that banks have to have equity capital of a certain percentage of all of their loans and other exposures as a cushion for hard times. Hence, every time the bank makes another home mortgage loan, it has to have equity capital against that loan, unless it sells existing loans to the company, in which event it can make more home loans and maybe also make a profit out of the securitisation.

3.51 These transactions have their own surrounding subservient contracts, such as interest rate swaps and agreements to provide liquidity to smooth out payments on the bonds, which may not completely match the home loan repayments.

3.52 The location of the securitisation vehicle tends to be driven by legal and tax factors. The financing bonds are internationally mobile transactions.

3.53 One may also here mention loan transfers which are sales of a loan which a bank has made or a participation in a loan, typically to another bank of hedge fund. Because of restrictions on assignment in the original loan agreement, the loan transfer may be structured as a sub-participation under which the incoming buyer lends the amount of the loan concerned to the original lender on terms that the original lender only has to pay the incoming buyer amounts equal to the original lender's recoveries from the borrower if and when received. Hence, the incoming buyer takes the credit risk of the borrower (and the selling bank).

3.54 Factoring is a transaction where a business sells its receivables to a finance company so as to finance itself. Factoring transactions are now niche.

3.55 In all of the above transactions, the receivables can be anything from home loans, to trade receivables, to aircraft leases, to mobile phone receivables, to car loans.

3.56 Loan transfers and the factoring of receivables are internationally mobile transactions.

Foreign exchange contracts

3.57 The foreign exchange market is by far the largest in the world, running to hundreds of trillions. The counterparties are usually banks and the main currencies are the US dollar, the euro, and the Japanese yen, plus other currencies such as UK sterling and Swiss francs. The largest proportion have a dollar leg. Most of the contracts are very short-term, eg two days. Most are settled via CSL Bank, which is based in New York, although the market is mainly in London.

3.58 The contracts are internationally mobile but, outside standard bank terms of business or foreign exchange master agreements, the contracts do not always expressly select a governing law and courts.

Exchanges and central counterparties

3.59 There are plenty of market exchanges, from flowers and antiques to car boot sales. The largest by far are exchanges for securities. We are here concerned with formal organised exchanges, not the protean number of exchanges run by single investment firms or informal over-the-counter markets between dealers. There are formal or informal exchanges for practically all of the assets which I listed above in the taxonomy of the main assets.

3.60 The main features of a formal exchange are (1) to channel client orders via brokers and agents who deal with each other on the exchange so that clients do not have to search out for a buyer of seller, (2) to increase the likelihood that there are many buyers and sellers

42   SCOPE OF CONTRACTS

congregated together so as to provide 'liquidity', (3) to record prices so that everybody knows what the prices are (price discovery), (4) matching of transactions, that is, checking the transactions with buyer and seller, (5) arranging settlement, that is, arranging for the security to be transferred and the price paid, (6) orderly trading and the observance of rules.

3.61   All of these activities are covered in the rules of the exchange, which are contracts of considerable intricacy. In practice, they are not internationally mobile contracts, but are governed by the law of the place where the exchange is. Even that could be something of a generalisation in view of the fact that most exchanges are now electronic and do not have a permanent habitation. The rule books, however, will select a governing law and the means of settling disputes, either by the courts or by arbitration.

3.62   At the centre of most of these exchanges is a marvellous and magical fiction, unkindly referred to by some uninformed commentators as financial plumbing, as though it was a toilet. This is the central counterparty, which is a triumph of reason and an instrument more delicate than a rose petal in its subtle simplicity.

3.63   On the one hand, if dealers A, B, C, D, etc, then A1, B1, C1, D1, etc, then A2, B2, C2, D2, etc, all have transactions, such as the sale of a share, with dealer X, then, if X becomes insolvent, there could be no set-off and netting of all of those contracts between the multitude of dealers on one side and X on the other. They would not be mutual and you cannot set off non-mutual contracts. One person's claim would be used to pay another's debt.

3.64   On the other hand, if you set up a company owned by the members of the exchange and have a rule that, whenever A, A1, A2, etc have a contract with X, that contract will immediately be converted into two contracts in a chain, one contract between the dealer and this company, and then a mirror contract between the company and X, then the result will be that, when X becomes insolvent, all the contracts with everybody on the exchange with X will be a contract between the company and X. Therefore, the company will be mutual with X on all of the array of contracts. The company can then terminate all of those contracts, calculate the losses and gains, and set them off. The reductions in exposure are so huge that you could not operate a significant exchange without this company in the middle.

3.65   These companies are called central counterparties. All the members of the exchange agree to provide loans and a back-up fund if the central counterparty exceeds certain risk ratios, and also to provide collateral, called 'margin', if a member's exposure exceeds a threshold. This must be the case because the fact that all of the contracts are routed through the central counterparty means that there is an immense concentration of risk on this central party. It is also necessary for the surrounding legal system to allow instantly realisable collateral and also set-off and netting. The collateral is usually highly rated securities such as government bonds.

3.66   It should be noted here that most clearing systems for securities require commercial trusts. For example, in the case of bonds, a global custodian holds a global bond representing the whole of the issue for the benefit of the clearing company, such as Euroclear in Brussels. That is a trust in substance because the global custodian is the trustee holding the apparent title to the bond, but the bond really belongs to the clearing company, who is the beneficiary. However, it does not stop there. The clearing company holds its interest under the bond for participants in the clearing company, who are usually big banks and dealers who have the necessary systems and can handle large sums of money. But each of those participants will usually hold its interest for, say, a small dealer, who in turn holds its interest for clients. The clients need these chains because, of course, there is no way that retail clients could deal with the administration of their securities on their own—some experts further up do that for them, such as a pension fund investing the clients' pension money. The result is that you have a chain of trusts and sub-trusts, a chain which can be quite long and snake through other jurisdictions. If there is a break in the chain because, for example, one of the jurisdictions does not recognise the trust, then if the person at the snapping-point becomes insolvent, the client at the end of the chain, who may be a pensioner, widow, or orphan, may get nothing, the ultimate catastrophe. It is a disaster because this is a situation which should never have happened. The law is not supposed to do that to people, especially people, which is most of us, who have no idea what is going on.

3.67 I will come back to the central counterparties later on at paragraph 10.74.

Funds

3.68 These are collective investment schemes whereby a company, partnership or trust is formed to hold and manage investments or other assets on behalf of its shareholders or other participants. They involve enormous amounts, tens of trillions, and there are thousands of them. They have derisively been called the investment advisers to the poor because somebody else makes the decisions. Which is the whole idea.

3.69 They share the same simple structure, that is the constitution of the fund, the appointment of a manager to manage the fund for a fee, and the appointment of a depository or custodian to hold the assets being managed.

3.70 These funds are everywhere. They include public mutual funds in which the public participate, private equity funds who buy companies with a view to selling them at a profit in three to five years' time, venture capital funds to finance start-ups, hedge funds who typically take bets on the market, real estate investment funds, university endowment funds, sovereign wealth funds, and many others.

3.71 Some of these funds are set up as trusts for their participants or as limited partnerships. As with companies, these entities are not internationally mobile in the sense that you cannot choose the law of the constitution: the law which applies to the entity is normally the law of the place of its constitution. But, as with companies, the main contracts of these funds are usually internationally mobile, although the investments in them, like shares, are not. You cannot choose the law governing a share.

Other financial contracts

3.72 Other financial contracts include prime brokerage agreements (which are basically agency agreements), corporate finance advisory mandates, investment advisory agreements, insurance policies, bank standard terms and deposits, confidentiality agreements, outsourcing agreements, and agreements between credit card companies and merchants.

3.73 All of these are internationally mobile transactions.

Significant corporate transactions generally

3.74 A short list of significant corporate transactions, usually involving many satellite contracts, includes five main subsets.

3.75 All of these transactions require predictability, business orientation, insulation from foreign laws, freedom of contract for new transactions, exclusion of liability—especially arranger's liability in relation to private offering circulars to sophisticated investors—methods of mitigating the various insolvency risks, and avoidance of disproportionate regulatory and litigation risks. For various reasons to be explained, on the one hand, the intensity of the risks is often less than in financial transactions. On the other hand, corporations often have to recognise that the greater risks in financial transactions have to be taken into account in order to facilitate the financing of the corporate transactions.

Sale of corporate shares

3.76 This class includes takeovers and leveraged buy-outs of public companies, together with the sale and purchase of private companies. A takeover of a public company attracts the application of specific legal rules governing takeovers, either a code of takeovers, as in the UK, many other English-based countries, and the EU, or by a mixture of statutes and case law, as in the US. Otherwise, the transaction is simply the sale of an asset for a price in money or shares or both—in a takeover the contract is the form of acceptance signed by accepting shareholders. The buyers are either other corporations seeking to expand their empire, or else are private equity firms, venture capital firms, or the like. Mutual funds do not normally buy all the shares of a corporation and banks do not normally buy corporations outside the financial arena. Insurance companies normally do not buy companies in any other class of business and may often be prevented from doing so.

3.77 The main document in a takeover is an offer by the bidder to buy the shares of the target company. This sets out the terms of the offer plus information about the companies and the reasons for the bid. The main document in a private sale of all the shares of a company is a sale and purchase agreement between the seller and the buyer. This agreement sets out the terms of the sale and many pages of warranties by the seller as to the business and the financial condition of the target. Sometimes, part of the price is withheld for a specified period of time, partly to allow a reduction if any of the warranties should not prove to be correct or payable only if the target's earnings achieve a threshold amount.

3.78 Transnational corporate sales are common outside protected industries, such as defence companies. Theoretically, as with any other sale, the contracts are internationally mobile but the usual market practice in the case of public takeovers and purchases is to use the law of the market where the target's shares are listed. The same is not the case with most private sales, where the law of the seller's jurisdiction is often chosen.

Raising of equity capital

3.79 These transactions include initial public offerings, the raising of capital by companies privately or by initial public or private offerings, and other equity capital-raising, the flotations of private companies by issues of shares to the public and the listing of the shares on a stock exchange, rights issues to existing shareholders, and the conversion of bonds into shares. Included are the opposite transactions of reductions of share capital and the conversion of public companies into private companies after a takeover.

3.80 Unlike a bond, you cannot choose the governing law of an equity share. The share is governed by the law of the place of incorporation and the terms of the company's constitution. The rights and protections of a shareholder are also governed by the law of the place of incorporation, including voting rights and minority protections. A share is not internationally mobile in the sense of choice of law. Shareholders also lose everything on the insolvency of a company and are at the bottom at the bankruptcy ladder of priorities. For these reasons, shareholders are much less enthused than creditors, such as banks and bondholders, in creditor protections and their position on insolvency. They only have an interest if the company can be rescued, which in turn usually depends on the attitude of banks and bondholders.

Sale or merger of a business

3.81 The sale of the whole of a business of a company is usually part of a group reconstruction. In this event, the transfer of liabilities and their assumption by the buying company requires the consent of the creditors and other counterparties to whom those liabilities are owed. The alternative is a universal succession by the buying company to all of the assets and liabilities of selling company pursuant to a corporate enabling statute. The English courts recognise these universal successions provided that they are in fact universal, ie no assets or liabilities are left behind. A further alternative is a merger by fusion of the two companies.

3.82 A common case of these transfers of a business is a transfer of the assets, but not the liabilities, to a new company as part of an insolvency rescue plan achieved by the establishment of Newco owned by bank and bondholder creditors and capitalised by them. This is just a sale, but often sanctioned by a scheme of arrangement or by a corporate law plan sanctioned by insolvency law, approved in both cases by creditor voting.

3.83 A common method of restructuring a failed bank is to transfer its assets and deposits to a bridge company owned by the government rescue corporation pursuant to legislation for the resolution of bank insolvencies of the type found in most developed countries. This legislation is often based on the regime developed in the US in the 1930s after the Great Depression, operated in the US by the Federal Deposit Insurance Corporation. That model spread to the UK and the EU after the global financial crisis starting in 2007 and was effectively the nationalisation of the bankruptcy of banks, ie the procedure is controlled by a government agency, subject to minimal safeguards.

Joint venture agreements

3.84 These are agreements between companies to collaborate or jointly to promote a project, usually by means of subscribing for shares in a company whose purpose and operations are governed by the joint venture agreement. This agreement sets out the areas of collaboration or the proposed business and its capital and management, and gives the shareholders pre-emption rights if one of them defaults. In the case of projects, the motive is generally to combine skills, to attract financing on better terms, and to ensure that the project company and its liabilities, as well as security for those liabilities, are off the balance sheets of the shareholders and are not caught by negative pledges (prohibitions on the grant of security) and financial ratios in their bank loan agreements, eg because the project company is not a subsidiary or controlled by any one shareholder. In modern economies, much enterprise is carried out through these project companies. These joint venture agreements are standard in project finance for infrastructure, power stations, and the like. The project company is generally formed under the laws of the host government where the project is located—a standard requirement of host governments so that the project is within their control.

3.85 The consortium can be for any other kind of business, of course, eg a consortium bank or a project to launch and maintain a space satellite.

3.86 Joint venture agreements are internationally mobile transactions.

Typical commercial agreements

3.87 In the commercial sphere, the main subsets include the following:

- *Construction contracts.* These are contracts for the construction of all kinds of buildings, industrial premises, plant, power stations, roads, bridges, railways, airports, and the like. Construction contracts and accompanying bonds, are surrounded by supporting contracts with architects, surveyors, engineers, subcontractors, suppliers, and insurers.
- *Manufacturing contracts.* These are contracts for the manufacture of all kinds of goods, including ships, aircraft, rockets and satellites, chips and computers.
- *Sale of goods agreements.* As we have seen, goods form a massive class.
- *Lease, charter, licence, and use agreements.* Another massive class. They include pipeline agreements, tolling agreements for roads, tunnels, and bridges; intellectual property licences and software licence agreements; agreements for the use of satellite and cable capacity, phone roaming agreements, technology network agreements, service agreements for computers, agreements for the use of the cloud or servers; operating leases; charterparties; and publishing and media agreements.
- *Insurance.* Insurance against loss and liability are an embedded feature of modern societies for the reduction of risk. These contracts are usually international mobile so that the parties can choose the governing law and courts. I exclude life insurance and pensions from this subset.
- *Agency and broker agreements.* These include agency and distributorship agreements for goods, for electricity, for technology; and agency and broker agreements for most of the assets listed at the beginning of this chapter.

Most of the above are internationally mobile contracts. Employment agreements are outside our scope. 3.88

The relevance of the thirteen main risk factors, such as predictability, insulation, business orientation exclusion clauses, insolvency risk mitigants, regulation, and litigation will vary according to whether, for example, the party is a seller or a buyer, a debtor or a creditor, and whether the contract is long term or short term, and the legal infrastructure and political risks involved in the location of the parties. 3.89

Real property agreements

One must not forget real property agreements, for example, sales of real property, leases and tenancies of real property, and the grant of rights over real property. 3.90

These are not generally internationally mobile, mainly because land rights are typically registrable in a land register and the land register may not in practice accept agreements under a foreign law. 3.91

Comparison of General Risk Characteristics of Contracts

Risk factors

We have seen how protean are the proliferation of contracts, each with its own risk features which need to be taken into account by the law. Some generic comments are worth making at this stage before a more specific treatment of key indicators in later chapters. The comments below discuss some aspects of the relative degree to which the main governing law risk factors differ according to the class of contract. The risk factors built into the governing law include predictability, insulation, business orientation, freedom of contract, the validity of exclusion clauses, aspects of the impact of insolvencies, regulation, litigation, and the other factors outlined in Chapter 1. 3.92

Banks and bondholders versus corporate management

The risk factors are intensely important to banks making large international loans and to bondholders, and in this respect their interests may be opposite to the interests of the borrowers and debtors. The debtors are generally corporations, many of them larger than the banks. For example, the predictability of an event of default clause in a syndicated bank credit or a bond is of pre-eminent importance to lenders because that is the only way they can have bargaining power to be able to persuade the debtor to agree to a reasonable reorganisation of the business if the debtor gets into financial difficulties. This is the sole means in practice to get the debtor to the negotiating table to negotiate in good faith, other than withholding further finance, which may in fact be needed to protect both parties. This is how the creditors obtain a 'vote' on management. It is very uncommon for banks to accelerate a major loan unless the position is hopeless, because that would put the borrower out 3.93

of business—a mutually assured destruction. The directors would not be able to continue incurring debt. That in itself weakens the negotiating position of creditors, which intensifies their concern that their bargaining position is not prejudiced by a lack of predictability in the law as regards that power to accelerate on an event of default. Corporate debtors will, of course, take the opposite position.

3.94 Further, most bank term loans are outstanding for between five and fourteen years during which one can expect significant changes in the borrower's financial condition, either because of mismanagement or because of an economic depression, financial crisis, or political disturbances in the country of the borrower. You only have to take any decade from 1970 onwards to confirm how rarely people at the beginning of the decade successfully forecast the crises which occurred during that decade. Not many people in January 2020 predicted the events of the next couple of years. The events in the various decades could lead to moratoriums and exchange controls defeating the foreign money-lenders who are last in the queue for policy priority. The result is that insulation against these the local laws by an external governing law is a major protection of lenders. Again, corporate debtors have the opposite interest.

3.95 The same situation arises in relation to the business orientation of the governing law that it is not distinctively pro-debtor but also has regard to the interests of creditors. Further, freedom of contract in all of its manifestations is necessary for lenders to protect their position, including a free choice of governing law and an enforceable choice of courts, the ability to override dissentient hold-out creditors by majority voting of bondholders, the validity of non-assignment clauses in loan agreements to restrict transfers to creditors to, say, financial institutions having a similar interest, the ability to exercise self-help measures without court interference in such matters as security enforcement, the ability to carry out a work-out privately without being forced into a rescue proceeding by director duties to file on insolvency, and also thereby to avoid the trauma and destruction of formal insolvency proceedings.

3.96 It goes without saying that these preoccupations with the governing law do not necessarily interest corporations in their role as debtors to banks and bondholders. This is not because this is a battle of the weak against the strong—which is an out-of-date view of the wholesale sector in modern economies. As pointed out, the corporations may be larger than the banks who finance them.

Interdependence of banks/bondholders and corporations

3.97 Probably what sways the corporations most in recognising these needs of lenders as regards governing law risks is that corporations, private equity firms, hedge funds, promoters of securitisations, corporations depending on work-out finance if they are in difficulties, corporations wishing to carry out capital-hungry projects—all depend upon banks and bondholders being willing to supply very large amounts of capital. Indeed, the profits of these corporations often depend upon the leveraging-up effect of using other people's money in order to enlarge their profits. As lenders are ultimately financed by the money of the citizen, it is legitimate that they should be permitted by choice of governing law to protect other

Lenders versus shareholders

3.98 The attitudes of lenders on these points differ sharply, not only from those of corporate management, but also from those of shareholders. Shares are completely unlike bonds. One cannot choose the governing law of a share as a method of risk mitigation. A share and its characteristics are governed by the law of the place of incorporation. The result is that, in the case of a major subset of corporate transactions, which is the raising of equity capital, the protections afforded by a choice of governing law are far from the thoughts of shareholders or those who arrange equity-raising transactions.

3.99 The management of the various types of funds discussed at paragraph 3.68, such as private equity funds and hedge funds, are in a similar position to corporate management, just as their participants or investors are in a similar position to shareholders of a company. In both cases, the managers of funds and investors in funds have a much diminished concern with risk management via the governing law than banks and bondholders.

Other financial contracts

3.100 The need for predictability and other factors involved in the choice of governing law apply in much the same way to the other subsets of financial contracts, such as security agreements, title finance agreements, securitisations, and foreign exchange contracts. Thus, in the case of derivatives the ability to close out on a default, to net the transactions and to apply collateral if there is a shortfall must be undoubted and not curtailed by insolvency laws and subject to court intervention as to the express rights of the parties. This situation is even more crucial in the case of central counterparties, having regard to their systemic importance and the concentration of risk.

Commercial transactions

3.101 The parties to commercial transactions, depending on whether they are debtors or creditors or have long-term contracts, will have similar interests as those outlined above concerning predictability, insulation, business orientation, freedom of contract, and the other indicators. It will often be found that, unlike the chasm between banks/bondholder versus corporate management, both parties in commercial contracts have an interest in risk management via the governing law and courts.

3.102 Sellers commonly seek to protect payments in full and on time and therefore the predictability and discipline of payments is important to them, as well as the insulation of payments from foreign exchange controls, currency redenominations, and moratoriums. They often aim, by exclusion clauses or otherwise, to reduce the warranties they give, the disclosures they have to make, and their liabilities generally to the buyer. They are concerned about credit risks, especially the insolvency risk of the buyer. Buyers are concerned about disclosure of the features, defects, and quality of the asset they are buying, whether goods or investments or software or satellite capacity. They also have the credit risk of the seller if the asset does not match the contract specifications. Both parties have an interest in predictability and in the insolvency treatment of their contract. Both may have an interest in freedom of contract, eg a clause restricting assignments of the rights of the other party.

Significance of chains of contracts for predictability

3.103 In commercial life contracts are often linked in chains so that each party in the line is dependent on the other. These closely linked chains of transactions strengthen the need for predictability of contract. Home buyers are familiar with this when they are buying a house when the ability to move in depends on a chain of buyers and sellers down the line. The failure of one is the failure of them all. The fall of one domino topples the rest.

3.104 The links in a chain are crucial to the stability of major transactions in the economy. At its simplest, if borrowers from banks en masse fail to pay back their loans in a timely way, the banks might then be unable to pay their deposits and in the worst case might be exposed to a run on the banks with resulting contagion poisoning the banking system. If issuers of bonds fail to pay insurance companies their steady expected income of interest and capital, then the insurance company might become unable to pay its pensions and life insurance policies, and, in the worst case, this might compel a government bail-out at great cost. If a construction employer cannot pay the contractor, then the contractor cannot pay subcontractors. If a supply line for batteries or other equipment used in a mobile phone fails to perform, then the mobile phone will not be produced, just because of one broken link in the chain, if essential and not readily available elsewhere in the market.

3.105 Wherever you look in modern economies, you have these chains. Some are enormously important to the economy itself. An example is the purchase by a bank of government bonds so as to pass them on to meet a margin call by a central counterparty in a clearing system. A margin call is a call for collateral to secure the exposure of a central counterparty to a participating bank if the exposure increases by reason of changes in market prices. Central counterparties carry a colossal concentration of risk. If a member defaults on a margin call, this could be a devastating mechanism for transmitting distress across the financial system. All other members, such as banks, would receive a margin call to pay into the default fund so one weakness could threaten the rest. Even the supplier of marmalade to a supermarket may not be able to pay the rent if the supermarket does not pay diligently on time where the law is inclined to give the supermarket another month or two to pay.

3.106 Other examples include a payment from a sub-lessee to a lessee to a lessor, from a buyer to an agent to a seller, payments from a reinsurer to an insurer to the insured, and back-to-back payments on hedged derivatives—similar to insurance and reinsurance.

3.107 It follows from this that predictability of contract terms regarding such items as performance and termination rights so as, for example, to enable a non-defaulter to seek another contractor elsewhere quickly, can be crucial.

3.108 Chain contracts explain why clauses in the relevant agreements often prevent a paying party from setting off against the party to be paid since this can disturb the stable flow of payments. Pay now, litigate later. These agreements not to set off must be legally valid to avoid a surprise ambush and not be invalid as an unlawful exclusion clause.

Interdependence of contracts

3.109 The interdependence of contracting parties in many situations is another aspect of the risks of chain contracts. Again, predictability is essential. One of the most frequent cases is the carrying out of a project through a single purpose company set up in the host government's territory and engaged in, say, a project to supply renewable power and financed by a syndicate of commercial banks. Contract is king. The portfolio of contracts are intricately interlinked and have to match precisely in terms of time of performance, force majeure clauses, and payments. Indeed, the process is often called 'matching', which is part of the arduous process of ensuring that the contracts are 'bankable'. Thus, the supplier of generators and solar panels must supply on time so that the construction contractor can construct the project so that the operator of the power station can start producing electricity pursuant to the operating agreement so that the purchaser of the electricity, the off-taker, can sell the electricity to businesses and consumers, who pay the wholesale distributor of the electricity so that the project company can pay the banks whose loans were used to pay for the generators.

3.110 If interest rates go up and the bank which has agreed to pay the extra under an interest rate swap with the product company fails, the project company may itself fail. If anybody defaults in this exquisitely balanced network of contracts, then it is lights out for the consumers, and the financing banks have to use up their reserves, which depletes their ability to finance the rest of the economy.

3.111 Again, it is clear that, in this kind of situation, contractual discipline and meticulously accurate performance is required. This is weakened if a court can intervene to override the express terms of contracts on the ground that the court thinks that the contract is unfair or disproportionate or that a central clause is an invalid exclusion clause. The risk is worsened if the financing banks decide to terminate and enforce their security, but the enforcement was wrongful, notwithstanding the express terms of the security agreement, so that the banks have to pay compensation to the project company. A party may not know for years whether it still has a contract or not while the matter is litigated.

Multiple mutual contracts

3.112 Counterparties in all the major financial markets, from the foreign exchange market to the commodities markets, typically always have a large number of contracts outstanding between them at any one time. This is also true of derivatives.

3.113 If one of the counterparties becomes insolvent and defaults, then it must be possible for the non-defaulting party to terminate all of the contracts and then set off the losses and gains on each contract so as to end up with a net exposure. The inability to do that would vastly amplify the risks and in some cases prevent the market from operating at all. This topic is discussed in Chapter 11.

3.114 The situation is less true of corporate capital-raising transactions, where it would not be normal for the issuing corporation to have reciprocal contracts with prospective shareholders. In any event, shares are not eligible for set-off and netting.

Standard forms

3.115 Standard forms are very pervasive in wholesale markets and for contracts between business parties. Examples are the ISDA form for derivatives, the Loan Market Association forms for syndicated bank credits, standard forms for repos and for stock lending, and innumerable standard forms for construction contracts, let alone the model form for trade letters of credit, the UCP 600. The speed and number of deals make a standard form essential.

3.116 These standard forms are model forms which are capable of negotiation between the parties and which are frequently amended to suit the circumstances. They have typically been settled after months or years of meticulous work by lawyers and numerous market participants. This is not a case of the railway company or laundry slipping in some small-print exclusion clause on the back of a ticket or to be found at the company's office. It is therefore important that the standard forms, which in many cases are essential for enabling business to carry out the transactions at all in volume, should not be subject to laws nullifying exclusion clauses or clauses which conflict with the views of the local court as to what is fair. Business parties should be able to allocate risks in their contracts as they wish. As these contracts have been negotiated carefully by whole markets and conform with market practice, the courts should be slow to characterise the rights of the parties as abusive or contrary to the court's view of good faith in contract.

Transfers of Property on Sale

Contract and property

3.117 A large number of the contracts listed in this chapter are contracts for the sale of assets, whether securities or receivables or goods or land. A takeover of a public company is a sale of shares. A securitisation is a sale of receivables.

3.118 Typically, the governing law of a contract of sale does not necessarily cover the law which you have to apply to determine whether the transfer of property has validly taken place from seller to buyer. Very often, the law governing the validity of the sale is the law of the location of the property, ie the law of where the asset is when the property is transferred. This is a very inconvenient rule for assets which are invisible such as receivables or shares, for assets which shift their locations, like an aircraft flying over one jurisdiction to another, or goods in containers on board a ship in transit. The application of this rule would therefore limit the ability of the governing law to mitigate the risks of the location rule in problem jurisdictions.

3.119 This compulsory law of location does not affect the other terms of the contract, which can be controlled by the governing law in the normal way, as regards predictability, freedom of contract, etc.

The doctrine of false wealth

3.120 The reason historically that the world has ended up in a confusing quagmire on this question of the transfer of property springs from an ancient legal principle which is now considered out-of-date but which lives on to destroy some transactions and to put obstacles in the way of others.

3.121 This is the principle of false wealth, once called reputed ownership in English jurisdictions. This principle holds that it is a fraud on creditors for debtors and other counterparties to appear to have wealth sufficient to pay debts when in reality the apparent owner does not own the asset. This would happen if, say, an apparent owner had declared the trust of the asset secretly in favour of someone else. It would also happen if the holder had possession of an asset or was registered as the holder of an asset, but had already transferred the beneficial ownership of the asset to someone else, the buyer, so that the asset was no longer available to creditors of the seller.

3.122 The theory was that, in order to prevent that situation of having many possessions but no assets, the buyer did not get the beneficial ownership of the sold assets until the buyer publicised its ownership. Hence, all creditors could see with their own eyes who had what assets and not be cheated by an apparent or reputed or false ownership. Ownership coincided with publicity. According to this doctrine, it had to be transparent for the protection of creditors on insolvency that you could see who had the ownership. It was also necessary for certainty if there were competing priorities, as where a seller sold the asset twice and you had to decide which of the innocent buyers would get title. The winner was the buyer who got the best public title first.

Meaning of the best public title

3.123 In the olden days when this principle was first formulated, at least back to the Romans, the various ways of publicising the true ownership of an asset was by having possession of the goods physically or of the title deeds to land or, when registers developed much later, having yourself registered as the owner of the asset in a title register. There are many of these title registers now, including for land, ships, aircraft, intellectual property, and shares. Therefore under this theory you as the buyer did not get title if the seller became insolvent and if you had not registered yourself as owner because it looked as though the seller was still the owner.

Best public title for receivables

3.124 When receivables proliferated in the increase in trade, especially after the Industrial Revolution, lawyers searched for some technique to replicate the idea of publicity by delivery of possession of the asset or registration in a public register. Their solution to that problem was to require that the seller or buyer gave notice to the debtor on the debt so that everybody would know who now owned the debt. Otherwise the sale would be void on the insolvency of the seller. Effectively, the notice was compulsory, instead of just optional, eg in order to inform the debtor who to pay.

3.125 The objection to this is that creditors could not see the receivable and certainly could not see if notice had been given to the debtor. In the usual case of the sale of hundreds or thousands of receivables, it would be impossible to ask all of the debtors if they had received notice.

Objections to the doctrine of false wealth

3.126 There are at least three overwhelming objections to the proposition of false wealth in the modern world. The first is that creditors do not now rely on viewing, or trying to view, physical assets. They rely on financial statements prepared by professionals.

3.127 The second is that a major slice of the assets of corporations is invisible anyway, such as shares and other investments or contract claims.

3.128 The third objection is an issue of justice, of morality. This is that if a sale fails on the insolvency of the seller because the buyer has not satisfied the required publicity, then the seller is paid twice, once by receiving the price from the buyer and then again by receiving the asset back. This is a clear unjust enrichment of the creditors of the seller, to be paid twice. It is disproportionate if one takes into account the fact that it is often not realistic to pay only on publicity, to obtain possession of goods at the moment of payment, that registrars may take time to register the new owner, or that sellers and buyers often do not wish for good reasons to confuse debtors, such as customers or mortgagors of their homes, by notifying them that there has been a sale, eg because the parties want the seller to continue to administer the receivables since it is the seller who has the records and the relationship.

3.129 For all of these reasons, the limitation of the scope of a free governing law because of the doctrine of false wealth also does not seem appropriate in today's conditions. It arose in ancient times when the main assets were goods and land which had a location which was visible.

Comparative survey of false wealth for sales

3.130 Does it matter much? In the case of the sale of goods, it is considered to be generally true that the publicity of possession in the Anglo-American common law jurisdictions, in the Napoleonic jurisdictions, and effectively in the Roman-Germanic jurisdictions is now not required for the validity of the transfer. Hence, it follows that the governing law of the contract can determine the timing of the transfer of the ownership of goods simultaneously with the payment of the price.

In the case of the sale of investments, such as bonds and equity shares, the operations of clearing systems are so efficient and rapid that you do not often get a significant gap between sale and entering of the new owner in a share account kept by the clearing house. The clearing house can organise payment at that point to ensure delivery against payment. But there could still be a mismatch. This gap would in English-based jurisdictions and in American jurisdictions not prevent the transfer of beneficial ownership at the time of payment and entry in the account, but this may not be true of the civilian jurisdictions. **3.131**

In the case of assets which can be registered in a title register, the general position in English-based jurisdictions is that ownership can be transferred immediately, even though the seller becomes insolvent before registration of the buyer as owner. This is not generally true in the Napoleonic and Roman-Germanic jurisdictions, which typically insist on the publicity of registration to transfer ownership on the insolvency of the seller. **3.132**

The position in relation to receivables is much more complicated. One can only say that, in the English-based jurisdictions, the transfer of a receivable does not require to be notified to the debtor for validity on the insolvency of the seller. **3.133**

A further consequence of the requirement for publicity by possession, registration in a title register, or by notice to the debtor is that the asset concerned has to be specifically identified. This could be complicated with the commingling of, say, oil or wheat and not realistic where this doctrine of specific identification requires, for example, the express details of each sack of potatoes. **3.134**

Priorities; security interests

There are two points to add. **3.135**

The first is that priorities between competing sales and security interests are almost everywhere determined by the first to achieve the best public title to the asset—by physical possession, registration, or notice to the debtor. In practice, priorities are a lesser problem with corporations because double sales require a degree of fraud or at least gross negligence, which are both less easy in a corporation than in the case of an individual acting alone. **3.136**

The other point is that almost all jurisdictions outside the Roman-Germanic group insist on the filing of security interests in a file registered according to the debtor, usually a company, as well as any necessary registration of the mortgage in a title register so that in the case of security interests they subscribe whole-heartedly to the doctrine of false wealth. **3.137**

Conclusion on false wealth

A preliminary conclusion is that the law which governs the transfer of property, eg by way of sale or creation of a security interest or the establishment of a commercial trust, may in **3.138** many cases not be decided by the governing law of the contract but often by the law of the location of the asset. The false wealth doctrine in these cases may require that a buyer, for example, gets the best public title before the buyer can be sure it has a valid transfer which is enforceable on the bankruptcy of the seller. The false wealth doctrine is in various areas at its strongest in the civil code jurisdictions, but is significantly eroded in the common law jurisdictions.

Digital Contracts; Green Transactions

Cryptocurrencies, decentralised finance, and smart contracts

3.139 At one time, money was represented solely by coins and subsequently by paper notes as well. Then, most money was a record in a bank account. Now, wholesale money, that is, accounts held between banks and the central bank, and between banks, is solely electronic. The idea therefore of electronic money was taken in its stride by English law, and many other legal systems. The same happened to shares and bonds, ie at first they were wrapped in paper, and then they were dematerialised by being represented in an electronic account in a clearing system. Hence, in both these cases the form of an asset was switched from a physical form to an electronic form without any particular fuss.

3.140 Cryptocurrencies and decentralised finance, for example, a loan which you take out when you pay for your groceries, are not something special from the legal point of view. The fact that a currency is recorded on a distributed ledger or blockchain does not change the fact that it is still an asset and property, as has been held by the English courts. The nature of a transaction, whether sale, security, or trust or loan, will have to be determined by the intentions of the parties and the evidence, as normal. The location of the asset for legal purposes and the governing law will also have to be determined by using and extending existing principles. This is something which the English courts have been used to doing since the middle of the nineteenth century when they were the first to allow a transaction to be expressly governed by English law, even though the transaction and the parties had no connection with England.

3.141 The main functional issue for cryptocurrencies is whether they will be accepted as a means of exchange and a store of value, and how they should be regulated. Any switch to central bank digital currencies would have to be achieved by legislation.

3.142 The UK Law Commission in its paper 'Smart Legal Contracts' of November 2021 expressed the view that smart contracts do not present special problems under English law. Smart contracts are electronic programmes which automatically execute a contract, such as a money transfer on delivery of a bought asset.

Green transactions

3.143 The achievement of protections against climate change will require a large amount of new projects to generate electricity and the addition of massive new infrastructure. These projects will require predictability of contract, an enterprise and business orientation in the law, freedom of contract to be able to develop innovative solutions, and the ability of the parties to be able to define their own risk allocation without the courts overriding them by some good faith or other doctrine. The projects will require flexible corporate laws which also do not discourage directors by imposing disproportionate personal liability risks and which facilitate novel transactions. The law will need to support large amounts of loan finance by being realistic about equity capital requirements, by facilitating complex shareholding structures, and by not hurrying the corporations involved into an insolvency procedure as soon as something goes wrong with the project.

All of these subjects are explored later in this book, from which it will be seen that English law is one of the legal systems which is favourable on all of the above points. As with decentralised finance, these transactions are not really wholly new, but rather adaptions of existing transactions. **3.144**

4
GOVERNING LAW AND CHOICE OF COURTS

Introduction

Purpose of this chapter

4.1 The purpose of this chapter is to set out the essentials, the basic principles, governing the choice of law of a contract and the choice of the courts to hear disputes on the contract, or of arbitration.

4.2 I am assuming that in the ordinary case the parties make an express choice of governing law and courts since this book is mainly about the consequences of the choice and the risks involved in the choice of law and courts, as opposed to the detail of how you make the choice. However, the validity of these choices and their effectiveness is an important risk factor which I will take into account when I come to discuss the question of freedom of contract in Chapter 8.

Principles well-established internationally

4.3 It is true to say that governing law is a done deal legally in nearly all commercial jurisdictions and the principles are very well established internationally. However, choice of forum continues to be a battle ground between parties fighting for a familiar forum best suited to their interests.

Governing Law of Contracts

Free choice of governing law

4.4 It is now well settled in almost all jurisdictions that the parties have freedom to choose the governing law of their agreement, notwithstanding that there is no connection between the agreement and the jurisdiction concerned. This is sometimes called party autonomy.

4.5 For example, a German bank can agree to make loan in US dollars to a corporation in France under a loan agreement expressly governed by English law, and all three countries, plus New York, will recognise the choice of law as being English law. It is irrelevant that neither the German bank nor the French borrower has any business in England, that the currency of the loan is not sterling, and that dollar payments are made in New York.

Freedom of choice appeared finally in England by 1865 in relation to a ship charterparty between parties who had nothing to do with England: see *P & O Navigation Co v Shand* (1865) 3 Moo PC (NS) 272. Freedom of choice without requiring any connection between the contract and the chosen jurisdiction was accepted in Germany in the 1880s, in France in 1910, and finally in Switzerland in 1952. Jurisdictions in the US were slow to confirm complete freedom of choice and even now the question of whether there must be a reasonable relationship is not clearly established in some states. To set the matter at rest, in 1984 the New York General Obligations Law was amended to enable parties to choose New York law for transactions of more than US$250,000, whether or not there is a reasonable relationship to New York in the contract: see the New York General Obligations Law. However, the Uniform Commercial Code requires 'reasonable relationship' in transactions covered by the Code. **4.6**

This freedom of choice is codified in the EU by a regulation of 2008 on the law applicable to contractual obligations—usually called Rome I. Rome I applies in the UK notwithstanding that the UK is no longer a member of the EU, subject to amendments not relevant here. For the Swiss position, see the Swiss Act on Private International Law of 1987. There are conflicts codifications in many other states, such as Japan, as well as the Bustamante Code applying in a number of Latin American states. **4.7**

Jurisdictions in which the free choice of law is considered doubtful include Laos, Oman, Saudi Arabia, Turkmenistan, and Vietnam. None of these jurisdictions would generally be considered suitable for large international contracts for other reasons. **4.8**

In the EU and the UK, the effect of article 3 of Rome I is that if all of the elements of the contracts are located in a country other than the country whose law has been chosen, then the choice cannot prejudice mandatory provisions of law in that other country. This is to prevent evasion of a mandatory rule of law which would have applied to the contract which is otherwise purely local and domestic. **4.9**

The law must be that of a jurisdiction. You cannot choose, say, the law merchant, or (as in one case in 2004) 'the principles of the Glorious Sharia'a'. You can choose public international law, and indeed there are many cases in which the general principles of law have been implied, at least by arbitral tribunals, into agreements to which one of the parties is a government. The World Bank, for example, applies the general principles of law in its loan contracts. The choice of public international law would be rare in other contracts, usually on the grounds that the rules of public international law on treaties which are the equivalent of contracts or insufficiently developed for the types of situation contemplated by most business contracts. **4.10**

A choice of law which is to be made by the court at the time of the hearing is not a valid choice of law since there is no chosen law up to the time of a court decision. However, it is perfectly possible under Rome I to vary the choice of law: see article 3(2), and this is probably the case practically everywhere. **4.11**

Governing law in the absence of express choice

If the parties do not expressly choose the governing law, then most jurisdictions will apply various centre of gravity tests to discover the governing law, such as a choice implied by the **4.12** choice of courts, or tests based on substantial connection, dominant contacts, or the law of having the most significant relationship, and sometimes rigid presumptions in a hierarchy such as common residence, or the law of place of contracting or performance. There is a hierarchy of contacts in the case of Rome I. In the US, the tests are basically centre of gravity: see the US *Restatement of Conflicts of Law*, especially section 188. There are special rules for various classes of contracts in sections 189–197, eg contracts for transfers of interests in land and various insurance contracts. Similarly, in Rome I there are special rules for such items as employment, consumer, and insurance contracts, all of which are generally outside our scope.

Matters decided by the governing law

4.13 The governing law primarily governs the existence and validity of the contract, whether it complies with formal requirements, how the courts interpret the contract, how the contract is to be performed, the consequence of breaches such as damages or specific performance, and the extinction of obligations, such as by prescription and limitation, that is, rules limiting the time within which claims must be brought so that they do not become stale.

Matters Not Decided by the Governing Law

Narrowing of scope of governing law

4.14 Some crucial matters in our context are not decided by the governing law but rather by a different law. Others are mandatory, compulsory laws, or rules of basic morality—sometimes called public policy—and override the governing law: these will be applied by the court hearing the matter. The effect is that freedom of choice does not apply in these cases. Some of these cases are hugely significant: their effect is to erode and restrict the free scope of the law. The governing law gives freedom with one hand and takes it back with the other.

4.15 The main lesson which the practitioner should take from the list below is that each item represents the threat to the chosen governing law and courts. The practitioner who is seeking to protect her position and to reduce her risks should therefore choose a law and courts which have the most liberal and proportionate views on each of these items, having regard to the circumstances of the case and the location of the counterparty. Otherwise, there is not really a free choice of governing law because the free region of the scope of the governing law is no longer a grand open plain, but a narrow strip of rock and scrub.

Criminal law

4.16 A court in which proceedings are brought will always apply the mandatory criminal laws of the country concerned, eg its laws against bribery, its laws against tax evasion and tax frauds, its laws against insider dealing and market manipulation, its laws against fraud, such as known misrepresentation or misleading information. Although jurisdictions may differ on the outer boundary of these matters, naturally one can expect that the contract will be subject to laws of this kind. Less obviously, the criminalised laws will include exchange controls, trade sanctions, and embargos. Many of the above laws are extraterritorial in the sense that they apply to acts committed outside the territory. If the contract involves doing anything contrary to these laws, then plainly the mandatory laws will override.

Corporate law

4.17 Corporate and sovereign powers and authorisations are generally decided by the constitution of the corporation or sovereign. This is not commonly a problem since the law in most commercial countries protects third parties dealing with a corporation. In the case of sovereign states, one should naturally take care when one is dealing with a usurping authority who is not actually in charge.

4.18 You cannot choose the law of a share in a company. The governing law of a contract does not protect against such matters as the strength of the veil of incorporation of the company, director liability, the protection of minorities, the rights of management and shareholders, amalgamations, migrations and mergers, compulsory subordinations of debt, the maintenance of capital, any prohibitions on the company giving financial assistance for the purchase of its own shares, (sometimes) the conduct of takeovers, and the liability of a director for deepening an insolvency. These matters are decided for you. See Chapter 14. A contract which involves these matters will not be protected by the governing law. They may often come within the scope of the place of incorporation of the counterparty.

Court procedure

4.19 Matters of procedure, such as the filing of pleadings in litigation, the availability of class actions, rules as to who bears the costs and how they are ascertained, the discovery of relevant documents, the ability to appeal, and (sometimes) the remedies which the court can order, such as punitive damages and the proportionality of damages, are governed by the procedural rules of the court, not the governing law of the contract. But under Rome I article 12(1)(c), 'the assessment of damages in so far as it is governed by rules of law' is governed by the governing law. The US Conflicts Restatement section 207 is to similar effect. For some of the issues, see Chapter 16. Where the issue is procedural, the parties have the remedy of making sure that they choose the courts that they want by a forum selection clause.

Consumer law

4.20 A court will generally apply its own consumer laws if the contract involves consumers within the territorial ambit of the consumer laws, such as consumers who have their habitual residence in the location of the court. As discussed in Chapter 3, parties cannot usually control the ambit of these laws by a choice of governing law.

International conventions

4.21 Certain international conventions between sovereign states may override the governing law because they contain their own rules about conflict of laws: see eg article 25 of Rome I. An example is the IMF Agreement whose article VIII 2b (discussed in Chapter 6) can in some jurisdictions destroy the insulation by external governing law against exchange controls in the counterparty's jurisdiction. In the EU, some EU regulations are also overriding. Another example is the United Nations Convention on Contracts for the International Sale of Goods 1980, which was not accepted by the UK. The application of this Convention can sometimes introduce unpredictability into a sale of goods contract.

Contract law

4.22 In some jurisdictions, some contracts can be so offensive to the sense of justice that they will override the governing law. This is likely to be the case, for example, with contracts induced by economic oppression or duress. However, local contract doctrines, such as the doctrine of good faith studied in Chapter 6, may be adhered to with such fervour that they override the governing law in the local courts, even though a respectable governing law such as English law may take the opposite view about some excesses of the good faith doctrine in their opinion.

Transfers of property

4.23 Property transfers, such as delivery of ownership under sale contracts, the attachment of security interests, and the validity of trusts, may often be decided by another law rather than the governing law of the contract, most often the law of the location of the asset. These are transfers of property, not contracts. We shall see that even here in important respects the governing law is beginning to throw some shafts of the sunlight of freedom into this dark area of compulsory restriction. See Chapter 3.

Regulatory law

4.24 Regulatory laws, such as financial regulation, data protection, competition laws, and environmental laws are effectively criminalised. You cannot control the scope of regulation by choice of governing law. Regulation typically applies to acts which are committed within the territory of the jurisdiction concerned or which have an adverse effect in that territory, even though committed abroad. See Chapter 15. Hence, if the contract involves doing anything prohibited within the territory of the regulated jurisdiction (and sometimes extraterritorially as well), the governing law is likely to be overridden in the local courts.

Insolvency law

4.25 The shadow of the law of insolvency looms over all contracts and in some cases can operate to smash or disrupt or claw chunks out of contracts. Insolvencies have their own completely different set of rules about governing law. Insolvency is the wild beast of private international law.

4.26 The impact of an insolvency is likely to be most significant where the counterparty enters into insolvency proceedings. However, there is some scope in important areas for the dominance of the governing law, as will be discussed in Chapters 10 to 13.

Tort law

4.27 The law of tort (called delict in civil code systems) covers such wrongs as negligence, product liability (including mis-selling of financial products), misrepresentation in offering circulars, and breach of a statutory duty, such as duties under financial services regulation. A choice of governing law and a choice of courts are restricted and the scope for disclaiming liability is also limited since the victims are normally involuntary victims, whereas in the case of contract the parties enter into the transaction voluntarily. Liabilities under tort law can be enormous and hence uninsurable.

4.28 Since very often legal systems allow parties to sue in either contract or tort on the same issue, such as alleged negligence of an arranging bank regarding a syndicate offering memorandum, there can be a serious exposure to an unexpected tort action which side-steps the agreed allocation of risks in the contract. This is a major reason for avoiding a choice of courts which allow overreaching and aggressive litigation.

Mnemonic for overriding laws

4.29 A mnemonic for these overriding areas of law where the risks are not controllable by a choice of company is 6C–TRITO. This stands for:

- criminal law
- corporate law
- court law
- consumer law
- conventions
- contract law
- transfers of property
- regulatory law
- insolvency law
- tort law
- others.

4.30 The effect of these overriding laws is to narrow down and restrict the scope of the governing law's control of risk. The effect is that when you decide on the governing law and the courts, you are also deciding not just what the governing law gives you in terms of predictability, freedom of contract, business orientation, insulation, and the rest, you are also contacting into a regime which may narrow your freedoms under the 6C–TRITO formula, more so than in the case of another choice of law and courts. As said, the objective should be to aim for the governing or of a legal system which is tolerant and fair on the 6C–TRITO issues, which is not punitive and aggressive disproportionately, and which has a clear business orientation and a sense of the importance of freedom of contract, including of the wide role of the governing law.

4.31 A majority of the above issues are in one way or another contained in the thirteen themes discussed in the main chapters in this book and contained in the ungainly mnemonic PIB—FREISST—CoRCO. It is useful to look at the architectural structure from another angle to gain new insights.

Choice of law clause

4.32 A clause choosing the governing law of a contract is usually the shortest in the whole agreement. For example, a typical clause simply states: 'This agreement is governed by English law.' Seven words. Sometimes the choice of law may be extended to all claims in connection with the agreement, including claims in tort. The main purpose of this is to make sure so far as possible that an opponent does not side-step the chosen governing law clause by bringing a claim under a head other than contract, typically a claim in tort (non-contractual wrongs, such as misrepresentation) which may then attract governing law rules more favourable to the opponent.

Governing Law of Non-contractual Claims

Less freedom than contracts

4.33 Non-contractual claims have their own set of rules for the law which governs the liability. I can only go into these very briefly so that you can get a feel about how they differ from the governing law of contracts where freedom prevails. There is considerably less freedom in these cases. This is because the victim is usually involuntary, whereas in the case of contracts, the parties agree consensually to their rights and obligations.

Examples of non-contractual liabilities

4.34 Non-contractual liabilities include such matters as misrepresentation, negligence, mis-selling, breach of a fiduciary duty, and breach of confidence. The most common cases are motor accidents, product liability, and occupier's liability, which are of little interest in our context. But they do include environmental liability, various economic claims, such as intimidation, and infringement of intellectual property. In common law jurisdictions, these claims are called torts, and in civil law countries they are typically called delict.

The other main set of these non-contractual liabilities generally come under the head of restitution. They include claims for breaches of trust, such as misappropriation by a broker holding a client's investments, the recovery of mistaken payments on the grounds of unjust enrichment, recoveries of bribes and embezzlement, compensation for self-dealing and secret profits, restitution where it turns out that the contract is a nullity, or the liability arises out of pre-contract dealings, or the contract is unauthorised, or the liability for participating in an embezzlement. **4.35**

Codes on governing law of non-contractual liabilities

The law in Europe is based on an EU regulation of 2007 on the law applicable to non-contractual obligations, which is in many respects the codification of existing principles. This is called Rome II. It continues to apply in the UK post-Brexit, but it does not apply in Denmark. In the US, the matter is covered by the Second Restatement of Conflict of Laws. In the UK, the few matters outside Rome II are covered by the Private International Law (Miscellaneous Provisions) Act 1995. **4.36**

The general rule in these codes, widely reflected elsewhere, is that (as in Rome II) you first apply the law of the place of the tort or other wrong, strictly the jurisdiction in which the damage occurs, irrespective of the country in which the event giving rise to the damage occurred. However, there is an override in Rome II where it is clear that the tort or delict is manifestly more closely connected with another country, with various other fall-backs. **4.37**

In the case of unjust enrichment and restitution for acts without authority or pre-contract dealings, you generally refer first to the law of that contract, again with fall-backs. **4.38**

The US Restatement in section 145 adopts the basic rule that the governing law of the tort will be that which is most closely connected to the wrong in question, a principle which was largely developed in relation to guest passenger motor accidents involving people from one country travelling in another. See section 145. **4.39**

Free choice of governing law

In the case of Rome II, article 14 provides that the parties can agree in advance to submit non-contractual obligations to the law of their choice where all the parties are pursuing a commercial activity and the agreement is freely negotiated. This is an important way of mitigating tort risks by making an express choice of law. **4.40**

For example, the arranging bank of a syndicated bank credit can agree with the other banks and the borrower group that English law will apply to all matters in connection with the documents, whether in contract or tort, so as to limit exposure on the information memorandum and on the negligence of the agent bank. English law is restrained in liability for tort and seeks to reduce the risks of tort liability, and especially liability for economic loss. **4.41**

The choice of English law could also limit exposure to the excesses of the good faith doctrine in civil code systems which can give rise to surprising liabilities in contract, such as for wrongful termination notwithstanding the express terms of the contract, and liability for not negotiating the contract in good faith, notwithstanding that the contract is expressly stated to be not legally binding. See Chapter 5. Some civil code jurisdictions characterise these liabilities as arising in tort, so that the choice of law could be crucial.

4.42 Tort law is particularly dangerous where there is an aggressive litigation system, as in the US.

Scope of the governing law

4.43 Article 15 provides that the governing or applicable law will govern such matters as the extent of liability, the persons who are liable, any exemptions or limitations of liability, the assessment of damages, and the liability for the acts of another person, as well as whether an obligation can be extinguished by rules of prescription and limitation. Note that the assessment of damages is treated as a substantive matter covered by the governing law, so that quantification is not just a matter for the procedural law of the courts.

4.44 As usual, there are the typical overrides for mandatory rules in the location of the forum and public policy. See Rome II, articles 16 and 26. The mandatory rules could include some of the adverse good faith rules discussed in Chapter 5 on predictability.

Choice of Courts

Factors influencing choice of courts

4.45 Most commercial jurisdictions permit parties to a contract to choose the courts which will hear disputes in connection with the contract. Most large business contracts include a clause providing for named courts to have jurisdiction to hear disputes, either on an exclusive or non-exclusive basis.

4.46 There are compelling reasons why parties would want to choose the forum.

4.47 First, if the parties do not choose a specific forum having jurisdiction, then the other party could select a forum which might be favourable to the other party but against the interests of the first party. This is especially risky since courts generally have long-arm jurisdiction whereby they can take jurisdiction on the basis of very tenuous links between the transaction and the jurisdiction concerned.

4.48 It is quite common for defendants to endeavour to get the courts of their own country to hear a dispute, especially if the home country is biased in favour of its own corporations. You can therefore easily get a battle for jurisdiction, known as forum shopping.

4.49 Secondly, courts will invariably apply the mandatory rules of the country of the forum, which could include a moratorium on a party's obligations, such as a suspension of the duty to pay back a loan or bond, or an exchange control interfering with payment obligations, or some other local law which distorts the contract.

4.50 Although it is true that most commercial countries will be willing to apply a foreign governing law, the chosen forum should coincide with the governing law in order to confer great predictability. For example, a choice of English governing law should usually be accompanied by a choice of the English courts since the English courts are familiar with their own domestic law. Otherwise, a foreign court will have to call expert evidence as to the interpretation of English law in which event, apart from delay and expense, the opposing experts may disagree and back their own side.

4.51 Next, a material consideration is the standards of the court concerned, such as a judiciary which is impartial, time, costs, the ability to attach assets prior to the judgment to prevent them being removed from the jurisdiction, and a number of other important factors which we will consider in Chapter 16.

4.52 If a party voluntarily and expressly submits to the jurisdiction of a named court, then it is much more likely that a judgment of that court will be enforceable in other countries, eg where the debtor has assets. The courts of most commercial countries will typically not enforce a foreign judgment if the original court based its jurisdiction on some ephemeral long-arm rule instead of an express submission.

4.53 The ability of a defendant to complain that the chosen court should not exercise jurisdiction on the grounds of an inconvenient forum is reduced almost to vanishing point if there is an express submission. It is common for a defendant to attempt to switch jurisdiction to a more favourable court in a different country on the ground that another court is at the centre of the action and is therefore the most convenient court for everybody involved.

4.54 Where the defendant is domiciled in an EU Member State, a written agreement specifying another court is effective to contract out of the general rule that the courts of the defendant's domicile are to have sole jurisdiction.

4.55 Finally, courts apply their rules of conflict of laws, that is, what law applies to the particular issue—which may lead to an adverse result.

Jurisdiction clauses

4.56 Jurisdiction clauses in large wholesale agreements can run to nearly thirty lines but a short form clause in a bank credit agreement might provide as follows:

> The borrower agrees that the English courts will have jurisdiction in connection with this agreement and appoints Service Processing Ltd as agent in England for service of process. The English courts are exclusive in the case of proceedings by the borrower, but the bank may also bring proceedings in any other court of competent jurisdiction.

4.57 Jurisdiction clauses in civil code countries normally cover:

- an express submission to the jurisdiction of named courts
- the designation of a court of venue, such as Frankfurt
- the appointment of an agent or election of domicile for service of process within the jurisdiction

- whether the jurisdiction is exclusive or non-exclusive.

4.58 In practice, it is important in international agreements to ensure that a borrower, for example, or an issuer of bonds is prevented from bringing defensive proceedings in its home jurisdiction since this may attract the protective cover of a mandatory local moratorium or exchange control, especially if the sovereign state is also in financial difficulties. In the 1980s, over 40 per cent of the world's sovereign states, almost all emerging countries, were insolvent, and presently a great many important countries have exchange controls, including China and India. In the aftermath of the 2007/2008 financial crisis, three countries in the European area introduced exchange controls: Iceland, Cyprus, and Ukraine.

4.59 There is much case law on whether the jurisdiction is exclusive or non-exclusive so it is material to make this clear. There is also case law on overlapping jurisdiction clauses in several documents.

Summary of long-arm jurisdiction

4.60 There is substantial disparity between nations as to the exercise of jurisdiction on the basis of more fleeting connections with the forum—often called the long-arm, or extended, or exorbitant or excessive jurisdiction, that is, a transaction which has a glancing glissando of contact with the jurisdiction. Almost invariably in the case of the long-arm jurisdiction, courts have a discretion as to whether or not they will accept jurisdiction so that jurisdiction is not automatic. This jurisdiction is generally exercised on the basis of whether the courts concerned are the most convenient forum. In many parts of the world, the courts are quite slow to refuse jurisdiction if technically they have it, even though the real centre of the action is elsewhere, and this is particularly the case in claimant-orientated jurisdictions if the court considers that the claimant will have a better result in their courts than elsewhere, eg in terms of large damages awards. The result is a great deal of forum shopping, exacerbated where, as in the US, lawyers can take a substantial cut of the proceeds of the litigation.

4.61 The main heads of discretionary long-arm jurisdiction internationally are:

1. Transient presence locally of an individual debtor (England, US states). There have been cases where the process server serves the papers when the pilot confirms that the aircraft has now entered the territory of the jurisdiction concerned. In England, there is such a thing as the 'Heathrow writ'. The Maharanee of Baroda had a writ served on her at Ascot Races. There are many cases of videos of process servers throwing the papers at or thrusting them down in front of the target, sometimes with a translator shouting the import.
2. The debtor does business locally, eg through an agent. In New York, the cases have given a wide interpretation to the New York civil practice law and rules which confer jurisdiction over a defendant who in person or through an agent 'transacts any business within the state'. It is probably not enough that the agreement was actually signed in New York (a contact which is sufficient in England)
3. The transaction sued on has local connections, eg the contract was made locally (England, but not New York), or the contract is expressly or impliedly

governed by local law (England, but not New York—*Hanson v Denkla* 357 US 235 (1958)).
4. Local nationality of the *claimant* (France, Luxembourg (CC, art 14)), and Italy (subject to reciprocity—(CCP, art 4(4)), but not England, not most US states. This is a remarkable instance of legal nationalism in the sense that nationals have privileged treatment, regardless of the status of the defendant.
5. Domicile of the *claimant*, regardless of nationality: Netherlands, (CCP, art 126(3)) and Belgium (subject to reciprocity in the case of Belgium). Not England, not most US states. Another example of legal nationalism.
6. Local assets of the defendant, however small—the 'toothbrush' jurisdiction: Germany (ZPO—the Civil Procedure Order, article 25), Austria (paragraph 99(1) of *Jurisdiktionsnormen*), Japan, Denmark, South Africa, Sweden. The asset is usually a bank account. It seems that this class of jurisdiction is extremely widespread. In one remarkable case, a famous French skier was subjected to the jurisdiction of the Austrian courts in a patrimony on the basis of a pair of boxer shorts he left in a hotel. In Japan, the courts require more than a trivial local asset. In England, the presence of a local asset is enough only if the claim relates wholly or principally to property within England, subject to an exception for land; see CPR (Civil Procedure Rules) PD 6B 3.1(11). In the US, the leading case of *Shaffer v Heitner* 326 US 310 (1945) establishes that there must be some other 'minimum contacts' in addition to the presence of assets so as to 'satisfy the standards of traditional notions of fair play and substantial justice'.

In addition, courts exercise long-arm jurisdiction for procedural reasons, such as where one of the defendants is subject to the jurisdiction and it is desirable to join other defendants outside the jurisdiction because they are closely involved in the main action, eg guarantors. **4.62**

The result is that jurisdiction is based on a variety of connections of which the main connecting links are: **4.63**

- the presence in the jurisdiction of the defendant or, less usually, of the claimant, ie a party connection;
- the subject matter of the action has some connection with the jurisdiction, eg a contract is to be performed there, a tort was committed there or wrongful acts were done there, or property is located there or a trust is domiciled there;
- the defendant has an asset within the jurisdiction. In this case, the jurisdictional reach is justified on the ground that creditors should be able to reach assets of the debtor wherever they are;
- the extension of jurisdiction has procedural advantages, as in the case of joining multiple defendants who are all involved in the same transaction.

We do not have to go into the detail of all of these procedural rules internationally because parties to the contracts concerned will almost always include a jurisdiction clause in the contract. **4.64**

A private survey of 161 countries in 2014 in which I was involved showed that almost all developed countries respect clauses giving jurisdiction to a foreign court. Countries which did not included Egypt, Iran, Kuwait, Kyrgyzstan, Laos, Saudi Arabia, Thailand, and a few others. **4.65**

EU Judgments Regulation 2012

4.66 This European Regulation covers all twenty-seven EU Member States and is idiosyncratic but nevertheless is important and generally qualifies what is said above about what courts have jurisdiction. The Regulation no longer applies in the UK. A different version applies to Denmark.

4.67 It applies to civil and commercial matters, but not to revenue, customs, or administrative matters, nor to bankruptcies, compositions, and the like, amongst other things. There are exceptions for certain EU instruments and certain other treaties and conventions, such as the New York Arbitration Convention of 1958.

4.68 The basic rule is that persons domiciled in a Member State must be sued in a Member State. But article 25 allows submission to the jurisdiction of another Member State if the clause satisfies some fairly straightforward requirements.

4.69 There are exceptions to the domicile rule, for example, an action is allowed in the courts at the place of performance of a contract, or the place where the harmful event occurred in the case of tort, delict or quasi delict. As regards a dispute arising out of the operations of a branch, a person may be sued in the courts for the place where the branch is situated. In the case of certain trust actions, suit can be brought in the Member State in which the trust is domiciled: see article 7. There are further procedural exceptions in article 8. In addition, article 24 provides that Member States have exclusive jurisdiction, regardless of domicile, in special cases, such as proceedings relating to land, certain constitutional matters in relation to companies, the validity of entries in public registers, and the validity of intellectual property. In these cases, the proceedings have to be carried out in the location concerned.

4.70 If the judgment satisfies these requirements, the judgment is recognised and enforced in all other Member States (articles 36 and 39), subject only to an override if recognition is manifestly contrary to public policy in the Member State addressed.

4.71 There are special rules for insurance, consumer contracts, and individual contracts of employment.

4.72 The object is to restrict the waste and cost of battles for jurisdiction based on fine-trigger jurisdictional bases.

4.73 Non-domiciliaries are subject to the long-arm rules of each Member State with the result that judgments on the basis of those rules are enforced in all other states. The Member States of the EU therefore operate as a monolithic jurisdictional unit with the widest conceivable long-arm jurisdictional rules available to, say, a creditor over a debtor in a non-Member State.

4.74 The Member State where the action is first brought will generally have exclusive jurisdiction. The position in other Member States can be preserved by the wide availability of pre-judgment asset preservation measures, such as freezing orders.

Jurisdiction over torts

4.75 Torts (sometimes called delicts) and non-contractual claims in our context include, for example, negligence liability under offering circulars, mis-selling claims, environmental liability, lack of good faith in pre-contractual negotiations, and failure to fulfil a disclosure obligation prior to contract under the good faith doctrine prevailing in many civil code jurisdictions. These claims can be particularly dangerous for contracting parties because, as mentioned, the ability to choose the governing law is restricted (see paragraph 4.14) and this is also so in relation to choice of courts. The reason is that a tort victim is an involuntary victim and often there is no contractual relationship between the victim and a party to a contract. An example is the liability of an underwriter (in some jurisdictions) for a negligent prospectus for equity shares to a buyer in the secondary market who has no contract with the underwriter which can contain a choice of law and choice of courts. Also, it is often the case that, as in England, the victim can choose to sue either in contract or tort.

Under the European Judgments Regulation 2012 discussed above a tort victim can sue either at the domicile of the defendant alleged to have committed the tort in a Member State, or at the place where the harmful event occurred (article 7(2)), or under a jurisdiction agreement under article 25 of the Regulation. There is authority from the ECJ that the choice of courts under article 25 binds an assignee of a contract as well as the original contracting parties and this would seem to apply also to purchases of bonds or other securities in the secondary market in the case of a contract claim: see eg *Gerling Konzern Speziale Kreditversicherung v Amministrazione del Tesoro della Stato* (201/82) [1983] ECR 2503. There is argument as to whether this would apply to a tort claim, eg for misrepresentation in an offering circular. If this is not the case, then a party might find itself sued for a prospectus liability claim in every jurisdiction where there is an investor with the claim. See Case C-375/13 *Kolassa v Barclays Bank plc* ECLI:EU:C:2015:37, where the ECJ held that an Austrian investor who had a prospectus liability claim against a UK bank issuer could sue in Austria because that is the place where the harmful event occurred, ie the place where the investor suffered the loss. **4.76**

But it is considered that the English courts would hold that a purchaser in the secondary market leapfrogging its seller and suing an underwriter under a law allowing such a claim (which English law usually would not) would be bound by a clause in the terms and conditions of the bonds selecting a governing law and courts and expressed widely enough to include actions in tort. **4.77**

In any event, in England the European Judgments Regulation 2012 no longer applies but the English courts have jurisdiction if the defendant has agreed to submit to the jurisdiction or if the damage was sustained within England or results from an act committed within the jurisdiction. See the Civil Procedure Rules PD 6B. **4.78**

English tort law is marked by an opposition to disproportionate tort claims and damages. English law does not have the expansive civil code liabilities for lack of good faith in contracts and for pre-contractual dealings. A possible way therefore of managing tort risk is to choose English law and courts, while recognising that in the present tumultuous world of international litigation, you may not be able to stop an action in a risky court elsewhere. **4.79**

Hague Convention on Choice of Court Agreements 2005

This Convention applies between the Member States of the EU, the UK, Singapore, and Mexico. It is worth mentioning it because it enables UK judgments to be recognised and **4.80** enforced in Member States of the EU, but only if the chosen courts are exclusive. In many cases such as international syndicated credits and bond issues, the creditors can sue in any other court of competent jurisdiction so would not be within the Hague Convention: a non-exclusive clause is usually preferred.

Arbitration

4.81 Arbitration is a feature of old economy agreements, such as the sale of goods and construction, but is not common in the classes of agreements we are concerned with here. These are syndicated bank credits, international bond issues, derivatives, securitisation documents, prime brokerage agreements, corporate finance advisory mandates, asset management documents, specialised contracts relating to settlement systems, agreements documenting security interests, repos and financial leases, equity capital-raising documents, sale and purchase agreements for the sale of private companies, takeover offers, merger and demerger documents, joint venture agreements, or purchase or supply contracts involved in project finance.

4.82 In the past, some banks included in their credit agreements a right of the bank to choose arbitration instead of the agreed courts. The reason for this is that there may have been doubts about the enforceability of judgments of the English or New York courts against a borrower or issuer in its own country where most of the assets are likely to be. The New York Arbitration Convention of 1958, adopted by practically the whole world, provides that arbitration awards in a contracting state must be recognised and enforced in other contracting states, a feature which is often seen to be a major advantage of arbitration.

4.83 Having regard to the fact that the countries less likely to enforce foreign judgments are also those less likely to enforce arbitration awards in practice, some practitioners think that the disadvantages of arbitration outweigh the advantages of the 1958 Convention. There are many different views on this issue. See Chapter 16.

Insolvency override of jurisdiction and arbitration clauses

4.84 It is considered that the English courts will not permit a foreign bankruptcy court to override an express choice of the English courts or an arbitration seat in England by the foreign bankruptcy court insisting that the litigation or the arbitration is continued exclusively in the courts where bankruptcy proceedings are taking place. See eg *UBS AG v Omni Holding AG* [2001] 1 WLR 916. UBS sued Omni for damages and took as security an option agreement expressly governed by English law with a selection of the English courts. Omni went into liquidation in Switzerland and the liquidator claimed that the issue should be tried in Switzerland. *Held* by the English court: the claim should be tried in the English courts as agreed, and not the Swiss courts. This was a case dealing with the EU Judgments Regulation 2012, which contains an exception for proceedings relating to the winding-up of insolvent companies which no longer applies in the UK, but it is considered that the decision is of general application.

Note that article 18 of the EU Insolvency Regulation 2015 refers the question of the effects of insolvency proceedings on certain limited lawsuits to the law of the Member State in which that lawsuit is pending. The UK is also no longer bound by the 2015 Regulation.   **4.85**

5
PREDICTABILITY

Purpose of Predictability and Summary

Predictability as a legal value

5.1 Predictability and certainty are values which are highly prized in the law generally. At the most basic level, people require predictability and certainty in the criminal law so that they may be sure of the type of conduct which could attract a custodial sentence or attract a fine. They require predictability in taxation so that they know how much of their income is for themselves and how much they have to pay to the state. In road traffic law, they need to know what the speed limit is precisely, and exactly what their duties are at a pedestrian crossing. When they insure their cars, they need to know with complete security whether they are covered against third party liability, lest the results of a single mistake or moment of inattention bankrupt them and ruin their lives.

5.2 The same principle applies to wholesale contracts. People who engage in these contracts need to know with precision what their risks are because, if the law declines to permit parties to agree terms which are predictable, the costs of inability to determine the outcome in advance could be enormous and sometimes crippling. For example, if a party believes that it can net all its foreign exchange contracts or derivative contracts on the bankruptcy of that counterparty and then it turns out that the law prohibits this because of a lack of clarity in the law from the very beginning, that party might find itself with a gross exposure of millions or billions when it thought they were zero.

5.3 The management of large corporations and banks have a direct responsibility for managing risks since the failure of their firm would cause losses to shareholders where, for example, the shares are held in pension funds for employees, to creditors, such as suppliers, who otherwise would not get paid, and to their own employees who lose their jobs. A major collapse can have an adverse impact on a local area or region and thereby damage the livelihoods of the people who live there and its economy even the whole economy. If there are serious and unexpected risks which cannot be managed by contract, the legal system is failing them. Banks would not know how much to set aside in reserves and how much capital against losses. They would know the extent or duration of the exposures that they should insure (or hedge) in the derivatives market. Their financial statements would not be able to assess their contingent liabilities with reasonable accuracy.

5.4 If the law does not permit private parties to regulate their risks by their own contracts but insists on overriding contracts by principles whose application is inherently uncertain, such as what a particular judge thinks is unfair after the contract is entered into, then the legal system is doubly failing them, because, not only is it uncertain, but it prohibits and restricts firms from voluntarily building certainty into their contracts. The legal system is failing the people in relation to a fundamental value which is freedom, probably one of the most fundamental values which societies have.

The law is a moral structure and does not anywhere permit dishonest, unconscionable, or oppressive conduct. Legal systems universally restrain that type of conduct. Hence we are here concerned with conduct which is above the minimum standard but which is considered by some jurisdictions to be null and void on grounds of unfairness, and in other jurisdictions to be fair and therefore legitimate, even though there may be occasional abuse or opportunistic behaviour. **5.5**

In the areas of law we are concerned with here, we are dealing only with parties who are sufficiently well-informed, and have sufficient resources to be able to take legal advice, so as to look after themselves. We are not dealing with individuals or consumers. **5.6**

This chapter covers the first letter in the sequence of the thirteen themes expressed in the mnemonic PIB—FEISST—CoRCO, standing for *p*redictability, *i*nsulation, *b*usiness *o*rientation, *f*reedom of contract, *e*xclusion clauses, *i*nsolvency law, *s*et-off, *s*ecurity interests, *t*rusts, *co*rporate law, *r*egulatory law, *c*ourts, and *o*thers. **5.7**

Summary of key indicators

In this chapter, I consider first two factors which are often said to differentiate legal systems in their quest for certainty: the degree of codification, and the degree to which judges are obliged to follow the decisions of higher courts—the doctrine of precedent. These are considered to be useful key indicators, but are not considered key or central for reasons to be explained. **5.8**

Instead, I shall focus on what is known (misleadingly) as the doctrine of good faith in three major areas. These are termination clauses, clauses that heads of terms or a mandate are not legally binding until a formal contract is signed, and compulsory pre-contract disclosure. This is followed by a listing of other areas within the scope of the good faith doctrine but without dealing with them in detail. **5.9**

By way of summary, the conclusions are as follows: **5.10**

- The French courts will override an express termination of contract or acceleration on an event of default if the courts think the termination contravened their view of good faith. The German courts take the same view but perhaps with greater reluctance in the case of express clauses. The English courts will not normally override termination clauses on an express event of default and will allow immediate acceleration and close-outs if so provided. The position under New York law is similar to the English view.
- The French courts will override an express term in heads of terms or a mandate to the effect that a document its stated to be not legally binding if the courts consider that the terminating party was not acting in good faith. That party will incur liability in damages in that case. The position under German law is similar. English courts will not override such a clause on the ground that the terminating party was not acting in good faith during negotiations. The New York position is similar to the English position.

- The French courts will override an express clause stating that one party does not have to disclose material matters before contract or that the other party should rely on its own investigations exclusively where the clause conflicts with the codified duty of good faith. The position is similar under German law but perhaps less intense. English law does not have any general pre-contract duty to disclose information to the other party, except in well-defined circumstances such as in the case of fiduciaries or in the case of public offering circulars.

5.11 These conclusions are documented below.

5.12 The conclusions would seem roughly to match the pattern of 1357 proposed at paragraph 1.63, that is:

- England 1 (blue)
- New York 3 (green)
- Germany 5 (yellow)
- France 7 (red).

5.13 As before, New York is marked down somewhat because of the unpredictability of jury trials and the possible impact of judicial politicisation in the lower courts. As before, these rankings cannot be mathematically precise and are order of magnitude only.

5.14 The three tests would appear to satisfy have the requirements of the key indicators, that is, they are measurable, important, symbolic, or representative, and involve a clash of views between jurisdictions (MISC).

5.15 Before going into the detail on the good faith tests, I discuss codification and the doctrine of precedent.

Codification and Binding Judicial Precedent

Codification

5.16 It is often claimed that the civilian legal systems—mainly the Napoleonic and Roman-Germanic legal systems—are more certain because more of the law is codified than is the case with the two main common law legal systems, American common law and English common law. This seems a weak factor for several reasons.

5.17 The first is that in the common law jurisdictions, the classic law textbooks effectively synthesise, distil, and abbreviate contract law so that its essence may be grasped without having to read the innumerable multitude of cases. In the case of the US, practitioners can fall back on the Restatement (Second) of Contract and do not have to read the vast number of volumes of the mighty *Williston on Contract*, let alone the shelf-miles of US law reports. The second is that even in France, which places great emphasis on codification, especially in the case of contracts, it is the case law which gives meaning to the generalities. Thus, historically almost the whole of the French law of delict (torts), was built on one article in the Civil Code.

5.18 Secondly, important parts of the law are codified in all commercial states, such as sale of goods, bankruptcy law, property law and corporate law. Contract is codified in some common law jurisdictions, such as India.

5.19 It is also sometimes alleged that codifications tend to freeze the law and hinder its development. For example, the French Civil Code article on good faith in contract remained in force for more than two centuries after their enactment in 1804 until revisions came into force in 2016. The development of the law on the English universal fixed and floating charge was entirely by case law, unhindered by eighteenth century ideas of pledges and mortgages, as in France. A codification, it is said, can sometimes be relentless in the implacability of expression and fail to allow for the nuancing arising from different situations.

5.20 The degree of codification would seem not to satisfy the tests for key indicators which I have set. One can make too much of codification as a distinctive characteristic. it is true that there is a separate argument as to whether codification helps or hinders the law. What really matters is what the law says, not how it is written down.

Doctrine of judicial precedent

5.21 The predictability of English law is aided by the doctrine of judicial precedent whereby lower courts must follow the decisions of higher courts and whereby the Supreme Court imposes upon itself a rule not to depart from or overrule previous decisions except in very unusual cases.

5.22 On the one hand, the New York courts have a similar principle but the rule in New York seems to be undermined somewhat by jury trials which are notoriously unpredictable, by the proliferation of decisions, and perhaps because courts in New York are less disposed to maintain a common policy and are readier to distinguish previous decisions which the particular court (or the jury) does not like.

5.23 On the other hand, in the civil law groups case law has much less authority. In France, for example, there is no formal doctrine of precedent. The court system is not centralised and therefore there is less ability to establish a common informal consensus on policy. Higher courts are much less likely to reprimand a lower court for departing from the common line, something which is done with devastating courtesy by the Court of Appeal or Supreme Court in England.

5.24 Naturally, everywhere judges do not like being overruled or ignored by a higher court, but the delivery of a rebuke by the Supreme Court in England in such a public way can be humiliating to a junior judge, especially if it happens often. Decisions are poured over by academics and practitioners in the legal journals and the books who can also be ever so politely scathing. It is a badge of honour not to be overruled on appeal.

5.25 As pointed out by Professor Solene Rowan, the *Cour de Cassation*, which is the Supreme Court in France, is composed of six chambers and has more than 100 judges who deal with over 20,000 disputes a year in civil and criminal matters alone. There are thirty-three courts of appeal, with over 1,000 judges. It seems therefore more difficult than in England to work out what the law is, to decide which decisions represent the consensus, and to discover what principles are at work. There is a higher risk that decisions are inconsistent with each other so as to add to the sense of confusion and uncertainty. In addition, courts in France often do not provide the reasons for their decisions which are typically laconic and brief. The principles become obscure and hidden, thereby increasing the uncertainty. All of this follows from the deeply inherited culture in France that judges do not make the law. That must be left to the legislature who are, under this theory, the voice of the people, as opposed to unelected judges.

5.26 It is suggested that the position is similar in Germany, but perhaps to a lesser degree. Again, the courts in Germany are not centralised and again here is no formal doctrine of binding precedent.

5.27 I do not use the doctrine of precedent as a key indicator. It is significant but is hard to measure accurately.

Stability of the law

5.28 The stability of the law is also a possible indicator, that is, the frequency and abruptness of change and the extent to which the changes mark large reversals or shifts of attitude. A legal system is unstable if, for example, it persistently over-reacts to changes from right to left and back again in government politics or to some current scandal. The law books are not the place to rant and rave. They are our scriptures and require measured rationality.

5.29 Stability is highly relevant, particularly for long-term contracts, but the conservatism or volatility of a legal system and the effects of the instability would be quite speculative and hence could not satisfy the MISC tests.

Doctrine of Good Faith in Contract

Good faith doctrine generally

5.30 The deepest and widest chasm in contract law between English and New York law on the one hand, and France and Germany on the other, and therefore to a greater or lesser degree the members of their respective families of law, is the approach to what is called the doctrine of good faith in contracts. This doctrine is not general under English law. The English courts do not intervene to overrule the express terms of contracts between business parties on the grounds of an imposed view of fairness. In principle, the English courts do not believe that it is just that they should overrule and ignore what responsible parties have agreed, whereas the courts of France are interventionist and are prepared to remodel contracts if the court thinks the outcome would otherwise be unfair.

5.31 The English courts in effect take the view that it is unjust and bad faith for a parties in a business setting to seek to change an agreement after they have agreed to it under cover of the cloak of altruism and morality.

See generally the literature on this subject cited in the Sources and References under this chapter. For France, see especially the lucid text by Solene Rowan, *The New French Law of Contract* (OUP 2022) which also contains comparisons with English law. **5.32**

Good faith generally in England

English law has a strong business orientation and considers it just and fair in wholesale markets, particularly financial markets, that the parties should have freedom of contract to decide the terms of their contracts and to allocate their risks without subsequent court interference. English law considers that contract predictability is essential in view of the large amounts at stake, and the often systemic interdependence and links between parties and markets which have high concentrations of risk. **5.33**

The result is that in the English courts under English law the parties get what they agreed and are regarded as being responsible for their own agreements if between business parties, whereas that is not normally so in the civil families of law. In various cases in France and some other (but not all) jurisdictions in the Napoleonic and Roman-Germanic groups, the court can reform the contract which the parties thought they had negotiated between themselves. In that case the court decides the risk after the contract was entered into and the parties have less freedom to determine with predictability what their risks are in advance. Instead, it is decided for them. **5.34**

Good faith generally in France

In France, the courts may override express terms agreed by the parties on the grounds of non-compliance with their view of justice. Hence, French law is less predictable. This interventionist approach may originally have been based upon the view that contracts in commerce are a battle between the strong and the weak, the overmighty bank or corporation against the innocent farmer, the predatory capitalist against the ordinary citizen. This view now seems obsolete and out-of-date in relation to business transactions in the modern world where most of the population have a business or work in a business and consumers are protected by consumer laws. **5.35**

Examples of good faith laws

The first step is to describe the general declarations about good faith in the main jurisdictions, but noting that jurisdictions mean very different things when they refer to a duty of good faith. **5.36**

The idea of good faith when employed in English statutes refers to honesty, not what is considered commercially fair in a particular case. English case law consistently makes it clear that the courts do not generally adopt a universal good faith doctrine for contracts, except in specific cases. **5.37**

5.38 In France, article 1104 of the new Civil Code on contracts provides that contracts must be 'negotiated, formed and performed in good faith'. This is described as 'a matter of public policy' and therefore is mandatory and cannot be departed from by agreement. The 1804 code stated that contracts should be performed in good faith, but now in the 2016 codification of case law the principle is extended to cover pre-contract negotiations and the stage of the formation of the contract at the beginning. The new code does not contain a definition of good faith, but case law prior to the new code in 2016 is expected to remain relevant. Good faith has been held, amongst other things, to mean that the parties have a duty of loyalty, cooperation, and a duty to be 'coherent'. France has also expanded its doctrine of the abuse of rights. The meaning of the duty of good faith was deliberately left open so that the judge could control the loyalty of contracting parties and their good faith. The result appears to be that the parties themselves cannot define good faith and that essential elements of the contract can be unpredictable. The doctrines of good faith and abuse of rights were significantly enlarged by case law mainly from the 1980s onwards.

5.39 Many of the French principles are adopted in international contract law instruments which are intended to be non-binding models which reforming states can introduce if they want, in particular the UNIDROIT Principles of International Commercial Contracts and the Principles of European Contract Law. These instruments on the whole are products of academics.

5.40 In Germany, the principle has achieved a very high degree of penetration, often more than is the case in other members of the Roman-Germanic group. Section 242 of the BGB, which is the German Civil Code, states generally that, on the one hand, everyone must perform his contract in the manner required by good faith and fair dealing, taking into consideration the general practice in commerce. Based on this, the German courts have created numerous obligations of loyal performance of a contract, such as duty to cooperate, to protect each other's interests, to give information, and to submit accounts. On the other hand, it is said that the courts are reluctant to impose terms overriding the express terms agreed between the parties on the grounds only that the court believes the imposed terms to be fairer and more equitable.

5.41 Provisions laying down a principle of good faith in the performance of the contract are found in article 1134 of the Civil Codes in Belgium and Luxembourg (based on the old French code), in article 288 of the Civil Code in Greece, in article 1175 of the Civil Code in Italy (see also articles 1337, 1366, and 1375), in articles 6.2 and 248 of the Netherlands Civil Code, in article 762(2) of the Portuguese Civil Code, in article 1258 of the Spanish Civil Code and in article 57 of its Commercial Code. In Denmark, the principle is said to be recognised by the courts and legal writers. In the Netherlands, for example, the doctrine as expressed in article 6:2 and 6:248(2) allows the courts to change the contract so as to comply with a form which the court believes to be more fair and equitable. See Ole Lando and Hugh Beale, *Principles of European Contract Law* (Martinus Nijhoff 1995).

5.42 The principle is a mandatory in at least Germany, France, Belgium, Luxembourg, Greece, Italy, the Netherlands, Portugal, and Spain in the Napoleonic group, in Germany and the Netherlands in the Roman-Germanic group, and therefore probably in a great many other countries in those groups. That means that the doctrine is espoused with such fierce intensity that the parties lose the right to contract out of the doctrine so that the doctrine overrides so as to change the terms of the contract the parties have agreed. In order to give more teeth to this, Rome I on contract applicable law requires in article 3(3) that, in effect, in a domestic contract the parties cannot choose a foreign governing law to avoid these mandatory provisions, thereby making an inroad on the freedom of choice of governing law.

The idea of good faith is also found in the codes of Switzerland, Japan, Poland, and South Korea, all of which are civil code systems in this respect. In China, the Contract Law provides in article 6 that in exercising their rights and performing their obligations, the parties shall observe the principles of honesty and good faith. We can therefore assume with some confidence that the concept is probably almost universal, or at least very common, in the Napoleonic and Roman-Germanic jurisdictions, as well as other civil systems outside the American and English common law groups. We cannot assume that the outcome is the same in all civil code jurisdictions, especially in such cautious jurisdictions as Sweden, Switzerland, and Japan. **5.43**

Good faith generally in the United States

In the US, section-1 304 the Uniform Commercial Code provides that: 'Every contract or duty within [the Uniform Commercial Code] imposes an obligation of good faith in its performance and enforcement.' A definition in section 1-102 states that good faith means 'honesty in fact and the observance of reasonable commercial standards of fair dealing'. Although this duty applies only to contracts within the UCC, the courts have extended the good faith principle to other contracts. See eg the Restatement (Second) of Contracts section 208. **5.44**

In the leading case of *511 W.232nd Owners Corp v Jennifer Realty Co* 98 NY 2d 144, (2002), the court said that under New York law 'all contracts imply a covenant of good faith and fair dealing in the course of performance'. The court added that this duty requires that 'neither party shall do anything which will have the effect of destroying or injuring the right of the other party to receive the fruits of the contract'. **5.45**

However, New York law narrows this duty so that it is of limited practical effect. The duty does not override express discretions given to one party and does not override express termination rights. Contrary to the position under French law, the courts does not intervene to decide whether the discretion or the termination right was exercised in good faith. The case law on this is decisive and voluminous. Thus, in *Triton Partners LLC v Prudential Sec. Inc* 301 AD 2d 411, the court said that it will not allow a claim for breach of the implied duty of good faith that is 'merely a substitute for a nonviable breach of contract claim'. The court will not use good faith to preclude reliance on a 'bargained-for clause that allows a party to exercise its discretion': *Paxi LLC v Shiseido Americas Corp* 636 F Supp 2d 275 (SDNY 2009). See also *Moran v Erk* 11 NY 3d 452 (2008) where the court held that the implied covenant of good faith and fair dealing should not be judicially imposed where it would modify or negate the express terms of the parties' agreement, including where the contract expressly permits one party to act in its 'sole discretion'. That case has been followed several times. See, for example, *Veneto Hotel & Casino v German American Capital Corp* 160 AD 3d 451 (1st Dept 2018). **5.46**

5.47 In Canada, a case heralded the adoption of 'reasonable contract performance', but this turned out to be no more than the principle of honesty which everybody accepts: see *Bhasin v Hrynew* 2014 SCC 71. The Australian courts appeared to adopt the main tenets of the English ideology. They have held that there is a duty to cooperate, which means that discretions must be exercised reasonably and not capriciously or for an extraneous purpose: *Renard Constructions v Buller Coal* (1992) 26 NSWLR 234. The Canadian and Australian applications are far different from the French and German. Singapore follows the general English position, it seems: *Ng Giap Hon v Westcomb Securities Pte Ltd* [2009] 3 SLR (R) 518.

English right to choose good faith voluntarily

5.48 In France and Germany, the rule is mandatory and there is no freedom to contract out of the duties if the parties want. Under English law numerous cases have held that the parties can provide for the application of the good faith doctrine in their contracts if they want to: see, for example, *Horn v Commercial Acceptances* [2001] EWHC 1757 (Ch). There are plenty of cases which describe what the effects are if they do choose to apply it.

5.49 In the ISDA master agreement, the term 'good faith' appears several times. Accordingly, English law preserves freedom on this point, and does not subscribe to the view that the courts should override what eligible parties have agreed.

Universal basic contract standards

5.50 In no jurisdiction do parties have complete freedom to behave as they like. There does not appear to be any commercial jurisdiction which does not require in its contract law some basic standards of morality, a kind of basic set of human rights which cannot be overridden by a contract between the parties. Very obviously no jurisdiction will allow contracts to murder, rape or rob, or to commit a fraud, to manipulate a market, or which are racist or grossly discriminatory. Nor will they allow a party to engage in dishonest conduct, such as lying or giving false information or making misleading statements. They will not allow a party to induce the other to enter into the contract by making a knowingly false statement, ie one that is fraudulent, not just negligent. They will not allow a party to exercise coercion, duress, or oppression, or grossly undue influence, or extortion. There are prohibitions on the imposition of penalties if a party does not perform, penalties which manifestly bear no relation to the actual loss which that party would suffer, eg a payment of a million dollars if you fail to deliver a loaf of bread. The rules in England for contract penalties are very tolerant: see *Cavendish Square Holding BV v Makdessi* [2016] AC 1172.

5.51 Many local statutes provide a duty of fairness. For example, under the British Companies Act 2006 shareholders can make an unfair prejudice application if they are subject to oppression. A creditor can make such an application protesting at unfair prejudice in an insolvency administrator's management of a restructuring under insolvency legislation. Employees may claim compensation for unfair dismissal. There are many other examples.

There is also another common core of principles which applies in all contracts probably everywhere, for example, that a contract fails if unforeseen circumstances occur which frustrate the contract, or contracts where a party is a fiduciary, such as a trustee or agent, and breaches its fiduciary duties. In both these cases, however, the law usually allows the parties to contract out in business situations. The conclusion therefore is that all relevant jurisdictions have a notion of good faith, including in English law, and the main question is the extent of the scope of the good faith concept and the degree to which it to which it restricts predictability. **5.52**

We can now deal with a number of specific situations against which one can test the credentials of a jurisdiction on this issue. **5.53**

Contract Terminations

Typical termination clauses

Most contracts, other than short-term spot contracts, contain provisions for a termination of the contract if the other party defaults or it is obvious that it will default. **5.54**

These events of default typically include a failure by the other party to make payments or perform its other obligations or if it breaches a representation or warranty in the contract, or its creditors attach its assets, or it becomes actually insolvent, or insolvency proceedings are commenced, or if the contract becomes illegal, or sometimes if there is a material adverse change in the financial condition of the other party, such as in a corporate takeover offer in the case of syndicated bank agreement. **5.55**

In the case of insolvency or creditor attachments, the events of defaults are anticipatory, ie there is no point in waiting since insolvency is the stroke of midnight usually. Some contracts, especially bank credit contracts and bond issues, contain a cross-default clause which provides that it is an event of default if a borrower, say, fails to repay other loans owed to other lenders This is an equality clause designed to ensure that creditors have equal rights since if the borrower defaults towards one lender, then other lenders are next. They should all be at the negotiating table at the same time so that one lender does not get priority of payment. In project or construction contracts, typically one party can terminate if the project is abandoned, or if completion does not occur by a prescribed long-stop, or a prescribed force majeure event occurs and continues for a prescribed period. **5.56**

Sometimes, these events of defaults apply only to one party, such as the borrower in a syndicated bank credit, and sometimes they apply to both parties, as in the case of the ISDA master agreement. Sometimes they are non-symmetric, as in the case of host government concessions for a project, ie each party can avail itself of different events of default. **5.57**

The party terminating can terminate and claim compensation, stop performing itself, accelerate a loan or bond, cancel the commitment to make future loans, take possession of collateral or sell it, take possession of a ship or aircraft, step into a project, use a construction contractor's equipment on the site, call guarantees and demand bonds, cut off the exercise **5.58** of rights under a intellectual property licence, or close-out and net contracts under a derivatives or foreign exchange transaction.

5.59 I deal here only with express termination clauses, not with situations where the parties have failed to put in events of default. The reason for limiting the scope of the discussion is that parties usually do insert express events of default so that there is little point in cluttering up the discussion with situations which are usually irrelevant in the real world of business contracts.

5.60 In summary, the English courts will very rarely interfere in an express termination clause on a business contract.

Symbolic case of *The Laconia*

5.61 The English approach is symbolised in the famous Monday/Friday case of *The Laconia* [1977] AC 850. The ship charter hire fell due on a Sunday. The charterer paid on the Monday. The shipowner sent the money back and repossessed the ship at once on the Monday. The hire was payable in advance so it should have been paid on the previous Friday. This was an express event of default and the charter stated that time was of the essence. The reason for the termination could have been that charter rates had gone up and evidently the shipowner wanted to get the ship back so that it could charter out to the ship to somebody else at a higher rate. If that was the reason, then many would regard the termination as a commercially abusive and opportunistic termination. *Held* by the English House of Lords: the shipowner was entitled to repossess. The charterer could have negotiated a grace period but did not.

Policies of upholding immediate termination clauses

5.62 In *The Laconia*, what was the court to do—three days, three weeks, three months, who knows? The court said it was up to the parties to agree their risks, eg a grace period after notice, as is commonly done. If there was any doubt about whether the shipowner could repossess and the shipowner was wrong, then it would be liable for very substantial damages for wrongfully taking over the ship.

5.63 This was an extreme case. Bondholders hardly ever call 'Snap!' and pounce, at least not before extensive negotiations and only then when all is lost and the position is hopeless. It is common market experience that responsible banks regard an acceleration as an absolutely last resort since the result is to put the borrower out of business and to make a rescue impracticable: everybody else would call in their same money at the same time and the directors will have to cease business in case they incur liability for deepening the insolvency. The same is considered to apply in practice to most commercial contracts.

5.64 The crucial point here is that, if there is any uncertainty in whether or not the termination is allowed and the court holds that the termination clause is invalid, then the terminating party could face serious consequences and damages for its own non-performance or interference in collateral or other assets of the counterparty. The effect of that would be to suspend the right potentially over whatever is the maximum period a court could impose. In practical terms, the termination clause could be practically useless because of the risks that the terminating party incurs.

One question therefore is: how much abuse can a legal system tolerate in order to sustain some higher objective, which in this case was the need for predictability in contract? The answer the English courts give to that is that the business community is prepared to put up with occasional opportunistic conduct, so long as the legal system keeps its promise about predictability. No doubt if it became habitual for banks or shipowners or others to abuse their rights, then that implicit deal with the law would change. 5.65

There are times where derivative counterparties or other parties need to act swiftly, eg in fast-moving markets where minutes or even seconds can count in relation to a close-out or sale, or there is a threatened attachment, or a set-off must be exercised as against a deposit being withdrawn by a borrower, or an aircraft or ship is fleeing its creditors, or the issuer is insolvent and the assets might be siphoned off. The legal system considers predictability is justified because creditors should not have to run the risk of substantial damages for wrongful interference or large losses in a plunging market. 5.66

The effect is that the parties are in charge of and control the documents which they negotiated. English law does not rewrite legitimate contracts on this point. 5.67

Further, in a world where the financial interconnections globally are intricate, involve enormous amounts and are sensitive to confidence, parties must make payments on time and in the full amount. There has to be discipline about this and there is little room for sloppiness. Otherwise there could be a serious knock-on or contagion effect, eg in relation to central counterparties, or foreign exchange or derivatives or securities markets, or where banks or corporations rely on large payments being received by them so that they can make corresponding payments or retrieve collateral. Even the strawberry pickers for the omnipotent supermarket want to be paid on time so that they can buy food for the family and pay the rent. 5.68

The Monday/Friday case is a litmus test—will a jurisdiction in a civil code group consistently replicate the result on the same facts? The answer is often, no. 5.69

Other English examples of terminations

Another example of the English view is the *Shepherd and Cooper v TSB Bank plc* [1996] 2 All ER 654 (1996) where a UK bank was held entitled to accelerate and enforce a secured loan immediately on a default in payment. The bank sent in receivers one hour after demanding payment. *Held:* the appointment of the receiver was valid. It was clear that the borrower could not pay. 5.70

There is a long and consistent line of English cases to the same effect up to the present day. In *Bank of Baroda v Panessar* [1986] 3 All ER 751, that court rejected the approach adopted in, say, Canada that the debtor is given reasonable time for payment. All that is required is that the debtor has time to arrange the mechanics of payment, assuming 5.71

that the debtor has the cash available. It was held that the appointment by the bank of a receiver one hour after the making of a proper demand was valid. No doubt in that case the demand did not appear out of the blue and the position was hopeless. In *The Angelic Star* [1988] 1 Lloyd's Rep 122 (CA), the court upheld the immediate acceleration of a secured ship loan pursuant to a clause allowing the bank to accelerate on an event of default. In *Nicholson v HSBC Bank* [2001] EWCA Civ 548, that court said that on demand means on demand. Hence, according to English law, if the contract states that it can be terminated immediately, that means immediately, not next Wednesday, not next Wednesday week.

5.72 In another charterparty case the charter payment was $80 short because an intermediary bank had deducted its costs from the hire payment. The shipowner was held to be entitled to cancel the charter under a clause allowing cancellation if payment was not made in full on the due date: *The Chikuma* [1981] 1 All ER 652. The House of Lords upheld the termination, even though the amount involved was small. If you were buying groceries, it is unlikely that the person at the till would accept a payment which is ten cents short. Nor would a taxi driver.

5.73 In *Union Eagle Ltd v Golden Achievement Ltd* [1997] AC 514, on appeal from Hong Kong, the buyers of a flat paid 10 per cent of the price of a flat costing HK$4.2million. Completion was fixed for 5 pm. The buyers arrived ten minutes late. Prices were going up and the market was volatile. The sellers cancelled the contract and forfeited the deposit, as allowed by the contract. *Held*: the sellers were entitled to do so. Five o'clock meant five o'clock. In these cases the courts have pointed out that, if they did not have a firm rule, a party could be left for years not knowing whether the contract was in being or not while the matter was litigated.

5.74 This was an extreme case, but the court made an important point. The remedy of parties is to arrive on time for an important transaction. Other linked transactions may depend upon punctuality. If there is a risk, agree a grace period and see the reaction when you propose being late. If a train leaves at 7.12 am, you can't complain if you are ten minutes late and the train has gone. Why should the rule for closings of large transactions, which can involve huge amounts, be any different?

5.75 In a series of recent cases the English courts have held that the doctrine of good faith does not apply to express terminations. There is no duty of rationality in this case: see, for example, *UBS AG v Rose Capital Ventures Ltd* [2018] EWHC 3137 (Ch). That kind of discretion is not subject to a rule which is often applied in England to the exercise of discretions, ie that they must not be arbitrary, capricious, or irrational. They do not have to be reasonable objectively. If there were, there would be endless litigation, cost, and delay, while the non-defaulter is left in limbo and the debtor receives an uncertain grace period which was never agreed.

5.76 The New York position is similar, subject to minor qualifications. See paragraph 5.44 above.

5.77 It is considered most unlikely that Germany, let alone France, would come anywhere near following the discipline of the English security enforcement cases mentioned above or the short-payment case or the Hong Kong ten-minute case.

Terminations under French law

The same consistent result from courts is not predictably available in the case of France. **5.78**

It was only in 2016 that the French Civil Code recognised a right of a non-defaulting party to terminate the contract pursuant to an express right in the contract, subject to various conditions: see the Civil Code, article 1224. Until then, under article 1184 of the Civil Code (which is still in effect in many Napoleonic jurisdictions) in certain situations in effect the court controlled whether termination was justified—an arresting situation to a lawyer in the common law tradition where express remedies of this sort are self-help. This role of the court over termination was seen as a necessary protection protect the defaulter because it meant that the court could ensure that the termination was legitimate within their view of the doctrine of good faith and could also verify whether the contract could be saved. Belgium and Luxembourg still do have article 1184. It is found also in article 1124(3) of the Spanish Civil Code and so it would appear to be widespread in the Napoleonic group. On article 1184, see generally John Bell, Sophie Boyron, and Simon Whittaker, *Principles of French Law* (2nd edn, OUP 2008) 357–359. **5.79**

Now under the new article 1224 of the French Civil Code a non-defaulter can terminate the contract by itself if it has an express right to do so. The right to terminate cannot be a general right but must specify precisely which are the obligations whose breach will entitle the other party to terminate. Hence we commence with unpredictability—how specific is specific? The new termination regime is still protective of the defaulter by virtue of safeguards in the new article 1226. The non-defaulting party must put the defaulter on notice that performance must be effected within a reasonable period of time, after which termination will follow. This applies except where there is urgency. In effect, the defaulter is given another opportunity to perform. Further if the defaulter continues to be in breach at the end of the period, the non-defaulter must give the defaulter another notice that the contract is at an end, also stating the grounds for termination. In effect, the defaulter can examine these grounds to see whether the termination can be challenged. If the defaulter does challenge the termination the court has power to overrule the termination and compel performance so that the contract remains in being. So the other party might have to wait a year or two before the court gets round to it and decides whether there is or is not a contract, leaving the non-defaulter in limbo. The court can grant the defaulter a grace period in which to perform. Defaulters can also invoke the doctrine of good faith to protect themselves against termination without good cause: previous case law on this is likely still to remain in effect so that for example an opportunistic termination would be regarded as a disloyal speculation. In 1994, the Limoges Court of Appeal (Civ (3) 12 Jan 1994, no 91-17023) held that it would not enforce a termination clause where the non-defaulter had attempted to rely on the defaulter's breaches and so to exercise a termination right as a pretext for agreeing more profitable transactions with third parties. The decision was upheld by the Court of Cassation. The exercise of a right to terminate may be curtailed by the separate doctrine of abuse of rights. For example, it has been held in France that a principal must have a legitimate basis for exercising a right to terminate an agency contract, even though the power to terminate was expressly unilateral and exercisable whenever the principle liked: Com 3 July, no 98-16.691. **5.80**

5.81 Under English law, there are no similar procedural requirements since the non-defaulter only has to tell the defaulter in accordance with the contract which typically contain its own notice procedures, or otherwise orally or in writing. The defaulter is not entitled to a court-imposed grace period, but only whatever grace periods are agreed in the contract, which they often are. The English courts specifically exclude a duty to act in good faith in relation to the exercise of an express termination right.

French legal interventionism elsewhere

5.82 The interventions by the courts in France in the case of contract terminations is consistent with an interventionist judicial surveillance in other areas as well. For example, self-help remedies of private sale of collateral on default are standard in both English and American common law systems, whereas in most of the Napoleonic jurisdictions, the opposite is the case. France is now more relaxed on this issue. Most sales of assets, outside investments with a clear value and outside financial collateral, require a court order and often a public auction in Napoleonic jurisdictions based on the French model. Again, the motive appears to be the protection of vulnerable debtors. The requirements are inconvenient in wholesale financial markets and of doubtful value even in other contexts. The effect is to give debtors de facto grace periods possibly running to years, depending on the court queue. In general, the Napoleonic group is the family group which is least sympathetic to security interests. See Chapter 12.

5.83 More tellingly, in the case of the main French insolvency rescue procedure the *redressement judiciaire*, introduced in 1985, the court exercises an interventionist command and control. The court has the sole right of decision as to what the plan should say. The plan is largely driven by a desire to protect employment and creditors do not vote on the plan. The court can impose a moratorium on debts and in a few cases the courts imposed a period of more than twenty-five years. In the case of safeguard proceedings introduced in 2006 the court still holds the whip-hand, even though there is creditor voting. Pursuant to a 2010 law, the safeguard scheme may be imposed on all creditors by the court, whether or not they agreed to the plan. Creditors for that reason seek to avoid insolvency proceedings if they can. But even then they can be compulsorily defeated by the rule that, if the company is actually insolvent, the directors are personally liable unless they apply for a judicial proceeding. It is worth investigating whether this dirigiste situation was modified by the French implementation of the European Restructuring Directive 2019.

5.84 France prohibits non assignment clauses in commercial contracts, thereby limiting freedom of contract: see paragraph 8.55.

5.85 As noted, another example of the preference for court interventionism in France is the risk of personal liability of directors for deepening an insolvency which forces the company into the trauma, delays, and expense of insolvency proceedings instead of permitting a private work-out, which is usually the best solution. See paragraph 14.82.

5.86 The number of examples of judicial intrusion in France seems to indicate a distrust of private self-help as opposed to court surveillance and control, an antipathy towards business.

By contrast, in England in these cases, the law encourages self-help, while allowing the parties to resort to the court if they wish.

Terminations under German law

In German law, the exercise of the right to terminate must be exercised in accordance with the general duty of good faith in section 242 of the BGB. There must be no abuse of the right to terminate. The cases suggest that the breach of contract must normally be fundamental and not trivial. It is probably the case that if a non-payment has been cured before termination, then it is too late to terminate and hence it is unlikely that the German courts would allow the termination of the charterparty in the same circumstances as *The Laconia*. **5.87**

The German approach appears again to be in the middle between England and France. **5.88**

Termination clauses on insolvency

The most devastating impact on the freedom to terminate a contract comes from insolvency doctrines which freeze terminations of contracts in the interests of rescuing of an insolvent debtor. Nearly all developed countries have this freeze in their insolvency laws. One of the least savage versions is contained in English insolvency laws and the freeze is rare in traditional English jurisdictions. I will be examining this important subject in Chapter 10. **5.89**

Mandates and Heads of Terms

Market practice

It is standard practice in the case of a complex contracts in the wholesale sphere for the parties to set out the main commercial terms for negotiation on the basis that they are not legally binding. For example, an arranger of a syndicated bank credit or an international bond issue will obtain a mandate letter from the borrower or issuer authorising the arranger to arrange the transaction and setting out the main financial and commercial terms, often with a provision that other terms will be in accordance with market practice. The practice is similar for long-term sale agreements and construction contracts. **5.90**

These heads of terms are typically stated to be not legally binding, except sometimes for specific clauses such as a confidentiality and the payment of specified costs. A bank loan offer may be made subject to credit approval by the bank or one of the parties may need to carry out a feasibility study. In English common law jurisdictions it is common to say that the heads of terms are 'subject to contract'. The parties intend that the heads of terms are there to enable negotiations to be completed by the drawing up and execution of a formal agreement and they do not expect to be held to the bargain legally before that happens. **5.91**

In addition, agreements contain detailed conditions precedent before the contract comes into force, such as the production of authorising board resolutions of the counterparty, **5.92** official consents and permits, the execution of related contracts such as security agreements, and the delivery of formal transaction legal opinions as to the enforceability of the transaction. Thus, in syndicated bank credits, the credit agreement will state that the borrower may not borrow any loans until these conditions precedent have been satisfied in form and substance satisfactory to the agent bank.

5.93 If heads of terms are easily converted into binding agreements, then a party finds itself bound by contract to which it has not agreed. In addition, if a party has to pay damages for wrongful conduct, then there is yet another head of unexpected liability.

5.94 I am dealing here only with situations where the parties, as is normal, provide that the heads of terms are not legally binding. It is not therefore necessary to deal with cases where the parties failed to make this provision for taking the contract outside the law. We can leave aside the vast law as to whether the parties intended to be bound, and whether the terms are sufficient to form a contract. We are also not dealing with a cases of 'gentlemen's agreements' where the parties never intend to enter into a legal contract but simply to rely on trust and honour outside the law.

International summary

5.95 By way of summary, English and New York law will not normally override an express term that the letter of intent is not legally binding, but French law and German law can both impose a liability for damages if a party was not negotiating in good faith. Technically, this is treated as a tort or delict because it is a non-contractual liability. It should therefore normally be governed by the law of the intended contract: see Rome II, article 12.

5.96 Under English law, the occasions when the courts override an expense provision that the heads of terms are not legally binding are rare. There are a few cases where the parties were deemed to be bound, because it is possible for parties to waive that term. In these cases, the parties typically have already done a large part of the work as if there had been a contract. This is a wholly different situation from cases where one party was held not to be negotiating in good faith.

5.97 In *Walford v Miles* [1992] AC 128, sellers of a business entered into negotiations with buyers which were in principle only and expressly 'subject to contract'. They agreed that they would only negotiate with one of the potential buyers if the buyers got their bank to send a comfort letter, which the buyers did. The sellers cut off negotiations with third parties, but ultimately decided not to sell to the proposed buyers and sold the business to a third party. *Held* by the House of Lords: the lock-out agreement was too uncertain to be enforced because it did not state how long the sellers were prohibited from negotiating with others. There was no implied term that the sellers had to negotiate in good faith with the proposed buyers for as long as they wanted to sell the business. The court said: '[W]hile negotiations are in existence either party is entitled to withdraw from these negotiations, at any time and for any reason. There can thus be no obligation to continue to negotiate until there is a 'proper reason' to withdraw.'

5.98 In the US, as a general rule the duty of good faith does not normally apply to negotiations before the contract is made. The courts allow a party freedom of negotiation and relieve a party of risks arising during negotiation. Parties should not be discouraged from entering into negotiations and they should not be subjected to the unpredictability of liability on the grounds that they did not bargain in good faith in the view of the court. In special cases in the US, there may be pre-contractual liability, for example, where there is an unjust enrichment resulting from the negotiations, such as the misappropriation of confidential ideas, or one party makes a misrepresentation or specific promise during the negotiations, or the parties have agreed to negotiate in good faith. The special cases do not seem to challenge the normal principle of no liability.

5.99 The situation is wholly different in the main members of the civil code group in Europe, a view which was inspired partly in the nineteenth century by the German writer von Jhering, who took the view that each party had a duty of care during pre-contractual negotiations. The doctrine was given a Latin title to guarantee its ancient authenticity. It was and still is called *culpa in contrahendo*—fault in contracting. The overall result is that a failure to negotiate in good faith or the breaking of negotiations otherwise than in good faith (as decided by the court) can give rise to liability, notwithstanding that the parties agreed that the heads of terms were not legally binding.

5.100 The principle is adopted by the courts in Germany and Austria, and also Greece (see CC, articles 197 and 198), Portugal (CC, article 227), Italy (CC, article 1337), Spain (CC, article 7(1)—the general good faith article). France, Belgium, and Luxembourg tend to use CC, article 1382, which deals with delict (tort) liability. The German Supreme Court has held a person liable if, without good reason, that person refuses to continue negotiations after having conducted the negotiations in such a way that the other party had reason to expect a contract to come into existence on the basis of the content which had been negotiated. Ditto in Austria, Belgium, France, the Netherlands, Portugal, and Italy, but not ditto in England or New York. A special area of risk in the civil code countries is where a party continues negotiations without telling the other party that the doubtful party may not continue, a situation which in practice is not uncommon in negotiations.

5.101 In France, the 2018 version of article 1112 of the Civil Code provides that the 'commencement, continuation and breaking-off of precontractual negotiations are free from control', but then goes on to state that they 'must mandatorily satisfy the requirements of good faith'. It gives with one hand and takes with the other. The article adds that in 'case of fault committed during the negotiations, the reparation of the resulting loss is calculated so as to compensate neither the loss of benefits which were expected from the contract that was not concluded nor the loss of the chance of obtaining those these benefits'. For example, French courts have held that conducting parallel negotiations with several potential parties is bad faith if a negotiating party is induced to believe the negotiations are exclusive. There is bad faith if a party continues to negotiate having taken the decision not to do so. In another case, a French company conducted lengthy negotiations for a dealership agreement with a US company, including an expensive trip to the US. The US party terminated the negotiations abruptly in a shorter phone call with no explanation. The Court of Cassation upheld a decision that there had been an improper breaking off of negotiations: Com 20 March 1972. Loss can include wasted expenditure or injury to feelings for the vexatious manner in which the negotiations where ended. The loss can also include the loss of chance to contract with a third party where the other party prolonged the negotiations, thus preventing them from entering into the contract with a third party. The loss does not include the loss of the expected contract itself since then the victim would be in the same position as if the contract had been concluded.

5.102 The position therefore seems to be that in a multitude of cases a negotiator would have to consult a lawyer expert in this area as to whether or not negotiations can be broken off. It often happens that there is a period of uncertainty as to whether or not a party will go ahead, especially where an internal approval is required. Hence, the position seems to be quite unrealistic in terms of the practical impact on negotiations of commercial deals.

5.103 Note also that in France under article 1116 of the Civil Code an offer may not be withdrawn before the expiry of any period fixed by the offeror or, if no such period has been fixed, the end of a reasonable period. The withdrawing party is liable to pay damages which do not include the loss of profits from the contract. Under English law a party can withdraw an offer at any time before acceptance.

Pre-contract Disclosure

Background

5.104 The questions here are whether during negotiations for a contract, each party is under any duty to disclose material information to the other party, and whether this duty can be excluded.

5.105 The exclusion of this principle is necessary in fast-moving markets, such as at the market sale of securities or foreign exchange where seconds count. It would obviously be impracticable in most other situations for parties to be under a duty to point out all the risks to the other party. Business would come to a halt if each contracting party had to file the equivalent of a prospectus about the deal each time or to list the risk factors. If there were such a duty about whether the disclosure was adequate, there would be no end to the arguments, no end to the unpredictability of whether a contract would or would not be invalidated for non-disclosure. The question of whether a party has a contract could drag on for years.

5.106 We can safely assume that in all jurisdictions a deliberate lie or the giving of information which is knowingly misleading because of its omissions or because it is falsified by later events will always give rise to liability because that is a fraud. We can expect also that where it is obvious to one party that the other has misunderstood the transaction, there might be a duty to correct the misapprehension.

5.107 I deal later in Chapter 9 on exclusion clauses with the question of whether a clause excluding a liability to give information is effective.

English law on pre-contract disclosure

Under English law, mainstream case law since the nineteenth century has consistently established that there is no general duty for one party to disclose risks to another party voluntarily prior to contract or to disclose latent defects eg the 'sick pigs sold with all faults' case of *Ward v Hobbs* (1878) App Cas 13 (which echoes the modern liquidator's sale of 'where is, as is'). The basic rule is *caveat emptor*—'beware the buyer'. You must inform yourself. When you buy a car, you ask questions, and nowhere is it possible for the party replying to exclude liability for an answer known to be wrong (fraud). Accordingly, parties must carry out their own due diligence and, if necessary, seek expert advice. We are dealing with situations where the parties have the resources is to take expert advice. There is only such a duty in special cases such as insurance, partnerships, public prospectuses, or where there is a fiduciary relationship (such as in the case of trustees and agents). As Rix LJ put it in *ING Bank NV v Ros Roca SA* (2012), 'Silence is golden, for where there is no obligation to speak, silence gives no hostages to fortune'.

5.108

French law on pre-contract disclosure

In France, article 1112-1 imposes a general duty to provide information. The article states that where a party knows information that is decisively important to the other's consent, he must share it wherever the latter is legitimately ignorant or relies on him. The duty does not extend to the value of the promised performance. If a party fails to provide the necessary information, the party can be liable in damages and the contract might be annulled, if the information was withheld with an intention to deceive: see article 1130 of the Civil Code. Parties cannot limit nor exclude the duty. The duty does not extend to the value of the performance. For example in the *Baldus* case (Civ (1) 3 May 2000), a seller sold photographic negatives at a considerable undervalue, not knowing that's the photographs were taken by a famous photographer. The buyer knew of the seller's ignorance but said nothing. The court held that the seller could not nullify the contract because no duty to inform had arisen. Note that the relevant party must have actual knowledge of the information and does not have to check. In addition, the duty applies only if the ignorance is legitimate, not where parties are expected to take responsibility for finding out through research, obtaining advice or other means. In this case, the victims have only themselves to blame. Notwithstanding these limitations it can be difficult in complex negotiations to have the expertise to be able to work out exactly what has to be disclosed. Traders are not lawyers and they cannot be expected to have an expert lawyer sitting by their side in all negotiations.

5.109

Pre-contract disclosure elsewhere

As in France, case law in Belgium and Luxembourg has held that there is a duty to disclose information known to one party and not the other, and a party who deliberately keep silent is liable. In German law, keeping silence may amount to fraud under BGB section 123. Many of the cases have concerned defects in a car known to the seller but not disclosed to

5.110

the buyer. There are similar duties to disclose in Austrian law, in Greek law (CC, article 147), in Italian law (CC, article 1349), Netherlands law (BW, article 3:49), and Portuguese law (CC, article 253).

5.111 The situation is worsened in many civil countries by the doctrine of mistake whereby one party's mistaken view of the facts may allow that party to avoid the contract. The result is an increased instability of contract. The doctrine of mistake in English law is much more limited in the interests of the security of transactions.

Other Good Faith Situations

Consents and discretions

5.112 It is very common in contracts for one party to be vested with a discretion to give a consent, or make a valuation, or to modify the other party's obligations. For instance, one party may need a consent to assign its rights. Syndicated credit agreements are replete with relaxations if the majority banks consent. Contracts generally may provide that the refusal of the consent must be 'reasonable', or 'reasonable in the opinion of' the consenting party.

5.113 Under English law the general position is that a contractual discretion must not be arbitrary, or capricious. This is called the Braganza duty after the leading case *Braganza v BP Shipping Ltd* [2015] UKSC 17. See also *British Telecommunications plc v Telefonica 02 UK Ltd* (2014) UKSC 42. The courts do not require that the decision is reasonable objectively so it is a minimum standard. The English chords have stated that establishing that a decision is irrational is a 'high hurdle'. It has to be so outrageous that no reasonable decision-maker could make that decision. There are many cases. It is possible to exclude even the duty of rationality: *Bates v Post Office Ltd (No 3)* [2019] EWHC 606 (QB).

5.114 As shown, under English law, this duty not to be arbitrary or capricious does not apply to a right to terminate a contract.

Agreements to negotiate in good faith

5.115 In England, agreements to negotiate in good faith are void because they are considered meaningless: *Walford v Miles* [1992] 2 AC 128. However, the courts have given effect to a provision that the parties must engage in 'friendly discussions' prior to arbitration: *Emirates Trading Agency v Prime Mineral Exports Private Ltd* [2014] EWHC 2104 (Comm).

Duties to cooperate

5.116 The duty of good faith in France includes a general duty to cooperate in commercial contracts to achieve the common goal of the contract. In one case approved by the Court of Cassation (Com 3 Nov 1992, no 90-18.547), the oil major BP had an agreement with a service station to sell petrol. BP decided to sell petrol through its own agents and gave them more favourable prices. The service station was unable to compete and alleged that BP had broken the distributorship contract. The court held that there was an implied duty on BP to provide the service station with the ability to compete, even though this was not expressly set out in the contract. The court held that there had been a breach of good faith. This is so notwithstanding that an implied duty not to compete would come as a great surprise for many commercial contractors.

Hardship clauses

5.117 It is common in commercial contracts such as sale contracts and construction contracts to contain an express clause dealing with force majeure or undue hardship. In the case of syndicated bank credits there is no such clause, apart from an illegality clause, and such a clause is unknown in international bond issues, apart from the clause in the typical subscription agreement allowing the underwriters to cancel if there is a change in financial conditions. In the ISDA master agreement there is a specific termination event in the case of subsequent illegality. Either party may also terminate affected transactions if its compliance with the transactions becomes impossible or impractical by reason of force majeure or act of state.

5.118 The reason that force majeure clauses generally do not appear in financial contracts is because of the wish not to give a borrower, for example, a right to challenge its duty to repay a loan on some vague grounds of economic depression, strikes affecting its workforce or burdensome taxation. The reason that the clause appears in the ISDA master agreement is attributable to the fact that derivatives are sometimes physically settled so as to attract the contract practice of sale of goods and other assets, a practice which generally includes force majeure clauses. Another reason may be the fact that derivative master agreements are reciprocal so that each side has an interest in protecting itself.

5.119 Under English law unless the parties specifically provide for force majeure, the subsequent events must satisfy the narrow doctrine of frustration of the contract in order to discharge the contract. Mere hardship is not enough. Even in the case of frustration, the court cannot keep the contracts alive and adapt them. The rationale for this is that English law takes the view that the parties themselves should anticipate how circumstances might change and agree the consequences in their own contract, rather than leaving this to the uncertainties of court intervention. Force measure clauses are standard in most commercial contracts.

5.120 In France, a new provision in article 1195 of the Civil Code gives the court broad powers to adjust the contract when unforeseen circumstances have made the bargain unduly costly. The article provides that, if a change of circumstances that was unforeseeable at the time the contract was made, renders performance excessively onerous for a party and that party had not accepted the risk of such a change, the party may ask the counterparty to renegotiate the contract. If the renegotiation is refused or fails, the parties may agree to terminate or ask the court to revise the contract. Where the parties fail to come to an agreement within a reasonable time, the court may on the request of one party revise the contract or terminate it on such a date and subject to such conditions as it determines. Under the old regime dating from a decision of 1876, the *Canal de Craponne* decision of the Court of Cassation, the court could not use the passage of time or changes in circumstances as grounds for inserting new terms that the parties had not agreed. This is roughly the present English position, but later the courts were prepared to intervene in long-term contracts in the case of hardship and often justified this on the ground of good faith. The idea was to promote contractual justice. The article is less important than it might seem because it is open to the parties to contract out of article 1195.

Other cases

5.121 There are manifold other cases, such as the English filling-in of inadequate contracts to give them business efficacy or duties in civil systems to cooperate by supplying information.

6
INSULATION OF CONTRACT FROM FOREIGN LAWS

Summary

Unilateral changes of contract

If a sovereign state as the debtor to foreign creditors can change its laws unilaterally to reduce or annul contract obligations or to reduce or annul the obligations of its important corporations to foreign creditors, then foreign contractors are the mercy of the debtor sovereign. The moment the economy of the sovereign is in trouble, out comes the legislative wand to pass a blocking exchange control or moratorium. Sovereigns will almost always protect their own populations before the foreign gougers. 6.1

However, under English law the English courts will not recognise a foreign law which attempts to change an English law contract. The EU Member States, as well as probably all other commercial jurisdictions, will adopt the same rule. In other words, the choice of an external legal system as the governing law of the contract will insulate the contract against these interfering laws. A Venezuelan law cannot change an English law contract, so far as the English courts are concerned. 6.2

The US arrives at broadly the same result but by different route. But obviously a Venezuelan court would apply its own mandatory laws and indeed the English courts will apply the Venezuelan law if the English courts are called upon to adjudicate a Venezuelan contract. 6.3

This chapter covers the second letter in the sequence of the thirteen themes expressed in the mnemonic PIB—FEISST—CoRCO, standing for *p*redictability, *i*nsulation, *b*usiness orientation, *f*reedom of contract, *e*xclusion clauses, *i*nsolvency law, *s*et-off, *s*ecurity interests, *t*rusts, *co*rporate law, *r*egulatory law, *c*ourts, and *o*thers. 6.4

Article VIII 2b of the IMF agreement

However, there is a crucial difference in the case of exchange controls because some countries interpret article VIII 2b of the IMF agreement to override the foreign governing law if the debtor country passes a complying exchange control preventing payment abroad or converting the currency of the debt into local currency payable locally. In that case, the insulation of the contract is potentially destroyed since the debtor country can unilaterally change the contract by passing an appropriate exchange control, something which would be disastrous in the case of a loan or bond issue. 6.5

6.6 These countries include France, Luxembourg, and possibly Germany, but not England, the US, Belgium, nor a few others which do not apply the article—Australia, Mexico, and Sweden. Most other countries do not have any law on subject so the position in those countries remains in doubt. Hence if a very high degree of predictability is required for insulation, then a party is effectively restricted to choosing English, New York (or another US state law), Belgian, Swedish, or Australian law as the governing law. One can speculate that at least the English-based jurisdictions, such as Singapore and Ireland, are likely to follow English law on this point because of the overall attitude to the protection of contracts, but this remains to be proven.

Insulation as a key indicator

6.7 It is considered that the insulation discussed below is a key indicator which satisfies the MISC tests, that is, it is measurable, important, symbolic, and shows a clash of policies. The fact that two of the most important civil law countries, France and Germany, as opposed to England and New York, do not insulate the contract in this case is consistent with the analysis of wider areas of relevant law, such as on predictability of contract terms and most of the areas to be discussed in subsequent chapters of this book, where the law is more protective of creditors under English and New York law than is the case with the law of France and Germany.

Background history of destabilising laws

6.8 We can start with some historical observations. The most common changes of law protecting national debtors have been: (a) legislation imposing a moratorium on foreign obligations; (b) reduction of the interest rate by legislation; (c) requirements that repayment must be made in local currency to a local custodian; and (d) exchange controls. The risk may be increased where the borrower is a state or is state-related or is nationally important. These interferences often arise either because of political upheavals or belligerence and wars, or because the state is insolvent—all of which are events against which the private contractor seeks some defence. Probably around half of sovereign states have been bankrupt since 1980, some of them more than once.

Latin American republics in the 1970s

6.9 A number of Latin American countries argued in the 1970s in the early days of the euromarkets that their syndicated bank credits from foreign banks should be governed by their own law and contain an arbitration clause. They said that they were not constitutionally allowed to submit to foreign law and courts—an element of what is known as the Calvo doctrine inspired by nineteenth-century imperialist gunboat diplomacy to collect bondholder debts. In those days, many Latin American countries were serially insolvent, a situation which has been maintained by Argentina to this day. With very few exceptions the foreign banks refused to lend on that basis and in the end English or New York law and courts were agreed with very few exceptions. The same conversation took place in my experience at the time in bond issues to Quebec (to finance the Montreal Olympic Games in 1976) and loans to Turkey and elsewhere, with the same outcome.

Greek bankruptcy in 2012

That issue surfaced again in 2012. One of the most hard-fought decisions in the case of the bankruptcy of Greece in 2012 was whether the new rescheduled bonds issued by Greece in exchange for its old bonds (which it was unable to pay) would be governed by English law, which is what the bondholders wanted, or by one of the seventeen eurozone systems of law, which is what Greece and the eurozone wanted. The intensity of the dispute was heightened by the unlikely argument that, if eurozone countries gave in on this issue, then bondholders might in the future require that all of the internationally held public debt of eurozone states should be governed by an external system of law—in practice domestic sovereign debt is usually governed by local law. **6.10**

It was considered essential by practically everybody involved that the deal put to the bondholders by Greece had to be acceptable to bondholders in order to promote the stability of the euro, amongst other things. A legal memorandum produced at the time on behalf of the bondholders explained that the governing law of the bonds could not be Greek law because Greece could change its law unilaterally. If an external eurozone legal system was chosen, then that external law had to meet two tests which were essential to the then structure of the deal—whether the jurisdiction had a trust and whether it had protective case law on an Article VIII 2b of the IMF Agreement, otherwise allowing countries to escape their obligations by enacting exchange controls. Only English law passed both tests. None of the seventeen passed both of the two tests—some passed one of them but not the other, and some did not pass either. Germany and Luxembourg, for example, did not pass either. So in that case English law was agreed by all parties to be the most suitable for the deal. English law was used also for other intergovernmental financial contracts with Greece from EU countries, including an EU Commission bond issue and the loans to Greece by a eurozone intergovernmental body, the predecessor the current European Stability Mechanism. A bilateral loan to Greece by a German financing body was also governed by English law. **6.11**

Insulation by External Governing Law

Insulation under English law

If, say, the borrower's system of law is chosen, a lender may be subject to changes in the local law. This conclusion flows from the rule that the governing law applying to the agreement is the law as it exists from time to time: see *Re Helbert Wagg & Co Ltd* [1956] Ch 323. As the House of Lords stated in *Kahler v Midland Bank* [1950] AC 24, [1949] 2 All ER 621: 'the proper law, because it sustains, may also modify or dissolve the contractual bond'. The law which is chosen is liquid law, the law as it is in the future as well as the present. The parties have to flow with the local river wherever it may take them. **6.12**

6.13 The point is illustrated by contrasting English cases:

In *Re Helbert Wagg & Co Ltd* [1956] Ch 323, a subsequent German moratorium law required a German borrower to make loan payments under a loan contract governed by German law to a government agency in Berlin in German marks instead of in pounds sterling. *Held*: the German law was effective to discharge the borrower. The German moratorium law arose under a German contract. On the other hand, in *National Bank of Greece and Athens SA v Metliss* [1958] AC 509 (HL), a Greek decree reduced the interest rate on bonds issued by a Greek bank and subject to English law. *Held*: the Greek law was disregarded and the borrower was liable to pay arrears of interest. The English governing law insulated the contract from changes in Greek law. Similarly, in *Kleinwort Sons & Co Ltd v Ungarische Baumwolle Industrie AG* [1939] 2 KB 678 (CA), a Hungarian firm declined to pay amounts owing to an English bank under an acceptance credit which were payable in London on the ground that Hungarian exchange control legislation rendered it illegal for the Hungarian firm to remit money abroad. *Held*: this was no defence to the claim of the English bank, since English law was the governing law of the contract which was to be performed in London. In *Libyan Arab Foreign Bank v Manufacturers Hanover Trust Co (No 2)* [1989] 1 Lloyd's Rep 608, the defendant bank argued that a US presidential decree freezing assets of the Libyan government was effective to block payment from the London bank account of LAFB with the bank because the governing law of the bank account was New York law. *Held*: the governing law was English law and the US decree was no defence. Also payment did not have to made in New York because it could have been made in cash in London, however unlikely.

6.14 The simple rule that under English law insulation requires that an external system of law is necessary be shown by various Russian Revolution cases. Where, by Soviet legislation, rights under an insurance policy were annulled, the courts dismissed an action on the policy where the policy was governed by a Russian law: see *Employers' Liability Assurance Corpn v Sedgwick Collins & Co* [1927] AC 95. See also *Wight v Eckhardt Marine GmbH (Cayman Islands)* [2004] 1 AC 147 (PC).

6.15 The *Helbert Wagg* case is striking because of the purity of the principle. Britain was only eleven years away from a horrific war with the Nazis and it was a German statute in 1933, the year that Hitler came to power, that blocked the payment of the loan to the English merchant bank. Nevertheless, the court, with absolute clarity of vision, declined to be swayed by politics or national resentments. The court upheld the principle which had already been established and which was perfectly correct.

6.16 The result is that in England the foreign lender can, by choice of external law, have complete certainty in knowing that the borrower's country cannot unilaterally alter the obligations by a change of local law. The piece of paper, at least, is inviolate and retains its bargaining power. That piece of paper, whether a credit agreement or bond or whatever, is all the creditor has to represent the money, and plainly the creditor's position is somewhat weak if that, too, is destroyed.

6.17 It is surmised that all European Union jurisdictions would arrive at the same result, ie that one of their legal systems as an external law will protect against legislation in the debtor's country. This is because Rome I on the law applicable to contracts, which applies in all European Union jurisdictions (as well as the UK subject to minor modifications) provides in article 12 that the governing law applies to the interpretation, performance, and discharge of a contract, subject to a public policy exception in article 21, and subject in some countries to the overriding effect of article VIII 2b of the IMF agreement cutting down the insulation of an external governing law.

Insulation under US law

Similar results have been reached in the US. Thus, the courts have denied recovery by a creditor if the bonds are governed by the debtor's law and the block is enacted by the debtor's country.

6.18

> In *Mayer v Hungarian Commercial Bank of Pest* 21 F Supp 144 (EDNY 1937), the Hungarian Government in 1931 enacted legislation blocking the payment of foreign currency bonds abroad. Instead, the foreign bondholders were limited to claiming amounts due on their bonds in Hungary in Hungarian currency. A bondholder's claim in New York on Hungarian municipal bonds failed because the bonds were governed by Hungarian law. In *French v Banco Nacional de Cuba* 23 NY 2d 46, 242 NE 2d 704, 295, NYS 2d 433 (1968), a New York court denied recovery on Cuban government certificates of indebtedness governed by Cuban law and therefore subject to a Cuban government decree suspending payment of the certificates.

But if the contract is governed by a US law, such as New York law, then a foreign interfering law will not be recognised.

6.19

> In *Central Hanover Bank & Trust Co v Siemens & Halske AG* 15 F Supp 927 (SDNY 1936), a trustee for bondholders succeeded in a claim on German municipal bonds whose payment in foreign currency abroad had been blocked by a subsequent German law which required that they be paid only in German scrip. The bonds were governed by New York law and were therefore insulated from the German law. A Russian repudiation was similarly defeated where Russian treasury notes were governed by New York law in the case of *United States v National City Bank of New York* 90 F Supp 448 (SDNY 1950). See also, *Bank Leumi Trust Co v Wulkan* 735 F Supp 72 (1990).

However, in other cases the US courts have applied the act of state doctrine which is a well-established and commonly applied principle of international law. This doctrine mainly applies to expropriations and holds that a country cannot expropriate assets situated outside their territories. They can, however, expropriate assets within their own territory, subject to exceptions in international law, such as the payment of prompt, adequate, and effective compensation. The situs of the debt is determined variously, mainly on centre of gravity principles, with the place of payment playing an important role. England applies this doctrine to expropriations transferring the right to the debt, but not to exchange controls or moratorium which only modify the terms of the debt, eg the currency or date of payment.

6.20

6.21 The overall effect is sometimes not quite so certain as the English law test because you have to weigh up a number of factors as to where the debt is situated, whereas under the English law doctrine the matter is decided simply by the governing law. This has not mattered much in practice because, since many of the situations involve payment in US dollars, the place of performance, and hence the location of the debt will be in New York, where payments commonly have to be made in US dollars.

> In *Weston Banking v Turkiye Guaranti Bankasi AS* 57 NY 2d 315, 442 NE 2d 1195, 456 NYS 2d 684 (1982), a Turkish bank owed a debt to a Panamanian bank payable in New York in Swiss francs. The Turkish bank failed to pay on maturity of the note, claiming that it was prevented from doing so by the imposition of Turkish exchange controls. On suit by the Panamanian bank in New York, the debtor raised a defence of the act of state doctrine based upon the governmental action taken by the Turkish Ministry of Finance. *Held*: the act of state doctrine is not applicable to debts located outside the foreign state whose act is being raised as a defence. The debt involved in this case was not located in Turkey because that state did not have the power to enforce or to collect it. Hence the Turkish bank was liable. In *Libra Bank Ltd v Banco Nacional de Costa Rica* 570 F Supp 870 (SDNY 1983), a bank syndicate had lent US$40 million to a bank wholly owned by the Costa Rican Government. The Costa Rican Government adopted a resolution limiting repayment of external debts and the loan was not paid. *Held*: the act of state doctrine may only be used as a defence to preclude judicial enquiry where the act of the foreign sovereign occurs within its own territory. The situs of the debt owed by the Costa Rican bank at the time of the resolution passing the exchange controls was in the US because: (i) under the terms of the loan agreement the Costa Rican bank had consented to the jurisdiction of the New York courts, (ii) New York law was the governing law, (iii) payment of interest and principal had to be made in New York through a New York bank, and (iv) the Costa Rican bank had assets located in the US. In *Allied Bank International v Banco Credito Agricola de Cartago* 757 F 2d 516 (2d Cir 1985), US banks sued nationalised Costa Rican banks on promissory note loans. Costa Rica, being insolvent, had passed exchange controls prohibiting the payment of foreign currency debts. *Held*: the Costa Rican exchange controls did not affect the debts and the Costa Rican banks were liable to pay. This was because the debts were payable in New York and therefore the situs of the debt was outside the territory of Costa Rica.

6.22 If the situs of the debt is in the territory of the legislating state, the US courts have refused to interfere by reason of the act of state doctrine. Thus, when Mexico imposed exchange controls prohibiting the payment of foreign currency debts (because Mexico was insolvent), bank actions in the US to enforce US dollar certificates of deposit were unsuccessful because the debts were payable in Mexico and were therefore situated within Mexican territory. The US courts could not question acts of state over local assets.

6.23 See *Braka v Multibanco Commermex* 589 F Supp 802 (SDNY 1984); *Callejo v Bancomer* 762 F 2d 1101 (5th Cir 1985); *Riedel v Bancam* 792 F 2d 220 587 (6th Cir 1986); *Grass v Credito Mexicano SA* 797 F 2d 220 (5th Cir 1986).

Stabilisation clauses

It is probably not possible by contract to stabilise the law, eg that the governing law is that at the time of the contract. The fluctuating governing law must still be ascertained and will apply to this term of the contract. A change in the governing law will override. However, a contract can provide that an invalidating change of law will constitute an event of default (although the change of law might override the ability to recover or the event of default itself). These points are commonly encountered in project finance concessions entered into by a host government and in sovereign bond issues. The terms of bilateral investment treaties may provide a remedy of a sort: these treaties usually provide for at an external arbitration in the case of claims of this type. **6.24**

Article VIII 2b of the IMF Agreement

Text of article VIII 2b

Article VIII 2b of the IMF Agreement burst into this tidy state of affairs in 1944, scattering shrapnel everywhere. The article provides as follows (emphasis added): '*Exchange contracts* which involve the currency of any *member* and which are *contrary to the exchange control regulations* of that member maintained or imposed consistently with this Agreement shall be *unenforceable* in the territories of any member.' **6.25**

The main drafters of this article were the English economist, John Maynard Keynes, and the American, Harry Dexter White, two men of very different character and political view. One of their objects was evidently to introduce a prototype of a bankruptcy freeze or stay in the case of insolvent states which had to introduce exchange controls in order to protect their economies. The objection to the concept was that it puts it entirely in the hands of the states concerned whether they could postpone or discharge their obligations, provided that the exchange control regulations were consistent with IMF rules. **6.26**

Article 25(1) of Rome I provides that Rome I shall not prejudice the application of international conventions to which one or more Member States of the EU is a party. Hence, the IMF Agreement overrides Rome I. **6.27**

Most states are members of the IMF. Australia, Mexico, and Sweden have not introduced this article into their law. **6.28**

As to exchange controls maintained 'consistently' with the IMF Agreement, the Agreement has rules restricting exchange controls for current transactions (eg trade payments and interest on loans) but allows them for capital transactions. **6.29**

Subsequent exchange controls

A possible interpretation is that the article applies only if the contract infringes exchange controls at the time the contract is entered into so that the subsequent imposition of **6.30**

'Exchange contracts'

6.31 An agreement will not be subject to art VIII 2b if it is not an 'exchange contract'. There are two basic views as to the meaning of this term:

1. The narrow construction that an 'exchange contract' is a contract to exchange the currency of one country into the currency of another and so would not catch a loan agreement or bond issue. This construction enables the courts to side-step the article which is frequently used by debtors seeking to escape their obligations. That effect of this is to neutralise the adverse impact of the article and declining to allow exchange controls to override the obligations under the contract, other than foreign exchange contracts, if at all.
2. The wide construction that an exchange contract is one which in any way affects a country's exchange resources, and so would catch a loan agreement or bond issue, because the country's exchange resources are affected: the debtor must sell domestic currency to pay for foreign currency in order to pay the debt. The effect of this is to allow the exchange controls of a country to override the debt obligations in a contract with a resident.

6.32 England adopts the narrow construction, and thereby does not permit exchange controls of a country to override the obligations under a contract with the residents of the country imposing the exchange controls. The result is that an English governing law remains inviolable.

In *Wilson, Smithett & Cope Ltd v Terruzzi* [1976] QB 703 (CA) an Italian resident owed sterling to English metal dealers in respect of metal dealing contracts on the London Metal Exchange. Payment was prohibited by Italian exchange controls. *Held*: the IMF Agreement was no defence. A wide definition would run contrary to the second paramount purpose of the IMF Agreement, namely to facilitate and promote international trade, and it would be extremely difficult, if not impossible, for contracting parties carrying out ordinary international contracts concerning goods or service or debts to satisfy themselves that all necessary permissions had been obtained. In the result, international trade would be hampered. As it happened, the Italian courts declined to enforce this judgment.

6.33 US courts uphold the narrow construction. See *Libra Bank Ltd v Banco Nacional de Costa Rica* 570 F Supp 870 (SDNY 1983) (loan not barred by Costa Rican exchange controls); *Banco do Brasil SA v AC Israel Commodity Co* 12 NY 2d 371, 190 NE 2d 235, 239 NYS 2d 872 (1st Dep't 1963), cert denied, 376 US 906 (1964); *J Zeevi & Sons Ltd v Grindlays Bank Uganda Ltd* 37 NY 2d 220, 333 NE 2d 168, 371 NYS 2d 892 (1975) (a letter of credit is not an exchange contract); *Weston Bank Corpn v Turkiye Guaranti Bankasi* 57 NY 2d 315, 442 NE 2d 1195, 456 NYS 2d 684 (1982); *Callejo v Bancomer* 764 F 2d 1120 (5th Cir 1985).

6.34 The Belgian Commercial Tribunal at Courtrai in *Emek v Bossers and Mouthaan, ILR* (1955) 722 also adopted the narrow construction in the case of an international commodities contract.

Other foreign decisions have preferred the wider interpretation. In some of these cases the courts seem to have taken into account that the stated primary object of the IMF Agreement was 'to promote international monetary co-operation' and that this objective could only be achieved by means of the policy of art VIII 2b if one interpreted 'exchange contracts' to mean any contract which has an effect on the financial situation of the member or in any way affects the currency resources of that country. This interpretation involves ignoring the word 'exchange'.

6.35

The wide interpretation has been adopted by:

6.36

- The West German Court of Appeal in *Lessinger v Mirau* 22 ILR (1955) 725: an action was brought in Germany by former Austrian residents to enforce a loan for a new system of roulette. The loan was in violation of Austrian exchange control regulations. The Austrians lost the money at the tables, but article VIII 2b absolved them from repaying the loan. The court said that a loan agreement is an 'exchange contract'. Other German decisions have treated all contracts as exchange contracts, eg guarantees, bills of exchange, sales commissions, and patent licence agreements. However, in 1988 the Federal Supreme Court held that a sale of goods contract was not an exchange contract. In a judgment of a Frankfurt court in March 2003 (Case 2-21 O 294/02) the court refused to apply art VIII 2b to Argentinian bonds which were subject to German law. The court said that the article related only to exchange contracts, not payments in connection with capital transactions. The bonds belonged to a category of capital transactions because they were used to raise capital of DM1 billion with a repayment period of nine years, making it economically significant and a long-term holding. The Federal Supreme Court had previously held that a loan is a capital transaction if it is to be repaid over a long period of time and if it is economically significant. A bond must be categorised as a capital transaction if it conforms to both of these conditions.
- A Luxembourg court in *Société Filature et Tissage X Jourdan v Epous Heynen Binter* 22 ILR (1955) 727: a contract of sale of poplin by a French firm to Luxembourg residents was held to be an 'exchange' contract.
- The Paris Court of Appeal in *de Boer, Widow Moojen v von Reeichert* 89 J Droit Int'l 718, Court of Appeal, Paris 1962, where a contract of sale of shares of a French company for French francs between a Netherlands resident as seller and a German resident as buyer which contravened Dutch exchange control regulations was held to be an 'exchange contract' and therefore null and void, since the Netherlands had an interest in the repatriation of foreign currency obtained from the sale of the shares. A French decision has also treated a commission agreement as an exchange contract: see Court of Cassation, 7 March 1972, Rev Crit 1974, 486.

Exchange control regulations

The exchange controls must be consistent with the IMF agreement, which basically means that all capital controls are permitted, but controls on current transactions have to be

6.37

approved by the IMF (which they sometimes are). German case law limits the scope of the article to exchange controls violating current transactions, which are defined in the IMF agreement, but not capital transactions.

Conclusion on article VIII 2b

6.38 The article is considered to have been a mistake. It allows sovereign states unilaterally to change their obligations. It would allow a politician like President Putin to assist Russia's war effort against Ukraine by passing capital exchange controls and to switch its liabilities on foreign bonds into roubles. It confers a monstrous privilege on international pariahs.

6.39 Sovereign states already enjoy exorbitant privileges when they are insolvent or wish to cancel the foreign money-lender as a gouger. Unlike the rest of us, the domestic assets of the sovereign states are immune from attachment or realisation to pay creditors (as must always be the case). Notwithstanding the usual waivers of sovereign immunity in bonds and loan agreements, the external assets of sovereign states are also de facto immune because their foreign assets are held by separate state entities who are not responsible for the obligations of the state, such as central banks, in the absence of manifest commingling or shadow directorship. In this respect, sovereign states are above the law. It is only the forceful sanctions and seizures by foreign states which can forestall these depredations and restore the rule of law.

6.40 If the framers of the article wanted to impose a kind of Chapter 11 for sovereign states, this was not the way to do it, and any such imposed solution would have to take into account the extraordinary immunities already available to sovereign states. The leading governing laws do not accept the article in their case law. The article is an embarrassment.

6.41 At present, the case law in Germany, France, and Luxembourg makes it more difficult for their legal systems to be used by the international business community, as was demonstrated in the case of the Greek bankruptcy in 2012. The main jurisdictions should speak with one voice on this matter. The article should be abandoned.

Other Aspects of Insulation

No external assets; local insolvency proceedings

6.42 One limit on the insulating effect of the choice of external law is that here may be no external assets capable of attachment to satisfy a judgment against the borrower. If the action were brought locally, the local courts are likely to ignore the foreign governing law to the extent it conflicts with local overriding law, including the very laws (such as an exchange control) against which the lender sought to be insulated.

6.43 Another limitation in practice on the insulation may be that the borrower has entered into local insolvency proceedings where all its assets are, in which case again it is highly likely that the local courts would apply local mandatory laws, such as an exchange control or moratorium, to any claim for the debt in the local insolvency.

6.44 English law has unusual protections against the interference in contracts under local insolvency law so long as the party concerned does not participate in the local insolvency proceedings: see paragraph 6.53.

6.45 It will be recalled that the main principles which narrow down the scope of the governing law and hence the power of the governing law to insulate against foreign laws are encapsulated in the mnemonic 6C–TRITO, that is, criminal law, corporate law, court procedural law, conventions, consumer law, contract law, transfers of property, regulatory law, insolvency law, tort law, and other laws. See paragraph 4.29.

6.46 One result is that in a modern inter-dependent world, it is hard to build a fortress to withstand every assault, every missile, from the hostile attackers outside. Transactors should be alert to choose a law and courts which mitigate the risk of the most dangerous raiders from destroying legitimate contracts and transactions.

Illegality at place of performance

6.47 Rome I gives the court a discretion if the contract is illegal at the place of performance, that is illegal where it must be performed, such as the law of the place of payment. Article 9(3) provides That effect 'may be given to the overriding mandatory provisions of the law of the country where the obligations arising out of the contract have to be or have been performed, in so far as those overriding mandatory provisions render the performance of the contract unlawful. In considering whether to give effect to those provisions, regard shall be had to their nature and purpose and to the consequences of their application or non-application'. Overriding mandatory provisions are defined in article 9(1).

6.48 Section 202 of the US Conflicts Restatement provides that the effect of illegality upon a contract is determined by the governing law, but, when performance is illegal at the place of performance, the contract will usually be denied enforcement.

6.49 Under Rome I, if the contract is lawful by the applicable law and lawful at the place of performance, then it is immaterial that the party liable to perform would by doing so violate the laws of the foreign country in which he is resident or carries on business or of which he is a national.

6.50 See *Trinidad Shipping Co v Alston* [1920] AC 888 (PC); *Toprak v Finagrain* [1979] 2 Lloyd's Rep 98 (CA); *Cargo Motor Corpn Ltd v Tofalos Transport Ltd* 1972 (1) SA 186; *Kahler v Midland Bank Ltd* [1950] AC 24; *Fox v Henderson Investment Fund Ltd* [1999] 2 Lloyd's Rep 303.

6.51 The result is that a borrower or lender, say, could be committed to perform a contract even though performance of that contract violated the laws of the country of its incorporation, eg an exchange control law or an embargo, provided that there is an external proper law and the illegality does not arise where payments have to be made. Many international loan agreements contain an illegality clause to protect the lender against this eventuality, but not the borrower.

6.52 The legal approach seems reasonable. If a state imposes an exchange control, moratorium, or embargo to protect its economy or to inflict its foreign policy, it is not unreasonable that foreign courts should ignore these local expressions of power if the contractor has not chosen the law of the legislating state. If the debtor wished to write in an express contractual excuse for non-payment in those events, naturally no international lender would lend to it. The legislating state then has to accept that its subjects will be compelled to do abroad what is criminal at home.

English protection of contracts on insolvency

6.53 The English policy to protect contracts on the insolvency of a counterparty is so strong that it applies on a foreign insolvency. The general proposition established in the cases is that a debt governed by English law cannot be discharged or compromised by a foreign insolvency proceeding, unless the creditor has submitted to the foreign insolvency proceeding, for example, by participating in the foreign proceeding. Discharge of a debt under the insolvency law of a foreign country is only treated as a discharge in England if it was a discharge under the law applicable to the contract.

6.54 This principle was settled in the case of *Antony Gibbs & Sons v Société Industrielle et Commercielle des Métaux* (1890) 25 QBD 399. This principle will, for example, prevent the recognition of a restructuring plan under foreign insolvency law which reschedules payments under a contract, or a foreign insolvency law which prohibits the termination of a contract under that insolvency law. Both of these interferences in contracts are common in the insolvency laws of the world's jurisdictions. It is often said that this *Gibbs* principle conflicts with international comity on insolvency, intended to give debtors a freer rein. However, insolvency law does not exist only to protect debtors.

7
BUSINESS ORIENTATION

Introduction

Promoting economic development

One of the most remarkable changes over the last century has been the acceleration of economic development and prosperity brought about by the growth of the number of businesses in the world and the movement away from agricultural pursuits. Nowadays, certainly in developed countries, very few people work on the land and the proportion of GDP derived from agriculture is often around 2 per cent or so. The proportion dedicated to manufacturing is usually not much greater than 25 per cent and the rest, the bulk of the economy, is services, such as information technology, research knowledge, construction, insurance, medicine, banking, other financial services, law, accountancy, and retail. People now work in offices. Most live in cities. Apart from government, their business is business. The question therefore is whether the laws have kept up with this dramatic change in people's lives and has encouraged businesses, instead of regarding them with hostility as a danger and harmful to the good life. If the law does not promote economic activity and prosperity, that is, businesses which are the main generator of prosperity, then the law is opposed to what most of the people do and what supports them economically. 7.1

The lack of business orientation is often characterised as theoretical law against practical law, ancient scholastic or metaphysical principles which are irrelevant in the modern world or obsolete or outdated. The lack of business orientation is more properly a conservatism which is unsympathetic to economic development, productive ventures, and innovation in terms of the commercial techniques needed to promote welfare. 7.2

In the good old days, life is often portrayed as being an existence of bucolic simplicity and a rural idyll. That is not what it was really like. At one time, not all that long ago, the lives of ordinary people were tormented by disease and pestilence. They lay on their beds, panting with fear, in a fever and a sweat, knowing what was coming and that there was no remedy. Famine and extreme poverty were the order of the day. If there was no food, you starved to death, wasted and emaciated from the hunger. Most people had no running water and there was a stench of sewerage in the house and in the streets. More than half the children died before the age of five, leaving their families riven with grief and despair. There was no personal safety, and robbers and muggers preyed on the people. Men spent their summers fighting ludicrous wars, from which they returned disabled and gashed, even if they returned at all. The excavations of archaeologists show the viciousness and cruelty of the mass graves. The only light at night was a guttering oil lamp. It involved enormous efforts, beyond most people, to travel anywhere to get away from the misery and destitution. This is still what life is like for billions of people on the planet. 7.3

110 BUSINESS ORIENTATION

7.4 That is why the law should serve enterprise and invention, why it should show discipline and innovation, why it should not be used as a means to degrade, to lay waste, or to destroy.

7.5 In most of the developed economies, most of the businesses by number are small businesses. But these small businesses are normally completely outstripped by a comparatively small number of very big corporations who together can account for half of employment and half of aggregate turnover. There is statistical evidence that large firms commonly pay better, have better conditions, and are more productive.

7.6 This chapter covers the third letter in the sequence of the thirteen themes expressed in the mnemonic PIB—FEISST—CoRCO, standing for *p*redictability, *i*nsulation, *b*usiness orientation, *f*reedom of contract, *e*xclusion clauses, *i*nsolvency law, *s*et-off, *s*ecurity interests, *t*rusts, *co*rporate law, *r*egulatory law, *c*ourts, and *o*thers.

Measurement of business orientation

7.7 Business orientation is a generic topic and requires the specificity of narrow key indicators to pin it down. I have chosen two indicators which are technical and perhaps unexpected, but which are symbolic in quite a piercing way and represent larger attitudes, as I shall explain. They also appear to satisfy the MISC eligibility tests in that they are measurable, important in practical transactions and in economic effect, symbolic or representative, and in conflict with or clashing with different approaches in the world's legal systems. Because they are narrow, they are sharp like a stiletto blade.

7.8 The two indicators are first the compulsory need to give notice to a debtor of a transfer or assignment of a receivable or debt in order for the assignment to be valid on the insolvency of the seller or other transferor. This notice is required in probably one-quarter to one-third of the world's jurisdictions.

7.9 The second key indicator concerns situations where ordinary commercial transactions might conflict with the anti-deprivation rule on insolvency that requires that, after the commencement of an insolvency, the assets of the insolvent debtor cannot be removed by individual creditors so as to deprive the body of creditors generally of the asset.

Historical examples of business orientation

7.10 Some of the most significant examples historically of the lack of a business orientation and anti-business attitudes in legal systems included the following:

- An objection to usury ie to the charging of interest on loans and unpaid debts by outright prohibitions. These still remain in Islamic jurisdictions but practically nowhere else, but there remain limits on the interest rates which can be charged (still prevalent in some US states) and the charging of compound interest, that is, interest on unpaid interest, which is often seen as a penalty
- An objection to stock exchanges and trading in securities which were regarded as gambling, considered to be a serious social evil. This objection has now virtually disappeared

in commercial jurisdictions because of the importance of corporations and the need for them to raise money from the public. Vestiges may live on in the slowness in some jurisdictions to allow derivatives. English law accepted the advent of derivatives in the 1980s with ease and soon developed a sophisticated set of cases on the ISDA master agreement.
- One of the clearest expressions of the objection to receivables as a form of property was presented by the very narrow scope of and restrictions on negotiable instruments which was seen as the merchant's way of escaping the generally restrictive and hostile view towards receivables and other debt claims. Negotiability is different from assignability: for technical reasons negotiability enables rapid and safe transfers in securities markets without formalities. The hostile view was expressed most noticeably in the Geneva Convention on Bills of Exchange and Promissory Notes of 1930 which imposed over-strict conditions on bills of exchange which was accepted by many civil code countries but not common law countries such as the English-based jurisdictions and the United States. The civil code countries which adopted it included Belgium, Denmark, France, Germany, Greece Netherlands, Russia, Sweden, and Switzerland. Both the English Bills of Exchange Act 1882 and Article 3 of the US Uniform Commercial Code were and remain much more liberal.

7.11 When it came to negotiable bonds which never complied with the technicalities of promissory notes, the English courts were quick to follow the markets in accepting the negotiability of bearer bonds. A court in a 1902 English case said that the time had passed when the negotiability of bearer bonds could be called into question in the courts: 'the existence of usage has so often been proved and its convenience is so obvious that it might be taken now to be part of the law': *Edelstein v Sculer* [1902] 2 KB 144. In 1892, a judge said that, in a matter of this sort, 'it is not, I think, desirable to set up refined distinctions which are not understood or are uniformly and persistently ignored in the daily practice of the Stock Exchange': *London Joint Stock Bank v Simmonds* [1892] AC 201. Bonds of a foreign government work first recognised as negotiable by English law in 1824 and those of a foreign corporation in 1892.

7.12 Under article 8 of the US Uniform Commercial Code any instrument in bearer or registered form which is 'commonly recognised as a medium for investment' is a negotiable instrument. In other words, the courts will follow a sensible market practice without allowing legal technicalities to get in the way.

7.13 Bills of exchange and promissory notes are no longer important in international financial transactions but the negotiability of bearer bonds remains significant in international bond issues, A negotiable bearer bond is held by a global custodian for the benefit of the clearing companies which in turn hold the bond for the benefit of investors according to their divided shares, represented by accounts kept by the clearing company.

Compulsory Notice of the Assignment of Receivables

Reasons for notice of assignment

7.14 Our first key indicator of business orientation concerns compulsory notice to the debtor of an assignment of a receivable owed by the debtor.

7.15 For lawyers in the common law group, a very unexpected rule in a large number of civil code jurisdictions is the rule that it is necessary to give notice of the assignment or transfer of a contract claim to the obligor liable to pay the claim in order for the assignment to be valid on the insolvency of the *seller*.

7.16 It is well enough known in all jurisdictions that there are number of practical reasons why a buyer should voluntarily and optionally give notice of the transfer of a receivable, eg to ensure that the debtor pays the buyer, to ensure that the former seller and the debtor do not vary the receivable, to ensure that further claims do not arise between the seller and the debtor which the seller could set off against the buyer, or to protect priorities in the case of double-assignments by the seller of the same debt. All of these are optional and frequently the buyer is prepared to accept these risks because the parties prefer to keep the sale silent. Very often the seller may want to maintain its relationship with its debtors and not confuse them about who to pay. An example would be the sale of a portfolio of mortgage loans where it is intended that the seller bank will continue to administer all of the mortgages for the buyer. This would be typical in the case of a securitisation. Another example is where a bank takes a general charge over all of the assets, including the receivables, of a company, but the parties wish the selling company to continue to collect and administer the receivables on behalf of the bank. Otherwise, debtors to the selling company might be confused and alarmed when they learned that the creditor has sold off their debt to someone else.

7.17 However, if the notice is compulsory in order to ensure that the sale is valid on the insolvency of the selling company, this is a serious risk for the buyer. From the justice point of view, it must come across as an extraordinary situation that the law annuls the sale because it would mean that in the normal case the seller would be paid twice, once by the price for the sale, and then again when the bankrupt seller's creditors recover the sold receivable. What could justify such an obvious unjust enrichment of the seller's creditors?

7.18 As regards financial transactions, compulsory notice to the contract debtor inhibits:

- the free transferability of intangible property
- security interests and the use of bulk receivables or other contract claims to raise finance
- the factoring and discounting of trade receivables
- securitisations, eg sale of loans to a finance vehicle in return for the price (it is normally impracticable to notify these bulk transfers)
- bank loan transfers.

7.19 It is not only financial assets which are affected—the rules apply to ordinary trade receivables, any receivables in fact.

International position on compulsory notice of debt assignments

7.20 The international position is portrayed in the author's *Maps of World Financial Law* (2008) map 24 on page 105. In summary:

- Most common law jurisdictions do not require mandatory notice of a sale, eg England and the US, but UCC, Article 9 in the US (and the equivalents in common law Canada) require public filing for the sale of certain accounts.
- Most Roman-Germanic jurisdictions do not require mandatory notice, eg Germany (BGB, section 398 ff) and Switzerland (CO, article 167), but the group is split into two on this issue. Thus, for example, Japan (CC, article 467), Korea (CC, article 450) and the Scandinavian jurisdictions do require notice: Sweden, Promissory Notes Act, sections 510, 531; Denmark, see the Instrument of Debt Act. Scotland requires the notice. China might require notice, but the point is unclear: see Contract Law 1999, article 80. The Netherlands reintroduced the requirement in 1994 and abolished it in 2004. In Sweden, the notice can be informal.
- Most Napoleonic jurisdictions require mandatory notice, eg those based on the old France CC, article 1690. See, for example, Luxembourg CC, article 1690; Italy CC, article 2800; Spain CC, article 347; Quebec CC 1641; Colombia CC, articles 1959–1972; Ecuador CC, articles 1868–1876; and Venezuela articles 1549–1557. Mandatory notice was abolished in Belgium in 1994 and also in France itself.

There are an increasing number of carve-outs, especially for securitisations, eg in Argentina, Italy, and Japan, all in the 1990s. **7.21**

In some countries, the notice must be formal, eg in traditional Napoleonic jurisdiction, still retaining the old French CC, article 1690, the notice must be served by a court official, the *huissier* or bailiff, or the assignment must be accepted by the debtor under a formal *acte authentique*. In Luxembourg, the requirement for a bailiff has been abolished but notice must still be given. In France, the inconvenience could be side-stepped by subrogation whereby the assignee pays the creditor and is thereby subrogated to the claim paid, but for various reasons, this does not solve all problems. **7.22**

Hence, at least eighty out of the 320 jurisdictions have this ambush, and perhaps quite a few more. **7.23**

Criticism of compulsory notice of debt assignments

The ideology of mandatory notice is based on a metaphysical idea called false wealth, a doctrine which creeps underground as an invasive root in nearly all jurisdictions in one way or another, sometimes almost eradicated but at other times leaking danger into the fertile land. See paragraph 3.120. The principle of false wealth is that the debtor has many apparent possessions but no assets, thereby allegedly inducing false credit. This concept is obsolete in most cases because, apart from land and goods, the other assets of corporations are largely invisible, such as their receivables and their investments or bank accounts. The rule is based on the need to publicise to the world who owns the assets. In the old days, in the case of goods you could only do this by transferring goods into the possession of a buyer or else by entering large chattels, such as ships, in a title register. Land registers have the same purpose of publicity. The giving of notice of the transfer of debt replicates the publicity of the delivery of goods but is futile as publicity because the debt and the giving of notice are invisible to third parties. The ideology is therefore obsolete. We will return to this darkly rooted **7.24** doctrine of false wealth in a larger context in Chapter 13, where we will see that it is one of the main reasons why more than half of the world jurisdictions do not recognise trusts over all assets, such as the custodianship of securities. That is why I use this example as a key indicator of the approach of legal jurisdictions. It is measurable and it is also representative of other transactions. It involves very large amounts and is economically important. It shows a collision of policy. It therefore satisfies all of my criteria for a key indicator.

7.25 The presence of a mandatory notice or other publicity evidences a policy to restrict dealings in contract claims, or a distrust of financial assets as a form of property, or a desire to protect debtors against a change of creditor ('know thy creditor'), or all these things and hence is debtor-protective. It shows a fundamental lack of business orientation. This key indicator is symbolic of other deficiencies springing from the same obsolete concept of false wealth, such as the absence of the commercial trust in many of the jurisdictions concerned: see Chapter 13.

Conflict of laws on compulsory notice of debt assignments

7.26 The international rules on the law which applies to this issue of whether you have to comply with the compulsory notice requirement is crucial for determining the risk that you take. This is because if you end up in a court which applies the location of the debt, which is usually where the debtor is located, such as a bank account, then you could get a very different result from simply applying the governing law chosen for your contract. If on the other hand the issue is decided by the governing law of the debt, then to escape this adverse result of invalidity for non-compliance, you need to choose a governing law which does not require compulsory notice, such as English or New York law. Note that courts apply their own rules where there is a conflict of laws so that in turn influences the courts which you choose to hear disputes. Quite a complicated situation.

7.27 As regards absolute transfers of receivables (there are different rules for transfers by way of security), there is little international agreement as to whether publicity by 'notice to the obligor' should be determined by the law governing the debt which is subject to the security, or the law of the fictional location of the debt, which will often be the law of the obligor's location.

7.28 Outside bankruptcy, article 14 of Rome I (which governs the applicable law of contracts in all European Union countries and also the UK) provides as follows:

1. The relationship between assignor and assignee under a voluntary assignment or contractual subrogation of a claim against another person (the debtor) shall be governed by the law that applies to the contract between the assignor and assignee under this Regulation.
2. The law governing the assigned or subrogated claim shall determine its assignability, the relationship between the assignee and the debtor, the conditions under which the assignment or subrogation can be invoked against the debtor and whether the debtor's obligations have been discharged.

3. The concept of assignment in this Article includes outright transfers of claims, transfers of claims by way of security and pledges or other security rights over claims.

7.29 Under Rome I, you therefore should apply the governing law of the claim assigned to decide whether notice to the obligor must be given for the validity of the assignment. This at least is the English position:

> In *Raffeisen Zentralbank Oesterreich AG v Five Star General Trading LLC* [2001] QB 825, CA, a shipowner mortgaged a ship and its insurances. A cargo-owner attached the proceeds of the insurances in France on the ground that notice of the assignment had not been given to the insurers. The insurances were governed by English law. *Held*: the question of whether notice was necessary for the validity of the assignment was determined by the law of the contract assigned. Since this was English law and since English law does not require notice to the obligor for validity of an assignment, the mortgagee was entitled to the insurances.

7.30 The position at English common law outside Rome I is considered to be the same. In the case of the former French rule requiring formal notification to the obligor for validity, German and Swiss decisions have determined the applicability of this requirement in accordance with the governing law of the debt assigned—the same as the English view. However, under former French law, if the obligor who owes the debt was in France and the assignor became bankrupt, the French courts in pre-Rome I decisions insisted on the formal notification so that, if it was not duly effected, local creditors could attach the debt and ignore the assignment and the assignment would be invalid on the assignor's bankruptcy in France. Hence, French courts applied the law of the location of the debt (obligor's place of business) and this may be still followed in other Napoleonic countries (France has abolished the compulsory notice requirement). The French position was derived from the fact that the notification rule was designed not only to protect unsecured creditors against false wealth, but also to protect the obligor who owes the receivable. It is understood that the Japanese conflicts code, reversing previous law, applies the governing law of the assigned receivable.

7.31 In summary therefore, to escape the compulsory notice requirement, you need the receivable to be governed by a law, such as English law, which does not impose this requirement, and you also need to avoid courts which apply the law of the debtor's location to decide this issue, as opposed to the governing law.

Deprivation of the Assets of a Bankrupt Corporation

Joint ventures

7.32 The English attitude to business orientation and the protection of commercial transactions is exemplified by a key indicator involving a principle of bankruptcy law, which is universal, that after the commencement of a bankruptcy, creditors are not permitted to take away the assets of the bankrupt. A creditor cannot walk in and remove a desk, a sofa, or a computer from the bankrupt's premises. All assets are frozen so that they can be sold and the proceeds distributed to creditors.

7.33 However, the English courts seek to maintain normal commercial transactions in defiance of this rule where this seems fair in order to preserve proper commercial bargains. It is not only bankrupts who deserve protection. Societies also need protection against bankrupts. Legal systems are not built solely to protect bankrupts and their creditors, nor should normal commercial transactions be disfigured and maimed because of the demands of bankrupts and their creditors. For example, it is standard in joint venture agreements between companies that on the insolvency of one of the joint venturers, the other joint ventures can buy out the shares of the insolvent company. The effect is that they can avoid having to accept into their club some stranger to whom the liquidator sells the shares. Thus, a provision in a company's articles that a shareholder is compelled to transfer his shares at full value to the company's nominees on his bankruptcy is valid, provided the price is fair and is fixed equally for all shareholders alike: see *Borland's Trustee v Steel Bros & Co Ltd* [1901] 1 Ch 279. See also *Money Markets International Stockholders Ltd v London Stock Exchange* [2002] 1 WLR 1150 (stock exchange rule forfeiting a member's share on the member's insolvency was valid—the share was not transferable and was inseparable from membership).

> In *Butters v BBC Worldwide* [2009] EWCA Civ 1160, two companies M and G entered into a joint venture agreement which set out the terms upon which one of the companies and another company BBC Worldwide held their shares in the joint venture company. The joint venture company was the sole shareholder of a company, the licensee, which would be granted a licence by BBC Worldwide of intellectual property rights under the terms of a licence agreement. The licence agreement and the joint venture agreement provided that if either of M or G as joint venture members suffered an insolvency, then M was on notice obliged to sell its shares in the joint venture company to BBC Worldwide for a price which was to be determined on the basis that the licence agreement had terminated. M then went into administration and the administrators contended that the above provisions were void because they infringed the deprivation principle. *Held*: by the Court of Appeal there had been no breach of the anti-deprivation principle.

The effect of the cancellation of the licence when a party became bankrupt was that the value of the shares was substantially diminished so that the non-defaulting joint venturer could take them over cheaply, therefore depriving the bankrupt other joint venturer of its property. However, the Court of Appeal decided that the provision for termination of the master licence did not involve the vesting of property belonging to the insolvent company in a third party: it merely involved a limited interest coming to an end since the licensor, BBC Worldwide, was entitled to grant the licence on any terms it wished to agree with the licensee. The provision for transfer of M's shares in the joint venture company, even if it might otherwise have constituted a deprivation, did not fall foul of the rule because they were to be transferred at market value. Each of the relevant clauses were unobjectionable on their own and they did not become objectionable by being linked.

'Flip clauses' as a deprivation

7.34 The differing attitudes of the English at New York courts to the anti-deprivation rule is neatly illustrated by cases on exactly the same facts in both jurisdictions, involving a common market clause called a 'flip clause'. In many transactions, such as securitisations, assets are charged to bondholders and the proceeds of realisation of the collateral are distributed to various creditors in a priority order, often called a 'waterfall'. It is common in these clauses to vary the waterfall if a party becomes bankrupt so that the bankrupt party gets less than it would otherwise have done. In England, this flip clause was held to be valid.

> In *Belmont Park Investments Pty Ltd v BNY Corporate Trustee Services Ltd* [2011] UKSC 38, the UK Supreme Court concluded that the anti-deprivation rule did not apply to invalidate the contractual 'waterfall' provisions in a Lehman Brothers structured finance transaction which operated to make the priority of certain creditor payment rights conditional upon whether or not an event of default had occurred with respect to the relevant creditor, in this case Lehmans. The court placed significant emphasis on its view that the arrangement in question was a bona fide commercial transaction and that its main purposes did not include an intention to evade insolvency law.

The US Bankruptcy Court went the other way on the identical facts and did not accept the validity of a flip clause in the case of *Lehman Brothers Special Financing Inc v BNY Corporate Trustee Services Ltd*, case No 09-01242 (Bank SDNY). In yet another Lehmans case, *Lehman Bros Special Financing Inc v Bank of America Nat'l Assoc* (Bankr SDNY 2016), the US Bankruptcy Court for the Southern District of New York held that subordination clauses in certain swap transactions were not invalid under the Bankruptcy Code where the ranking of payments to a swap counterparty in the priority of payments remains indeterminate until determination of the swap transaction, even if this was after the commencement of the bankruptcy. Hence, there is some division of authority on flip clauses. 7.35

Turnover subordinations

This contrasting case law is considered symbolic of a wider approach to allowing the claws of insolvency to override ordinary commercial transactions and to destroy bargains. Apart from the importance of these clauses in joint venture agreements, a similar problem could arise in some jurisdictions in relation to turnover subordinations. Under a turnover subordination, a junior creditor of a common debtor agrees to turn over its recoveries on the junior debt until the senior creditor is paid in full. This is the most common way of achieving a ranking of creditors, who would otherwise rank equally on an insolvency and is otherwise purely an arrangement between the senior and the junior creditors. If the junior creditor becomes insolvent, then practitioners in some members of the civil code families, such as Belgium, have suggested that a future transfer of proceeds from the junior creditor to the senior creditor would violate the anti-deprivation rule, thereby invalidating the subordination. This would not be the case under English law. 7.36

Post-commencement proceeds of security

A similar point arises in relation to add the recovery by a secured creditor of proceeds of the collateral coming into existence after the commencement of the debtor's insolvency, such 7.37

as future interest and dividends and rights issues in respect of shares. This is not a problem under English law but it can be elsewhere. The position is intricate.

7.38 These somewhat technical situations are all markers of the extent to which bankruptcy is allowed to override ordinary commercial and business expectations.

Other Indicators of Business Orientation

7.39 The key indicators chosen above are useful in the accuracy with which they can display business orientation and the protection of transactions. There narrowness and technicality should not hide other indicators considered in this book which could fairly be regarded as indicators of business orientation in general.

7.40 These include predictability discussed in Chapter 5, the insulation of contracts against adverse foreign laws discussed in Chapter 6, freedom of contract discussed in Chapter 8, exclusion clauses discussed in Chapter 9, various insolvency indicators discussed in Chapters 10 to 13, and aspects of corporate law, regulation, and litigation law discussed in Chapters 14 to 16.

7.41 One of the objectives of the law is to save and sustain productive work and enterprise wherever it can, rather than to destroy or degrade without good reason.

8
FREEDOM OF CONTRACT

Freedom as a Value

Freedom generally

Freedom is a basic human value, highly prized, and the centre of human happiness. In constitutional law, freedom includes the right to free elections, freedom from arbitrary arrest and freedom of expression. The concept is idealised in the stirring allegorical painting on a huge scale *Liberty Leading the People* by Delacroix, painted in 1830, which we discussed in Chapter 2. It is that same Liberty, also made in France, which stands majestically at the foot of Manhattan Island. **8.1**

The law is a restriction but the law should restrict us only in order to liberate us. There is always this tension between necessary restriction and the desire to be free. **8.2**

Freedom of contract is an important expression of the basic idea of liberty. It is an audacious idea that the law will enforce some private bargain in order that people may have the assurance of enforceable bargains, and the boldness of this idea is considered justified in principle. But clearly there are limits to the freedom and hence there is a spectrum from the iron grasp of control through to the utmost liberty, yielding only to basic notions of proper conduct. **8.3**

Because freedom is such a large concept, it is necessary again to be specific and particular and to adhere to our rule that the specifics or key indicators must be measurable, important, symbolic, and conflicting between jurisdictions. **8.4**

This chapter covers the fourth letter in the sequence of the thirteen themes expressed in the mnemonic PIB—FEISST—CoRCO, standing for *p*redictability, *i*nsulation, *b*usiness orientation, *freedom of contract*, *e*xclusion clauses, *i*nsolvency law, *s*et-off, *s*ecurity interests, *t*rusts, *co*rporate law, *r*egulatory law, *c*ourts, and *o*thers. **8.5**

A theory of law based on liberty versus restriction

We have already summarised in very broad terms the main areas of law which restrict the freedom of the governing law in the mnemonic 6C-TRITO at paragraph 4.29. We could go on adding other letters representing areas of law which can be disproportionate or oppressive, such as an autarchic constitutional law (another C), producing 7C-TRITO. We would then begin to have a holistic theory of law based on the elemental struggle between despotic restrictiveness and the liberty which is what everybody in Delacroix's painting were fighting for. Any such theory would have to develop the ideas of whether freedom includes the freedom to oppress, or the freedom of the strong against the weak, or the freedom of the **8.6** few against the many. These larger philosophical questions must always be born in mind when we discuss freedom, even freedom of contract.

Freedom to choose predictability without court intervention

8.7 We have already seen that jurisdictions differ on predictability of contract, ie whether the courts will give effect to what the parties have agreed in accordance with their freedom (subject to a certain universal basic principles) or whether the courts will intervene to curb and control that freedom.

8.8 Thus, the new article 1102 of the French Civil Code departs from the 1804 Code by an express enunciation of the principle of freedom of contract. It provides that everyone is free to contract or not to contract, to choose the person with whom to contract and to determine the content and form of the contract, but adds ominously that this freedom is within the limits imposed by the law. It goes on to add that the parties cannot derogate from mandatory rules. This principle of freedom is seen as so fundamental that symbolically it is the very first rule after the definition of contract itself. Yet we have seen that in contract the law in France allows much greater regimentation and control of contract than English law, notably in relation to the doctrine of good faith. The good faith doctrine has such a high degree of prominence in French contract law and is considered so fundamental that it is mandatory as a matter of public policy. Article 1104 provides that contracts must be 'negotiated, formed and performed in good faith'. French and English law differ sharply on the question of what is in fact fair and just, and the concept of good faith means two very different things in those legal systems.

Key indicators of freedom of contract

8.9 The three key indicators I have chosen to illustrate freedom of contract are, first, limits on the choice of governing law and courts; secondly, the international position on prohibitions on clauses restricting assignments of rights under contract; and, thirdly, bondholder voting clauses.

8.10 The first issue—restrictions on the free choice of governing law and courts—is a fundamental subject in this book. The second, concerning legal prohibitions on clauses restricting assignments or transfers of contract rights, involves a direct clash between two potent principles, that of the need for the marketability of all assets as against the concept of freedom of contract. The third key indicator discusses a financial democracy, a topic which is particularly instructive when you compare the rules of political democracies. A comparison of how jurisdictions deal with these major concepts must be regarded as innately significant and important, so that any clashes at all on these basic principles is bound to be of interest.

8.11 We have to be selective in the choice of key indicators since we cannot deal with them all. Most of this book is in fact a meditation on the contest between liberty and restriction, a contest which is revealed in almost all areas which I review, from predictability, insulation, business orientation, freedom of contract, and exclusion clauses, through to insolvency law, regulation, corporate law, and litigation; indeed, all of the areas represented by the gawky mnemonic of our main areas PIB–FREISST–CoRCO announced in Chapter 1, and all of the (somewhat overlapping) areas summarised in the mnemonic 6C–TRITO explained at paragraph 4.29.

Free Choice of Governing Law and Courts

Free choice of governing law

8.12 As discussed in Chapter 4, in almost all commercial countries parties to a contract have the free choice of governing law. However, this freedom may be limited where the choice of law is evasive and intended to avoid the mandatory provisions of the jurisdiction which would otherwise have applied. This concept has been curtailed in Rome I and now appears in article 3(3):

> Where all other elements relevant to the situation at the time of the choice are located in a country other than the country whose law has been chosen, the choice of the parties shall not prejudice the application of provisions of the law of that other country which cannot be derogated from by agreement.

8.13 These are not necessarily public policy objections: they apply to rules which cannot be overridden by contrary agreement, eg the overriding doctrine of good faith, a contract penalty clause or an invalid exculpation clause or lack of consideration. All the elements must be connected with another country (except the express choice of law) and even then it is only mandatory forum rules which override. The provision is intended to prevent the use of an artificial applicable law in order to avoid otherwise mandatory rules, but clearly limits the freedom of choice to avoid mandatory laws. It is no surprise, therefore, that the English courts would seek to narrow the restrictive scope of article 3(3) as they did in a case involving the ISDA master agreement for derivative transactions. The effect is that the use of the ISDA cross-border form for a swap will almost invariably mean that the swap is not within article 3(3) and will almost always be an internationally mobile transaction.

8.14 In *Dexia Crediop SpA v Comune di Prato* [2017] EWCA Civ 428, the English Court of Appeal held that an Italian local authority could not rely on local mandatory laws to invalidate an interest rate swap entered into with an Italian bank. In its ruling, the court emphasised that swaps entered into on ISDA form documentation, where these are related to back-to-back hedging transactions, form part of a market which is inherently international. Following the approach in its decision in *Banco Santander Totta SA v Companhia Carris de Ferro de Lisboa SA* [2016] EWCA Civ 1267, the Court of Appeal endorsed the view that article 3(3) of the Rome I Regulation is a very limited exception to the principle of party autonomy to choose the governing law.

8.15 Between 2002 and 2006, Dexia and Prato entered into a number of interest rate swaps under the ISDA master agreement and confirmations incorporating an express choice of English law and jurisdiction. Rates went against Prato and it took steps to avoid the agreements. Dexia brought a claim in the English Commercial Court for payment and declaratory relief as to the validity of the swap and prior swaps. Prato's defence and counterclaim were based primarily on Italian law arguments relating to its capacity to enter into the swap and mandatory provisions of Italian financial services law, which, Prato argued, applied by virtue of article 3(3), both of which rendered the swaps invalid or unenforceable.

8.16 The Court of Appeal upheld Dexia's claim that the swaps were not invalid. The court followed the approach in its decision in *Banco Santander Totta SA v Companhia Carris de Ferro de Lisboa SA* [2016] EWCA Civ 1267 and asked whether, other than the English governing law and jurisdiction clause, 'all other elements relevant to the situation are connected with one country only', ie Italy.

8.17 In its evaluation of the elements relevant to the situation, the Court of Appeal held that the following were important factors:

- the choice of ISDA documentation, which was itself an international element rather than a domestic element associated with any particular country
- the Multi-Currency Cross Border form contemplates more than one currency and the involvement of more than one country. The ISDA master agreement was in English, despite it not being the first language of either party
- the back-to-back swaps entered into by Dexia were routine and 'the fact that they were made with banks outside Italy shows just how international the swaps market actually is'.

8.18 The Court of Appeal expressly recognised that the ISDA master agreement is used precisely because it is not intended to be associated exclusively with any one country and forms part of an international swaps market. The presence of back-to-back hedging contracts was 'highly significant' and supported the need for certainty in the scope of application of mandatory local rules in an international market. The Court of Appeal said that, if mandatory local laws of a party are to be applied to an individual swap contract in isolation, there is a 'real risk that the back-to-back security will quickly become illusory'. The court therefore endorsed the approach to narrow down article 3(3) as an exception to the principle of party autonomy to choose the governing law. The court also held that the swap did not breach Italian law.

8.19 One of most important consequences of this case is that the mandatory rules of the doctrine of good faith in, say, France, Belgium, Luxembourg, Italy, Spain, and Portugal in the Napoleonic group, and in Germany and the Netherlands in the Roman Germanic group, are side-stepped so that they do not, for example, override termination rights or insert overriding pre-contract disclosure duties or override exclusion clauses in relation to the ISDA master agreement and presumably also the other main standard market master agreements. This therefore is a good reason for choosing the English courts, instead of a court of a civil code jurisdiction in Europe. Otherwise, these other legal systems would succeed in imposing a narrowing of the scope of the governing law, and therefore in effect the free choice of governing law, in relation to a rule of law (the overreaching doctrine of good faith), which is not accepted by the largest combined family group.

Non-symmetrical jurisdiction clauses

8.20 We have already seen in Chapter 3 that courts in commercial countries give effect to an express choice of courts by the parties to a greater or lesser degree. This rule is adopted by article 25 of the EU Judgments Regulation 2012.

8.21 In the leading US Supreme Court case of *The Bremen v Zapata Off-shore Corpn* 407 US 1 (1972) 92 S Ct (1907 32 L Ed 2d 513) it was held that the courts, in determining the effectiveness of an exclusivity clause, should give effect to freely negotiated private international agreements unaffected by undue influence or overweening bargaining power. The court said (Burger CJ at 9):

> The expansion of American business and industry will hardly be encouraged if, notwithstanding solemn contracts, we insist on a parochial concept that all disputes must be resolved under our laws and in our courts ... We cannot have trade and commerce in world markets and international waters exclusively on our terms, governed by our laws and resolved in our courts.

8.22 The court further held that the old doctrine whereby a choice of forum clause intended to oust a court of jurisdiction was now void and was 'hardly more than a vestigial legal fiction'. See also *Scherk v Alberto-Culver Co* 94 S Ct 2449, 417 US 506 (1974).

8.23 In New York, the General Obligations Law, section 5-1402 provides that, if a contract with a foreign party choosing New York law involves at least US$1 million, the choice of a New York forum for the adjudication of disputes under the contract must be given effect by the New York courts. This overrides the ability of the court to dismiss the action on principles of inconvenient forum.

8.24 One-way jurisdiction clauses (sometimes referred to as hybrid or asymmetric jurisdiction clauses) are a common feature of many financial documents. The clauses restrict debtors to bringing proceedings in a single named country, but the banks or other creditors can freely bring proceedings in any court anywhere which has jurisdiction. The creditors have certainty about where proceedings may be brought against them, but flexibility to bring proceedings elsewhere.

8.25 This makes commercial sense because the lenders should not be exposed to the serious risk that the debtor may try to bring proceedings first in its home country where there is a moratorium or exchange control, or in some other country where its obligation to pay may be weakened or rescheduled. This risk has been called the 'torpedo', ie a pre-emptive strike by a debtor to frustrate a creditor. It is important to lenders that the obligations should be shielded or insulated from local adverse laws, a risk which is heightened by the fact that most jurisdictions can claim jurisdiction on long-arm or exorbitant grounds by virtue of very tenuous connections. The risk is further heightened by the fact that often there are multiple creditors internationally, such as a syndicate of banks from many countries or numerous bondholders.

8.26 However, creditors need to be able to reach assets of a borrower or issuer wherever they may be, otherwise they restrict their recourse to assets only in the territory of the chosen court or else be put to all of the complications and doubts about enforcing a judgment elsewhere. It would seem therefore that one-way clauses are justifiable and fair in the normal case and are not an unjust discrimination by giving one party an advantage which the other party does not have.

8.27 The market practice is that bank loan agreements and international bond issues typically have one-way clauses in favour of the lenders. The Loan Market Association Standard forms contain one-way jurisdiction clauses. The standard jurisdiction clause in section 13 of the 2002 ISDA Master Agreement is essentially non-exclusive.

8.28 However, the French courts have invalidated certain one-way jurisdiction clauses.

> In *Ms X v Banque Privée Edmond de Rothschild* French Supreme Court, 26 September 2012, number 11-26.022 the agreement provided for disputes to be submitted to the exclusive jurisdiction of the Luxembourg courts but the bank had the right to sue the client in the courts of her domicile or any other competent court. The client brought proceedings in France. The court held that the one-way jurisdiction clause was contrary to the object and finality of the extension of jurisdiction permitted by article 23 of the Brussels Judgment Regulation (now article 25). The ground was that an obligation conditional upon an event within the control of one party only is void. In *ICH v Crédit Suisse*, No 13-27264, (French Supreme Court, First Civil Chamber, 25 March 2015) the French Supreme Court again invalidated a one-way jurisdiction clause in a loan agreement between a French borrower ICH and a Swiss bank Credit Suisse under the similar article 23 of the Lugano Convention.
>
> The French borrower entered into two facility agreements with the bank via an English company, acting as a financial intermediary, for financing repair works on a farming business. These facility agreements were secured by a first demand guarantee issued by a French bank. The borrower started court proceedings in France against all the parties to the transaction for breach of their duty to inform and advise the borrower. The Swiss bank and the French bank challenged the jurisdiction of the French court. In particular, the Swiss bank relied on the jurisdiction clause included in the facility agreements, which provided: 'the borrower acknowledges that the exclusive forum for any judicial proceedings is Zurich or at the place where the relationship with the bank's branch is established. The bank is, however, entitled to bring a claim against the borrower before any other competent court'. The French Supreme Court, following the *Rothschild* ruling, held that this clause was invalid in its entirety, as it was contrary to the objectives of predictability and legal certainty in article 23 of the Lugano Convention. The ruling explained that the rationale underlying the *Rothschild* ruling was not the protection of the consumer, but a more general prohibition of imbalanced clauses, irrespective of the status of the contracting parties. in *Rothschild* the borrower was an individual, in this case it was a corporation. In November 2015, the French Supreme Court again considered an asymmetric jurisdiction clause in *eBizcuss v Apple Sales International* and found it to be enforceable as it was sufficiently foreseeable. The clause in question was different to the standard jurisdiction clauses generally seen in commercial documentation (and considered in *ICH* and *Rothschild*). It seems that the Supreme Court was willing to uphold it on the basis that it allowed the identification of the courts that would potentially have to resolve any dispute that might arise and that it therefore complied with the foreseeability principle. This would not be the case for a jurisdiction clause that allows one party (the lender) to sue another party (the borrower) in any other court in the world without any geographical limitation. This

might mean that a one-way jurisdiction clause that gives one of the parties the option to sue another party before a limited number of courts could be valid. this is still some way from market practice.

8.29 By contrast, in January 2014 the Luxembourg District Court expressly upheld the use of an asymmetric clause under the forerunner to article 25. The court dismissed the argument based on the French decision that a pledge that conferred jurisdiction on the courts of Luxembourg and gave the lenders the right to bring proceedings 'before any competent court' was void. The Luxembourg court noted that the contracting parties had equivalent bargaining power and concluded that the court should give effect to the parties' bargain.

8.30 English courts have also upheld asymmetric jurisdiction clauses:

> In the English case of *Commerzbank AG v Liquimar Tankers Management Inc* [2017] EWHC 161 (Comm), the court held that an asymmetric (or hybrid) jurisdiction clause is valid under the Judgments Regulation. The refusal of the courts in certain EU Member States, including France, Bulgaria, and Poland, to uphold them left a question mark hanging over their validity. Liquimar applied under the EU Judgments Regulation to stay proceedings brought in England by Commerzbank pending the determination of parallel proceedings commenced by Liquimar, in breach of an asymmetric jurisdiction clause, in Greece. The asymmetric jurisdiction clause restricted Liquimar to commencing proceedings in England only. The court found that asymmetric jurisdictions clauses are compatible with the Judgments Regulation, notwithstanding the French cases to the contrary. The court held that an asymmetric jurisdiction clause is an exclusive jurisdiction clause for the purposes of the Judgments Regulation.

> In *Perella Weinberg Partners UK LLP v Codere SA* [2016] EWHC 1182 (Comm), the English High Court held, albeit obiter, that an asymmetric (or hybrid) exclusive jurisdiction clause falls within the definition of 'exclusive' for the purposes of the anti-torpedo provision in the Judgments Regulation. The clause stated: 'Codere agrees for the benefit of Perella that the courts of England will have non-exclusive jurisdiction to settle any dispute which may arise in connection with this engagement.' In *Mauritius Commercial Bank Ltd v Hestia Holdings Ltd* [2013] EWHC 1328 (Comm), the English Commercial Court confirmed the enforceability of hybrid jurisdiction clauses under English law. Mauritius Commercial Bank lent money to Hestia, both domiciled in Mauritius, under a facility agreement governed by English law including a hybrid English jurisdiction clause. Hestia defaulted. Hestia argued that the jurisdiction clause was too one-sided to be compatible with English law on the grounds of equal access to justice. *Held*: the jurisdiction clause was governed by English law and was valid.

Conclusion on governing law and choice of courts

8.31 The above indicators show a strong adherence by the English courts to the idea of the freedom of parties to choose the governing law, with the minimum limits placed on that freedom of choice. The key indicator is indicative of English attitudes to freedom of contract in other contexts and so the key indicator is symbolic and representative.

8.32 The limitations in France and elsewhere in continental Europe on asymmetric jurisdiction clauses are consistent with the French view in relation to predictability of contract: France restricts contract freedom in favour of protecting debtors by using the doctrine of good faith, as shown in Chapter 5. This would tend to show a reduced enthusiasm in France for the market and for the business orientation of the law.

Prohibitions on Clauses Restricting the Assignment of Receivables

Restricting bans on assignments

8.33 Legal restrictions overriding clauses which limit or prohibit the assignment or transfer of rights under a receivable are a useful key indicator because the policies involve a sharp conflict or clash between two very powerful legal policies. These are the need for the free marketability and transferability of property as against freedom of contract. A restriction on assignments and transfers is a threat to one of the principles of market economies which include the freedom to market and sell assets and to use them as collateral, but to the detriment of the freedom of contract whereby parties to a contract can limit the range of the ultimate contractual parties they have to deal with. It will be seen that English law characteristically allows, subject to a minor exception, the freedom to restrict assignments of commercial receivables and hence gives priority to freedom of contract, compared to many other jurisdictions, including France and Germany and also New York, Canada, and Australia.

Historical background to the marketability of property

8.34 A substantial proportion of jurisdictions have strong policies in favour of the marketability of all assets and resist attempts to tie up property by private agreement. The most momentous example of this policy historically was the attempt by aristocratic landowners to arrange things so that that their land, especially the family manor house or castle, remained within the family forever. They did this mainly by the use of the trust. It was the trustees who owned the palace but under the trust the heirs could live in and use the palace during their lives. The effect therefore was that indeed you had a generation-skipping palace which was forever the inheritance of the families. But they could never sell it. In the result, the people who worked on the land found they could never buy it so that just a few families monopolised ownership of large portions of the land in country. The rest of the people, many of them serfs and peasants, could not buy the most valuable resource of all. Hence it was no surprise at the time of the French Revolution that this whole idea of trusts was abolished. The English approach was less violent, but they achieved a similar result by a mixture of laws requiring the property to vest absolutely after a prescribed period of time such as eighty years or else by taxation. So if you want to know why the trust disappeared in civil code jurisdictions but not in England, that is one of the reasons, but not the only one. In any event, the idea of the free marketability of all property as a major social objective took root after the Industrial Revolution which was also a social revolution. It never really applied to goods because it was simply too difficult to enforce controls on marketability. Apart from family heirlooms, nobody wanted controls anyway or needed them for perishable assets.

When it came to intangible property, such as receivables, it was often the case that the contracting parties did not want the other party to sell its rights and so they inserted a provision to that effect. Accordingly, the prevalence of these restrictions meant that receivables could less easily be traded and, in particular, could less easily be used to raise finance by way of creating a mortgage or charge over the receivables or by way of debt factoring—the sale of receivables to raise money. Instead, in order to achieve marketability, you had to represent the receivable by a bill of exchange or promissory note which was trickier to do because of the tight conditions necessary to qualify as a negotiable instrument, such as certainty and unconditionality. In the case of bonds, the negotiability requirement was side-stepped by laws or, in England, court decisions ensuring that bearer bonds at least could be traded as if there were negotiable instruments, ie much more safely. In the case of companies, it was recognised from the very beginning that the owners wanted to restrict transfers of the shares to people they approved of and that still remains the universal rule. In the case of public companies raising money from the public, then of course there could be no restrictions because the whole object was that the owners of the shares could trade them. **8.35**

Nowadays, the definition of property propounded by the legal theorists is that property must be identifiable, must be capable of being used or consumed and destroyed by the owner, and that it must be capable of being transferred—whether by way of gift, sale, or security interest. **8.36**

Reasons for restricting the marketability of receivables

The example of private company or close company shares points to a rift in this neat policy because there is another side to the question of compulsory transferability. It collides with another very fundamental principle of freedom of people, especially in their dealings with their assets, to restrict transfers. In this context, we have to have in mind that the most significant difference between land and goods, on the one hand, when compared to intangible property such as shares, bonds, and trade receivables, on the other hand, is that intangibles need two people to create the asset. In the case of land, people do not have to be involved at all and that is also the case with goods. We mere mortals are irrelevant to them. The world can roll round on its diurnal course in the darkness and in the silence and exist without us, even though we love the land and we love our goods (or some of them). Land and goods just don't care. **8.37**

For intangible property the situation is different since there is nothing there, they are a void, a nullity, a nothing, unless you have two people, such as a lender and borrower, a bank and a depositor, insurance company and an insured, a company, and shareholders, so that the identity of the other party is crucial in many cases. This two-person requirement is true **8.38** even of intellectual property, like patents, where the two people are the owner of the monopoly right on the one side, and everybody else in the world on the other.

8.39 In addition, the ban interferes with freedom of contract. Contract is everywhere, not just sale contracts for goods, but project contracts (such as construction, power purchase, supply), charterparties, lease of all kinds of assets, custodianship, intellectual property licences, joint venture agreements, network and satellite agreements, collaboration agreements, etc. Parties often wish to limit assignments for legitimate reasons, eg to preserve the business relationship, to prevent the receivables from coming into the hands of an aggressively hostile party or competitor, to protect the brand, to preserve commercial confidentiality, to protect the ranking of security, to discourage the trade in litigation claims, especially in countries with aggressive litigation procedures, and to ensure that an incoming party is bound by the obligations, as well as benefitting from the rights.

Set-off and netting are prejudiced by assignments

8.40 Further, the set-off and netting of contracts can be more complicated if disturbed by assignments. This is because, if the claimant assigns its rights under a contract, insolvency set-off ceases to be available to the counterparty on the insolvency of the claimant because the reciprocal obligations are no longer mutual. The contract rights are now owed by the assignee who is a third party and who stands to lose if the right assigned is diminished by a debt owed by the assignor to the counterparty. It is true that in most jurisdictions a contract to set off is effective against an assignee as well as the original party, but the rules for setting-off against interveners, such as assignees, are much more complicated and hedged about with qualifications, eg because they often depend upon whether the counterparty had notice of the assignment—an event which can be uncertain. In rapid market dealings, a dealer may not realise that someone in another department has notice of the assignment and enters into a contract to set-off after that notice. The provisions about these set-off rights in the laws of states enacting versions of Article 9 of the Uniform Commercial Code (see paragraph 12.50) sometimes make the situation worse by cutting off these set-offs after notice.

8.41 In financial markets involving astronomical amounts, set-off and netting must be absolutely bullet-proof in all situations—you cannot have any gaps in the protection. See Chapter 11. It is for this reason that some of the bans on non-assignment clauses exclude contracts for financial services, eg Australia and the UK, as well as the UNCITRAL Model Law, subject to qualifications. The effect is that dealers at the desk have to take into account yet another piece of legal complexity—is their contract within the exclusion of financial services and what is the fidgety definition? It is impossible for dealers to check all that in all relevant jurisdictions (even legal specialists in this field are baffled) and so there is instability written into markets.

8.42 As is so often the case in the law, jurisdictions have to decide between competing policies and, in the light of the strength of the opposing views, it is not surprising that they come out differently on this issue.

8.43 The line-up of jurisdictions is so confused on this issue that you cannot simply slot the issue into family of law. Members of the three main groups, plus the United States, come to conflicting conclusions on the issue. Some of the statutes are unforgivably complicated and bring the law into disrepute. That is why I go into this issue in more detail than is normally bearable in a book which aims to make simple points simply.

English law mainly allows restrictions on assignments

The effect of a valid non-assignment clause in many jurisdictions, including English-based jurisdictions, is that a violating assignment is of no effect at all—it is not just a breach of contract. The right becomes wholly non-transferable. **8.44**

Subject to a small business exception (in regulations of 2018 No 1254 about business contract terms), in England an assignment contravening an express prohibition on assignments is void even if the assignee did not know of the restriction: see, for example, *Linden Gardens Trust Ltd v Lenesta Sludge Ltd* [1993] 3 All ER 417 (HL) (assignment of asbestos-removal contract with 'non-assignment' clause was void). But the proceeds when received by the assignor from the debtor would be bound by a trust in favour of the assignee even if the assignor is insolvent. For an example of a case where an express restriction on assignment did not prevent a trust of the claim (although in substance the effect was the same), see *Don King Productions Inc v Warren* [1999] 2 All ER 218 (assignment of restricted boxing promotion contracts to a partnership: *held* that the assignor held them in trust for the partnership). Effectively, the courts construe restrictions on transfer narrowly since the law prefers the free marketability of property. There is much other English case law in which the courts narrow non-assignment clauses so as to allow marketability. Nevertheless, it is simple to draft an assignment clause prohibiting any kind of disposition of a contract claim. **8.45**

Other jurisdictions allowing non-assignment clauses

Under article 1260 of the *Italian* Civil Code creditors can assign their claims, gratuitously or non-gratuitously, even without the consent of the debtor, provided that the claim does not have a strictly personal character or that the transfer is not forbidden by law. The parties can exclude the assignability of the claim, but the agreement is not effective against assignees unless it is proved that they knew of it at the time of the assignment. **8.46**

In *Spain*, clauses that restrict or prohibit the assignment of the parties'/creditor's rights under an agreement (*pactum de non cedendo*) are valid according to article 1112 of the Spanish Civil Code. The general principle is that contractual rights can be transferred without restrictions but the parties may agree otherwise and include in the agreement a provision that impedes or limits the assignment. **8.47**

In *Belgian* law, parties can stipulate in a contract that claims cannot be transferred, and those clauses are effective. Non-assignment clauses are not void. In *Sweden*, there is no ban or non-assignment clauses. In *China*, it seems that article 79 of the Contract Law allows parties to agree not to permit assignment of a contract between them and they must comply with such agreement or they would be in breach. **8.48**

8.49 In the *Netherlands*, it has been held by the Supreme Court that a non-assignment clause in a claim has a property effect in the sense that it prevents the validity of an assignment in violation of the restriction—it does not merely give rise to a right of damages for a breach of the contract. It has also been held by the Supreme Court that the same property effect applies to a pledge created in violation of a clause between the pledger and the pledgee prohibiting the encumbrance of the claim included in the collateral by a pledge in favour of a third party.

Jurisdictions prohibiting non-assignment clauses in financing transactions

8.50 A number of jurisdictions specifically nullify non-assignment clauses in contracts, in the case of financing transactions which are generally defined to include ordinary charges and also factoring and similar transactions which they see as a security substitute which should, according to this theory, be governed by the same rules as ordinary charges. Some examples are as follows:

- article 9-406 of the US Uniform Commercial Code (the article dealing with security interests). Article 9 has been highly influential in other countries
- the Australian Personal Property Securities Act 2009, section 81, based on article 9
- the Ontario Personal Property Security Act 1990 section 40(4), also based on article 9
- the UNCITRAL Model Law on Secured Transactions 2016, which is used as a basis for many statutes around the world and is also inspired by article 9
- The UNIDROIT Convention on International Factoring 1988, article 6. This has been adopted by Belgium, France, Germany, Hungary, Italy, Latvia, Nigeria, Russia, and Ukraine, but not all states have necessarily adopted this article—there is an opt-out.

8.51 In the US version, for financing transactions there is a complete ban in relation to the contracts caught. However, in other jurisdictions, eg Canada, Australia, and those based on UNCITRAL, the effect is that the assignment is effective despite the ban but this does not prevent the assignment from being a violation of the contract. Hence, the counterparty could sue for breach of contract (damages may often be small or nil) or declare an event of default or terminate the contract—a more powerful remedy. In some cases, the counterparty can declare a default but not terminate the contract.

8.52 The objective of the ban is to ensure that contracts can be covered by security interests and also in those countries which treat factoring and the sale of receivables as security interests, to encourage finance by this method. This favours the general marketability of property.

8.53 Other jurisdictions which have a ban on non-assignment clause in certain cases include the Czech Republic, Greece, and Slovakia (but this is worth checking). For others, see below.

8.54 Subject to exceptions, US UCC, section 9-406 provides that:

> a term in an agreement between an account debtor and an assignor or in a promissory note is ineffective to the extent that it:
> 1. prohibits, restricts, or requires the consent of the account debtor or person obligated on the promissory note to the assignment or transfer of, or the creation, attachment, perfection, or enforcement of a security interest in, the account, chattel paper, payment intangible, or promissory note; or

2. provides that the assignment or transfer or the creation, attachment, perfection, or enforcement of the security interest may give rise to a default, breach, right of recoupment, claim, defence, termination, right of termination, or remedy under the account, chattel paper, payment intangible, or promissory note.

Section 9-407 deals similarly with restrictions on assignments by lessor or lessee under lease agreements for goods. See also UCC, section 2A-303 to similar effect. Section 9-406(f) extends the ban to restrictions arising by law, statute, or regulation in relation to an account or chattel paper.

Other jurisdictions nullifying non-assignment clauses

In *France*, in 2001 a law introduced—in the Code de Commerce—various provisions protecting contractors against certain 'abusive commercial practices'. Among these is an article (article L.442-6 II c) of the Code de Commerce) which states that any clause in a commercial agreement where one party prohibits the assignment of claims which the other party has against it, is null and void. This prohibition of non-assignment clauses probably only applies when the beneficiary of the non-assignment clause acts in a commercial capacity (because of a clash with CC, new article 1321). **8.55**

Under the *German* Commercial Code, clauses which restrict or prohibit the assignment of a monetary claim do not produce a legal effect and result in an ineffective assignment, provided that the legal transaction that justified this monetary claim is a commercial transaction (ie commercial business) for both parties or the debtor is a legal entity under public law or a special fund under public law. **8.56**

The current Civil Code of *Japan* has a complex compromise. Clauses in ordinary contracts which prohibit or restrict the assignment of the rights of a party to be paid are generally effective and assignments in breach of such contractual restrictions are considered void. **8.57**

However, given the frequent use of assignment of receivables as security (collateral), this rule was modified under the amended Civil Code, effective in 2020. Under the new Civil Code, assignments in breach of such contractual clauses will be treated as effective, ie the restriction does not make the assignment void. However, if the assignee was aware (or was unaware due to gross negligence) of the contractual restriction, the debtor will have the right to refuse to pay the assignee and to continue to pay the original obligee (assignor). This is a compromise position making assignments in breach of non-assignment clauses effective, but giving certain effects (to protect the debtor) to the non-assignment clauses without making them void outright. The assignment is void in the case of claims for the repayment of deposits with banks and credit institutions, provided that attachment in an enforcement action will be permitted notwithstanding the contractual restriction. **8.58**

Conclusion on bans on non-assignment clauses

The single conclusion we draw from the above key indicator is that the conflict of policies can be so acute that legal systems of all stripes are splintered and twisted in their results and **8.59**

132 FREEDOM OF CONTRACT

it is difficult to find patterns which fit all jurisdictions and their family groups. It is, however, perceptible in this case that English law on this issue is consistent in its pursuit of freedom of contract subject to a minor exception, and that France and Germany give priority to the marketability of property over freedom of contract. So at least perhaps there is still a symmetry, although partially buried under the rubble of the attacks and counter-attacks.

Bondholder Democracies

Collective action by bondholder voting

8.60 The third key indicator is intended to measure freedom of contract in a way which demonstrates a significant lesson in the formation of legal systems and how they react to extreme stresses. This indicator is bondholder voting, which is a form of collective action which usually arises when the issuer is in financial difficulties.

8.61 We do not only have political democracies, we also have financial democracies. These include shareholder voting, syndicate democracy clauses in syndicated bank credit agreements, and creditor voting on an insolvency restructuring plan under a bankruptcy law designed to rescue the debtor. Bondholder voting is another of these democracies.

8.62 Financial democracies are property democracies. You have to have a bond or a share or a claim against a debtor to vote.

8.63 Collective action is necessary in the case of bondholders. A minority of bondholders could refuse to agree a restructuring plan approved by majority, and destabilise the plan by declining to accept 'holding out'. Bondholders are often dispersed and their identity changes. They may have conflicts of interest. They often do not have time or the skill to develop a plan. They are often a heterogeneous group. The bonds are often held through clearing systems and via depositories which are obstacles to easy communications.

English law on bondholder collective action

8.64 English law freely permits the appointment of a trustee to act on behalf of bondholders. This is achieved by a parallel covenant by the issuer to pay both the bondholders and also the trustee, except that payment to the bondholders is deemed to be a payment to the trustee so that there is no duplication. The trustee can require payment to the trustee itself if there is a default so that the trustee can then sue for the amount owed and monitor pro rata payment. The trustee is empowered to sue and collect.

8.65 Under a 'no-action clause', bondholders cannot sue or petition for insolvency unless, say, one-fifth of the bonds so require. The purpose of this clause is to prevent a race to the courthouse door and the preferential payment of a bondholder, and to prevent a destabilisation of the issuer when this might be adverse to the interests of bondholders generally. This reduces the hold-out powers of minority activists. No action clauses were upheld in the English case of *Re Colt Telecom Group plc* [2002] EWHC 2815.

8.66 The trust deed can set up whatever voting provisions it likes and there is virtually complete freedom of contract about what terms of the bonds can be changed and by what majorities, and the disqualification of votes by the issuer and its related parties. Market practice is to distinguish minor matters from major matters, such as a change to payments, which require typically at least 75 per cent of the votes cast at a quorate meeting or by written resolution.

8.67 Case law shows that the resolution can be attacked if, for example, there is unfairness or oppression of the minority or bribes, or secret payments are given to a bondholder. For example, English case law holds that a resolution will be invalid if the bonds of dissenting bondholders will be reduced effectively to zero if they do not vote in favour of the resolution: *Assenagon Asset Management v Irish Bank Resolution Corporation Ltd* [2012] EWHC 2090 (Ch). However, a success fee payable only to the majority voting in favour does not by itself invalidate the resolution if the fee is payable equally to all holders who wish to vote in favour, is disclosed and is not designed to oppress the minority. Resolutions must, of course, be within the express powers of the bondholders set out in the trust deed or the bond itself.

8.68 It is apparent that political democracies do not necessarily build in the protections which are standard in financial democracies.

US law on bondholder collective action

8.69 The position in the United States is very different. The Trust Indenture Act of 1939 provides in section 316 that the indenture must not impair or affect the right of a bondholder to receive payment of principal and interest on the due date without the consent of each bondholder, with a minor exception for interest. Hence, private work-outs are difficult unless all bondholders agree. The payment covenant is the most important covenant which needs to be modified if the issuer is in trouble. Binding bondholders can be achieved by a restructuring plan under a Chapter 11 insolvency rescue proceeding under the Bankruptcy Code of 1978 which involves the trauma and expense of a formal proceeding.

8.70 This policy was adopted because the view was taken, for example, by William O Douglas, then chairman of the Securities and Exchange Commission in the United States, that, amongst other things, collective action clauses allowed Wall Street insiders, especially banks, to take advantage of small bondholders by rescheduling bonds so that that insiders could more easily collect their private loans. The English no-action clause is not allowed and each bondholder can accelerate, sue for unpaid amounts, and file an insolvency petition.

8.71 The market practice in the US to get round this inconvenient restriction is that, when a bondholder accepts an exchanged and rescheduled bond, the holder agrees to amend certain of the old bond's non-payment terms so as to make them less attractive to hold-out dissentient bondholders, who are therefore given an incentive to accept the resolution These are called exit consents. Examples are the removal of listing so that the old bonds are less liquid, the removal of negative pledges, other non-payment covenants, and events of default (other than non-payment). The bond is stripped of all other protections, except the obligation to pay. There is much case law in the US as to whether these exit consents are permitted; that is, whether they indirectly impair the payment covenant. See eg *Greylock v Province* *of Mendoza* (SDNY, 8 February 2005), where the court upheld the deletion of the negative pledge (prohibition on the creation of security interests by the issuer), events of default except non-payment, and the modification of the waiver of sovereign immunity by the issuer.

8.72 These provisions apply only to regulated indentures, ie broadly those involving the public. They do not apply to sovereign issuers and hence the use of wider collective action clauses is permitted in that case.

Bondholder collective action clauses elsewhere

8.73 Bondholder collective action clauses are widespread in other jurisdictions. In each case, it is worth checking whether the statute applies only to issues by locally incorporated companies, for example, as in France and Switzerland. In Switzerland, the statute also applies to a company having a business establishment in Switzerland. It is unusual for these bondholder community statutes to prohibit changes to the financial terms, although they often do have an exclusive list of the changes which may be made and specific rules as to majorities.

8.74 Germany introduced a bondholder community statute in 2009, which vests rights of action in a common representative (not a trustee) and allows a no-action clause. The statute is fairly liberal, but there is some question about whether bondholder resolutions fall within the prohibition in Germany forbidding derogation from certain mandatory norms in contracts that are not individually negotiated, especially exclusion clauses in standard business terms.

8.75 The Japanese bondholder community statute applying to joint stock companies is contained in the Companies Act, articles 715–742.

Relevance of this key indicator

8.76 Why is this key indicator chosen and what is its relevance to the issue of freedom of contract?

8.77 It is not merely because the Trust Indenture Act of 1939 inhibits freedom of contract in a most unexpected way, and in a way which is inconsistent with the features of legal systems in the United States, including New York. That is obvious. The real reason that this indicator is relevant is that it demonstrates the ease with which a mature and sophisticated legal system can be knocked off balance by a crisis which feeds irrational dreads and fears, in this case that predatory banks were cheating the innocent citizen.

8.78 It is also relevant in that it shows how long the shadow of a bad law born out of a bad crisis can be, and how a law which is wildly inconsistent with the general consensus of a mature jurisdiction can remain defiantly on the statute book—now for nearly a century with no sign from anybody that anything is wrong.

9

EXCLUSION CLAUSES

Background to Exclusion Clauses

Exclusion clauses generally

This chapter discusses exclusion clauses generally in the context of our scope of internationally mobile business transactions and in particular the degree of freedom that parties have in excluding a degree of their liability in order to manage their risks. As always, I exclude transactions with individuals and consumers. **9.1**

The inability to control transaction legal risks would significantly decrease the potential liabilities of contracting parties and is an essential part of the pricing of the performance that they undertake. Effectively, the question resolves itself into the issue of whether each party can self-insure their risks by free contract since in many cases in our field conventional insurance is often not available or very expensive for this type of risk. Insurance would in any event significantly add to transaction costs. **9.2**

Hence, this is not only an issue about freedom of contract. It is also an issue about predictability in business arrangements which can typically involve extremely large sums of money and in some situations devastate a company if an exclusion clause should turn out to be invalid. **9.3**

Apart from the normal case of limiting commercial liability, there are also a number of specific specialist cases where it is commercially proper for all liability to be excluded. For example, an insolvency administrator selling the assets of a bankrupt company needs to be able to wind up the company quickly and to be free of continuing liabilities under sale warranties which would prevent an early distribution of the assets. Therefore, there can be no ongoing warranties about the assets sold and these sales are typically on an 'as is, where is' basis. **9.4**

Another example is that, in order for a project to be bankable, the contracts of the purchaser of the project power or other product must often be 'take or pay', that is, the purchaser must pay for the power even if it does not receive it from the project company since this is the only way the banks can be paid back without the purchaser having actually to guarantee the financing. **9.5**

Summary of key indicators

After an initial general discussion of exclusion clauses on a comparative basis, I review the key indicators for exclusion clauses, which are: **9.6**

- the exclusion of the liability of bank arrangers of syndicated bank loans for information memoranda prepared by the borrower to invite banks to participate in the loan used by the arranger
- the exclusion of the liability of the arrangers or underwriters for an unregulated offering circular for securities prepared by the issuer, that is, an issue to sophisticated investors which is not caught by the restrictions on public regulated prospectuses and offering circulars
- the liability of an underwriter for an offering circular covering a public regulated issue
- the exclusion of the liability of a bank for the sale of a derivative.

9.7 The measurement of these key indicators is difficult, partly because of the dependence on a wide range of different facts and partly because of the apparent absence of a large body of case law outside English and New York law in relation to syndicated credits, international bond issues, and derivatives. The liabilities are, however, significant for arrangers and underwriters because the amounts involved. There do, however, appear to be symbolic patterns consistent with attitudes to freedom of contract, predictability, and business orientation. There also appear to be clashes of policy.

9.8 This chapter covers the fifth letter in the sequence of the thirteen themes expressed in the mnemonic PIB—FEISST—CoRCO, standing for *p*redictability, *i*nsulation, *b*usiness orientation, *f*reedom of contract, *exclusion clauses*, *i*nsolvency law, *s*et-off, *s*ecurity interests, *t*rusts, *co*rporate law, *r*egulatory law, *c*ourts, and *o*thers.

General Review of Exclusion Clauses Internationally

English law on exclusion clauses

9.9 The usual approach of the English courts is to uphold clear and properly drafted exclusion clauses in contracts between commercial parties. In other words, they generally permit parties to allocate their own risks of liability so that each party knows what due diligence it has to carry out and what advice it should take where is clear that it is not entitled to rely on the other party. Note that below I make no distinction between the liability under contract and the liability in tort—there are differences which need not concern us at present.

9.10 As in all cases, it is assumed that the clause is properly drafted so that there is the minimum scope for the possibility that the court might interpret the clause strictly against the party which is relying on the exclusion clause. For situations where the parties do not do this, see the books on contracts. An important technique in drafting is to define the limited scope of the duties which one party will perform, instead of imposing a wide duty and then excluding liabilities. Thus, an agent bank in a syndicated credit agreement defines its duties as administrative and mechanical so as effectively to exclude the normal due diligence and other fiduciary duties of an agent.

9.11 The main limits in English law on exclusion clauses are found in the Unfair Contract Terms Act 1977 which basically requires exclusion clauses in business contracts to be reasonable. The courts have neutered this provision in normal cases by finding that the test of reasonableness is satisfied, in the absence of fraud and except in the most manifest case of outrageous conduct.

A Court of Appeal judge summarised the English view as follows: 9.12

> Where experienced businessmen representing substantial companies of equal bargaining power negotiate an agreement, they may be taken to have had regard to the matters known to them. They should, in my view, be taken to be the best judge of the commercial fairness of the agreement which they have made ... They should be taken to be the best judge on the question whether the terms of the agreement are reasonable: Chadwick LJ in *Watford Electronics Ltd v Sanderson Ltd* [2001] EWCA Civ 317.

The 1977 Act in any event excludes contracts relating to insurance, land, intellectual property, the constitution of companies, or the rights or obligations of its members, the creation or transfer of securities or any right or interest in securities, certain charterparties and other maritime contracts, and contracts for the international supply of goods. The contract must have some substantial connection with England and does not apply where a contract has chosen to apply English law which would not otherwise have applied. Consumer contracts are covered by the Consumer Rights Act 2015. 9.13

A few illustrative cases will suffice. In *Photo Production Ltd v Securicor Transport Ltd* [1980] AC 827 (HL) the court held that, in commercial matters generally, when the parties were not of unequal bargaining power, and when risks were borne by insurance, Parliament's intention in the Act seemed to be one of 'leaving the parties free to apportion the risks as they think fit ... respecting their decisions'. This foundation case was followed in *The Zinnia* [1984] 2 Lloyd's Rep 211. 9.14

In *National Westminster Bank plc v Utrecht-America Finance Co* [2001] EWCA Civ 658, [2001] 3 All ER 733, a bank bought another bank's participation under a credit agreement. The purchaser acknowledged that 'the seller shall have no liability to the purchaser, and the purchaser shall bring no action against the seller in relation to the non-disclosure of [a specified category of] information'. *Held*: the clause was reasonable under the Unfair Contract Terms Act 1977. The clause had been freely negotiated between the parties who were of sophisticated and equal bargaining power. 9.15

The 1977 Act does not apply to 'any contract so far as it relates to the creation or transfer of any right or interest in securities': schedule 1, paragraph 1. This provision has been given a wide interpretation, eg *Micklefield v SAC Technology Ltd* [1991] 1 All ER 275, 281. 9.16

In *Nobahar-Cookson v The Hut Group Ltd* [2016] EWCA Civ 128, and *Transocean Drilling UK Ltd v Providence Resources plc* [2016] EWCA Civ 372, the Court of Appeal handed down judgments on literalism in exclusion clauses. Exclusion clauses are upheld in commercial contracts. Commercial parties often seek to limit their contractual liabilities towards their counterparties, whether by shortening limitation periods, narrowing, or qualifying definitions of loss, or any of the myriad other devices found under the umbrella 'exclusion clause'. The court suggested that parties might successfully, and without fear of interference, mutually exclude liability for any breach of a given contract if it is clear. As long as the language of 9.17

the contract clearly states the parties' intention to give up rights and remedies, the principle of freedom of contract dictates that it should be interpreted plainly. Parties are entitled by exclusion clauses to allocate their risks in business contracts.

9.18 In *AXA Sun Life Services plc v Campbell Martin Ltd* [2011] EWCA Civ 133, the court upheld an entire agreement clause so as to exclude liability in litigation involving claims by AXA against its appointed insurance representatives, all of whom had entered into agreements with AXA in a standard form and who alleged that, inter alia, they had been induced to enter into the agreements with AXA by negligent and fraudulent misrepresentations and collateral warranties. AXA relied on an entire agreement clause, which was contained in each of the agreement, arguing that it precluded the defendants from making these claims. The clause stated that the documents referred constituted the entire agreement and understanding between the parties in relation to the subject matter thereof and superseded any agreements, representations, etc. The reasonableness test in the Unfair Contract Terms Act was satisfied. All defendants were financial advisers accustomed to dealing with written agreements. They could have been expected to read the contracts, in which the clauses were clearly marked. The provisions were not unusual in the insurance industry. See also *Peekay Intermark Ltd v ANZ Banking Group Ltd* [2006] EWCA 1551, [2006] 2 Lloyd's Rep 511.

9.19 A similar result is achieved in the case of the exclusion of liability for misrepresentation (except for fraud). For example, under the Misrepresentation Act 1967 which imposes a test of reasonableness for contract exclusion clauses.

Exclusion clauses in civil code countries

9.20 In the main civil code countries the control of exclusion clauses is based initially on the doctrine of good faith and its related concepts. In addition, there are number of special statutes, most of which apply to a business contracts with much stricter rules for consumer contracts. One of the most prominent of these special contracts statutes is that German Act on Standard Terms (AGBG) of 1976 whose target was standard terms but which applies to any contract where the terms were not individually negotiated. The initial rationale was protecting the strong against the weak, regarded as part of the mission of social justice. Later, it was realised that many businesses use standard terms and that the real problem was that parties were disinclined to negotiate them and therefore the courts were justified in policing them. The AGBG has black and grey lists of clauses presumed to be unfair unless the contrary is shown, and those always deemed to be unfair.

9.21 A test which applies to any contract which is not individually negotiated could, for example, apply to international bond issues which are negotiated solely between the issuer and the arrangers, but not by the bondholders themselves, let alone bondholders in the secondary market. One would have to consider whether the very large number of standard forms used in financial markets, such as the credit agreements of the Loan Market Association, the ISDA master agreement, and the forms for foreign exchange contracts, repos, and stock lending, might be caught. Often they are individually negotiated, but sometimes they are not. That immediately invites unpredictability, unless there is a cluster of positive court decisions on that issue, which is often not the case, typically because many of these agreements are subject to English or New York law and courts.

9.22 Elsewhere, see the general principle of good faith and good mores in Greece CC, articles 178, 179, and 281, Belgium where clauses may be declared invalid under the public policy test of CC, articles 6 and 1131 or constitute an abuse of rights, or in the Netherlands BW, article 6:284 (2), which invalidates unfair clauses if they are contrary to reasonableness and equity (see also article 6:23 ff), and Austria ABGB, section 879. Often, a distinction is made between liability for gross negligence which cannot be excluded, and liability for ordinary negligence which can: see Italy CC, article 1129 and Spain CC, articles 1102, 1256, and 1476.

Exclusion clauses in France

9.23 In France, outside consumer law, there are three provisions which needs to be taken into account. See especially Solene Rowan, *The New French Law of Contract* (OUP 2022).

9.24 Article 1170 states that any 'contract term which deprives a debtor's essential obligation of its substance is deemed not written'.

9.25 Article 1171 (2018 version) provides that in 'a standard-form contract, any term which is non-negotiable and determined in advance by one of the parties and which creates a significant imbalance in the rights and obligations of the parties to that contract is deemed not written'. One issue could be whether the ISDA master agreement or any of the other standard forms used in financial or commodities markets could fall within this definition.

9.26 Article L442-1 of the Commercial Code, dealing with unfair competitive market practices, provides that in commercial negotiations parties are liable to make reparation for loss caused by 'obtaining or trying to obtain from the other party an advantage … manifestly disproportionate having regard to the value of what is agreed in return' or 'subjecting or attempting to subject the other party to obligations creating a significant imbalance in the rights and obligations of the parties'. A party probably cannot claim under article 1171 if the Commercial Code article applies. The Commercial Code article is not limited to standard form contracts, the main subject-matter of the contract is not excluded and the substance of the bargain, including any financial imbalance, can be taken into account, so that the Commercial Code is much wider than article 1171.

9.27 There is some controversy as to whether the old interventionism remains after the 2016 amendments which dropped the requirement that a contract must have 'cause'. This generally means some reason for the contract, such as payment for the sale of goods, often called 'consideration' in English law. In any event, the notion of 'cause' is found in the Quebec Civil Code and in the Italian Civil Code. The basic concepts of 'cause' seem to have reappeared in article 1170 (depriving a debtor's essential obligation) and in the guise of significant imbalance in articles 1171 and L442-1 and to raise the question as to whether the courts can intervene if the price is too low. This is probably unlikely but, nevertheless, it is the courts who assess significant imbalance, not the parties, and so it is the courts who become involved in what is properly a commercial decision in wholesale contracts.

9.28 Prior to the reforms, in the *Chronopost* case (Com, 22 October 1996), a courier company failed to deliver letters responding to a request for tender within twenty-four hours, which resulted in the sender's letters not being considered for the tender. The contract limited the courier's liability to the cost of delivery. On the one hand, the Court of Cassation held that day limitation of damages was void because timely delivery was an essential obligation. On the other hand, in the pre-reform case of *Faurecia II* (Com, 29 June 2010), the software company Oracle breached a contract to design and deliver an integrated software system. It relied on a limitation clause limiting its liability to a small sum. The limitation was deemed to be valid because the contract had been the subject of tough negotiations and the low limit on Oracle's liability was held by the court to be counterbalanced by a significant discount on the contract price and other benefits.

Exclusion Clauses in Unregulated Offering Documents

Syndicated bank credits

9.29 The arrangers of syndicated bank credits generally assist the prospective borrower to prepare an information memorandum to circulate to potential participating banks to ascertain if they wish to participate. This information memorandum contains details of the loan in principle and then of the borrower, often by cross-referral to information such as the financial statements of a listed company. The information memorandum for project finance will contain an extremely detailed analysis of the financial feasibility of the project, plus numerous expert reports.

International bond issues

9.30 Similarly, arrangers of an international bond issue to sophisticated investors assist the issuer in the preparation of a much more formal offering circular about the issuer which will be circulated to potential investors. The bonds are usually listed on a stock exchange, although most dealings in this type of bond issue are off-exchange between institutions directly. Because the bonds are not issued to the public generally, the listing standards of disclosure and underwriter liability are relaxed.

Unregulated disclosure documents

9.31 In most commercial countries, these disclosure documents are generally unregulated, that is, they do not have to contain prescribed information, are not subject to restrictions on exclusion clauses, and do not have to be publicly registered because the lenders or investors are sophisticated investors, such as banks and insurance companies, as opposed to the general public. If the bond issue or other offer is made to the public, then the disclosure requirements are intensified and it is not possible to exclude liability. In most commercial jurisdictions, there is a detailed definition of sophisticated investors who are outside the scope of intensified regulation, with the result that exclusions of liability are sometimes possible.

Issuer liability

9.32 We are only dealing with exclusion clauses by the arrangers of these deals. It is not the practice for the issuer to exclude liability for the accuracy of the information they provide and it would not be acceptable for them to do so. However, experts may be responsible only for the information which they provide themselves.

No exclusion for fraud

9.33 One may assume that in all jurisdictions it is not possible to exclude liability for fraud, that is, a statement which the arranger knows is false, either because it is known to be untrue or because it is misleading and the arranger knows this. The result is that it is only liability for a negligent misrepresentation which is the risk, that is, where the arranger does not carry out effective due diligence to check the information.

Sources of law

9.34 You would think that the law of lies would be as simple as one of the bullet points in the list of ten sent down from the mountain. Not so. Case law or statutes dealing with falsities or negligent fibs is piled up in jumbled heaps of words, in contract law, in misrepresentation acts, in fraud regulations, in theft acts, in legislation about unfair contract terms, about the issue and sale of securities prospectuses, about market manipulation and market abuse. Each has its own quirky scope or damnatory nuance. In any particular case you have to search out if there is any slit or crevice of escape. In the books, you will find lists of these laws which the writers explore with fascinating and effusive finesse. I have to limit my own remarks so that at last we can proceed to the next subject.

Big pocket liability of arrangers and underwriters

9.35 The main risk for arrangers is the risk of big pocket liability, that is, the misrepresentation is found out when the borrower or issuer becomes bankrupt and so is unable to pay the losses of investors. In that event, the lenders or investors turn to everybody else involved in the offering material as the only pockets left to pay. They see the arrangers and underwriters as accomplices. The argument is that they were there at the scene and earned fees. They are seen as gatekeepers who should have made further investigations. The opposing policy view is that it was not their misrepresentation, that sophisticated institutions should rely on their own investigations where there is an express clause allocating this responsibility, and that hindsight makes the error more obvious than it was at the time.

Corporations as black bags

9.36 These disclosure documents are everywhere in transactions involving loans or issues of bonds or shares for the simple reason that corporate borrowers and banks are like a black bag which you cannot see into. It is not usually possible to walk around and look at their physical assets, let alone their liabilities. Their assets and their liabilities can only be described in words. Offering circulars are descriptions and summaries of the assets and liabilities hidden in these black bags and invisible to human sight and touch. You cannot smell the fragrance or hear the sound of a debt. You can only see the letters of an alphabet or numbers on a page or on a screen. But even those are blurred by the fogginess of meaning.

Liability of an arranging bank for a syndication offering memorandum

9.37 In most commercial countries, an offering memorandum for participations in a loan is outside compulsory disclosure required by securities regulation, either because it is private, or because it is issued only to sophisticated investors, or because the borrower is a government, or because the participations in the loan agreement are not 'securities' within the securities legislation.

Liabilities of arranging banks in England

9.38 Under English law, a properly drafted exclusion of liability will normally protect the arranger except for fraud. A few cases are representative of this policy.

9.39 In *IFE Fund SA v Goldman Sachs* (2006) EWHC 2887 (Comm), Goldman Sachs acted as the arranger in the provision of a syndicated credit facility for a company to take over another company. IFE was a participant. Goldman sent an information memorandum to IFE, which annexed accountants' reports prepared at its date. The information memorandum contained a standard disclaimer in relation to the information provided in the memorandum, stating that it had not been independently verified, that Goldman was not making any representation in relation to the information's accuracy, and that it should not be assumed that the information would be updated. Very shortly after the acquisition, the financial position of the target turned out to be worse than that shown in its audited accounts. Prior to closing, there had been some concerns expressed by the accountants that they were not getting sufficient information. *Held*: the information memorandum was a document issued to financially sophisticated entities operating in a specialist market in which the participants should be left to determine their own respective risks and responsibility. On the one hand, there was no duty on Goldman to investigate the matter further in light of the terms of the disclaimer in the information memorandum. If, on the other hand, Goldman had had actual knowledge that the information previously supplied was misleading, then it would be necessary for Goldman to disclose this. A mere possibility was not enough.

9.40 This trend was continued in *Springwell Navigation Corpn v JPMorgan Chase Bank* [2010] EWCA Civ 1221. Springwell lost an appeal against JPMorgan Chase (Chase) for misrepresentation. Springwell was the investment vehicle for a group of shipping companies owned and controlled by Mr Polemis and his family. Springwell invested heavily in notes issued by Chase, which were referenced to underlying bonds issued by the Russian Federation known as 'GKOs'. As a consequence of the Russian financial crisis in 1998, the value of these investments was marked down heavily and effectively the portfolio collapsed. Springwell claimed over US$700 million in damages. *Held*: Chase was not liable for negligent mis=statement. Mr Polemis was a sophisticated investor who understood the significant risks attached to the GKOs. In using the term 'conservative', Chase's employee was merely giving his opinions on the qualities of the GKOs as a salesman to a sophisticated investor, rather than stating any fact. There was no general duty of care on Chase to give advice. Further Chase's contractual documentation precluded any successful misrepresentation claim being made and exempted Chase from liability. Springwell had contractually agreed that the relevant Chase entity was not assuming any responsibility for statements made by the Chase employee. The exclusion clauses were not unreasonable under the Unfair Contract Terms Act 1977.

9.41 In *Raiffeisen Zentralbank Österreich AG v Royal Bank of Scotland* [2010] EWHC 1392 (Comm), the English High Court dismissed a claim that the Royal Bank of Scotland entered into a syndicated loan as a result of various implied misrepresentations in the information memorandum and other documents relating to the loan. The disclaimer in the information memorandum was effective and the court said that the allocation of risk is well established and understood by banks operating in a sophisticated market.

9.42 The protection of arranging banks in England also extends to agent banks of a syndicate, whose duties usually stated in the documents to be solely administrative and mechanical. Cases where the agent bank is acting pursuant to an intercreditor agreement for two or more tiers of lenders show that the English courts give the agent plenty of room to make decisions where there are arguments between senior and mezzanine lenders, as there often are when the borrower is in trouble. See, for example, *Saltri III Ltd v MD Mezzanine SA Sicar* [2002] EWHC 3025 (Comm) and *Torre Asset Funding Ltd v Royal Bank of Scotland plc* [2013] EWHC 2670.

Liability of arranging banks in the US

9.43 The various sections under the Securities Act of 1933 imposing liability for misrepresentation in relation to offerings of securities do not apply to an offering memorandum in a bank syndication because a bank loan is not a security.

9.44 An exclusion clause was upheld in the US case of *Bank of the West and Valley National Bank of Arizona* 94 CDOS 8867 (23 November 1994): the participant was bound by clear language that it should rely on its own due diligence and not rely on the lead bank. See also *Banque Arabe et Internationale d'Investissiment v Maryland National Bank* 819 F Supp 1282 (SDNY 1993) and 850 F Supp 1199 (SDNY 1994).

Underwriter liability for unregulated bond prospectuses generally

9.45 International bond issues to sophisticated investors normally outside the special regulation of issues to the public and therefore the ordinary rules of contract misrepresentation apply.

Underwriter liability in England for an unregulated prospectus

9.46 The English courts will normally, in the absence of fraud, uphold a usual disclaimer clause by the arrangers in the offering circular. Securities are outside the Unfair Contract Terms Act 1977. An example of the English approach is as follows.

9.47 In *Taberna Europe CDO II plc v Selskabet* [2016] EWCA Civ 1262, the Court of Appeal held that the issuer of subordinated notes was not liable to a secondary market professional investor for damages for misrepresentations made in investor presentation/roadshow slides and a quarterly results announcement. There was a wide disclaimer. The defendant, an insolvent Danish bank, issued subordinated notes under a Euro Medium Term Note Programme. They were originally issued to Bank A in December 2006 and subsequently marketed to prospective investors, including Bank B. Taberna, an Irish investment vehicle, purchased notes from Bank B on the secondary market for just over €26 million. The issuer suffered severe financial difficulties shortly after the purchase, and defaulted under the notes. Taberna sued the issuer in England for damages for misrepresentations in an 'Investor Presentation Roadshow' published around the same time as the report. *Held:* the disclaimers about the roadshow were effective. Commercial parties are entitled to make their own bargains and have the court interpret the relevant clauses accordingly. The Court of Appeal found that there was no ambiguity in the relevant exclusion clauses and it was quite clear that no responsibility was being accepted for the information in the roadshow presentation. The English courts will not normally, in the absence of fraud, uphold a usual disclaimer clause by the arrangers in the offering circular.

US underwriter liability for an unregulated prospectus

9.48 In the US, underwriter liability in negligence for an unregulated prospectus also appears unlikely if there is a proper disclaimer. There is no liability under section 11 of the Securities Act of 1933—this applies only to regulated prospectuses. There is probably no liability under section 12(2)(a) (liability of sellers to buyers in initial distribution) because section 12 evidently does not apply to rule 144A offerings which are offerings to sophisticated investors. Section 12 of the US Securities Act of 1933 imposes liability on any person who offers or sells securities by means of any written or oral communication which mis-states a material fact or omits a material fact necessary to make the statements made not misleading under the circumstances: see section 12(a)(2).

9.49 This provision applies to mis-statements or omissions in any form, in any securities transaction and whether or not subject to the registration provisions of the 1933 Act. All that is required is that there is some use of the mails or facilities of interstate commerce in the course of the transaction: see *Franklin Savings Bank v Levy* 551 F 2d 521 (2d Cir 1977). The action is not available for private placement memoranda to sophisticated investors under rule 144A (a rule exempting issues to sophisticated investors): *Gustafson v Alloyd & Co* 513 US 561 (1995). The purchasers can only sue the persons from whom they bought the security or the soliciting broker and cannot therefore sue an issuer if the purchasers bought the securities from an underwriter: see *Collins v Signetics* 605 F 2d 110 (3d Cir 1979); *Pinter v Dahl* 486 US 622 (1988). The majority of courts have held that the section does not catch professionals, such as lawyers and accountants, who merely help to prepare the prospectus. The section is available only to persons buying securities in the initial distribution, not purchasers in the secondary market: *Gustafson v Alloyd Co* 513 US 561 (1995). The sale must be made 'by means of' the misleading communication. The purchaser need not show that the communication had a decisive effect on his decision but must show at least some causal relationship to the decision: *Jackson v Oppenheim* 533 F 2d 826 (2d Cir 1976). The purchaser does not have to show actual reliance on the mis-statement: see *Johns Hopkins University v Hutton* 422 F 2d 1124 (4th Cir 1970). Sellers have a defence if they can establish that they did not know, and in the exercise of reasonable care, could not have known, of the untruth or omission. The remedy is primarily rescission, otherwise damages.

Universal liability for fraud

There is always liability for fraud everywhere, that is, where the arranger or underwriter knew of the dishonest statement. For example, the famous US anti-fraud rule 10b-5, promulgated under section 10b of the Securities and Exchange Act of 1934, provides: **9.50**

> It shall be unlawful for any person, directly or indirectly by the use of any means or instrumentality of interstate commerce, or of the mails, or of any facility of any national securities exchange,
> - to employ any device, scheme or artifice to defraud
> - to make any untrue statement of a material fact or to omit to state a material fact necessary in order to make the statements made, in the light of the circumstances under which they were made, not misleading or
> - to engage in any act, practice or course of business which operates or would operate as a fraud or deceit upon any person
>
> in connection with the purchase or sale of any security.

The section applies to any purchase and sale of any security regardless of whether or not the transaction has been registered and regardless of whether or not the 'security' is exempt from certain of the registration provisions of the Act. **9.51**

Knowledge of the falsity is required but probably recklessness is enough. Negligence is insufficient: *Ernst and Ernst v Hochfelder* 425 US 185 (1976). **9.52**

Liability is civil as well as criminal. The civil liability is grounded on a breach of statutory duty: *Kardon v National Gypsum Co* 69 F Supp 512 Ed Pa (1946). Plaintiffs need not show **9.53** that they relied on the statement—the Supreme Court has presumed reliance: *Basic, Inc v Levinson* 485 US 224 (1988). See also *Blue Chip Stamps v Manor Drug Stores* 421 US 723 (1975); *TSC Industries Inc v Northway Inc* 426 US 438 (1976); *Herman & MacLean v Huddleston* 459 US 375 (1983). Aiding and abetting liability imposed on underwriters was severely limited by the following case:

> The Supreme Court case of *Central Bank of Denver NA v First Interstate Bank of Denver NA* 511 US 164 (1994) refused to impose aiding and abetting or secondary liability under the fraud provision in rule 10b-5. To be caught, the party has to be intricately involved in the mis-statement, not just a party to the transaction or advising, so as to attract primary liability. Central Bank was the indenture trustee of bonds secured on property. The bonds required that the property be valued at 160 per cent of the bonds. The issuer defaulted. Investors maintained that the appraisals of the properties were wrong. *Held*: the trustee was not liable under rule 10b-5. The rule does not impose liability on those who do not actually make the mis-statements but mainly on those give a degree of aid to those who do. The court said that any person, including a lawyer, accountant, or bank who makes a material mis-statement on which a purchaser relies may be liable as a primary violator under rule 10b-5 if the requirements of the rule are met.

9.54 This rule 10b-5 liability is more or less matched by intentional and dishonest deceit under English common law and under the English Theft Act 1968, section 19 and the Financial Services Act 2012, sections 89 and 90.

Liability of underwriters on an unregulated prospectus elsewhere

9.55 A Belgian case may be noted:

> In *Aroute v Fortis Banque* (Brussels Court of Appeal, 8 March 2002, Forum Financier 2002/IV 234), a large Canadian insurance company Confederation Life in the early 1990s issued subordinated eurobonds in Belgium led and managed by Fortis. Some bonds were bought by small investors. The company collapsed eighteen months later, largely because of exposure to the fallen property market. The investors who bought in the market, otherwise than from the managers, sued the lead manager for lack of due diligence. They had to sue in tort under CC, article 1382. *Held*: the lead manager was not liable. A lead manager must verify the information but is not obliged to conduct independent due diligence, notably of the financial statements, nor personally to re-do the work of the auditors to establish solvency. At the time of the issue the company enjoyed high standing in Canada and was rated AA by Standard & Poor's. The lead manager had received a comfort letter from a leading firm of auditors. It was not to know of some anxieties expressed internally by management or to the regulator. The fact that, unbeknown to the lead manager, an insurance analyst had reported unfavourably on the company and that an internal analyst at the bank had noted the exposure to the property market was not enough to cause doubts.

Underwriter Liability on Regulated Prospectuses Generally

Intensification of liability

Specific securities statutes enhance disclosure and liability for regulated prospectuses, mainly those for issues to the public, excluding wholesale or sophisticated investors. **9.56**

There are great variations, but typical features of statutory rules include: **9.57**

- the prospectus must contain prescribed information. This is deemed to be material. Usually, this information is what would be expected in any event
- there is a general duty of full disclosure of all material facts (as with insurance policies)
- there is an express duty of due diligence, ie a positive duty to make reasonable enquiries
- the onus of proof for due diligence/no knowledge may be shifted on to the person alleged to have made the misrepresentation
- there may be absolute liability on the issuer, regardless of knowledge or the absence of negligence
- exclusion clauses are prohibited
- liability is extended to persons other than the issuer, eg directors, managing underwriters, co-managers, auditors, lawyers, and other experts, and (sometimes) controlling shareholders
- sometimes there is no necessity for the investor to prove reliance or inducement, eg if the investor did not read the prospectus. Reliance is usually necessary in ordinary misrepresentation actions
- the statute often gives investors the same direct rights, regardless of whether they bought direct from the issuer or underwriter, or bought from someone else in the secondary market. The investors do not have to show contract privacy, ie that they purchased directly from a person responsible for the prospectus. They do not have to rely on 'proximity' tort doctrines, eg that a lead manager owed the investor a duty of care. This direct liability normally substantially improves the investor's claim
- class actions are available in Australia, Canada, and the US, but seem patchy elsewhere. Class actions do not normally depend on whether the claim arises under the ordinary law or under a special statute
- the statute often sets out limitation periods for the investor's claims—these are often quite short
- jurisdiction is often wide, eg where the prospectus was sent from, where the investor received the misrepresentation or acted on it, or sometimes where the principal market is.

Underwriter liability for a regulated prospectus

The key indicator here is whether mandatory regulation imposes negligence liability on the underwriters or arrangers of a regulated prospectus. The arguments in favour of this are that the underwriters are often closely involved in the preparation of the prospectus, that they are paid large fees, that there is a need for a gatekeeper as an incentivised monitor, the **9.58**

148 EXCLUSION CLAUSES

underwriters have the resources and expertise, and the liability enhances confidence in capital markets.

9.59 Some of the disadvantages are that the prospectus is the issuer's document and a misrepresentation by the issuer is not an underwriter misrepresentation, the liabilities are potentially huge (in the case of the WorldCom bankruptcy in the early 2000s, the underwriters settled for more than US$6 billion), the collapse of a major underwriter could be a threat to the banking system, especially in the US where punitive damages are common in mass tort litigation, and that the risks are uninsurable.

9.60 In any event jurisdictions take opposing views on the policy choice.

US regulated prospectuses

9.61 The US Securities Act of 1933, section 11 imposes negligence liability on underwriters: each underwriter's liability is limited to the published offering price of the securities which it underwrote. Section 11 of the 1933 Act applies only to registered offerings and exemplifies a tough approach to misrepresentation in public securities transactions.

9.62 The section provides that if any part of the registration statement filed with the SEC (which includes the prospectus) when it became effective, contained an untrue statement of a material fact or omitted to state a material fact required to be stated therein or necessary to make the statements therein not misleading, any person (which includes purchasers in the secondary market) acquiring the security may sue (among others) every person who signed the registration statement, directors, experts (accountant, engineer, appraiser or professional expert who is named by consent as having prepared or certified any part of a registration statement or any report used in the registration statement), underwriters, and any person who 'controls' a person who is liable: see section 15. The purchaser does not have to prove reliance, but cannot sue if he knew of the untruth or omission: see section 11(a).

9.63 The list of parties liable is exhaustive and will not be extended to others, eg on the basis that they aided and abetted the mis-statement: *In re Equity Funding Corpn of America Securities Litigation* 416 F Supp 161 (CD Cal 1976).

9.64 The term 'material' is defined in rule 405 to mean 'matters as to which an average prudent investor ought reasonably to be informed before purchasing the security registered'. By section 6, the registration statement must be signed by the issuer, its principal executive officers, its principal financial officer, its comptroller, and the majority of its board of directors, except that a security issued by a foreign government or a political subdivision need only be signed by the underwriter of the security. By section 15, controllers of a party liable under section 11 are also liable, subject to various good faith and due diligence defences. The liability is joint and several, with rights of contribution (except in case of fraud). According to the SEC, controller means somebody who has direct or indirect power to direct management and policies. The object of including controllers was to leapfrog the use of dummy directors of an issuer.

9.65 By section 14, the parties cannot contract out.

9.66 The issuer has no defence so that issuer's liability is virtually absolute, even for innocent misrepresentations: see *Herman & MacLean v Huddleston* 459 US 375 (1983). However, each other person has a defence if, amongst other things, he proves that he had, after reasonable investigation, reasonable ground to believe and did believe, at the time the registration statement became effective, that the statements were true and there was no omission. Experts such as accountants, engineers, and valuers are responsible only for the portion prepared or certified by them, but the others are responsible for all errors. Persons other than experts do not need to prove reasonable investigation of the accuracy of the expert's statements (but they do need to prove that they had 'no reasonable ground to believe' the information was inaccurate) so that the registration statement is divided into 'expertised' and 'unexpertised' portions. The standard of reasonableness is 'that required of a prudent man in the management of his own property'.

9.67 The section contains detailed provisions for the calculation of damages. The damages are not 'rescission' damages (the whole cost of the security) but the difference between the price the plaintiff paid (but not more than the public offering price) and the price at which the plaintiff disposed of the security or—if the plaintiff still owns it—its value at the time of suit: see *Beecher v Able* 435 F Supp 797 (SDNY 1977); *Akerman v Oryx Communications, Inc* 810 F 2d 336 (2d Cir 1987). The damages are reduced if the decline is attributable to other factors, eg general economic depression. In the case of each underwriter (other than those receiving more than a proportionate share of commissions, etc.) damages are not to exceed the total price of the securities underwritten by the underwriter and distributed to the public.

9.68 Originally, action had to be brought within one year of discovery of the misrepresentation but not later than three years from the public offering. The Sarbanes-Oxley Act of 2002 extended these periods to two and five years for frauds.

9.69 The first fully litigated decision on section 11 was the celebrated case of *Escott v BarChris Construction Corpn* 283 F Supp 643 (SDNY 1968). BarChris was a small company engaged in the construction, equipping and sale of bowling centres. It filed a registration statement for the sale of US$3 million worth of 5.5 per cent convertible subordinated debentures in 1962. The plaintiffs brought an action under section 11 against three classes of defendants: the directors, the accountants, and the underwriting group. The alleged misrepresentations related inter alia to errors in the accounts, non-disclosure of officers loans, use of proceeds in a manner not disclosed in the registration statement and additional undisclosed business activities. Parts of the registration statement, it was alleged, gave the impression that the bowling industry and BarChris were healthy when in fact they were on the brink of disaster. *Held*: the mis-statements were material; the defendants, not having exercised due diligence, were all liable under section 11.

9.70 A US commentator observed that it seems that only the postman who mails the fraudulent prospectus and the company which manufactured the paper on which the violating documents are printed will escape liability.

9.71 One result of the above situation, coupled with fraud risk under rule 10b-5 is that underwriters receive a letter from their lawyers called a 10b-5 letter giving them comfort on the offering circular, a letter which involves enormous time and cost, but is regarded as indispensable.

English law on regulated prospectuses

9.72 In England, apart from the limited educational liabilities of a listing sponsor, there is no general underwriter liability for negligence in relation to regulated prospectuses unless the underwriter authorised the prospectus (unlikely). If there were liability for negligence, then contracting-out is possible and also liability to purchasers in the secondary market is probably restricted by the test that they are not within the range of person to whom a duty is owed—an English test for restricting liability. There obviously is liability for fraud, ie participation in knowing or reckless mis-statements.

Regulated prospectuses elsewhere

9.73 The US approach appears also in jurisdictions influenced by that approach, eg Ontario (and presumably other provinces), Japan, South Korea, and Brazil (regulations of 2003). There is underwriter liability in Australia (Corporations Law—but not sub-underwriters), Singapore (Securities and Futures Act 2000 as amended—underwriters, issue manager, but not sub-underwriters) and also in China.

9.74 The EU Prospectus Regulation 2017 does not impose specific liability on underwriters but member states may do so. Liability is in any event imposed on persons asking for the admission to trading on a regulated market: see article 11(1). This will usually be the issuer. It seems that there may be some underwriter liability, at least for the lead underwriter involved in the prospectus, in France, Germany, the Netherlands, and Italy, but there is surprisingly little direct case law and there are a range of opinions in the books, depending on a variety of situations: see, for example, Danny Busch and others (eds), *Prospectus Regulation and Prospectus Liability* (OUP 2020); Pierre-Henri Conac and Martin Gelter, *Global Securities Litigation and Enforcement* (CUP 2019). The matter should be investigated.

9.75 Some European countries seem to take a different view from the English position on limited underwriter liability.

9.76 A leading case in the Netherlands is the *Coopag* case decided by the Dutch Supreme Court (HR, 1994, NJ 1996, 246). In this case a Dutch subsidiary of a German parent issued bonds listed in Amsterdam and guaranteed by the parent. The financial statements omitted to consolidate 214 companies, but they did not need to be consolidated under German accounting law. The prospectus contained a statement by the arranging banks that, so far as they were aware, the information provided by them was accurate. About three months after the issue, the group got into financial difficulties and the bondholders sued ABN-Amro, the lead manager, on the basis of liability rules in the civil code stating that a person who publishes a statement relating to goods or services offered by himself or a person for whom he acts in the course of a business is liable if the statement is misleading. *Held*: the bank was liable. It was irrelevant that the financial statements were supplied by the accountants—the bank could not unconditionally rely on the auditors. The disclaimer was not clear enough to exclude responsibility for the accounts. Note that now the Amsterdam Stock Exchange requires sponsors to conduct due diligence.

9.77 In the *Bond Finance* case decided by the Frankfurt Court of Appeal on 1 February 1994, the company issued bonds in Germany—and listed them there—in mid-1988. The bonds were guaranteed by its Australian parent, the Bond Corporation. The Bond group collapsed less than two years later. The prospectus gave the impression of a highly successful business with a bright future, when in fact the group was already in trouble. It failed to mention that the parent was about to undertake a highly risky transaction. The German Stock Exchange Law made the banks who signed the prospectus liable for knowing mis-statements or if they were grossly negligent. *Held*: the lead bank had been grossly negligent and was liable to investors.

9.78 But compare the Denmark *Hafnia* case decided by the Danish Supreme Court in 2002 where the investors did not succeed. The company issued shares and collapsed a month later as a result of the collapse of its very large holding of investments in real estate. Investors sued the lead arranging bank, the auditors, the chairman, and the managing director. In the absence of a specific liability statute, they relied on the general law. *Held*: the parties sued were not liable. The prospectus made it clear that the investment was very risky and also recorded a recent massive loss in the value of the company's investments. The investors' losses were not attributable to any errors in the prospectus.

9.79 In Switzerland, liability is covered by the Financial Services Act 2020, which expressly imposes liability on the issuer but not expressly on underwriters. But such a liability could arise under the general law of delict.

Derivatives Liability

Typical forms of disclaimer

9.80 Derivatives are like insurance (although not technically insurance) in the sense that a people can 'insure' against the risk that, for example, the interest rate they pay goes up, or value of their investments crash. A form of derivative called a credit default swap is very similar to a guarantee of a bond. The result is that it is possible for banks, insurers, and corporations to insure their exposure to risks. As with conventional insurance, the ability to ensure these risks by derivatives depends upon there being somebody in the market who will take on the risk, just as an insurer can reinsure. The sellers of derivatives are often speculating, but they are essential to the business of limiting exposures.

9.81 Many derivatives are risky. They are not suitable for unsophisticated investors or ordinary consumers. In practice they are only appropriate in wholesale markets where people know what they are doing or at least have the resources to obtain expert advice.

9.82 It is essential in these markets that the derivative seller does not incur liability if the bet goes wrong since this would disrupt the market and sellers of derivatives would disappear. It is up to the buyers of derivatives to determine the risks which are invariably forecasts about the future. Everybody knows that the future is not determinable with absolute confidence, at least in the markets we are discussing.

9.83 Dealers usually endeavour to obtain confirmation from sophisticated counterparties to the effect that: (1) the counterparty relies on its own independent judgment and not on the dealer or on any statements about the transaction made by the dealer; (2) the counterparty is able to assess the merits of the transaction; and (3) the dealer is not a fiduciary or adviser to the counterparty. There is standard language in the ISDA master agreement in the schedule, as well as in the ISDA equity derivative definitions.

English law

9.84 The English courts are slow to impose implied duties on banks to advise sophisticated or professional customers about the prudence of a transaction. The customer should take its own advice. The general rule is that banks are under no duty to advise on the prudence of a transaction from the customer's point of view, unless the bank clearly undertook to advise the customer. Blanket written disclaimers will usually be upheld. The position is different in relation to unsophisticated individuals and consumers.

9.85 The underlying policy is that if a client does not understand a transaction, the client should obtain and pay for its own advice and not seek instead to annul the bet after it had gone wrong. It is obvious that when you buy a car from a dealer, you should not rely on what the dealer says, and this must be even more the case if the dealer hands you a notice stating that you are not to rely on the dealer. In the case of cars, purchasers customarily rely on their own investigations, and it is not odd that, in the case of sophisticated people with the necessary resources, the rule for derivatives is similar. There is much case law on this subject and a few English examples can be mentioned.

9.86 In *Williams & Glyn's Bank v Barnes* (1981) Com LR 205, an experienced businessman borrowed £1 million from the bank and his company was heavily indebted to the bank. The company became insolvent and the bank called in the personal loan. The businessman claimed that the bank had breached its duty to him in lending the personal loan when the bank knew the company was in difficulties. *Held*: the bank had no duty to advise unless there was a clear assumption of responsibility. The relationship of lender and borrower is not normally fiduciary.

9.87 In the English case of *Bankers Trust International plc v Dharmala* [1996] CLC 518, a bank entered into complex interest swaps with an Indonesian company Dharmala. The company incurred losses and the bank claimed them. The company defended on grounds of lack of authority, deceit, and breach of duty of care. *Held*: the company was financially sophisticated. The bank owed no duty to advise them, because there was no fiduciary relationship or duty of care. On the facts, there had been no actionable misrepresentation by the bank. However, in *Morgan Stanley UK Group v Puglisi Consentino* [1998] CLC 481, the bank entered into a derivatives transaction with an individual client involving US$10 million of which the client borrowed US$9 million from the bank. The client had net assets of between US$500,000 and US$2 million. The structure of the deal was complex and risky for the client. *Held*: the contracts were unenforceable because they were unsuitable for a private customer under the current regulatory regime.

9.88 In *Peekay Intermark Ltd v ANZ Banking Group Ltd* [2006] EWHA 386, an investment fund located in the Isle of Man alleged that it was induced by the bank to enter into a transaction involving a currency speculation of the US dollar against the Russian rouble by a representation that it was a transaction of one sort, when in fact the actual transaction which was signed was of another sort. *Held*: the investment fund could not overturn the transaction on the grounds of misrepresentation. Although the original transaction may well have been represented as being different from the final transaction, the documentation was clear and indeed the representative of the Isle of Man investment fund did not even read them. In addition, the contract contained an acknowledgement that the investment fund had not been induced to enter into the contract by representations and that they had read the documents and understood them: this clause would be upheld. See also *JP Morgan Chase Bank v Springwell Navigation Corp* [2010] 2 CLC 705 (bank not liable for derivative transaction based on Russian currency investment).

9.89 In *Titan Steel Wheels Ltd v Royal Bank of Scotland* [2010] EWHC 211 (Comm), the English High Court held that a bank which sold two foreign exchange derivative products did not owe a duty of care to the purchaser because the duty was precluded by the terms of the agreement between the parties, which provided that the bank would not provide advisory services. The purchaser was financially sophisticated. Even if the exclusion clause was controlled by the Unfair Contract Terms Act 1977, the exclusion clause was not unreasonable. For one thing, it was not difficult for Titan to take separate advice.

9.90 In *Thornbridge Ltd v Barclays Bank plc* [2015] EWHC 3430 (QB), the High Court rejected an interest rate swap mis-selling claim for losses allegedly arising as a result of the bank having acted negligently, in breach of contract or in breach of statutory duty. The court held that the bank had not assumed an advisory duty; it was only under a duty not to provide inaccurate or misleading information. In light of the historically low interest rates since the 2008 financial crisis, this case was considered to be a 'case based on hindsight'. The court said that a salesman has no obligation to explain fully the products which it is trying to sell. Further, there was an exclusion clause in ISDA's standard form.

9.91 In *African Export-Import Bank v Shebah Exploration and Production Co Ltd LCT* [2018] 2 All ER 144, it was held that ISDA master agreements with a schedule varied according to the counterparty did not constitute a standard form agreement within section 3 of the Unfair Contract Terms Act 1977. This provides that, where a party deals on the others written standard terms of business, certain contract terms are enforceable only to the extent that they are reasonable. Hence, that restriction did not apply.

US law

9.92 In the 1990s, large US cases on alleged mis-selling, eg *Gibson Greetings v Bankers Trust Co* (1994) and *Procter & Gamble v Bankers Trust Co* (1994), were settled before judgment, perhaps for many millions of dollars. Both cases involved allegations of misrepresentation and non-disclosure to corporates who had lost heavily on the deals. *Orange County Investment Pool v Merrill Lynch and Co* (1995) also involved allegations of unsuitability; Orange County had lost US$3–5 billion. The cases turned on whether banks had a statutory duty to disclose risks and a duty to advise on suitability under securities regulation.

9.93   In the Tennessee case of *Power & Telephone Supply Company v Suntrust Bank*, US District Court, WD Tennessee, 10 May, 2005, affirmed 447 F 3d 923 (6th Cir 2006), a borrower had entered into interest swaps with a bank in connection with a loan. The company made substantial losses on the interest swaps and alleged breach of fiduciary duty by the bank, breach of contract, agency, misrepresentation, negligence, common law unsuitability and various other claims. *Held*: a fiduciary relationship must be established through written documents and the company had failed to produce any. There was no intentional misrepresentation. The bank had stated that it was not acting as an adviser and that the company should make its own determination without reliance on the bank or its affiliates. The fact that the bank's marketing documents referred to the parties as 'financial partners' and described the bank's 'capabilities and capacity to assist' the borrower in managing interest rate risk and growing credit needs was not sufficient to establish a fiduciary relationship and a duty upon the bank to advise the company. There were no material written documents to establish that the bank had put itself in the position of an agent of the company. As to the negligence claim, the bank did not have a duty of care to the customer. As to the claim for intentional misrepresentation, the court held that this was similar to a claim for fraud and had to be pleaded with particularity which it had not been. As a result, the company could not avoid the transaction.

German law

9.94   In contrast to the English and US cases cited above, the German courts have taken a more stringent approach to liability for derivatives. It is worth investigating whether the sellers of the derivatives concerned had agreed a market form of disclaimer of liability with the buyers.

9.95   In the leading German BGH decision dated 22 March 2011 (the *Ille* case) the court held that banks have to disclose the so-called initial negative market value of a swap. The court defined the initial negative market value as the sum of the profit and cost components structured into a swap transaction, ie roughly the bank's gross margin. The court said that the existence of a negative market value reflects a severe conflict of interest for the bank while advising its customers. Customers assume that banks profit only from interest rate movement, not from an initial built-in profit.

9.96   Relying on the *Ille* decision, many companies, individuals, and municipalities lodged claims for damages. Several appeal courts reached inconsistent conclusions on how far-reaching the disclosure obligation is. In April 2015, the BGH held that a bank must disclose the initial negative market value irrespective of the complexity of the swap transaction, but also clarified that no such disclosure duty exists if the sole motivation for an interest-rate swap is to hedge risks arising from interest rates under a corresponding loan agreement.

9.97   In a judgment dated 22 March 2016, file No XI ZR 425/14, the BGH held that a 'corresponding loan agreement' must be agreed between the same parties as the swap agreement.

The swap will only be considered as an instrument to hedge risk if the amount and the term of the swap is equal to, or at least does not exceed, those of the loan agreement, presumably meaning that the buyer of the swap is insuring an actual exposure, as opposed to making a speculative bet. Under these circumstances, the advising bank does not need to disclose the initial negative market value to a client. The BGH also found that clients cannot claim damages if they knew about the existence of the initial negative market value but did not show any interest in its exact amount. The rationale behind this is causation: a client's absence of interest in the exact amount of the negative market value reveals that it was not a decisive factor for the conclusion of the agreement.

Conclusion

9.98 The main conclusion from the above is that, as regards arranging bank and underwriter liability, the English courts are sympathetic to exclusion clauses in wholesale markets. The US position seems to be similar, except that the liability of underwriters for a regulated public prospectus is significantly increased, probably by reason of the passions aroused after the Great Depression in 1929 generating a bitter resentment of banks, repeated after the global financial crisis in 2008 onwards.

9.99 Standing back, the English attitude to exclusion clauses in general seems more welcoming than in Germany or France. There may well be a consistency between the key indicators of offering circulars and derivatives and the approaches of the four main jurisdictions to exclusion clauses in general. In that event, the key indicators would be symbolic or representative of wider policies and would also reveal a conflicting clash of policies.

10
INSOLVENCY LAW INDICATORS AND RISKS

Why Insolvency Law is Relevant

Importance of insolvency law

10.1 Insolvency law is fundamental in this study because of the role it plays in legal systems in our context.

10.2 A debtor is insolvent when it is unable to pay its debts as they fall due. The debtor may also be deemed insolvent when its liabilities exceed its assets. Insolvency has a major impact on transactions and the rights of the parties.

10.3 A broad conclusion is that insolvency attitudes are, to a greater or lesser extent, correlated to the general attitudes of the legal system towards wider themes, including the degree of freedom of contract, business orientation, and state intervention via the law in private transactions.

10.4 Insolvency law yields many key indicators which are particularly revealing of the choices which jurisdictions make in a crisis. The main key indicators I have chosen are three in number—insolvency set-off, security interests, and commercial trusts. They are crucial because each of the claimants can reduce its risk to zero on the insolvency of the counterparty if it can exercise these rights to the full extent of its claim. Jurisdictions which support these triple super-priority claims can be regarded as creditor-friendly. Those which support none or only one of them can be regarded as debtor-friendly. These three claimants are considered in Chapters 11, 12, and 13. Other key indicators are summarised at the end of this chapter in outline.

10.5 This chapter covers the sixth letter in the sequence of the thirteen themes expressed in the mnemonic PIB–FEISST––CoRCO, standing for *p*redictability, *i*nsulation, *b*usiness orientation, *f*reedom of contract, *e*xclusion clauses, *insolvency law*, *s*et-off, *s*ecurity interests, *t*rusts, *co*rporate law, *r*egulatory law, *c*ourts, and *o*thers.

Insolvency rules are mandatory

10.6 The essential difference between the governing law of contracts and the governing law of insolvencies is that in the case of contracts you can choose the governing law but in the case of insolvencies most of the rules are mandatory. In that case you have to accept what the local insolvency rules do to your transaction, eg whether they smash it or strive to preserve it.

10.7 Of course, on an insolvency of a counterparty you as a creditor will not be paid in full and indeed in the normal case unsecured creditors on a liquidation receive only a small percentage of what they are owed, if anything.

10.8 The reason for the stern view taken by the law in virtually all commercial jurisdictions that the rules of insolvency are largely compulsory is that insolvency has a devastating effect on people's lives and their transactions. Creditors are not paid so that they lose their assets without compensation. Contracts are shattered and their terms interfered with or negated. Employees lose their jobs and sometimes their pensions. The collapse of banks and insurance companies destroys the savings of the citizen unless the government steps in to bail them out. When there is a depression, the economy of the whole society itself may be sapped. Bankruptcy is a destroyer and a spoliator.

10.9 One tests the credentials of a jurisdiction in its commercial and financial law by its approach to insolvency, in particular where the jurisdiction stands on a straight line from creditor-friendly to debtor-friendly. This is because at last the law has to choose who to support and the choice cannot be side-stepped or evaded. There is not enough money to go round and therefore the law must ruthlessly decide who is to bear the risk. There is a winner and a loser, a victor and a victim. The choices are relentless in their results and, since there will always be losses borne by someone, bankruptcy is the great driver of commercial law. That also explains why jurisdictions insist that their own law applies and are not willing to allow freedom of choice so far as they can.

10.10 In these chapters on bankruptcy, I deal with the bankruptcy of mainly corporations and not individuals, although the principles are often very similar. The focus in this book is on business-to-business transactions. I use the terms insolvency and bankruptcy interchangeably. The technical usage of these terms differs in many jurisdictions, but these are not important for our purposes.

Understanding Insolvency Law

Essential elements of bankruptcy

10.11 This section is a primer on bankruptcy law.

10.12 A final bankruptcy has three essential features:

- Legal actions by creditors individually to seize assets through attachment or execution are frozen. Creditors cease to be able to grab assets in a disorganised race for the courthouse door. Instead, each creditor is left with the right to claim for a dividend out of the pool of the proceeds of the assets.
- The assets of the bankrupt are sold and the proceeds are distributed to creditors. In other words, bankruptcy is collective.
- Creditors are paid according to a ladder of priorities. They are not paid equally out of the proceeds. The rank of a creditor on this ladder is by far the most important differentiator between legal systems and the source of the greatest dissension and disharmony.

That is because if you are high up at the top of this ladder you often get paid, sometimes in full. But if you are at the bottom of the ladder you do not get paid at all.

Impact of the bankruptcy of corporations on legal systems

10.13 One does not have to look very far back into history to discover why bankruptcy drives the legislator to wave the legal wand.

10.14 The bankruptcy of banks in the global financial crisis beginning in 2007 led to a massive surge in regulatory law in an attempt to mitigate the risk of a recurrence. Regulatory law probably doubled in the following decade in the major jurisdictions. It certainly became much more intense as legislators expressed their indignation at the cost to the taxpayer of the debacle. A notable outcome was the widespread nationalisation of the law governing the insolvency of banks via 'resolution' statutes, with the result that the authorities could take virtually complete charge of a bank insolvency without giving creditors the normal recourse to the courts.

10.15 This leap in the quantity of law has been a feature of numerous periods where banks have become bankrupt stretching all the way back into the nineteenth century. The same has happened whenever any industry essential to the public becomes bankrupt, whether the early American railroads (which precipitated the first permanent bankruptcy statute in the US in 1898) or the failure of an airline, or of a major employer, or of a large company which engaged in doubtful practices. An example of the latter is the failure of the US corporation Enron in late 2001, resulting in creditor losses of around US$11 billion, which in turn led to the passage of legislation rendering senior executives personally responsible for the financial statements of a company, the Sarbanes-Oxley Act of 2002. This Act was up to then unthinkable in US corporate law.

Summary of methods of insolvency risk mitigation

10.16 There are a number of ways in which parties can escape the consequences of the mandatory rules of bankruptcy:

- They can take security from a counterparty to secure its obligations. Often this is not possible in the case of large corporations because of prohibitions in their credit agreements (called 'negative pledges'). If they do take security, their position depends on the scope of the security and the ease with which it can be enforced. If the security is effective, then they are outside the bankruptcy—they are separatists.
- In a few crucial cases they can improve their position on the ladder of priorities by choosing a governing law of a transaction which gives a priority, such as English law, even though local law does not normally recognise the priority under its own law. Two examples are set-off and trusts. These claimants are also separatists.
- It is sometimes possible, but very expensive, to move the principal office of the debtor (often called its centre of main interests) to a jurisdiction which is more favourable to the creditor's position. This has to be done before official insolvency takes over

and generally requires the consent of other creditors via a scheme of arrangement or other plan.
- The governing law of a contract cannot usually be ignored by an insolvency representative as regards matters such as predictability, although sometimes the local law regards good faith and similar doctrines as mandatory overriding rules, regardless of governing law.
- A creditor may be able to commence insolvency proceedings in another jurisdiction where there are assets so as to attract rules which are more favourable to it. This is not usually an attractive option for an ordinary creditor because the main assets will normally be where the main insolvency proceedings are taking place.
- In the case of most financial difficulties, creditors typically endeavour to agree a private restructuring with the debtor (called a 'work-out') in which creditors can theoretically agree what they like. But in practice the ability of other creditors to institute an insolvency proceeding or the frequent requirements of creditors to submit the work-out agreement for approval by a court to legitimise it, prevents one creditor from negotiating a position which it would not have had if there were a normal insolvency.

Three methods of handling insolvencies

There are three main ways in which insolvencies of a corporation can be dealt with. **10.17**

The first is a private voluntary restructuring or work-out agreement between the debtor and its creditors without recourse to the courts. Small companies do not usually have the resources to pay for legal advice or to pay restructuring specialists and so either they agree a rescheduling with their bank or they go into liquidation. The practice in the case of large companies is often to try and organise a work-out privately as an alternative to the trauma of court proceedings. The statistics are poor but it is considered that most financial difficulties in the major economies are dealt with in this way, at least initially. **10.18**

The second method is to institute a formal rescue procedure in the courts. These rescue proceedings normally have rules for voting by creditors on a reorganisation plan which does not require unanimity but can bind dissentient 'hold-out' creditors. Virtually all the major jurisdictions have a statutory rescue now, with very few exceptions. A large number of emerging countries have instituted these rescues. They can generally be commenced by a debtor unilaterally. Rescue procedures were installed rapidly worldwide after the propagation of Chapter 11 under the US Bankruptcy Code of 1978, followed by a tough version in France in 1985, a moderate version in Britain in 1986, and then a torrent of similar statutes in the following two decades. After that, legislators were preoccupied more with bank resolution statutes after the financial crisis in order to rescue banks. In recent years, the tinkering with these rescue statutes was resumed, especially in the UK and continental Europe. The main reason for legislative interest is to protect jobs. **10.19**

The third method is by a liquidation where the business is sold and creditors are paid a dividend out of the proceeds. **10.20**

10.21 A liquidation is a last resort when the position is either hopeless or is too chaotic to control. A liquidation generally destroys the value of a business. On the one hand, the advantages of rescue statutes are that the business can be kept going, hold-outs can be bound by majority voting, creditors are subject to freezes on individual creditor actions, there is less risk of director personal liability for deepening the insolvency, international recognition may be improved, and debt-equity conversions are generally easier. On the other hand, some disadvantages are that that the announcement of insolvency is very damaging to businesses. They lose customers and employees, credit dries up, suppliers demand cash up-front, counterparties terminate their contracts, landlords cancel leases, management may lose control completely or partially, creditors lose control to the court, court proceedings are more time-consuming and much more expensive, and the disclosure of information is more formal. There is much less scope for creditors to take security for their existing debt and hope to outlast the preference avoidance period. There are other reasons too.

10.22 Hence, rescue statutes have not enjoyed the hopes that were placed on them and the number of successful cases in most jurisdictions has been small compared to work-outs or liquidations. They are often no more than a slow-motion liquidation, chosen because the debtor's position against creditors is improved compared to a liquidation, such as freezes on the enforcement of security and the ability of the debtor to prevent the termination of contracts. They are more useful for big companies with many classes of creditor. They are too expensive and too complicated for small companies.

10.23 There are many hybrids between a work-out and a judicial rescue. For example, some countries require very little court intervention beyond opening the proceedings and approving a plan. Most commonly in a big case the creditors involved and the debtor negotiate the work-out agreement between themselves and then apply to the court to approve it under an expedited procedure, ie put a court stamp on it to give legitimacy to the work-out agreement. This is called a 'pre-packaging' or a 'prepack' in the jargon.

Work-outs and judicial rescue plans

10.24 A private work-out and a reorganisation plan voted on by creditors under a rescue statute typically involve similar measures. Both will normally provide for a rescheduling of bank debt by stretching maturities or by exchanges of bonds for old bonds or for defaulted bank debt, by a sale of all or part of the business to slim it down, or a merger with a stronger company, or a conversion of debt into equity. In each case, it is common for the restructuring to be effected by a Newco structure. Thus, the insolvent company sells all its assets to a newly formed company owned by the banks and bondholders as main creditors. Newco in return issues shares to the creditors in return for them giving up their claims against the old shell company. In this way, the former creditors own a new company clear of all liabilities other than those which are dragged along by law such as employees, and at the same time the company is restored to solvency by the debt equity conversion.

10.25 In both cases, there will be a range of contracts which must be governed by a governing law and be subject to the jurisdiction of a court. A reorganisation plan itself in a judicial proceeding will be governed by the law of the jurisdiction where the proceedings are taking place, but, especially in the case of work-outs, this need not be the case. In work-outs, there can be a great many documents, such as the work-out agreement itself signed by participating creditors, new credit agreements, new security agreements, any disposal of assets or merger documents, a standstill agreement amongst creditors, and intercreditor agreements, as well as a disclosure document with any accompanying disclaimers of liability. Group companies are likely to be involved, sometimes dozens of them. In a large international case, it will often be found that the underlying bank loan agreements and bond issues will be governed by English or New York law, so that the rescheduling of these agreements, and hence the whole work-out agreement, will also be governed by the same law. Work-out agreements are internationally mobile.

Creditors involved in work-out and judicial rescue plans

In the case of both work-outs and judicial rescue plans, the main participants in a big case are usually banks, bondholders, and hedge funds. Some may be secured or may be subordinated to other creditors. Other creditors, such as trade creditors and employees, will not be involved, but will continue to be paid out of bank money to keep the business going. In that event, bank money is used to pay employees and trade creditors. In some countries, employee pension trustees have claims which have to be settled by the group. Reorganisation plans are document-heavy. **10.26**

International diversity of insolvency approaches

The law of contract in most jurisdictions is a done deal in the sense that the number of areas of serious divergence and disharmony are relatively limited compared to insolvency law. We have already studied some of these differences, such as predictability, business orientation, and freedom of contract. But in the case of bankruptcy law the range of differences is vast and in violent conflict on the most basic issues. Further in the case of contracts, the question of what law applies to a particular issue is well-settled in all but a few narrow cases and similarly the upholding of free choice of courts is more or less established in most commercial jurisdictions. Although some progress has been made in these areas in international bankruptcy law, the consensus is much less than that applying in the case of contracts and hence one of the requirements of our key indicators, that of a clashing conflict, is easily satisfied. **10.27**

The diversity of these solutions in bankruptcy law intensifies the degree of international legal risk and ambush. **10.28**

Harmonised International Insolvency Laws

EU Insolvency Regulation and UNCITRAL Model Law

The two main international instruments dealing with conflict of laws on insolvency are the EU Regulation on Insolvency Proceedings 2015, replacing a former regulation, and the **10.29**

UNCITRAL Model Law on Cross-Border Insolvency adopted in 1997. The Model Law has been absorbed by a great many countries including the US, the UK, Japan, Mexico, Poland, Romania, South Africa, New Zealand, Australia, South Korea, Canada, Greece, Chile, and the Philippines, subject often to reservations.

10.30 The EU Regulation applies in all twenty-seven Member States of the EU, excluding Denmark but including Austria, Belgium, Croatia, the Czech Republic, the Baltic countries, Germany, Greece, Hungary, Ireland, Italy, Finland, France, the Netherlands, Poland, Portugal, Luxembourg, Romania, Slovakia, Spain, and Sweden. It does not apply to the UK as a result of Brexit. The UK has a highly developed set of conflict of laws rules dealing with international insolvencies and has also adopted the UNCITRAL Model Law.

10.31 Other than the above, the landscape is bare of treaties, other than a Nordic treaty and a couple of Latin American treaties of limited scope.

Summary of the EU Insolvency Regulation 2015

10.32 The Regulation applies to all types of collective insolvency proceedings and to all debtors, except certain insurers, banks, and mutual funds.

10.33 The main principle of the Regulation is that the courts of the Member State where the debtor has its centre of main interests, which is usually its place of incorporation or principal office, has jurisdiction to open insolvency proceedings and first opener has exclusivity. Those proceedings are then automatically recognised throughout the EU so that the freezes on creditors and the judgments in relation to the proceedings must be recognised and enforced throughout the EU, subject only to a public policy exception. The Regulation only applies if the centre of main interests of the debtor is in the EU. If the debtor's centre of main interests is outside the EU, then each Member State has whatever jurisdiction it has outside the Regulation.

10.34 If the debtor's centre of main interests is situated in a Member State, then secondary proceedings can be opened in another Member State if the debtor has an establishment there. This is roughly a branch which has some permanence. These secondary proceedings are restricted to the assets concerned. The freezes of the establishment state do not apply to external assets. The insolvency practitioner in the main proceedings has power to influence the secondary proceedings, eg liquidation or rescue.

10.35 There is no power to open proceedings in the Member States if there is anything less than an establishment, such as the mere presence of assets locally like a bank account.

10.36 So the EU concentrates the proceedings in the main jurisdiction of the debtor. This is considerably more audacious than the Brussels Regulation of 2012 on judgments because, under the Brussels Regulation, the parties can contract out of the jurisdiction of the defendant's domicile and choose courts anywhere else they like, whether in the EU or elsewhere, such as the US. In addition, the Brussels Regulation has many exceptions to the domicile. The Insolvency Regulation has an exception for local branches, but that is it. A party will therefore be dragged into the mandatory insolvency law of the counterparty.

A potentially bankrupt company can change its centre of main interests but that is complicated and expensive.

10.37 The insolvency is separate for each member of a group, each of which is treated as a separate entity with its own centre of main interests. In other words, the treatment typical of financial statements of a group of parent company and subsidiaries as being a consolidated single entity is shattered and explodes into its component pieces, thereby greatly complicating the insolvency. There are loose cooperation provisions for members of the same group.

10.38 The second fundamental principle of the Regulation is that the law of the opening state, whether main or secondary, determines the conditions for the opening of the proceedings, their effect, their conduct, and their closure. See article 7. In particular, it determines what debtors can be bankrupted, the assets of the estate, powers of the debtor and insolvency practitioner, the effect on contracts and creditor proceedings, the lodgement and treatment of claims, priorities, the effect of closure and a discharge by a composition, and voidable preferences ('detrimental acts'). See article 7(2). It probably also determines director liabilities for deepening the insolvency, but probably not other prior mismanagement liabilities under corporate law.

Exceptions to opening state applicable law

10.39 Under the EU Insolvency Regulation, there are major exceptions to the uniform application of the insolvency law of the opening state, whether main or secondary. The most important relate to:

- third party rights in rem (proprietary rights) in assets situate in other Member States (mainly security interests including floating charges, liens, leases, restitution, beneficial interests under trusts, and title rights recorded in title registers— article 8);
- set-off. If insolvency set-off is not permitted under the local law, it can be admitted if the law of the debtor's claim allows set-off— article 9);
- reservation of title for assets situate in another Member State (article 10);
- contracts to acquire or use immovable property (law of the Member State where the immovable property is— article 11(1));
- payment and settlement systems and financial markets (law of the Member State where the system or market is— article 12);
- effects of insolvency proceedings on title registered land, ships, aircraft (law of Member State where the register is— article 14);
- voidable preferences subject to another law and not challengeable under that law (article 16).

10.40 The shift of the mandatory governing law from the law of the opening state to some other law, such as the law of the location of an asset, is of very great importance in our context and will be dealt with in the subsequent three chapters.

10.41 Various previous insolvency conventions between Member States are overridden, but certain other conventions are preserved. See article 85.

10.42 The EU has separate directives for the insolvency of banks and insurance companies.

Summary of the UNCITRAL Model Law on Cross-border Insolvency

10.43 The Model Law provides for the recognition in the enacting state of foreign collective insolvency proceedings (not out-of-court work-outs), whether liquidation or rehabilitation. It is contemplated that the insolvency of banks, insurers, and other entities can be excluded. The insolvency administrator is called a foreign representative. See article 2.

10.44 The Model Law divides foreign proceedings into main and non-main proceedings. Main proceedings are those commenced at the debtor's centre of main interests. See article 2. In the absence of proof to the contrary, the debtor's registered office (or habitual residence in the case of individuals) is presumed to be the centre of the debtor's main interests. See article 16(3). Non-main proceedings are those taking place where the debtor has an establishment—broadly a non-transitory branch. See article 2. A main insolvency has much better recognition than a non-main. A foreign insolvency where there is less than a branch (eg only local assets) is not entitled to recognition. So far, the Model Law shares many features of the EU regulation.

10.45 After foreign recognition, the enacting state may open local proceedings only if there are assets locally—it need not be a branch. See article 28. The stays in the local proceeding have primacy over the stays in the foreign proceeding recognised locally so that they could be more or less: see article 29. The Model Law does not state what law applies to the local proceedings, but normally it will be local law, including its conflicts rules.

10.46 Foreign creditors have the same rights to commence and participate in local proceedings as local creditors. See article 13.

10.47 The Model Law has two central concepts: (1) recognition of the foreign proceeding, and (2) cooperation between courts and representatives of concurrent proceedings.

10.48 Foreign main proceedings will normally be recognised. Once a foreign main proceeding is recognised, then three basic stays come into effect locally: (1) on individual actions and proceedings; (2) on execution against the debtor's assets; and (3) on disposals of the debtor's assets. See article 20. But a local proceeding may be commenced. See article 20(4). The scope of the stays can be limited by local law. See article 20(2). Examples of exempted stays might be the potential stays on security interests, lease repossessions, reservation of title, other rights in rem, contract terminations, and set-off—if indeed caught by the automatic stay.

10.49 The scope of the stays is the main battleground of the Model Law and the most controversial in implementation. The full range of stays would be dramatically debtor-protective and contrary to the insolvency policies of many jurisdictions.

10.50 The Model Law does not prevent the court from refusing to take action if manifestly contrary to the public policy of the enacting state. See article 6.

10.51 International treaties and other state agreements prevail.

10.52 Unlike the EU Insolvency Regulation, the Model Law does not set out any rules as to what law is to apply to particular issues. These matters have to be covered by the conflicts rules of the jurisdiction of the opening court.

Insolvency jurisdiction and applicable law outside the treaties

10.53 Outside the EU Insolvency Regulation, the UNCITRAL Model Law on Cross-Border Insolvency and, apart from other treaties, the general position is that courts have jurisdiction over insolvencies where the debtor is incorporated or where its centre of main interest is or where it as a branch or usually where it has local assets or local business activities. The jurisdiction can be very tenuous. What usually happens, therefore, is that insolvency proceedings are started at the principal place of business and then opened in various other countries where there are assets. Often there is there is a race between local creditors, especially tax creditors, as against the insolvency representative in the main proceeding.

10.54 Hence, the insolvency of a group with many interests abroad looks like a moon against a background of stars. One must not forget that each company is usually treated as a separate entity, subject to separate insolvency proceedings (although occasionally a pooling order is possible). This must be the case since it would be unrealistic normally to merge all creditors and all assets and to override the overwhelming importance of the veil of incorporation. That is one reason why financial statements wildly diverge from the reality of insolvency and are of interest only if the group is a going concern. Some groups have thousands of subsidiaries.

10.55 People often complain of the time and cost of insolvency proceedings. The main reason for the delay and cost in a big case is litigation. The insolvency of the Bank of Credit and Commerce International in 1991 lasted for twenty years. The insolvency of Lehmans commencing in 2008 lasted for at least twelve years. By comparison, the insolvency of Greece, which involved about the same amounts as Lehmans, was resolved in nine months because, for one thing, there is no judicial bankruptcy for sovereign states. There are a few lessons there.

Insolvency of corporations, banks, and sovereign states compared

10.56 Despite the commonality of the condition of insolvency and its consequences for the debtors and creditors concerned, the legal approaches differ quite fantastically in the case of the three great classes of debtor—corporations, banks, and sovereigns. These approaches or chasms part on practically every issue.

10.57 Sovereign states can become de facto bankrupt in the sense of being unable to pay their debts as they become due, just like everybody else. The number of sovereign states that have not been bankrupt over the last century is tiny. In the case of banks, the insolvency law has been nationalised in the leading countries. The law is dirigiste. Effectively, the insolvency is controlled be an organ of the state such as the central bank or a regulator. They decide the method of resurrection or obliteration. Creditors do what they are told. Control by the

10.58 courts or creditors is swept away or limited. There are only a few cowering clauses beneath the blaze of machine gunfire and missiles offering safeguards, for example, that no creditor should be worse off as a result of the procedure.

10.58 By contrast, there is no bankruptcy law at all in the case of sovereign states, apart from EU legislation as to the inclusion of bondholder collective action clauses, mainly majority bondholder voting on plans, in most EU sovereign issues. Hence, sovereign financial problems are resolved solely by negotiation between the parties to a rescheduling agreement—usually an offer by the debtor to exchange new rescheduled bonds for the old bonds, the terms of which depend entirely on the bargaining strength of creditors and the debtor, especially the geopolitical importance of the sovereign debtor and the ability of creditors to withhold further finance for a debtor state. Freedom of contract reigns.

10.59 Corporate insolvency proceedings are in the middle, with very complicated bankruptcy laws about liquidations and reorganisations. Creditors are subject to the supervision of the courts but they are still given much scope on the details of a plan.

10.60 There are many reasons for these striking differences. But there is a plain outcome. This is that in the case of corporations and banks, the conflicts of law on insolvency are decided nationalistically and compulsorily by the law of the forum state. As we have seen, in most cases the creditors cannot choose the governing law of a particular issue, as they can in the case of contracts. The theoretical argument is that freedom might give rise to unequal treatment, but the real argument is that the ideologies are so intensely held that countries insist on applying their own law. In the case of bank insolvencies, the forces to protect local depositors and creditors are so overpowering that international cooperation agreements are weak or non-existent.

10.61 It is therefore ironic that. in the case of sovereign insolvencies, the effect of a rescheduling transaction is determined by the governing law and the courts expressly chosen by the parties in the documents. This choice is normally free. We must not give up hope that liberty may triumph over expediency. Freedom can work.

Key Indicators of Insolvency Law

Triple super-priority insolvency claims

10.62 The most important indicators of insolvency law, which also pose the greatest risks on insolvency if they are not available, are the three triple super-priority insolvency claims. They are:

- set-off and its companion netting, examined in Chapter 11;
- security interests, such as pledges, mortgages, and charges, examined in Chapter 12;
- trusts, such as the custodianship of investments by banks and other depositories, investments held by a clearing company, and a trustee holding collateral for bondholders or a syndicate of lending banks. These are examined in Chapter 13.

10.63 The amounts involved in each of these legal constructs are so enormous that their absence or an unexpected invalidity in which a large institution, such as a major bank, is implicated could have systemic consequences. A systemic consequence is typically one where the insolvency and collapse of one party has a knock-on, domino, or contagious impact on other parties, such as a bank run, thereby prejudicing the system.

Each of these indicators are tested only an insolvency since they are intended as a bulwark and safeguard against bankruptcy. Set-off is irrelevant if both parties can always pay. Security interests are designed to provide a recourse against assets if the party granting security becomes unable to pay. The efficacy of a trust is vital on bankruptcy when it is tested. It is irrelevant that all of these institutions work only when the relevant party is solvent. In addition, the loss if one of these arrangements is invalid can be measured with great predictability, much greater predictability than would be the case with, say, an unpredictable contract. 10.64

If set-off is disallowed on bankruptcy, the loss to the creditor is the amount which could have been set off compared to the amount which the creditor receives on the debt owed to it by the bankrupt debtor. If a security interest fails, the loss is the value of the collateral compared to the dividend received by an unsecured creditor—which is often a tiny percentage or nothing at all. In the case of a trust, the measure is similar. Thus, if the beneficial owner of investments does not get back those investments held in custody by a bank, ie on trust for the owner, and the trust fails on the insolvency of the bank, then the loss is the value of the investment compared to the dividend received by the beneficiary as an unsecured creditor. 10.65

General attitude of the legal families to the three super-priority claimants

The line-up of the three main legal families is reasonably clear. The Napoleonic group are the least favourable in general to all of the three super-priority claimants. The Anglo-American group are strongly in favour of all three. The Roman-Germanic group are relatively favourable to insolvency set-off and to security interests, but not favourable to trusts. These are generalisations which are subject to erosions, clefts in the rocks, and different declivities. In particular, there is a widening gap between the traditional members of the Napoleonic group and the economically advanced jurisdictions in this group, especially Belgium. 10.66

The triple super-priorities satisfy the eligibility tests for key indicators

The three super-priority claims easily satisfy the tests I have laid down for the eligibility of key indicators. Each one is measurable, either precisely in a quantifiable figure, or (in the case of security interests) to a sufficient degree to enable reasonable quantification of the risk. Each one is economically important: each involves many trillions, manifestly more than world gross domestic product (GDP) (and in the case of set-off and netting, a multiple of world GDP). 10.67

Each is symbolic and representative. The position of the three great legal families are internally consistent and distinctive. There is also quite a high degree of correlation between the approach of a family to the three super-priority claimants and the approach of the family to 10.68

other key indicators, such as the role of predictability in contract, business orientation, and freedom of contract.

10.69 Thus, as said, in all three cases the English common law group strongly favour all three, the Napoleonic jurisdictions do not favour any of them (but subject to major reservations), and the Roman-Germanic jurisdictions are broadly in the middle between the two wings. This matches the 1 3 5 7 ranking proposed in Chapter 1—England blue, New York green (because of the greater pro-debtor bias in its insolvency laws compared to England), Germany yellow, and France red.

10.70 It is clear also that the attitudes of the three major families conflict intensely on the underlying policies. The policies vary between each of the claims, but they have a single commonality, that is, that by virtue of their super-priority on an insolvency, the three claims defy the equality of creditors. Effectively, they take away assets of the insolvent. There are convincing reasons why they should do so, but the explanations are not accepted by the dissenting jurisdictions. Accordingly the competition is between satisfying the claimant (and its creditors and shareholders) or enlarging the estate of the debtor available to its creditors.

10.71 The contrasting *chiaroscuro* of policies are deeply embedded in the profound depths of history, so deeply in fact that one sometimes feels that the present day has forgotten the reasons for their ideology.

Role of the contract governing law in achieving super-priority

10.72 We have seen that insolvency rules of the place where the insolvency proceedings are opened are treated as mandatory and override any contract to the contrary. Nevertheless the governing law of a contract can in some jurisdictions legitimise an insolvency set-off which would otherwise not be available under the law of the insolvency forum. In a wider number of cases, the governing law can legitimise recognition of the trust in a non-trust jurisdiction. In the case of security interests coverage is more complicated for the governing law to improve a security interest in a jurisdiction which is not sympathetic to security interests. Nevertheless, there are some steps which can be taken to strengthen the security interest by the use of a governing law.

10.73 In all three cases, to improve the position it is necessary to choose a governing law which is that of a common law jurisdiction, such as English or New York law because it is only this group which normally supports all three of the super-priority claimants universally, or at least without having to rely on finicky carve-out statutes for financial markets in refusing jurisdictions. New York law is somewhat less enthusiastic than English law in the case of set-off and security interests. I discuss the detail in the following three chapters.

Central counterparties and the triple super-priority claimants

10.74 The three super-priority claimants of insolvency set-off, security interests, and commercial trusts are crucial in the case of central counterparties. These entities are discussed at paragraph 3.62.

Set-off and netting are at the heart of the reduction of risk, as will be explained in Chapter 11. Security interests, mainly over financial collateral, are essential to cover any remaining exposures of participants. In clearing systems for securities, the clearing company holds the benefit of the securities in trust for participants. **10.75**

A typical structure is that the clearing company holds investments, such as bonds, in trust for large institutions who are members of the clearing system and they in turn hold in trust for smaller banks and other institutions. These smaller institutions may themselves hold in trust for brokers, pension funds, mutual funds, or others, and these in turn may hold in trust for the ultimate investors who could include individuals. Sometimes the chain is even longer. **10.76**

It follows that the trust, for example, must be legally recognised at each level in order to avoid a break in the links, which would mean that the ultimate investor has no direct claim against the issuer and is an unsecured creditor of whoever is just above the break in the chain. This would be a most unexpected disaster for that investor. In addition, set-off on insolvency looks through the chain of trusts from the investor to the ultimate issuer so that the ultimate investor and the issuer of bonds are in a mutual set-off relationship, subject to any liens or breaks in the chain. Mutuality is based on absolute beneficial ownership, that is, who is the ultimate beneficial owner of a claim. In order to have mutuality for set-off, each debtor-creditor must be personally liable for the debt it owes and beneficially entitled to the debt owed to it. Thus, the ultimate investor may owe a loan to the issuer of the bonds which is a bank owing a deposit to the ultimate investor so that you have two reciprocal claims eligible for set-off on the insolvency of, say, the bank. **10.77**

In addition, security interests granted by any party in the chain must be inviolable. **10.78**

It follows from this that the jurisdiction must recognise the triple super-priority claimants at every stage in the chain. In continental Europe, the Settlement Finality Directive 1998, dealing with clearing systems and central counterparties, and the Financial Collateral Directive 2002 between them forcefully legitimise insolvency set-off and netting, security interests, and commercial trusts in relation to clearing systems at least. But they only apply to a limited set of eligible institutions and not to everybody in the possible chains. Hence, the walls of the fortress may have gaps, particularly at the lower end of chains with the results that the fortress is not impregnable. In order to achieve bullet-proof protection, the protection of the three super-priority claimants should be universal, applying to everybody. This is normally the case in English common law jurisdictions, as will be seen in the next three chapters, but it is not the case in almost all of the civil code systems. **10.79**

Similar principles apply in the case of central counterparties not involving securities, such as those for derivatives or metals or commodities trading. **10.80**

Bankruptcy ladder of priorities

I now turn to other significant bankruptcy key indicators which are material in showing the approach of a jurisdiction, particularly as regards the measure of creditor or debtor friendliness. I do not deal with any of these in detail. **10.81**

10.82 The first of these is the bankruptcy ladder of priorities, probably the most hard fought areas of bankruptcy law with everybody clutching for the top to gasp in the last bubble of air. Many commentators prize bankruptcy for its equality of treatment as everybody faces a disaster, but nothing could be further from the truth.

10.83 The ladder has dozens of rungs, but broadly the main list, split into sub-rungs, includes the following, with large differences between jurisdictions as to who comes where:

1. *super-priority claimants*, such as claimants with a set-off, secured creditors, beneficiaries under a trust, and creditors with security substitutes, such as retention of title to goods, financial leases, repos, and other forms of title finance. These claimants are typical of English common law jurisdictions;
2. *priority claimants*, such as the costs of the insolvency administration, taxes, employee remuneration, and others. There is much contest as to whether these rank ahead of security interests;
3. *pari passu creditors* such as bank creditors, bond creditors, and trade creditors, as well as tort claimants, eg for personal injury or property damage or misselling. These creditors will typically receive a tiny dividend so that in the usual case this rung and lower rungs are below the water and drowned. The jargon is that 'value breaks' at this point;
4. *subordinated creditors*, such as creditors subordinated by law, post-insolvency interest, and creditors who have agreed to be subordinated. The most important of these creditors who are compulsorily subordinated are creditors who are subordinated for misconduct under the *Deep Rock* doctrine in the US, and, in Germany and a number of other countries, shareholder loans made at the time when the loans should have been equity shares to rescue the company. See Chapter 14. These doctrines do not apply under English law. This class may also include foreign creditors who are not entitled to be paid before local creditors, as in the case of the bankruptcy of a New York bank;
5. *equity shares*, notably shares in the company, ranked according to their own internal hierarchy, such as preference shares before equities;
6. *excluded claims*, including, for example, late claimants, foreign revenue and penalties, and claimants who have lost their property because they are beneficiaries under non-recognised trusts. In almost all jurisdictions the claims of creditors in a foreign currency are converted into the local currency at the commencement of a liquidation, so that if the local currency is depreciating, for example, in a depression or in the case of a sovereign insolvency, then the claim may become worthless. Top-ups are very rare.

10.84 Each rung will typically include numerous other classes, and also the classes are internally ranked. The differences between jurisdictions very considerably.

Contract and lease terminations on insolvency

10.85 The test here is whether the insolvency administrator can prevent the termination of contracts and leases on the insolvency of the debtor and can then transfer the contracts to a third party. This is probably one of the most violent actions which can be taken in terms of the destruction of contracts in the interests of in financing the debtor at the individual expense of the contract counterparties who are affected. Probably the most aggressive jurisdictions on this point include France and the United States, and England one of the least aggressive amongst developed countries.

10.86 This power is available in very many jurisdictions, including in the EU. In the UK, a mild version was slipped through under the cover of Covid-19 in 2020, which, however, excluded the financial arena, as well as protecting set-off and netting arrangements. The usual tough version overrides express termination clauses. These measures are intended to enlarge the debtor's estate to increase the chances of a rescue. However, what happens in practice is that the administrator terminates the non-profit-making contracts and keeps the profit-making contracts. The non-defaulter is denied an advantage granted to the debtor, who is the defaulter. In addition, the defaulter is often unable to perform in any event, with the result that the ability of the counterparty to find an alternative is merely held up. That counterparty has to live with whoever the debtor decides to transfer the contract to. As discussed in Chapter 3, the networks or chains of linked contracts can be mortally disrupted by the bankruptcy of a link in the chain, which makes it even more necessary that the counterparty can itself replace the link quickly, without the delays of an insolvency administrator maximising a bankrupt's assets at the risk of everybody else.

10.87 Most catastrophically, the ban on the ability to terminate the contracts destroys the ability to net contracts to lower risks and to mitigate exposures, except to the extent that set-off and netting are parked off into yet another unintelligible carve-out statute. If you want to quantify benefits to the estate of the debtor against the damage to the legal system, you would think that the result would be open and shut. For the variety of contracts which might be affected, see Chapter 3.

Other insolvency key indicators

10.88 Other key indicators which are worth exploring in the insolvency arena and which very often exhibit significant differences between jurisdictions include:

- the *avoidance of preferences* on insolvency. This criterion would distinguish between those jurisdictions with a high claw-back risk and those where the risk is reduced. The core issue is the retroactive disruption of transactions in favour of insolvency equality, as against the predictability of transactions and the protection of private workout agreements. The English regime is probably the lightest, and the American and Napoleonic regimes the toughest;
- *creditor control* of the proceedings as against management of the debtor or the court. See paragraph 5.83 for the command and control by interventionist courts in France in relation to plans;
- the compulsory priority of *post-commencement financings*, that is, the degree to which existing creditors can be compulsorily subordinated to post-commencement secured loans to finance a rescue. English law does not allow existing creditors to be subordinated without their consent;
- the *invalidity of the sale of contracts and receivables* if the debtor in respect of the contract or receivable has not been notified prior to the insolvency. This is discussed in Chapter 7. English and New York law do not adopt this invalidating doctrine;

- the *entry criteria* for a rescue proceeding. In the United States, a debtor can file without showing insolvency;
- the *ability to trace* stolen or delinquent money through transformations and mixtures on the insolvency of the final holder, such as the recovery of money by virtue of a claim for embezzlement, mistake, or misappropriation of assets by a director or other fiduciary. Many of these are unjust enrichment claims or claims for proprietary restitution or real subrogation. This tracing is blocked in most civil code countries and it is one of the chief nuancing key indicators available in common law jurisdictions;
- *director liability*, studied in Chapter 14, especially personal director liability for deepening the insolvency. The English approach is moderate. in France and Germany there are compulsory duties on directors to file when a company is insolvent;
- the *support of work-outs* which do not involve the trauma of judicial rescue proceedings, especially the absence of criminal liability for the grant of preferential security for existing debt often granted in workouts, and the absence of direct liability for deepening the insolvency. The overall English approach favours free work-outs, but both German and French insolvency law hurry the debtor into an insolvency proceeding: see paragraph 14.82 ff. New York law does not permit bondholders to be bound by a work-out which changes payments, thereby discouraging work-outs. See paragraph 8.69;
- the *approval of reorganisation plans*, including the court ability to override the vote of a dissenting class, called a 'cram down';
- the scope of the *anti-deprivation rule* preventing the forfeiture of assets of the estate and thereby inhibiting normal business transactions. See Chapter 7;
- the relative ease or difficulty of *debt-equity conversions*;
- the intensity of the prohibition on a company giving *financial assistance* in connection with the purchase of its own shares. See Chapter 14;
- an example of *lender liability* is where lenders are liable for abusive credit, that is, continuing to grant credit to an insolvent debtor without informing third parties of the true situation. This surprising doctrine originated in France in the 1970s by case law and presented great dangers to banks who were endeavouring to rescue a company. A 2005 statute restricted the liability but the risk still applies in the case of blatant interference in management or if and the security obtained is out of all proportion to the funds. There is also Austrian case law on abusive credit.

10.89 It is not feasible in the space to explore all of these, but they need to be taken into account in any overall weighting of the insolvency regime.

Conclusion

10.90 As a rough guide, English insolvency law is creditor-friendly on most of the indicators. The triple super-priority claimants are firmly embedded and the regime on most of the other key indicators supports creditors. The English view is that, although debtors need protection from their creditors, creditors and society as a whole need protection against bankrupts.

10.91 US bankruptcy law honours the triple super-priority claimants, but otherwise US bankruptcy law is debtor-friendly, notably as regards the rights of management to stay in possession during a judicial rescue, the problems of rescheduling bondholders outside a proceeding, the formidable claw-back of preferences, and the severe regime whereby the administrator controls the destiny of contracts.

French insolvency law is considered highly debtor-friendly by comparison. Insolvency set-off is very weak and security interests are not particularly strong initially and are weakened further on insolvency. The personal liability of directors for failing to file on insolvency discourages work-outs. There are other reasons. **10.92**

Germany similarly imposes personal liability on directors for failing to file on insolvency. The German approach to the non-termination of contracts on insolvency is tough and rescue proceedings involve a large deduction from the proceeds of security. German law is not sympathetic to the commercial trust in general. Again, there are other reasons. **10.93**

These generalisations are considered to be often true of the members of the family groups represented by the Big Four jurisdictions. **10.94**

The above broad analysis would seem to support a ranking of 1 3 5 7, that is, England blue, New York green, Germany yellow, and France red, on insolvency indicators. This would be consistent with the overall ranking for all thirteen themes of 1 3 5 7 suggested in Chapter 1. **10.95**

11
INSOLVENCY SET-OFF

Essentials of Insolvency Set-off and Netting

Insolvency set-off and netting as a key indicator

11.1 The first of the three super-priority claims on insolvency to be discussed is insolvency set-off and netting. The issue is eligible as a key indicator because it is measurable with relative ease, because it involves colossal amounts and is economically crucial, because it is symbolic and representative of consistently different other approaches between families of jurisdictions, and because it demonstrates a clash of conflicting solutions. Hence, the MISC tests are satisfied with a provable conviction. Insolvency set-off is a particularly potent key indicator.

11.2 We also cover a couple of sub-indicators in relation to insolvency set-off.

11.3 This chapter shows that the choice of governing law can significantly mitigate a risk of the absence of a local insolvency set-off and plays a crucial role in other cases of set off.

11.4 This chapter covers the seventh letter in the sequence of the thirteen themes expressed in the mnemonic PIB–FEISST–CoRCO, standing for *p*redictability, *i*nsulation, *b*usiness orientation, *f*reedom of contract, *e*xclusion clauses, *i*nsolvency law, *s*et-off, *s*ecurity interests, *t*rusts, *co*rporate law, *r*egulatory law, *c*ourts, and *o*thers.

What is insolvency set-off?

11.5 If, on the one hand, two parties owe each other debts of 100 each, and one of them becomes bankrupt, then if the other can set off the two claims, the non-defaulter is paid in full by the set-off. The defaulter does not receive the 100 owed to it. Hence, set-off is a form of payment or discharge of a debt. The two claims cancel each other out to the extent of the smaller claim. The set-off reduces the creditor's risk. If you throw two stones into a lake, then when the two ripples meet, they cancel each other out and the lake is smooth again.

11.6 If, on the other hand, set off is not available on insolvency, then the non-defaulter has to pay its 100 into the estate of the defaulter. The non-defaulter then claims in the insolvency for the 100 owed to it by the defaulter on which it will be paid only a dividend, typically a tiny amount or nothing at all. Hence, if the set-off is allowed, the creditor is paid 100. If not, the creditor loses 100 and is not paid.

What is netting?

Netting is somewhat more complicated. When two parties have several open contracts with each other which still have to be performed on both sides (often called 'executory contracts'), eg to buy or sell goods or securities or foreign exchange, and one of the parties becomes bankrupt (which usually means that it will be unable to perform), then the non-defaulter will normally wish to cancel the whole row of contracts between them and to work out on each one what the losses or gains are. On the one hand, often the solvent party will have losses on some of the contracts so that the defaulter owes those as damages to the solvent party. On the other hand, it may be the defaulter who has experienced losses and the solvent party has a gain. In that case the solvent party can set off the losses which the defaulter owes to the solvent party against the losses which the solvent party owes to the defaulter on all the contracts.

11.7

Set-off is one step. Netting is three steps: cancel the contracts, calculate the losses and gains either way, and then set off the losses and gains. Cancel, calculate, set off. In the case of debts, such as loans against bank deposits, only set-off is necessary. In the case of executory contracts, such as sales or derivatives contracts, both parties still have to perform (one delivers the goods, etc. and the other pays for them), it is necessary to cancel the contracts first, then work out the losses and gains, and then set off.

11.8

In the case of netting it is therefore necessary that there is no freeze or stay on the termination of contracts on the insolvency of a counterparty. A large number of jurisdictions do prevent the non-defaulter from terminating contracts on insolvency, which in turn destroys the possibility of netting.

11.9

Two-way payments

Strictly, if the solvent party can keep its gains, while also paying the losses to the defaulter, the solvent party does not need the set-off. The gains compensate for the losses. This is sometimes called a 'walk-away clause'. We can ignore this for the moment because in many jurisdictions capital adequacy regulation of banks requires that each party pays gains to the other party, and this is also customary in formal markets because of the desire for reciprocity. That is called 'two-way payments'. Outside those situations, English case law strongly favours the walk-away, that is, the keeping of the profits by the non-defaulter.

11.10

Policies of insolvency set-off and netting

The main policies in favour of set-off and netting include the colossal reduction in risk in markets, the reduction of the cost of credit, a reduction in capital adequacy costs, and a reduction of transaction costs, such as maintaining credit lines and collateral for gross exposures.

11.11

11.12 In view of the amounts involved in foreign exchange markets, derivatives markets, securities markets, commodities markets and, and even the amounts involved between small businesses (which are large to them), it is clear that if we did not have set-off and netting, there would be nothing on the plate for breakfast. It would not be possible to maintain all of these markets if the exposures were gross.

11.13 Set-off and netting disturb creditor equality on insolvency but, as is also the case with security interests, the need for set-off and netting is overwhelming in modern societies. In any event, nowhere is there equality between creditors. Always there is a ladder with many steps.

11.14 From the moral point of view, it seems wrong that the defaulter is paid but does not pay. There seems no reason why a creditor set-off should be used to rescue an insolvent debtor and its creditors. In the words of the old maxim, the person who wants equity must do equity. If you owed a loan to your bank and the bank owed you a deposit which comprises your savings, and the bank became bankrupt because of gross mismanagement, you would keenly feel the injustice of the situation if the bank were so hopelessly bankrupt that you received nothing on your savings deposit, but you still had to pay your loan back to the bank in full.

11.15 Set-off is everywhere. It does not just favour habitual creditors like banks and insurance companies. A small trader can be just as much devasted by the loss of set-off as a big bank and it would seem strange if the legal system treated the small trader as a second-class citizen.

Carve-out statutes

11.16 Nearly all advanced countries have adopted special carve-out statutes to validate set-off and netting on insolvency in financial markets because of the risks involved. The statutes typically disapply a ban on insolvency set-off, permit contract terminations, provide that contract netting and set-off are effective against assignees and the like, disapply preference avoidance rules, and implement various other technical items. In many cases the netting validation is available only if the payments are two-way, ie the insolvent is credited with gains. In the case of some countries, particularly in the English common law group, the netting statute is the declaratory of the position for the avoidance of doubt.

Jurisdictions having carve-out statutes

11.17 At least sixty countries have these carve-outs, thereby covering many more jurisdictions out of the 320. They include the US, the UK, all Member States of the EU, Australia, Canada, Israel, Japan, Mexico, Russia, South Africa, South Korea, and Switzerland.

11.18 EU Member States have additional carve-outs resulting from implementation of the EU Settlement Finality Directive 1998 as amended (applying to recognised payment and securities clearing systems), the EU Financial Collateral Directive 2002 as amended (applying to a financial collateral arrangements between eligible business parties involving investments, cash and credit agreements), and the EU Directive on the Reorganisation and Winding up of Credit Institutions 2001. The EU Bank Recovery and Resolution Directive 2014 for the insolvency of banks allows the resolution authorities to implement rescue tools which could override set-off and netting, but there are protective carve-outs.

Excessive intricacy of carve-out statutes

11.19 The obvious problem with these statutes is that they are excessively intricate and over-detailed so that in a global world it is out of the question for traders on the floors to master the detail internationally. Even experts have to rely on traffic light systems which are bound to blur the detail. They are intricate because the carve-outs have different definitions of the parties and the transactions involved, sometimes depending on definitions within definitions.

11.20 If your case is protected by one of the carve-outs, then you do not need to explore other protections. But it is an immense task to find out whether you are protected internationally. I give an example of a carve-out in France. Article L 431–437 of the Monetary and Financial Code provides:

> Debts and claims resulting from all transactions on financial instruments, to the extent that such transactions are conducted in the context of the general rules of the *Autorité des marchés financiers*, or to the extent that they are governed by one or several master agreements complying with the general principles of national or international market master agreements, and governing the relationships between at least two parties, one of which is an investment services provider, or a public entity or an institution, an undertaking or an establishment having the benefit of the provisions of Article L. 531-2, [the definition also includes credit institutions, local authorities, clearing houses and international organisations of which France or the EU is a member; none of the parties may be a natural person] or a non-resident establishment with a comparable status, may be netted in accordance with the valuation procedures provided for in such rules or master agreement(s) and may give rise to the calculation of a single netted settlement amount.

> If there exist two or more master agreements between the parties, these parties may link them together so that the settlement amounts resulting from the netting that would be effected in respect of each master agreement pursuant to the preceding paragraph could then in turn be netted among themselves.

> Whenever any of the parties is subject to any of the proceedings contemplated under Book VI of the Commercial Code [believed to be amicable and judicial insolvency proceedings], the said rules or master agreements may provide for the automatic termination of the transactions referred to in the first and the second paragraphs of this Article.

> The termination, valuation and netting procedures contained in the rules or master agreement(s) referred to in the preceding paragraphs are effective vis-à-vis attaching creditors. Any termination, valuation or set-off effected on grounds of civil execution proceedings will be deemed to have taken place prior to the said proceedings.

> The assignment of claims arising under transactions governed by the master agreement(s) referred to in the first paragraph of this Article is effective vis-à-vis third

parties upon written consent thereto by the person whose obligation is assigned. In order to secure the obligations arising out of the master agreement(s), the parties may also provide for collateral arrangements, either by transfer of ownership, by way of security and fully effective vis-à-vis third parties without further formalities, of instruments, securities, notes, receivables or cash, or the creation of security interests over such assets and rights, enforceable even if one of the parties is subject to one of the proceedings referred to in the third paragraph of this Article. Debts and claims relating to such transfers and security interests and those relating to such transactions may then be set-off in accordance with the provisions of the first and second paragraphs of this Article.

The provisions of Book VI of the Commercial Code shall not interfere with the application of this Article.

11.21 This provision is not by any means the longest or the most complicated. That crown is taken by the US.

Protection of Insolvency Set-off by Governing Law

Free contract choice of insolvency set-off

11.22 In many cases, jurisdictions will apply their own rules as to set-off if the insolvency proceedings are opened in their territory. However, the EU Insolvency Regulation 2015 states in article 9(1) that, although set-off is governed by the law of the opening state, if that forum disallows the set-off, then the creditor obtains the set- off 'where such set-off is permitted by the law applicable to the insolvent debtor's claim'. It follows from this that a creditor can contract into insolvency set-off in a jurisdiction which does not otherwise permit the set-off by choosing a governing law, such as English law, for the debt owed to the insolvent since English insolvency law is probably one of the strongest jurisdictions permitting insolvency set-off. A similar rule applies to set-off between solvent parties under article 17 of Rome I on applicable contract law.

11.23 The Regulation applies to all debtors, except certain insurance undertakings, credit institutions, investment firms, and collective investment undertakings. See article 1. It does not apply in Denmark or, as a result of Brexit, in the UK (irrelevant because all UK jurisdictions allow insolvency set-off). The EU Directive on the Reorganisation and Winding up of Credit Institutions 2001 article 23 is virtually the same as the above article 9(1) and there is a similar provision in the corresponding directive of 2001 for insurance undertakings. The Credit Institutions Directive is dominated by bank resolution instruments in the EU which generally allow the authorities to override set-off and netting in the case of banks, subject to safeguards.

11.24 Austria, Belgium, Germany, and Spain, and perhaps some other EU Member States, apply the same rule as article 9(1) of the EU Insolvency Regulation to situations where the Regulation does not apply, eg because the centre of main interests of the debtor is outside the EU.

11.25 In addition, in the case of some jurisdictions the parties can contract into insolvency set-off by an agreement to that effect, eg in Belgium and Luxembourg. These two are jurisdictions which do not normally permit insolvency set-off.

11.26 Further, in some number of jurisdictions such as France and Spain, insolvency set-off is allowed if the claims are connected so that free contract might improve the connexity. This is still nowhere near the English mandatory set-off.

Other EU protections

11.27 Some other special protections in the EU should be noted. Article 12(1) of the EU Insolvency Regulation provides that, without prejudice to article 8 dealing with certain property rights, 'the effects of insolvency proceedings on the rights and obligations of the parties to a payment or settlement system or to a financial market shall be governed solely by the law of the Member State applicable to that system or market'.

11.28 Articles 25 to 27 of the Directive 2001/2001/24/EC on the reorganisation and winding-up of credit institutions are remarkable provisions which, like set-off, effectively allow the parties to choose their insolvency law for netting, repos and regulated market transactions. According to recital 26, the Settlement Finality Directive of 1998 as amended, is overriding.

11.29 Article 25 provides: 'Netting agreements shall be governed solely by the law of the contract which governs such agreements.' This is subject to the Bank Recovery and Resolution Directive 2014 article 68, that crisis measures may not of themselves lead to termination; and article 71 to the effect that resolution authorities have the power temporarily to suspend termination rights.

11.30 Article 26 provides: 'Without prejudice to article 24, repurchase agreements shall be governed solely by the law of the contract which governs such agreements.' This is subject to BRRD articles 68 and 71.

11.31 Article 27 provides: 'Without prejudice to article 24, transactions carried out in the context of a regulated market shall be governed solely by the law of the contract which governs such transactions.' It is not stated that these transactions must necessarily involve a credit institution. Some commentators have suggested that the governing law of these contracts must be the law of an EEA state, but this does not seem to be warranted.

11.32 It follows that, in all these cases, the governing law could play a role in attracting a law which allows set-off and netting. One would have to investigate precisely how these protections are implemented by Member States and how the various EU instruments interlock with each other.

11.33 Under the EU Settlement Finality Directive 1998 as amended, eligible payment and securities settlement systems designated by Member States as benefiting from the enhancements of the Directive, such as set-off and netting, must be governed by the law of a Member State chosen by the participants, and in practice in most of these Member States, regulated markets will be governed by the local law of a Member State. The UK has its own equivalent protections.

Comparative Survey

Armour-plated protections in English set-off

11.34 Probably the most protective set-off rules in the major jurisdictions are the English law rules. They are universal and you do not have to rely on a carve-out which is limited to restricted parties and restricted transactions, as opposed to all parties and all transactions. The exceptions are rare and those that exist are clear. The set-off rules cover all valid claims both ways (including contingent claims), make the set-off automatic, and allow it in rescue proceedings where there is a distribution to creditors. They make the set-off mandatory so that the court cannot override the set-off on the grounds that there was some pre-existing agreement not to set off—which there often is. The mandatory nature of this set-off is not available in any of the other families of jurisdiction, although it is shared by some members of the English group.

11.35 Outside the English common law group, in all of the other families and in the US, insolvency set-off is often considerably weaker for various reasons, particularly in that the law allows only the normal solvent rules to continue into insolvency so that, for example, there can be issues about whether claims which are contingent at the commencement of the insolvency, such as claims under guarantees, can be included in the set-off.

11.36 In addition, contrary to the position in most other permitting jurisdictions, the English suspect period preventing the build-up of set-offs in the suspect period prior to the commencement of proceedings is virtually zero: see paragraph 11.78.

11.37 The restrictions in the Corporate Governance and Insolvency Act 2020 on termination of contracts on the insolvency of a counterparty does not include any financial contracts, and set-off and netting arrangements are specifically allowed.

11.38 The provision in English law preventing restrictions on the assignment of contracts—which might prejudice set-off—is limited to small and medium-sized businesses and excludes all manner of financial transactions. This is less commonly the case with other jurisdictions which override non-assignment clauses. See Chapter 8.

11.39 The statute relating to the resolution of banks has special safeguards for set-off and netting arrangements.

11.40 The UK adoption of the UNCITRAL Model Law on Cross-Border Insolvency blocks the recognition of stays on set-off.

11.41 The English courts do not recognise judgments in foreign insolvency proceedings which interfere with contracts, such as by preventing their termination contrary to their terms, unless the party concerned participated in the foreign proceedings. See paragraph 6.53.

11.42 Set out below is a brief survey of the international groups, with specific mention of some of the main jurisdictions which are relevant to the governing law issue.

EU Restructuring Directive 2019

11.43 This directive provides a stay on certain insolvency proceedings of individual enforcement actions. Article 7(6) allows Member States to exempt netting arrangements. The precise implementation in each state should be checked.

Insolvency set-off in the US

11.44 All the US states have a basic insolvency set-off by virtue of BC 1978 section 553. However, it is stayed on commencement by section 362, although subject to adequate protection in the same way as a security interest. There are a number of carve-out provisions.

11.45 In the US, section 553 of the Bankruptcy Code does not create an independent right of set-off. Rather, it incorporates any pre-existing set-off right that may exist under state law. In practice, it is highly desirable that parties wanting a set-off should contract for the set-off pre-petition.

11.46 This is illustrated by the case of *Bank of America v Lehman Bros*, a decision of the US Bankruptcy Court, South District of New York in November 2010. Lehmans owed overdraft loans to Bank of America plus a large number of other claims, eg under derivatives. Bank of America owed a large deposit for around US$500 million to Lehmans, covered by a collateral agreement intended specifically to protect Bank of America in respect of the overdrafts it had granted to Lehmans. Lehmans went into a Chapter 11 bankruptcy proceeding in September 2008. There were no overdrafts at the time and Bank of America purported to set off other liabilities, eg on derivatives, owed by Lehmans to Bank of America against the collateralised deposits. *Held*: the set-off was only available for the special purpose of securing the deposit, not the other liability. In addition, Bank of America had violated the automatic stay on set-off contained in Chapter 11. Instead, it should have applied to the court for relief from the stay. In the circumstances, Bank of America lost its set off and had to hand back the US$500 million to Lehmans' estate. This would not have happened under English law.

11.47 The section preserves set-offs under state law, eg New York's Debtor and Creditor Law section 151. Section 362 freezes the debtor's estate at the time of the filing of the petition in bankruptcy. In particular, the commencement of a case in bankruptcy operates as a stay of 'the setoff of any debt owing to the debtor that arose before the commencement of the case ... against any claim against the debtor': see section 362(a)(7).

11.48 The effect is to require the intervention of a court to allow a right of set-off after the commencement of a bankruptcy case. The automatic stay does not defeat the right of set-off but postpones it pending an orderly examination of the debtor's and creditor's rights. It ceases to be self-help.

11.49 Hence, the party with a set-off has the protections available to a secured creditor in bankruptcy. If the creditor has a valid right of set-off, it will be treated as cash-secured to the extent of the creditor's right: see section 502. In the Supreme Court decision of

Citizens Bank of Maryland v Strumpf 516 US 16 (1995), it was held that a creditor may *temporarily* withhold payments owed to a debtor to the extent of its claim pending resolution of its set-off rights. The creditor must avoid any manifestation of intent permanently to settle accounts, eg by recording a set-off in its books and records at the time of the administrative freeze. Also, the creditor should seek relief from the automatic stay at or promptly after the imposition of the administrative freeze. Further, the set-off is treated as cash collateral and under section 363 the debtor would have to provide 'adequate protection' before using the funds. If the estate cannot provide adequate protection, relief from the automatic stay should be granted under section 362(d)(1). The overall effect is that, despite some wobble, the economic effect of set-off is preserved, most of the time. Nevertheless, the route to achieve this is tortuous and labyrinthine and the outcome is much less assured than in England. In England the set-off is mandatory and automatic.

11.50 Netting requires the ability of a party to terminate contracts with an insolvent counterparty. But in the US, there is a stay on contract cancellations on insolvency: BC 1978 section 362(e) provides that (subject to carve-outs) an executory contract may:

> not be terminated or modified ... at any time after the commencement of the case solely because of a provision in such contract or lease that is conditional on:
> (A) the insolvency or financial condition of the debtor at any time before the closing of the case;
> (B) the commencement of a case under this title; or
> (C) the appointment of or taking possession by a trustee in a case under this title or a custodian before such commencement.

11.51 Hence, netting in the US depends on the complicated carve-outs for financial markets.

Set-off in the English common law jurisdictions

11.52 It is believed that almost all the jurisdictions in the English common law jurisdictions have insolvency set-off based on a Bankruptcy Act going back to the earliest codification in England in 1705, repeated in around a dozen subsequent versions. The present form was more or less settled in BA 1869, which made the set-off mandatory. It was this form or its successors (often BA 1914) which was introduced into the law of British colonies and adopted in Australia and New Zealand.

11.53 In *England*, the present provisions are in IA 1986 section 323 for individuals, IR 2016 r 14:25 for company winding-up and IR r 14:24 for administrations. The set-off is not stayed on an administration and is required by case law to be honoured in schemes of arrangement. As mentioned above, the set-off is universal and mandatory.

11.54 In *Singapore*, the winding-up provisions in the Companies Act chapter 50 absorb the insolvency set-off provisions of BA 1995 section 88: see CA section 327(2). Set-off is not stayed on a judicial management and ordinary solvent set-off applies: *Electro Magnetic Ltd v Development Bank of Singapore* [1994] 1 SLR 734. For *Hong Kong*, the Companies Ordinance absorbs the set-off in the Bankruptcy Ordinance section 35. For *Australia*, see the Corporations Act 2001 section 553C. For *Israel*, see the Companies Ordinance absorbing set-off in the Bankruptcy Ordinance as decided by *Haspaka Central Agriculture Corpn Ltd v Agra* CA 4316/90, 49(2) PD 133. Check if the set-off might be stayed under the Companies (Second Amendment) Act 2002. For *India*, see the Insolvency and Bankruptcy Code 2016. In *Ireland*, see now CA 2014, which absorbs the Bankruptcy Act set-off. Unlike England, the set-off is not mandatory. In *Barrington v Bank of Ireland* (26 January 1993, unreported) a bank had agreed to rely solely on security given by a customer without further recourse and so was held to have waived its set-off—this was a non-bankruptcy case. The set-off is not stayed on an examinership.

11.55 In *New Zealand*, the corporate set-off clause is in CA 1993 section 310. However, the statutory management for banks under the Reserve Bank of New Zealand Act 1989 section 122 and under the Corporations (Investigation and Management) Act 1989 section 42 both stay set-offs, subject to carve-outs.

11.56 The set-off is mandatory in at least Australia, Bermuda, England, Hong Kong, Northern Ireland, and Singapore. The advantage of this is that a court cannot find, for example, that a creditor has waived the set-off since the mandatory set-off overrides any prior agreement not to set off.

11.57 In *Canada*, the set-off preserves provincial rights of set-off but does not create an insolvency set-off. See the Bankruptcy and Insolvency Act section 97(3) and the Companies' Creditors Arrangement Act section 18.1.

11.58 In *Mauritius*, the Insolvency Act 2009 provides in section 309 for a compulsory insolvency set-off of mutual claims on the lines of the English set-off clause.

11.59 It is also believed that most jurisdictions in this group do not have general rules nullifying the termination of ordinary executory contracts on insolvency, apart from land leases, utilities, and any special legislation affecting banks and insurance companies. Australia freezes termination clauses in certain cases. There are stays on contract terminations in Canada and (unusually) in New Zealand. The freeze on termination clauses in the UK does not apply to the financial sector and exempts set-off and netting arrangements specifically.

Insolvency set-off in the Napoleonic jurisdictions

11.60 These jurisdictions either adopted or were influenced by the French bankruptcy legislation of 1807, 1838, and its successors which prohibited insolvency set-off, except (by case law) for transaction set-off and set-off in a single current account. A transaction set-off is a set-off which arises out of the same contract, such as where a buyer sets off a breach of warranty claim owed by the seller against the buyer's liability to pay the price. This is of little help for independent transactions. The prohibition was continued in French bankruptcy codes of 1889, 1955, 1967, and 1985. The prohibition is founded on bankruptcy code provisions which state that the debtor may not make any payments after bankruptcy (for France, see ComC L621–624) and on Civil Code provisions that set-off must not affect the acquired rights of third parties, eg Belgium CC article 1289. Set-off is considered a form of payment and is therefore prohibited on bankruptcy. The old Luxembourg ComC article 444 to that effect is typical of the Napoleonic tradition but Luxembourg itself now has insolvency set-off by contract. Since then, France has (by case law, codified in 1994—now ComC article L621–624) widened insolvency set-off to extend to connected transactions and this case law may influence other Napoleonic states, especially former colonies.

11.61 It is believed that the Napoleonic bankruptcy codes did not and do not nullify contract termination clauses on insolvency. However, statutory freezes were introduced in France (1985), Belgium (1998), Portugal (2004), and Spain (2003), subject in each case to netting carve-outs. Luxembourg has never had a freeze on contract cancellations. An EU Directive mandates freezes on contract terminations.

11.62 The carve-outs for contractual set-off and netting in Belgium and Luxembourg are extremely wide, but not as wide in France.

11.63 The main exceptions to the normal objection to insolvency set-off in this group are Italy, which in BA 1942 section 56 introduced insolvency set-off, Belgium, which by the Financial Collateral Act 2002 effectively introduced contractual set-off on insolvency for corporates, and Luxembourg, which did the same in the Financial Collateral Arrangements Law 2005 articles 18 and 19.

11.64 Spain allows transaction set-off on insolvency.

Insolvency set-off in the Roman-Germanic jurisdictions

11.65 In *Germany*, insolvency set-off is in IA 1999 section 947, recognising the ordinary solvent set-off rules in BGB sections 387–390 and explicitly contractual set-off. Check also the German implementation of the European Restructuring Directive 2019 – previously case law imposed a freeze on contract cancellations. There are some carve-out sections. The same rules apply to final bankruptcies and reorganisations.

11.66 Insolvency set-off in *the Netherlands* is found in BA 1896 article 53, which extends the Civil Code right of solvent set-off to insolvency proceedings. For *Sweden*, see BA 1987 sections 15–17. Reorganisation stays on contract cancellations in Sweden. In both cases, check the scope of implementation of the EU Restructuring Directive 2019. For *Switzerland*, see the Debt Enforcement and Bankruptcy Act articles 213, 214, extended to composition proceedings by article 297 (4) allowing set-off.

Insolvency set-off in the Mixed civil/common law jurisdictions

11.67 *Jersey* has mandatory insolvency set-off on English lines: Bankruptcy (Désastre) Jersey Law 1990 article 34, imported into creditor winding-ups of companies by the Companies (Jersey) Law article 166.

11.68 In *China*, IL 2006 article 40 states that 'a creditor who owes a debtor to the debtor prior to the acceptance of the petition for insolvency may set off his claim against a debt owed to him'.

11.69 In *Japan*, insolvency set-off is available under BL 2005 article 67 and, on different terms, under the Corporate Reorganisation Law 2003 and the Civil Rehabilitation Law 1999. There is carve-out netting legislation for financial markets.

South Africa does not have insolvency set-off, subject to a South African financial markets carve-out. See *Re Trans-African Insurance Co Ltd* 1958 (4) SA 324(W). **11.70**

Unlike the English insolvency set-off clause in the bankruptcy rules, the law in *Scotland* has no statutory regulation of set-off in the insolvency, but case law leads to broadly similar effects of set-off in Scotland on insolvency to those applicable in England. However, the Scottish insolvency set-off is not mandatory and it is not self-executing, ie it is not automatic. **11.71**

Bankruptcy law in Canada is federal and so *Quebec* is subject to this: see Canada under the English common law group. *Panama* was originally Napoleonic, but has insolvency set-off by statute. **11.72**

In all of the other groups, notably the Islamic and new jurisdictions, the allowance of set-off and netting is either unclear or unusual. **11.73**

Set-off mutuality

Virtually all jurisdictions which permit set-off on insolvency also require that the criss-crossing claims are mutual, that is, each party is the beneficial owner of the claim owed to it and is personally liable on the claim owed by it. If you could have a set of involving a claim owed to a third party, then the property of the third party would be used to pay somebody else's debt by the set-off, as in the case of set-offs between a bank on the one side and parent and subsidiary on the other. **11.74**

The establishment of mutuality is crucial for central counterparties in formal clearing systems, discussed at paragraph 10.74 and also in relation to group account netting. Both of these require elaborate structures to achieve mutuality and of course the set-off and netting will only work in a permitting jurisdiction. **11.75**

Most payment systems used to rely on non-mutual multilateral set-off, which were obviously void in the normal case on insolvency because the multilateral set-off led to an insolvent bank being deprived of a claim owed to it which was used up in a set-off between two other banks. The biggest payment system in the world, CHIPS in New York, is protected by a special statute, as is also the case under the EU Settlement Finality Directive 1998. Despite these awkward protections, most payment systems now do not rely on set-offs but rather require immediate payment of the gross amounts across the accounts of banks kept at the central bank. This is called 'real time gross settlement'. **11.76**

There are plenty of other key indicators related to the safety of set-off. I mention only two of them (next) but without getting into the international position in any detail. **11.77**

Avoidance of build-ups of set-offs

All permitting jurisdictions normally provide that if a debtor to a prospective bankrupt buys a claim against the bankrupt from a creditor in order to achieve a bankruptcy set-off at a time when it has notice of the actual insolvency of the prospective bankrupt, then this build-up of the set-off is not permitted. It is obviously a preferential arrangement. All the party owing money to the bankrupt has to do is to find a creditor of the potential bankrupt **11.78** who is probably not going to be paid by the bankrupt and therefore will be glad to sell its claim for a higher price to the party concerned. In fact, the suspect period for this build-up is very short in English insolvency law. The cut-off is when the creditor had notice of a winding-up petition or certain similar events: see IR 1986 rule 14.25. The position of a creditor is worse in the US on these build-ups because debts acquired by the creditor from a third party within ninety days of insolvency commencement are excluded from set-off, even if the acquirer did not know of the actual insolvency. This creates a three-month unpredictable risk period. In general, an improvement in set-offs in the ninety-day period is invalid in the US. See the Bankruptcy Code 1978 section 553.

Set-off against assignees and other intervenors

11.79 To be reliable, set-off must have no gaps in the law. It must be bulletproof.

11.80 A significant consideration is the situation where one of the parties to mutual debts assigns its claim to a third party. The effect is that the two criss-crossing claims are no longer mutual between the original parties and so the rules of insolvency set-off cease to apply. Instead, the creditor must be able to set off the claim owed to it by the original debtor against the claim now held by the assignee who, of course, will not wish the claim it has bought to be diminished in this way.

11.81 The issue depends upon the rules for set-off between solvent parties and the timing of a notice to the assignee of the assignment. The rules are extremely complicated but the situation can be controlled in many, if not most, jurisdictions, by a contract between the original parties allowing the creditor to set off because this contract will normally bind the assignee.

11.82 There are still some excruciatingly difficult questions as to the timing of these contracts and what constitutes notice with the result that the best way to avoid the risk is to forbid assignments altogether. Under English law, if there is a prohibition on assignments which is wide enough, then an assignment is void, apart from a minor exception relating to small businesses. However, in a great many other jurisdictions, as we have seen, this protection is missing because clauses prohibiting assignments can be void or restricted: paragraph 8.33.

11.83 You can get similar problems in other cases where other third parties take over and intervene in one of the claims so as to destroy the mutuality. These creditors can include those who take a charge over a receivable, an attaching creditor, undisclosed principals of an agent, and an undisclosed beneficiary under a trust. Under English law these can usually be prohibited, as in the case of assignees and, in the case of attachments (where the creditor cannot prohibit the attachment), English law is normally protective of the set-off.

11.84 Because English set-off is restricted where both parties are solvent, in order to protect the principle of 'pay now, litigate later', a party wanting a set-off should insert a clause to that effect. This is also desirable in other jurisdictions for a variety of reasons. Set-off clauses are found in the ISDA master agreement and are very common in syndicated bank credits.

Conclusion

The overall effect of the above is that insolvency set-off is strong in England and the English common law group, strongish in the US, fairly strong in the Roman-Germanic group, and weak or absent in the Napoleonic group and most of the new or transition groups. Insolvency set-off has been improved in France and even more so in Belgium and Luxembourg. In most developed countries, a carve-out statute authorises set-off and netting for eligible contracts and eligible parties, usually for financial markets. **11.85**

The international position on preventing the termination of contracts on insolvency is patchy. Netting is not possible where these provisions apply, unless there is a carve-out. England remains firm on both set-off and netting. **11.86**

12
SECURITY INTERESTS

What are Security Interests and their Key Indicators?

What is a security interest?

12.1 The second of the three super-priority insolvency indicators to be discussed is the security interest—mortgages, pledges, charges, and the like. The term 'charge' is a generic term in England for these. There are other terms in common use in various jurisdictions, such as lien, hypothecation, or encumbrance. The term 'collateral' is often used to refer to the assets covered by the security, but equally it is common to refer to a debt being 'collateralised', which means secured.

12.2 We must not be dragged into the obscure technicalities of definition which vary from jurisdiction to jurisdiction, except for one significant difference. In US jurisdictions, the law on the subject is codified in article 9 of the Uniform Commercial Code, a code whose central ideas have been borrowed by many other countries, including Canada, Australia, and New Zealand, but not including England. A crucial concept in the article 9 jurisdictions is that the rules relating to pledges and charges, etc. also apply to certain sale and lease transactions which have a similar effect to charges but are still sales or leases, such as sale and repurchases (repos), factoring, and the securitisation of receivables, financial leases, hire purchase, stock lending, sale and leaseback, and retention of title to goods. Article 9 lumps together core charges and pledges with these title finance transactions and calls them generically 'security interests'. This is now the most common generic term internationally and is the one which I adopt, although it will refer either to core charges and pledges or to these core transactions as well as title finance, according to the jurisdiction.

12.3 The fact that we have to spend time at the outset on these obscurantist definitions is a sign of the mess this subject has got into internationally. In addition, the world is in disarray on the legal policies. The cacophony of conclusions springs from the fact that creditors can voluntarily give themselves a super-priority over other creditors on insolvency simply by agreement with the debtor, without the consent of other creditors. The law is made unnecessarily even more complicated by the alleged profusion of situations, since there are at least fifty different classes of assets which the law thinks merit special treatment and since the number of legal issues which the law thinks it necessary to consider in putting together a security package is also somewhere around forty, many of them obsolete and overlapping, but depending on the jurisdiction.

12.4 This chapter covers the eighth letter in the sequence of the thirteen themes expressed in the mnemonic PIB—FEISST—CoRCO, standing for *p*redictability, *i*nsulation, *b*usiness orientation, *f*reedom of contract, *e*xclusion clauses, *i*nsolvency law, *s*et-off, *security interests*, *t*rusts, *co*rporate law, *r*egulatory law, *c*ourts, and *o*thers.

12.5 We will see that the governing law can play a material role in the mitigation of risks in relation to security interests.

Security interests are a protection against insolvency

12.6 Security interests are fundamentally a protection against the insolvency of a debtor. They are not needed unless a debtor can always pay. Sometimes commentators point to other advantages, including control and defence of the assets (a shield but not a sword), but these pale before the basic objective. Hence, security interests are like set-off—they only matter when somebody is insolvent and cannot pay.

Key indicators of security interests

12.7 In order to measure security interests on a comparative basis, it is necessary to identify the key indicators of security interests. These are considered to be the following:

- *Scope*: The indicator here is the assets which the security interest can cover, that is, the scope of the security, especially whether the assets have to be specifically identified as opposed to generically, thereby excluding future assets, especially floating assets such as inventory and receivables. A second limiting factor is whether the jurisdiction requires unfeasible possession of goods or virtual possession of receivables by the giving of compulsory notice to the debtor in respect of those receivables. A few jurisdictions, especially in the Roman-Germanic group (notably Germany) object to over-collateralisation which hinders the advantages of clean universal security suitable for, say, small corporates and single purpose companies. In substance, the key indicator is whether universal security over all present and future assets generically is or is not allowed.
- *Secured debt*: The indicator here is the scope of the secured debt, whether it includes all present and future debt generically or whether it is limited to debt which can be specified, with or without maximum amounts and maturity dates. Another issue is whether the debt can be expressed in a foreign currency or must be in a local currency. Other questions are whether prepayments can be disallowed (important for stability of the bond required for insurance companies paying pensions and others), whether capitalised or penalty interest is allowed, and whether interest stops on the commencement of an insolvency.
- *Publicity*: In most jurisdictions, security interests have to be publicised by actual possession where possible, notice to the debtor in respect of receivables, registration in an asset title register (such as for land, shares, intellectual property, ships and aircraft), or by registration in a corporate or other register indexed by debtor rather than asset. Sometimes all these methods are required, but there is much variation.
- *Priority over unsecured creditors*: As mentioned above, the whole purpose of security is priority on insolvency over unsecured creditors. The key indicator here is therefore whether some favoured creditors rank ahead of security, notably employee remuneration and benefits and taxes. This head includes the expenses of the insolvency

administration (which can be a significant percentage in some jurisdictions), and any post-commencement security for new rescue money allowed by insolvency law over the heads of existing secured creditors. This question is a matter resolved by the bankruptcy ladder of priorities.

- *Enforcement, especially on bankruptcy*: The final key indicator is how easily the security interest can be enforced, especially on the bankruptcy of the debtor. There is no point in taking security, however wide the scope, if obstacles are placed in the way of enforcement. The end is as important as the beginning. The main obstacles are a requirement for a judicial order for enforcement (which can operate as a grace period running into years), public auctions, freezes of sales on the commencement of the bankruptcy, rights of the insolvency administrator to use the assets without adequate protection, and exclusion of accessories to the collateral arising after the commencement of the insolvency, such as rights issues in respect of shares and future revenues. Together these can in some jurisdictions have a cataclysmic effect on a security interest. The law gives and then takes away.

12.8 There are other key indicators, but it is not feasible to explore them all. They include such items as the following:

- whether a trustee of security interests is allowed (a trustee facilitates the administration up security for a syndicate of banks or for bondholders and also facilitates loan transfers which involve an assumption of liabilities by banks)
- whether there are problems about guarantees or prohibitions on the grant of financial assistance by a company to purchase its own shares (both of these relevant to the financing of takeover bids for companies)
- whether the grant of security within the suspect period after the debtor has become actually insolvent is a voidable preference on judicial insolvency—a critical question for work-outs
- the priority of the security interest as against other secured creditors and buyers or of the collateral and previous owners. This is a weak indicator because, in practice, the difference between jurisdictions on these priorities is less than in the case of the main key indicators, so there is less clash. A short almost universal code for the priority hierarchy from junior to senior is: first in time, overridden by first to get the best public title for the asset (sometimes only if without notice), overridden by those claiming to improve the asset (such as a lien for repairs or a purchase money security interest, often known as retention of title to goods), overridden by a priority expressly or impliedly consented to by the secured creditor, such as the holder of an English floating charge (who inevitably consents to ordinary course of business sales of inventory and other floating assets)
- costs, stamp duties, and fees (often also a significant percentage).

International summary

12.9 An international summary ranking of the favour given to corporate security interests, excluding consumers, is first English-based jurisdictions (with some weakening in England itself), together with US common law jurisdictions; second Roman-Germanic jurisdictions;

and third Napoleonic jurisdictions. Mixed civil/common law jurisdictions depend on the dominant influence in the mix. Security interests in the new or transition jurisdictions vary considerably from the medium to the poor, but subject to a couple of advanced and sophisticated regimes, eg Moldova. In most Islamic jurisdictions security interests are undeveloped and the market relies on security substitutes, such as title finance transactions whose validity depends upon the severity of the relevant Islamic school of jurisprudence. More detail on these conclusions is given later in this chapter.

12.10 The main point for us in this chapter is whether a creditor taking security can minimise the risks and maximise the value of the security by a free choice of law and courts. In general, the key issues are decided by one of five legal systems. These are:

- the governing law of the security agreement, which is generally within the free choice of the parties but subject to mandatory overrides of the courts, which could include bankruptcy laws
- the governing law of an asset included in the collateral, especially contract claims where the parties to those contract claims can choose the governing law of their contract
- the location of the collateral. There is normally little scope for a secured creditor and the debtor to shift assets into a more favourable jurisdiction, but this can be done for bank accounts
- the location of the court adjudicating upon the issue which in our context will generally be the court adjudicating upon a bankruptcy in the opening state. Generally, a secured creditor will have little control over the location of the bankruptcy court, which is either at the centre of main interests of the debtor or where the debtor has a branch. Most insolvency issues are governed by the law of the bankruptcy forum, but some are parked off to the law of the location of the collateral. Either way, the secured creditor cannot usually control this issue by a free choice of governing law
- the prevailing law at the place of incorporation of the debtor. This law will obviously cover such matters as the powers and authorisations of the corporate debtor, which are generally straight- forward, but in a large number of jurisdictions the place of incorporation decides whether you have to register a security interest in a register indexed by debtor, as opposed to a title register such as a land register. Registration in one of these corporate registers is usually a straightforward matter which can easily be checked and complied with. The problems arise in jurisdictions which require collateral to be registered in the territory where the collateral is located, sometimes only if the debt corporation also has a branch there: these requirements can be hard to check.

12.11 The fact that there are so many competing jurisdictions and that jurisdictions differ fundamentally on who gets the right to apply their law makes a predictable approach infeasible in the case of situations where the debtor has many classes of assets scattered all over the world. It is even more problematic to carry out due diligence when in, say, a takeover, the target has subsidiaries in sixty or seventy jurisdictions, all granting security. However, even in this case there are methods of mitigating the risks. In those cases where the risk cannot be managed, then the risk simply has to be brought into account in the evaluation of the credit risk of the financing.

Use and Importance of Security Interests

Importance test of key indicators

12.12 One of the components of key indicators is the economic importance of the indicator. A useful way of obtaining a rational perspective on the importance and use of security interests is by summarising the type of situations in which security is most used, which in turn facilitates an examination of what risks can be managed by, for example, choice of governing law, and which cannot be managed by a secured creditor. In the main I disregard the special case of consumer finance of goods—in practice these goods are usually cars.

Home loans

12.13 Probably the largest sector comprises home loans which may amount to two-thirds of gross domestic product in many countries. The importance of this sector is shown by the fact that a bubble in home loans nearly brought down the world financial sector in the global financial crisis of 2007/2008. In this sector, secured creditors inevitably have to take whatever legal risks there are under the domestic law of where the homes are situated—such as the scope of local mortgages, restrictions on enforcement, and controls under bankruptcy and consumer credit laws locally. These transactions are not internationally mobile, although theoretically they could be.

Special purpose companies

12.14 Much enterprise finance on a large scale is now conducted through the medium of special purpose companies. These are companies set up to own and operate a project or a single ship, aircraft, or real property, or to make a bid for another company, or to act as a securitisation vehicle. These special purpose companies are formed mainly to ensure that the project or other business is insulated from the bankruptcy of the shareholders and that the shareholders are insulated from the bankruptcy of the new business. They do not usually have general creditors, they have a negligible number of employees and no pensioners, and they are not permitted to incur debt outside their single purpose operations and the finance for the project or other activity. Although the main assets of project companies tend to be concentrated in the territory of the host government, they can have assets elsewhere, such as bank accounts, and their contracting parties, such as construction contractors, suppliers and buyers of, say, the project product, can be anywhere. The security covers all of these contracts as well.

12.15 Ships and aircraft are of course experienced travellers.

12.16 Some securitisations can involve receivables owing by debtors in different jurisdictions. The special purpose company is usually incorporated in a tax haven jurisdiction which also has favourable laws relating to security interests, such as the Cayman Islands, which is an English-based jurisdiction.

The amounts involved in this class of secured credit for all types of special purpose vehicles are extremely large worldwide.

Small and medium-sized companies

These often create universal security in favour of the house bank to the maximum extent this is permitted in the relevant jurisdiction. These businesses tend to be local and therefore conflicts issues are less likely to arise. They are private companies which do not issue bonds to the public. Their financing needs are usually served by a single house bank so there is no need for the complications of common security. If they are dissatisfied, their remedy is to switch banks. The very large number of these businesses in developed economies is a significant political force which hence can drive pro-debtor policies by populist governments in relation to security interests, as well as insolvency law generally.

Publicly listed companies

Public companies do not usually borrow secured. Instead, they borrow from banks and bondholders unsecured but with a negative pledge, which restricts the group from creating security in favour of other creditors so as to ensure that the banks and bondholders are not subordinated. This means that the commanding heights of the economy are outside the debate.

However, these large companies do grant security in special situations and the charge is then as universal as it can be locally. If they get into financial difficulties, then the grant of security may be a condition of last resort finance from banks.

Secondly, public companies which are taken over are usually de-listed and converted into private companies and these companies may then give guarantees to the banks financing the bid and grant security over their assets for the guarantees, where this is permitted by rules against a company giving financial assistance for the purchase of its own shares or those of its holding company, or by director fiduciary duties. This would commonly be the case with public companies taken over by other public companies or by private equity funds. The result is that very substantial companies within a target group grant security to a syndicate of banks.

The syndicated credit agreements for public companies typically contain a clause providing for a mandatory prepayment if there is a change of control, so that very often existing banks will join a new syndicate to finance the target company and perhaps also make loans to the bidder to finance the takeover.

Sovereign states

It is unusual for sovereign states to grant security interests to creditors, although state-owned companies may do so, and infrastructure financing by other sovereign states through state-owned banks may involve security over concession land and related assets. If they do grant security, then this is usually a sign that the sovereign state is in financial difficulties or has a poor credit rating. Their bond issues, if any, will normally not permit security for other tradable bonds but typically will allow security to be granted to banks and others for non-tradable debt. The security may be granted over the proceeds in commodity bank accounts externally, perhaps by a set-off arrangement which would not qualify as a security interest.

Trade finance

12.24 Secured trade finance is probably a diminishing sector. Here, the bank of the buyer issues a letter of credit to the seller's bank, and the buyer's bank takes a pledge over the documents of title to the goods, plus the insurances and sometimes the benefit of the contract of sale. These are short-term security, often lasting no more than a few weeks at most. The amounts involved are tiny compared to the other sectors and the security is often extremely straightforward since it involves mainly a simple pledge of goods where the problems are well understood.

Financial markets

12.25 A major sector comprises the grant of security by banks and other financial institutions for their obligations in payment systems and in financial markets. The security may also be created by major corporations trading in these markets, including derivatives. The legal issues are simplified by the fact that the collateral is usually highly liquid: most of the collateral is a cash deposit or government debt securities since the collateral must have a readily ascertainable market value and be quickly realisable, often within minutes. In many cases, the security over investments is a sale and repurchase (repo) of the securities rather than a security interest. The finance is typically short-term, sometimes overnight only. Repos would be typical of central bank overnight finance to commercial banks.

12.26 Collateral is also required to secure exposures of participants to central counterparties whose object is to be insulated completely against risk so far as possible. These central counterparties are explained at paragraph 3.62.

12.27 An important sector of this market is collateral provided by hedge funds and investment banks to support commercial bank loans to finance proprietary trading in investments and derivatives.

12.28 Although the collateral may be simple, the complicating factor is that the amounts involved are extremely large so that a very high degree of predictability is required. Financial market security interests are so fundamental as a protection against systemic risks that some states have introduced sledgehammer legislation which in effect enables security interests in financial markets to be treated in accordance with the contracts of the parties and which override the interferences of insolvency law and publicity requirements. See, for example, the EU Settlement Finality Directive 1998 and the EU Financial Collateral Directive 2002, as amended.

Title finance

These transactions are effectively substitutes for security interests. The main title finance transactions are financial leasing, sale and repurchase ('repos'), sale and leaseback, securities lending, hire purchase, the factoring of receivables, securitisations, and retention of title of goods. Some of these transactions are big ticket such as the financial leasing of aircraft and repos in financial markets, while other transactions do not involve significant amounts. The retention of title to goods attracts an attention which is quite disproportionate to the amounts involved, which are considered small in relation to other sectors of title finance and trivial in relation to secured finance generally. **12.29**

One of the main conflicting issues in relation to title finance is whether the transaction is recharacterised as a security interest in relation to such issues as publicity, insolvency freezes on repossession, and duty of the financier to return the surplus proceeds of realisation to the debtor. Factoring is a niche method of financing. **12.30**

The financings based on large-scale receivables are usually achieved by securitisations where the originator of the receivables sells them to a special purpose company which finances the purchase by a bond issue and grants the bondholders security over the receivables and all its other assets. **12.31**

Conclusion

The effect of the above is that we can narrow down the important fields in the business sector (ignoring home loans) to (1) project finance and securitisations using special purpose vehicles, (2) privatised companies which have been taken over, (3) small and medium-sized companies which generally obtain all their finance from a single bank, (4) financial collateral in financial markets, and (5) big ticket financial leasing of equipment. The main exclusions are public listed companies and sovereign states. **12.32**

Notwithstanding the exclusions, it is clear that security interests are of enormous economic importance internationally and therefore that this eligibility test of the key indicators is satisfied. **12.33**

Comparative Law of Security Interests

Pros and cons of security interests

The rationale in favour of security includes arguments that the person who pays for the asset should have the right to the asset if that person is unpaid (the lender is normally in substance buying the assets for the debtor and the debtor should not keep the asset without paying for it), the need to protect creditors on insolvency (banks hold the money of the citizen and so indirectly it is the citizen who is protected), the encouragement of capital for enterprise finance, the reduction of the cost of credit, the encouragement of rescues (since the lender feels safer for longer or because the lender provides last resort money), and, **12.34** especially in project finance, security is a defence against attachments by unsecured creditors of essential assets, thereby holding the project to ransom.

12.35 The disadvantages are often said to be that the security violates bankruptcy equality, that security disturbs the safety of commercial transactions because of priority risks, the secured creditor that can disrupt a rescue by selling an essential asset, that security confers too much power on the secured creditor, and that security might encourage careless lending.

12.36 Where the charge can be universal, the arguments in favour of universality include the above, together with the reduction of transaction costs, that in practice trade creditors continue to be paid until the position is really hopeless, the business can be sold as a whole which enhances the value, the problem of competing security interests and overlaps are avoided, and it is not necessary to add new assets by lists and supplements.

12.37 The disadvantages are said to be that the security is monopolistic and gives the creditor too much power, that nothing is left for unsecured creditors, and that the automatic grasp of security over subsequently acquired assets is theoretically preferential.

12.38 All of these arguments are hotly contested, but the overall consensus internationally seems to be that security interests have a fundamental role to play in finance and enterprise. The main contests are not about whether security interests should be allowed, but rather their scope.

Security interests according to the families of jurisdictions

12.39 The strength of security interests worldwide falls into the now familiar classification of strong in the English-based jurisdictions, weak in the Napoleonic jurisdictions, and medium in the Roman-Germanic jurisdictions. There have been improvements in a few members of the Napoleonic group, especially in France and Belgium. In any event, the split three ways was part of the Triple Polarisation in the nineteenth century.

12.40 Security interests are of little value in most Islamic jurisdictions: they use title finance, such as conditional sales, as substitutes, with varying degrees of approval according to the Islamic school of jurisprudence (because of the prohibition on interest). They are episodic in the new jurisdictions. In the mixed/civil common law jurisdictions, the question turns upon the dominating family in the mix. On this issue, they usually fall into the Napoleonic or Roman-Germanic class, except for Quebec which has a universal security interest on North American lines. China has its own approach, which is codified.

12.41 On the one end, the traditional English common law jurisdictions (now with some qualifications in England) permit a company to create a universal charge over all of its assets, present and future generically (fixed over more permanent assets and floating over fluctuating inventory and receivables) to secure all its present and future debt owed to the creditor generically. The company can theoretically do this in ten lines and register it once only in a central registry kept by the registrar of companies. If so provided, the secured creditor can, on an express event of default on a few hours warning, call in all the moneys secured, and immediately by a simple letter, without the involvement of the courts, appoint a possessory receiver, usually an accountant, to manage the collateral—which is all the assets of the company. The receiver displaces the powers of the directors. The receiver can use and sell the collateral according to the secured creditor's timing. Enforcement is immediate and there is no need to switch off the power station.

A portion of the collateral—coming out of the floating charge over the bulk receivables and bulk goods in the main—is subject to the payment of prior unsecured preferential creditors, notably employee wages, taxes, and administration expenses. This universal security is available only to companies, not to individuals. Hence, it was able to develop its liberality and freedom without the pressures of protecting consumers. **12.42**

If you want to be able to raise money via this wide security, you have to incorporate but it is possible to have a one-person company so that the system is readily available to very small businesses with only one or two proprietors. It has an elementary simplicity and lack of formality. **12.43**

Regrettably in England this exceptionally simple regime, which worked so well in providing credit to the enterprise, which cheapened the cost of credit, and provided a swift and effective method of rescuing a business via a receivership, was weakened by the abolition of receivership in 2002 except for a few special cases (although replaced by a simple administration instead), by rescue rules which enabled the administrator to use the floating assets (but not the fixed assets) without formal adequate protection, and by a line of unsatisfactory cases ensuring that charges over receivables were always floating charges, hence being subject to the priority of preferential creditors, unlike fixed charges: see *Agnew v Commissioner of Inland Revenue* [2001] 2 AC 710 and *Re Spectrum Plus Ltd* [2005] 2 AC 680 (HL). The overall result did not have a significant adverse effect on recoveries but nevertheless revealed a tendency to obfuscate and fiddle with a system which was a model of efficiency and fairness in practice and therefore advantageous to businesses as well. **12.44**

At the other end of the scale are traditional Napoleonic regimes based originally on France (although now considerably improved in such countries as France itself, Belgium, and many others). Virtually none of the above is possible. For most of this group, it is not legally possible to create a security of all the assets generically to secure all obligations generically, largely because future assets are excluded and because assets have to be specified or because you have to take actual possession of assets, which is not feasible. Enforcement typically involves the courts and hence extensive delays and high costs. Because individual traders can grant the security, the restrictions were considered to be justified in the case of individuals and companies alike. There is a high degree of formality, eg notarisations. **12.45**

Meanwhile, the jurisdictions based on Germany, the Netherlands, and Scandinavia—the Roman-Germanic jurisdictions—developed a class of security interests between the two extremes of the traditional English and the traditional Napoleonic. Security interests in Germany and the Netherlands are almost as wide in scope as the English fixed and floating charge, and do not require public registration (everybody knows that small businesses are in hock to their banks and public listed companies do not borrow secured, so who is interested—the others are either financial collateral or else special purpose companies which do not have general creditors). Germany has a principle of over-collateralisation, which restricts the amount of collateral that can be taken to a percentage of the secured liabilities, based on the good faith doctrine. A big chunk of enforcement proceeds on **12.46** insolvency goes to unsecured creditors—generally 9 per cent but up to 25 per cent if one includes taxes. Japan and Korea also have quite wide security based on the German model, but not Taiwan. There are some general business charges in Scandinavia but they are not as wide as the English model, and Swiss security has less scope over floating assets than the German and Dutch equivalents. Most of these countries do not have a public register indexed by debtor for security interests over movables.

12.47 France liberalised its security interests over the past couple of decades, although there is as yet no generic universal charge over all present and future assets. However, security fares badly on bankruptcy by reason of the prior payment of preferential creditors and administration expenses, the power of the courts to impose a moratorium on debt, and the absence of adequate protection rules for collateral during a rescue proceeding. Luxembourg has a quite wide general business pledge. Belgium reformed its security interests in 2013 by introducing a reasonably comprehensive pledge of a business and providing for private sales of collateral over movable assets.

12.48 The US version is different: see below.

American and English security interests

12.49 The English and American regimes for security interests represent the greatest number of jurisdictions and the widest acceptance internationally. Both of these regimes espouse the need for universal security interests whereby a debtor can charge all its present and future assets generically to secure all its present and future obligations (but less so in the US), and each of them allows a relatively rapid enforcement via a private sale if so provided. They differ on some quite significant points. The US version was codified in article 9 of the Uniform Commercial Code.

12.50 The American regime applies in all fifty-one jurisdictions in the US and also in Puerto Rico, Guam, the Marshall Islands, Micronesia, Palau, and Liberia. It has been adopted in Australia, Canada (except Quebec), New Zealand, and about thirty-four other mainly small and low income jurisdictions, mostly in very slimmed down versions, eg Afghanistan. Its biggest converts are Mexico and (to some extent) Nigeria.

12.51 The American system can be best understood by its history.

12.52 When work was started on article 9 of the UCC in the late 1940s onwards, most states of the US at that time had extremely poor regimes for security interests. They had nothing anywhere approaching the simple English universal charge which would cover all present and future assets to secure all present and future debt generically. Instead, there was a medley of chattel mortgage statutes, accounts receivable acts, and various other provisions which in their requirements for specificity, control, and possession, their limitations and their problems with enforcement were not altogether different from the current regimes in many traditional Napoleonic states with poor security interests.

12.53 The problems were compounded by adverse case law, in particular the notorious case of *Benedict v Ratner* 268 US 353, 45 S Ct 566, 69 L Ed 991 (1925).

In *Benedict v Ratner*, Aaron Ratner made a loan to the Hub Carpet Company of US$30,000. As security for the loan, the company agreed to assign to Ratner all its present and future accounts receivable. The carpet company sent Ratner a list of the receivables monthly but continued to collect the receivables and to use the proceeds as it saw fit. The carpet company became bankrupt. *Held* by the US Supreme Court: the assignment of the accounts receivable to Ratner was in essence a fraudulent conveyance. Mr Justice Brandeis, deciding the matter on the law of New York, pronounced the basic legal proposition: 'Under the law of New York a transfer of property which reserves to the transferor the right to dispose of the same, or to apply the proceeds thereof, for his own uses is, as to creditors, fraudulent in law and void.' The court held that Aaron Ratner could not have a security interest because he had no ownership and because he had no dominion.

12.54 In contrast, the universal charge, as exemplified by the English universal charge, allowed the debtor to have full control and complete dominion of its assets so it could deal with them in the ordinary course of business, other than fixed assets such as land.

12.55 The result of this decision and the general regime was to torpedo US secured lending based on manufacturing assets such as inventory and receivables. The creditor had to have a degree of control and dominion, which of course was not possible.

12.56 As a result of this situation, financiers had to resort to all kinds of title finance transactions instead, such as leases, conditional sales, and retention of title. Hence, when the draftsmen of article 9, especially the eminent jurist Professor Grant Gilmore, came to prepare article 9 they were faced with the almost universal use of title finance transactions to escape the misfortunes of the law relating to security interests. It was natural that they should resolve to bring all of these devices, which they saw as evasive, within the scope of a security interest. The decision was therefore taken that all title finance would be recharacterised and treated as a security interest, including sales and leases of goods, including outright sales of receivables. This had a number of significant consequences, including treatment asset by asset—at least forty different classes of assets. It seemed to the legislator that each asset deserved special treatment, which in fact is doubtful. The result is that article 9 has the clunky feel of the Napoleonic regimes.

12.57 Article 9 covers only movables and then not all of them. It does not cover land, ships, or aircraft or rolling stock or insurances or most tort claims. It does not cover all intellectual property. The result of the splitting was that the American system requires separate security for these assets. The law of land mortgages in many US states is pro-debtor. For example, in some US states, a lender cannot claim for the unsecured balance if the proceeds of sale are insufficient to pay back the loan.

12.58 The English law regimes do not recharacterise title finance as a core mortgage and charge and maintain a strict division between core mortgages and charges and other financing transactions, even though the other financing transactions are very similar to core mortgages and charges. But the article 9 regime does. As mentioned above, title finance covers such transactions as: retention by a seller of title; sale of receivables in order to raise finance—commonly called factoring or discounting; sale and repurchase transactions; finance leasing; hire purchase; and sale and leaseback.

12.59 The issue is not whether title finance transactions are often very similar to security interests in substance, although the form is of a sale or lease. There is no doubt that often they are, but nevertheless a sale or lease is a sale or lease. It is not a loan secured by a charge on the sold or leased property. This is not just a question of where one should draw the line. The main question is whether title finance should be thrust into the cage of the law, particularly the bankruptcy law, relating to security interests, or whether it should be left to fly free.

12.60 Generally speaking, a creditor under a title finance transaction is usually worse off if the deal is recharacterised as a security interest. This is because it becomes subject to all of the restrictions on security interests and in particular the transaction loses the super-super priority it would often have on insolvency, even ahead of a secured creditor. The international position is intricate and varies from jurisdiction to jurisdiction, except that under English law the courts strictly do not treat title finance transactions as a security interest, with all its accompanying disadvantages, but the article 9 jurisdictions do.

12.61 Some of the adverse areas which have to be considered in relation to recharacterisation include registration or filing, freezes on enforcement on bankruptcy, loss of super-super priority by virtue of the ability to repossess ahead of secured creditors, compulsory grace periods, subordination to post-commencement financing, compulsory judicial public auctions instead of private sale, rules allowing an administrator to use, sell, or lease the collateral, rules that the financing party can use the collateral for its own purposes (which the finance party could do in the case of securities lending or a repo), vexatious challenges on acceleration and repossession, formalities of security interests and the use of notaries, plus higher costs, usury limits, and perhaps being subject to a worse priority right. The market practice is that financing parties are generally required by the documents to return excess proceeds of sale, as they would in a secured transaction.

12.62 In English-based jurisdictions, security interests by individuals are very poor in the case of movables. By far the largest demand for individual finance in most jurisdictions is for cars and other vehicles, and less so for household goods. The gap is filled by title finance, such as hire purchase and leasing.

Financial Collateral Directive 2002 and Settlement Finality Directive 1998

12.63 These two directives, as amended, apply to all European Union Member States and are absorbed into United Kingdom (UK) law. The Financial Collateral Directive dramatically enhances the validity and enforcement of both security interests and title transfers, including repos, in respect of investment securities, cash, and credit claims. It removes perfection by registration, allows immediate realisation on an enforcement event, thereby overriding public auction, solvency freezes, judicial orders, and the rights of an administrator to use the property, gives a right to use the collateral if so provided, and recognises title transfers and netting, amongst other things.

12.64 The parties must be financial institutions, insurance companies, central banks, and the like, but members can allow one of the parties to be any person but other than a natural person, if the other party is a prescribed institution. The UK implementation allows both parties to be any person other than a natural person so that the rules are not limited to financial institutions.

12.65 The Settlement Finality Directive 1998, as amended, sweepingly validates transfer orders, netting, and collateral in payment and securities settlement systems governed by the law of a Member State and designated as eligible by the Member State concerned. In effect, the directive overrides insolvency laws interfering with these matters, including in relation to central counterparties.

12.66 By way of contrast, the EU Restructuring Directive 2019 imposes stays on the enforcement of security, amongst other things.

Aircraft and ships

12.67 Note that a large number of states are contracting parties to the Cape Town Aircraft Convention 2001, including European Union Member States, the UK, and the US. This provides for the registration in Dublin and protection of international security interests and certain title finance transactions for aircraft.

12.68 As regards ships, the 1926 Brussels Convention on Maritime Liens and Mortgages regulates priorities for these maritime liens, maybe in favour of suppliers to the ship, and mortgages. The Convention was not accepted by many major maritime states, including many British-related jurisdictions, because of its protection for trade liens over the ship mortgage. This stance was characteristic of the English protection of financial creditors over trade creditors.

Governing Law and Security Interests

Role of the governing law of security interests generally

12.69 As discussed above, a secured creditor is faced with the reality that, apart from the financial terms of the secured liabilities, such as a loan or bond issue, most of the other important issues relating to security interests are not controllable by the governing law chosen in the security agreement. For example, everything to do with the scope of the security and the publicity necessary for the validity of the security is decided by the location of the collateral or place of incorporation of the debtor, neither of which is controlled by the governing law. Anything to do with enforcement, such as whether a court order is required for a sale, is decided by the law of the court where action is brought, not the governing law. Anything to do with bankruptcy proceedings, such as a freeze on enforcement, the right of the administrator to use the collateral, and the priority over unsecured creditors, such as employee benefits, taxes, and administration expenses, are decided by the law of the opening state or of the location of the collateral, not the governing law of the security agreement. These are generalisations, but, whatever the detail, the freedom of a creditor to manage the risks is dismally reduced. The objections to security are so powerful that, in practice, the law of the location of the security is dominant. Sovereign states are determined to control the law governing assets which are, or are deemed to be, within their territorial domain. We are therefore back to legal restriction and the mnemonic 6C–TRITO

12.70 The section discusses some possible methods of maximising the security of a secured creditor and minimising the risks by the choice of governing law and courts and by structuring the secured transaction.

Governing law of contract for security agreement

12.71 The parties can freely choose the governing law and courts for the credit agreement or other secured debt with the result that the terms of the secured debt, but not the security itself, will be governed by the governing law, except for mandatory laws of the forum and bankruptcy overrides. This contract will or should determine factors such as the financial terms, the covenants, the events of default, protections of the secured creditor, and the like. Hence, the parties can choose predictability, insulation of the obligations from local law, insulation from bankruptcy interference (if English law), the efficacy of assignment clauses, immediate acceleration and termination of commitment, exclusion clauses, and the scope of the governing law and its conflicts rules. English governing law is favourable on these matters.

12.72 The free governing law is subject to local court or location rules—the secured creditor cannot control these normally. As always, the powers and authorities of the debtor will be governed by the law of the place of incorporation of a corporate borrower, but these are not usually problematic.

12.73 It is common practice in international deals for the financial agreement to be governed by an external governing law, say, English law, with an accompanying a choice of courts which is non-exclusive for the creditor, but limited to, say, the exclusive English courts for the debtor. This agreement will typically grant universal security over all present and future assets generically for the secured debt and provide for the fullest self-help and other remedies available, including private sale and possessory management of the assets through a receiver to the extent permissible. The agreement will also provide that the debtor will grant the maximum security over foreign assets parallel with the general security granted by the main security agreement. These parallel documents may have to be in local form, eg in the case of title registers for land, ships, aircraft, and perhaps other assets.

12.74 If a security agreement fails for non-compliance with any requirements, notably those applicable at the place of the location of the collateral, then under English case law an agreement to grant security is treated by the English courts as the actual grant of the security, for what that is worth. Better than nothing.

12.75 For guarantees, see paragraph 14.123. For financial assistance by a company to buy its own shares, see paragraph 14.47.

Scope of security interests

In English-based jurisdictions the scope of the assets can be or present and future assets generically. Subject to a very few exceptions, this is not the case in most civil code jurisdictions because, almost invariably, future assets generically are not covered unless they can be specified—the degree of specification varies from 'all my potatoes in my warehouses in Frankfurt' to 'all my potatoes in sack 34 in my warehouse in Madrid at 25 Calle Prado'. Future assets have to be added by lists which involves preference risks, costs, and non-compliance risks. This specificity requirement preventing future assets plus impracticable publicity requirements for receivables and goods are the main methods by which civil code jurisdictions reduce their security so that it is not monopolistic. Germany has a principle of over-collateralisation and the Netherlands a principle of abusive security. It would seem that all of these matters are decided by location, which is not normally controllable by the governing law.   **12.76**

A different problem arises if the best forms of security can only be granted to locally regulated institutions, such as local banks. That is just a fact of life.   **12.77**

Scope of collateral and publicity

Generally, the scope of the assets which may be covered by security depends initially on compliance with the publicity requirements for that asset. In the first place you look to the publicity requirements for where the asset is situated. Very broadly one can usually expect that: **12.78**

- goods are situated where they are (except for goods in transit);
- assets registered as to title (such as land, ships, aircraft, shares, intellectual property, sometimes vehicles), where the register is;
- bank accounts, where the bank account is kept;
- receivables and other contract debts, where the debtor is located or where its centre of main interests is; and
- book entry securities, in most important countries where the destination account is (known as the 'place of the relevant intermediary approach').

It is not normally possible for the secured creditor to arrange for the location to be changed, except in special cases, such as bank accounts for projects, and sometimes the location of the warehousing of goods, where the asset can be moved to a more favourable location by the debtor. Thus, the proceeds bank account for a project will usually be located with a syndicate agent bank outside the territory of the host government.   **12.79**

In the case of civil code jurisdictions, it is almost invariably the case that a security interest over an asset in a title register must be registered in that title register if it is to be effective on the insolvency of the debtor, and very often this will apply to book-entry securities as well, subject in the UK and the EU to the relief available under the Financial Collateral Directive. In English-based jurisdictions this registration is not necessary for validity on insolvency but it is desirable for priorities against competing security interests and the like. In some   **12.80**

American jurisdictions it is necessary for validity on insolvency to register a mortgage of land, which is outside the article 9 filing system for movables. Also, in some civil code countries (but not the Anglo-American jurisdictions), outside title registered goods, the creditor has to take physical possession of the goods or of the documents of title. This is usually impracticable, especially for inventory and equipment, unless there is a provision for a debtor-indexed register discussed below (as there sometimes is).

12.81 In the case of probably all English-based jurisdictions for all assets and for article 9 movables in the US, subject in both cases to various detailed exclusions, all that is necessary is to register the security interest at the place of incorporation of the debtor. Quite a few English-based jurisdictions (but not England itself) require registration if the asset comes into the jurisdiction and the corporation has a branch there or is doing business there. In cases of doubt, the practice is to send the details of the security documents down to the local companies registry anyway if it is thought that there might be an asset there. In the US, if the debtor is located in a jurisdiction outside the US and that jurisdiction does not have a public filing system generally, then filing is in the District of Columbia: see section 9-307(c). The law of the place of incorporation is not within the control of the governing law of the security agreement and so the rules there have to be accepted by a creditor as mandatory.

12.82 Priorities is too big a subject to deal with here, but they will often be a matter for the law of location. The priority of a title registered asset will typically be the timing of the order of registration.

Recharacterisation of title finance as a security interest

12.83 Whether title finance, such as a repo or financial lease, is recharacterised as a security interest and therefore subject to the clutches of security interest law, ought to be a matter for the governing law of the security agreement which expresses the intention of the parties. However, in practice a filing or registration statute in the territory of the place of incorporation of the debtor, is likely to override, and various other aspects eg in relation to enforcement and bankruptcy treatment of title transfers, will be outside the governing law of the security agreement and not controllable by a party choice of governing law. There may be cases, such as with financial leases and repos, where English law might help if it is desired to ensure that there is no recharacterisation. This is because the English courts make a strict division between mortgages and charges on the one hand and title finance on the other, which is not recharacterised (retention of title to goods is more complicated).

Trustees of security

12.84 It is common for a security granted to a syndicate of banks or to bondholders to be held by trustees for the creditors. This topic is considered in Chapter 13 on trusts. Many jurisdictions in the civil code jurisdictions do not recognise the trust. In many cases, the position is improved if the governing law of the trust is that of a jurisdiction which recognises a trust over all kinds of assets, which is the case with English and New York law (and, indeed, all other common law jurisdictions except Zambia, which abolished the trust after independence in the 1960s).

Permissible secured debt

Generally, English-based jurisdictions permit the grant of security by corporations to secure all present and future debt generically. In civil code jurisdictions, they are often requirements excluding future unspecified debt, requiring local currency and limiting interest on interest. You would think that these ought to be matters for the governing law of the security agreement, but in practice they might be considered as mandatory overriding rules by a local court and not controlled by the governing law. **12.85**

Transfers of secured debt

It has been noted at paragraph 7.26 that a requirement for the giving of notice to the debtor of an assignment of the secured debt can sometimes be avoided by choice of governing law. This would point to the choice of a governing law, such as English law, which does not have this requirement and whose courts also treat this as governed by the law of the debt included in the collateral, not the law of the location of the debtor in respect of that debt. **12.86**

Enforcement remedies

The question of enforcement remedies outside bankruptcy, such as whether a private sale or the appointment of a receiver or foreclosure is possible is likely to be an issue to be decided by the court concerned. English law is liberal on enforcement remedies. Most jurisdictions in the civil code group require judicial public auctions, except for marketable securities, self-help collection of receivables, and certain other cases. The intervention of the courts can lead to considerable delays and costs. **12.87**

Bankruptcy

Security interests are intended to be a bulwark against bankruptcy and attaching creditors. Bankruptcy interferences include freezes on enforcement, the right of an administrator to sell or use the collateral, the priority of preferential creditors, such as taxes, employee benefits, and the costs of the administration, subordination to post-commencement new loans, the loss of post-commencement property arising in respect of the collateral, such as dividends and interest on debts, and the avoidance of preferences. **12.88**

One can expect some jurisdictions to decide these matters according to the law of the opening state, but in fact the opening states will often refer these matters to the law of the location of the collateral. Thus, the EU Insolvency Regulation 2015 provides that where the debtor's centre of main in interests is in the EU, the opening of insolvency proceedings **12.89** in the Member State concerned does not affect the rights in rem—which includes security interests—of creditors or third parties in respect of assets belonging to the debtor within the territory of another Member State at the time of the opening of the proceedings: article 8. In other words, the collateral is immune from the Member State's bankruptcy proceedings. The UK is no longer bound by this Regulation but English case law establishes that a secured creditor will not be prevented from enforcing its security abroad so that, again, the collateral is insulated: *Moor v Anglo-Italian Bank* (1879) 10 Ch D 681. However, the courts where collateral is located may have very similar bankruptcy interferences. Hence, in neither case can the secured creditor manage these risks via the governing law of the credit agreement.

12.90 The situation with regard to the avoidance of preferences is more complicated.

Corporate structures to minimise risks

12.91 A method of minimising risks on security interests, often used in project finance and available elsewhere wherever the assets are held by a single purpose company, is to arrange for the shares of the project company to be held by a second company whose shares in turn are held by a top company. The middle and top companies are incorporated in an English-based jurisdiction, such as Cayman, which allows possession of security interests via a receiver and otherwise has sympathetic rules about collateral. The top company, which holds the middle company shares, charges the shares to the financing banks under a charge which enables receiver possession of the shares and other favourable remedies on a default. If the project company gets into financial difficulties, then, instead of the banks being forced to sell the project assets—which might be complicated and subject to local interference—the bank can take possession of the shares and thereby control the project company and can also sell the shares more easily than selling the project assets. The choice of location of the holding companies has to take into account taxation and the availability of a bilateral investment treaty confirming protection against expropriation and other political risks where the project company is located.

Conclusion

12.92 It seems clear that the key indicator of security interests satisfies the MISC tests of measurability, economic importance, symbolism, and a clash of conflicting views. The question of the strength of security interests also appears to be symbolic or representative of more general attitudes of the jurisdictions concerned in other key areas and to be broadly consistent with the ranking of the Anglo-American common law jurisdictions on one side, the Napoleonic jurisdictions on the other, with the Roman-Germanic jurisdictions in the middle. These generalisations are subject to considerable divergence within the family groups.

13

COMMERCIAL TRUSTS

Background to Commercial Trusts

Non-recognition as unjust enrichment

13.1 This chapter discusses the third of our super-priority claimants—beneficiaries who claim their property from somebody who is holding their property and who has become bankrupt. Maybe half or more of the countries in the world do not allow the real owners of the property to get their asset back from the holder and it is gobbled up by the creditors of the holder. What can justify this injustice, and enrichment out of somebody else's property, a kind of legalised expropriation, a taking? The requirement of a key indicator that it involves a clash or collision of views internationally is well satisfied.

13.2 This is a problem which has been grumbling on for centuries. The jurists of the world have been peering around searching for a solution to this simple moral question as if they were in the dark, even though the sun is shining.

13.3 The main purpose of this chapter is to show that the choice of governing law is internationally a very important means of reducing the risk of the non-recognition of a trust on the insolvency of a trustee. As with set-off and security interests, the test is bankruptcy. If everybody can always pay, then one does not need insolvency set-off or security interests or trusts (in most cases).

13.4 This chapter covers the ninth letter in the sequence of the thirteen themes expressed in the mnemonic PIB—FEISST—CoRCO, standing for *p*redictability, *i*nsulation, *b*usiness orientation, *f*reedom of contract, *e*xclusion clauses, *i*nsolvency law, *s*et-off, *s*ecurity interests, *t*rusts, *co*rporate law, *r*egulatory law, *c*ourts, and others.

What is a trust?

13.5 The essence of the common law trust is that one person has the public title to an asset, but the asset belongs to someone else and is immune from the private creditors of the trustee. For example, a custodian, such as a bank, holds the investments of a client in the name of the bank, but if the bank becomes insolvent or a creditor attaches assets of the bank, the investments cannot be taken by the creditors of the bank—the assets are separate, immune, are not assets of the bank. The trustee is the bank, but the real owner is the beneficiary.

13.6 It is irrelevant whether you call this a trust, a fiducie, or a fiducia, or Treuhand, or deposit, or bailment, or revendication (the Belgian term in Euroclear), or an in rem claim, or a separable claim, or the man in the moon. It is not the name which matters, but the function—are the real owner's assets protected from the creditors of the trustee?

13.7 If the trust is not recognised and there is no equivalent, then, for example, securities held by a custodian would go to pay the creditors of the custodian on its insolvency. That would be a taking, an obvious unjust enrichment, a legal scandal. But that is the default position in civil code countries which commonly do not recognise the trust universally. You would have to have a compelling reason to legitimise that.

13.8 There is a twist in the story. This is that, so far as I know, if you store your goods in a warehouse, the warehouse has the public title, which is possession in this case. But if the warehouse becomes insolvent, you as the beneficiary get your goods back from the warehouse. They are not taken from you and sold for the benefit of the creditors of the warehouse. So that is in essence the function of a trust, although technically called a bailment or deposit. If Roman traders put their jars of olive oil on a ship from Tunisia, they would get them back if the shipowner went bust during the voyage.

13.9 You therefore get the illogicality that if you put your chairs in a warehouse, you get them back everywhere if the warehouse is insolvent, but if you put bearer bonds in a warehouse, such as a bank vault, you do not get them back in nearly half the world (outside carve-out statutes).

13.10 Common law jurisdictions all recognise universal trusts over all assets present and future but most civil code states do not. Instead, they either have limited special trusts and, if not, various other devices.

13.11 The availability of the trust or otherwise is therefore an attribute which can be measured as a key indicator.

What are trusts used for?

13.12 When asked what trusts are used for, a commentator Pierre Lepaulle responded in a book on the trust in 1932, 'Almost everything'. Another commentator responded in a 1999 book on the principles of European trust law edited by Professor David Hayton, 'One might almost as well ask what contracts are used for.' Those observations may be something of an exaggeration, but there is no question that the idea of the trust is fundamental to the legal structure in the modern world.

13.13 The non-family uses of trusts vastly outrank the family uses by a stupendous multiple, once you start including uses like securities settlement systems, such as the Depository Trust Corporation in the US (half the world's GDP) and Euroclear in Belgium (one and a half times the GDP of the EU). These two institutions are the biggest trusts in the world and are effectively custodians of the securities they hold. The shadowy Cede & Co, which holds the Depository Trust Company (DTC) securities, is by far the largest trustee the world has ever seen.

13.14 A bank may act as a custodian of investment securities for safe custody and administration. A holder of global debt securities holds the global note for a clearance system. A depositary holds the benefits of a bank cash account for the owner of the investments. The amounts concerned are large. Financial institutions are required by regulation in the UK and the EU, and no doubt elsewhere, to segregate client assets. Lawyers and notaries hold client money on trust for their clients. In the case of client portfolio investment, a depositary holds title to the investments and can therefore collect, vote, and switch.

13.15 A trustee for bondholders holds the benefit of the covenant to pay and any security for that covenant in trust for individual bondholders: it would be impracticable for them all to have a slice of, say, a mortgage of land or a heap of receivables. Similarly, an agent bank holds the borrower's covenant to pay plus the security on trust for the syndicate of banks. A parallel debt structure is the conventional common law arrangement whereby trustees of security held by agent banks for a syndicate or by a trustee for bondholders. In addition to the borrower's covenant to pay the banks or bondholders, the borrower also agrees to pay the trustee and grants security to the trustee for this payment covenant. If the borrower pays the banks or bondholders direct, as is normal, there are provisions to prevent duplication of payment to the trustee.

13.16 This agent bank trusteeship is essential for the transfer of participations in a loan by a syndicate of banks where it is necessary also to transfer the obligations under the loan agreement of the selling bank, such as the selling bank's obligation to the borrower to make new loans, or to indemnify the agent bank, or to share recoveries under a pro rata sharing clause. If the agent bank holds the security in trust, then there is no problem about introducing a new transferee by novation or assumption of obligations (these are not a simple assignment of rights): the new transferee is merely a new beneficiary under the agent bank trust of the security interest for the loans. But if the trust is not recognised, then the security itself in favour of the new transferee might fail—a disaster for that bank. In Napoleonic jurisdictions there is generally an article in the civil code which recognises the new novated bank's security, but this is not so in members of the Roman-Germanic group, such as Germany and the Netherlands, who do not recognise this kind of trust. The desperate legal contrivances to get around this problem are unproven, thereby leaving a surprise ambush in a normal transaction carried out with great frequency.

13.17 Investment trusts and mutual funds hold the investments on trust for investors via a depositary. Pension and employee retirement benefit trusts hold investments in cash on trust for pensioners. In an equipment trust or a real estate investment trust the assets are held by trustees for investors.

13.18 In the case of depositary receipts, a company in one jurisdiction issues equity or debt securities to a depositary bank, which issues listed depositary receipts to foreign investors backed by a trust of the original securities. An example is an American depositary receipt. This facilitates wider investment than permitted by the original jurisdiction since transfers and administration are located locally rather than in the issuer's jurisdiction.

13.19 When a seller of land or securities remains on the register as the apparent owner pending re-registration after receiving the price, the seller effectively holds the asset sold on trust for the buyer, even though this is unperfected or unpublicised.

13.20 In many countries an assignment of contract debts is invalid on the insolvency of the seller if notice of the assignment is not given to the debtor. The seller should be holding on trust for the buyer.

13.21 In all these cases of a sale, if the seller's trust fails (which it does in many civil countries), the seller remains as the apparent owner. An insolvent seller is then paid twice, once by the payment of the price and then again when the seller's insolvent estate gets the asset back on the seller's insolvency because it has not been publicised.

13.22 A broker or an ordinary agent, whether or not disclosed, often holds the sale contract on trust for the principal.

13.23 Third party beneficiary contracts are almost universal.

13.24 In subordinations of debt, the junior creditor holds the proceeds of its subordinated debt for the benefit of the senior creditor. These standard turnover trusts of proceeds fail in many civil code countries on the insolvency of the junior creditor because this is a trust. They sometimes justify the failure on the basis that, for example, proceeds to be turned over arise after the commencement of the junior creditor's insolvency and are hence a deprivation of the bankrupt's assets.

13.25 Bank deposit protection schemes may hold contributions to the fund to compensate depositors in trust for them. This may also apply to travel agents.

13.26 A seller of land may take an advance deposit for the price and landlords may take caution money. Money may be paid to an escrow agent or auctioneer.

13.27 In building contracts, the construction employer may hold retentions on trust for the contractor (with a right to apply them towards unpaid amounts owed on a default by the contractor) or for sub-contractors.

13.28 An unsuccessful litigant may deposit funds to compensate those injured by a mass tort. A litigant may deposit moneys with a court official as security for costs.

13.29 We can ignore will trusts and trusts by spouses of the matrimonial home. We can ignore charitable trusts of shares of a special purpose company holding securitised assets so that the company is not a consolidated subsidiary of anybody and just an orphan. Not to mention the ordinary altruistic trust for a deserving charity.

13.30 Accordingly, it is clear that trusts satisfy the second eligibility requirements of key indicators that they are economically important.

Breakdown of key indicators

13.31 I deal with the commercial trust as a key indicator on a somewhat generic basis. It would be possible to break the subject down into a series of specific key indicators, such as custodianship, bondholder trustees, and agent banks acting as trustees of security interests for the banks.

International Survey of Trust Recognition

Common law jurisdictions

13.32 All the common law jurisdictions have a universal trust—that is, more than 45 per cent of the jurisdictions of the world, including the US states and also including Louisiana and

Quebec (mainly as a result of university gifts by Paul Tulane and McGill, which might otherwise have been lost). The only country actually to abolish the English law trust recently was Zambia—in a flash of post-colonial resentment. Pakistan Bangladesh, Singapore, and Hong Kong are common law jurisdictions.

Civil law trust statutes

13.33 In the civilian group, there are a few jurisdictions which have a trust law, although often excluding land. These jurisdictions include China, Japan, France, and a few others. Otherwise, jurisdictions in these groups have introduced trusts in tatters and fragments, a medley patchwork which covers only portions of the body and still leaves the rest cold and wet. Thus, there is here a law allowing custodianship of securities or a regulation sanctioning a mutual there, a trustee of bondholders to the left, and some other patch to the right. For custodianship in particular, there are other solutions, dodging around the boundaries of the dangerous territory of trust. A favourite is the ring-fenced special purpose subsidiary, as in the Netherlands. Another is a complicated form of mandate requiring an unpredictable disclosure of the beneficial interests of investors, as in Spain.

Napoleonic group

13.34 In the very large Napoleonic group, France introduced an express consensual trust in 2007. This was a major turning point in the history of law and an important step in France towards recovering the mediaeval heritage of French law which they had gifted to the English via the Norman conquest in 1066 and via subsequent entanglements between the English and the French. Most of the Latin American countries have statutory trusts, usually registrable and limited to banks and sometimes limited in other ways. These were probably inspired by British nineteenth-century capital and then American capital in the twentieth century. There are trusts of securities in Egypt and Lebanon. The latter found time to deal with this matter despite all the violent sectarian banditry which goes on in that beautiful country.

Other family groups

13.35 In the Roman-Germanic group, Germany, Austria, and Switzerland have trusts for securities, mainly for custodianship. There are various trusts for specific purposes in South Korea.

13.36 In the mixed group, there are wider trusts in the Southern African cone group of six, and in Scotland. China has a trust law which is virtually a codification of the English consensual trust—another major turning point. Jersey and Guernsey have limited trusts by statute.

13.37 In the new or transition group, Russia has a narrow five-year trust and a wider trust for securities.

13.38 This survey is not exhaustive by any means.

Objections to the Trust

Background

13.39 The 'trust' for goods was not allowed in civil code countries for land, mainly because of the desire to free up land which aristocrats were holding in trust for future generations of the family so that the land never came up for sale. It was not allowed for intangibles, such as custodianship of bonds, because of a historical suspicion of debt claims and investments—seen once as wispy ethereal creatures of legal fiction and not property at all. The legal scholars had other theories to justify this alarming situation.

13.40 The theoretical objections were articulated especially by the nineteenth century French and German codifiers, who were jurists largely influenced by Roman law as codified after the fall of Rome, especially in Germany.

False wealth

13.41 The first main objection they had is that of false wealth, a doctrine which we have already encountered in Chapters 3 and 7. This doctrine holds that creditors are deceived if debtors appear to have many possessions and apparent riches because they hold the visible title to them but in fact they are held in trust for somebody else and are not available to creditors. Many possessions, no assets. This objection is met by the fact that, apart from land and buildings, most of the assets held by corporations now are intangibles—receivables, investments, goodwill—so creditors are not misled by appearances. They cannot see the assets. The necessary transparency is achieved now mainly by financial statements and, if absolutely necessary (which is doubtful), by registration like security interests. One the one hand, it is ironic that Roman-Germanic jurisdictions like Germany and the Netherlands do not require the publicity of registration of all security interests on a corporate file indexed by debtor so that false wealth cannot be a problem for them. On the other hand, common law jurisdictions are fanatical about registration of security interests but do not care one jot about the non-registration of trusts (apart from more recent requirements here and there to notify beneficial interests in shares and other investments, inspired, like Henry VIII, by the tax authorities, now joined by other indignant interests).

Priority risks

13.42 The second main objection is that the presence of secret hidden ownership rights might destabilise transactions and give rise to unpredictable priority disputes. How could a buyer or mortgagee be safe if a third party could come out from behind the curtain and claim the asset? The common law answer to that is to protect the buyer or mortgagee by the rule that the hidden owner loses priority if the third party has no notice of the hidden owner and often even if they do have notice.

Other objections

The other objections are a miscellany. The most prominent is that trust can aid tax evasion. But so can companies, more so. The English King Henry VIII endeavoured unsuccessfully to abolish the trust in 1535 to augment tax revenues. There is a fear of fraud and fraudulent preferences or a fear of hiding embezzled assets—the Russian oligarch syndrome. But companies are by far the most pervasive vehicle for concealment.

13.43

Another fear is that property would be tied up forever and cease to be marketable, especially land. This can be met by requiring trust property to vest within a certain period, a solution achieved by perpetuity acts in English-based jurisdictions.

13.44

Some jurisdictions object to litigation being brought by the non-owners of a claim and seek to prevent proxy litigation. Others fear that trusts could be used to defeat forced heirship or other compulsory heirship rights, the formalities of probate, and the regulation of a deceased's inheritances—all anxieties relevant only to succession.

13.45

It would seem difficult to justify why these objections cannot be easily dealt with or why they would be seen as justifying the expropriation of the real owner of assets.

13.46

Doctrine of specificity

One of the most metaphysical and scholastic consequences of the obsolete doctrine of false wealth was that, if you cannot identify an asset specifically, then you cannot warn creditors about false wealth. This doctrine was used to block transfers, trusts, and security interests over future or floating assets generically, and over fungible assets—which investments generally are. The doctrine has had a baleful impact on legal systems and seems irrational. This is because you can identify assets generically in order to determine them. In the case of fungible securities, it is everywhere the case that, when dematerialised (unwrapped from a piece of paper), it is enough to identify the issuer and issue and then to allocate ownership by mathematical proportions, eg US$100 or 10 per cent of the amount of a bond issue, just as you can allocate mathematically the ownership portions of grain in a silo or oil in a tanker.

13.47

Impact on the tracing of illegal proceeds

In the absence of a specific statute allowing the freezing of criminal proceeds, the doctrine of false wealth and the resulting objection to the trust, in virtually all civil code countries, also block the ability of a rightful owner to trace embezzled or fraudulent or trust assets through transformations and mixed bank accounts and claim them ahead of the creditors of the fraudster—as you can in common law countries. This must surely be the ultimate in unjust enrichment—the creditors of the fraudster get the stolen assets ahead of the real owner. In common law countries, lawyers call this tracing or proprietary restitution. This is

13.48

an obscure term for nothing simpler than getting your property back which is stolen from you or which you parted with by mistake.

Short history of the rejection of the trust

13.49 The idea of divided ownership was rejected by the Napoleonic codes in the opening decade of the nineteenth century, mainly (as mentioned above) because of the desire to free land from generation-skipping trusts set up by aristocrats to keep land in the family. There was also a fierce desire to define ownership as an absolute right to the enjoyment and disposition of a thing, to rid property of feudal burdens, to facilitate capitalism, and to exalt the emotional desire to have and to hold—a melange of meaningless aspirations which had the opposite effect.

13.50 When the German codes were drafted in the second half of the nineteenth century, the same solution was adopted, notwithstanding a lament by Professor von Gierke that it was 'a horrible legal blunder—a scientifically unmotivated notion'.

13.51 For an account of the process, see the classic article by Vera Bolgár at the University of Michigan, 'Why no Trusts in the Civil Law?' (1953) 2 Am J Comp L 204.

Impact on legal systems outside Western Europe

13.52 Western Europe exported its legal systems largely in the nineteenth century so that now more than 85 per cent of the 320 legal jurisdictions of the world have a legal system fundamentally based on a Western version—common law, Napoleonic, Roman-Germanic, or a mixture. So that is why so many of the world's legal systems do not have the universal trust and why we are still debating this issue in the twenty-first century.

13.53 It seems desirable that the Western nations that exported their systems in the past should now show how they should be updated. This need for the trust generally is one of those areas. Others which are part of the same trio of super-priority claimants on insolvency in the common law systems are insolvency set-off—which is weak in the Napoleonic group—and security interests, which can be weak in many civil systems. It makes no sense that the EU countries, which were once the unchallenged leaders of law in the world, an essential bedrock of modern societies, should now not be able to resolve these major problems of the Triple Polarisation of legal systems which happened in the nineteenth century. The three issues are systemic.

13.54 If the US, Japan, China, the UK, and India can get by with the trust, without causing anarchy, chaos, and economic collapse, why not continental Europe and the rest of the world?

13.55 As stated above, France boldly reinstated the fiducie in 2007 after the upsets of the Revolution in 1789. After all, it was France who exported the trust to benighted England back in 1066 when the Normans invaded. France actually picked it up from the Romans. So the trust is not English by origin. It is thoroughly European.

Maximisation of Trust Recognition and Risk Mitigation

Objectives

13.56 The object of this section is to explore possible methods whereby parties may maximise the recognition of a trust and minimise the risks that the trust may fail, potentially leading to significant losses. These losses are measurable as the difference between the value of the trust assets and the dividend that a beneficiary would receive as an unsecured creditor on the insolvency of the trustee. These losses could be enormous if, say, a custodianship of securities fails.

13.57 We are dealing here only with business trusts, not with family trusts or will trusts.

Governing law of the trust contract

13.58 Apart from the immunity of the trust assets, the contract contained in the trust instrument, such as the trustee's duties, exclusions of liability, and termination clauses, should be governed by ordinary principles of the governing law of a contract. It is true that article 2(1) of Rome I on contract applicable law excludes 'the constitution of trusts and the relationship between settlors, trustees and beneficiaries', but it is considered that similar principles apply to the contractual aspects of a trust as opposed to the proprietary aspects. The position is similar to a security agreement where very obviously you can separate the contract of loan from the grant of the security interest. The parties should therefore by choice of governing law be able to select such principles as predictability, freedom of contract, business orientation, and insulation from adverse foreign laws such as exchange controls and moratoriums, in relation to the trust contract itself.

Hague Trust Convention 1985: governing law of the trust

13.59 In the case of those jurisdictions that have implemented the Hague Convention on the law applicable to trusts and on their recognition of 10 January 1986 (often given its 1985 date), the immunity of the assets of the trusts from the private creditors of the trustee is decided by the governing law of the trust. Hence, the parties can minimise their risks of non-recognition of the trust by choosing a governing law which allows the trust, such as English or New York law, if the situation falls within this Convention.

13.60 Subject to relatively minor variations, the Hague Trust Convention applies in the UK (England, Scotland, and Northern Ireland) by virtue of the Recognition of Trusts Act 1987. Amongst common law jurisdictions, the Hague Convention has also been implemented by (amongst others) Australia, Hong Kong, Gibraltar, the Isle of Man, Canada, Bermuda, the British Virgin Islands, the Turks and Caicos Islands, and Montserrat.

13.61 Amongst civil code and non-common law jurisdictions, the Convention has been implemented by China, Italy, Liechtenstein, Luxembourg, Malta, the Netherlands, San Marino, Jersey, and Guernsey.

13.62 China, Liechstenstein, Malta, Jersey, and Guernsey have statutory trusts anyway, at least over movables for the last three.

13.63 A trust is 'governed by the law chosen by the settlor. The choice must be express or by implied in the terms of the instrument creating or the writing evidencing the trust, interpreted, if necessary, in the light of the circumstances of the case': see article 6. Hence, the Convention supports free choice of governing law. If the law chosen does not provide for trusts or the category of trust involved, the choice is not effective and the law specified in article 7 applies. Where no applicable law has been chosen, a trust is governed by the law with which it is most closely connected in accordance with various factors set out in article 7, broadly corresponding to centre of gravity tests.

13.64 According to article 11, recognition implies in particular:

  (a) that personal creditors of the trustee shall have no recourse against the trust assets;
  (b) that the trust assets shall not form part of the trustee's estate upon his insolvency or bankruptcy.

13.65 This reflects the essential immunity of the trust assets from the creditors of the trustee, a concept set out in article 2, which states that a trust has the characteristics that 'the assets constitute a separate fund and are not a part of the trustee's own estate' and 'title to the trust assets stands in the name of the trustee or in the name of another person on behalf of the trustee, as well as a trustee's duty to apply the assets in accordance with the terms of the trust'.

13.66 There are reservations in article 15, unimportant exceptions in article 16, and a public policy override in article 18.

13.67 Contracting states may reserve the right to apply the recognition requirements only to a trust the validity of which is governed by the law of a contracting state: see article 21. The UK did not make this reservation.

> In *Akers v Samba Financial Group* [2017] UKSC 6, it was held that the Convention would apply notwithstanding that the trust was in respect of assets located in a non-trust jurisdiction.

Location of trust assets under EU Insolvency Regulation

13.68 The law of the location of the trust assets may provide a further escape from lack of a trust, but only if the trust is located in a jurisdiction which recognises the trust.

13.69 The EU Insolvency Regulation 2015 generally provides for the application of the insolvency law of the Member State in which proceedings are opened. Proceedings must normally be opened at the centre of main operations of the debtor in the Member State concerned, but secondary proceedings where the debtor has an establishment can also be opened. The Regulation no longer applies in the UK.

13.70 Under article 8(1) of the EU Insolvency Regulation 2015:

> [t]he opening of insolvency proceedings shall not affect the rights in rem of creditors or third parties in respect of tangible or intangible, movable or immovable assets—both

specific assets and collections of indefinite assets as a whole which change from time to time, belonging to the debtor which are situated within the territory of another Member State at the time of the opening of proceedings.

13.71 One of the particular examples of the rights in rem which benefit from this provision is 'a right in rem to the beneficial use of assets'. See article 8(2)(d). This should include trusts. There are detailed rules in article 2(9) as to where assets are situated.

13.72 The effect of article 8(1) is that the opening of insolvency proceedings does not affect these rights in rem at all, which in our case means that the beneficiaries' rights would not be affected if the asset concerned is located in another Member State. Article 2(9) states that the Member State in which assets are situate means in the case of claims against third parties (except bank accounts) the Member State within the territory of which the third party required to meet them has its centre of main interests. It is somewhat unclear whether these claims are limited to ordinary debt claims such as contract claims, receivables, and the like or whether claims could include property claims by a beneficiary under a trust. The latter is preferable.

13.73 If under these location rules the trust asset happens to be located in the jurisdiction in which the insolvency proceedings are opened under the EU Regulation, then that jurisdiction will apply its own law; thus, the law of the opening state determines 'the assets which form part of the estate': see article 7(2)(b). This probably means its own substantive law, not its conflicts rules. But the Hague Convention may override pursuant to article 85(3) of the Regulation which reserves certain prior conventions.

13.74 The concept that the immunity of beneficiary assets under a trust should be decided by the governing law is underlined by the Hague Convention on Indirectly Held Securities 2003 and Article 8 of the American UCC, both of which deal with book-entry securities held in settlement systems—which are in substance trusts, by whatever name they are called. Both these instruments apply the law of the place of the relevant account to decide such matters as the validity of transfers, and in both cases the parties can normally decide the location according to the governing law of the account.

13.75 The article 8 exemption does not apply to assets situate outside Member States. Those assets are completely outside the Regulation: the opening state should determine the effects of insolvency in accordance with its own conflict rules, not the Regulation rules. In practice, the law of the location is predominant in most states in relation to property matters. For example, Australia, Belgium, Germany, and Spain have applied the Regulation rules to cases outside the regulation.

13.76 Other possibly relevant rules in the Regulation relate to payment and settlement systems (law of the Member State where the system or market is—article 12), and title registered land, ships, aircraft (law of the Member State where the register is—article 14).

Location of trust assets at domicile of trustee

13.77 Many jurisdictions may well follow the traditional view that the question of in rem rights, that is, rights to property as opposed to contract rights and including rights under a trust, is determined according to the location of the property, eg land where it is, goods where they are, and intangible claims where the debtor is. It would often not be feasible to track down the location of all the assets. Jurisdictions should arguably decide the location of trust assets as being situated at the office of the trustee—which could be in a common law country. This would be consistent with the location of bank deposit accounts and the international consensus that intangibles are located where they are enforced. This ought to apply to proprietary intangibles as much as it does to debtor–creditor claims. The beneficiary's claim under the trust is a different asset from the real asset and is often classified as a movable because it is realised in cash, even if it is land which is held on trust.

13.78 To strengthen this location argument, documents could state that the claims of the beneficiaries against the trustee are enforceable and situate where the trustee is located, and that the trustee must maintain these records and its administration of the trust in an approved trust country.

13.79 The Cape Town Aircraft Convention has its own regime on aircraft-related trusts. If the above analysis is correct, then the registered aircraft mortgage held by the trustee should be located at the place of the register in Dublin in Ireland which is a common law country recognising the trust.

13.80 The above arguments about location are presently tentative, but as a matter of prudent risk reduction it is better to have an argument which might succeed than no argument at all.

Recognition of trusts under a foreign governing law

13.81 If the trust is set up under a foreign governing law, such as English or New York law, the foreign trust may be recognised in a country which does not normally recognise trusts. An example is the groundbreaking *Belvedere* case of 13 September 2011 decided by the French Supreme Court.

> In the *Belvedere* case of 13 September 2011, the French Supreme Court recognised the right of a trustee of security under a trust agency governed by New York law and also a 'parallel debt' structure. A New York bank had filed a proof claim against Belvedere, a Polish company undergoing safeguard insolvency rescue proceedings in France, on behalf of bondholders owed £375 million. The security agent was appointed under a trust deed governed by New York law. Two other banks, acting as security agents filed proofs of claim of the same amount in their capacity as legal owners under a parallel debt structure. The argument that the security agent bank was just a proxy was rejected. Only the legal owner, or its specially appointed proxy, is entitled to file a claim in French safeguard insolvency rescue proceedings. The trustee had not been specially appointed as proxy, but the court held that under New York law the security agent bank was the legal owner and this did not contravene French public policy. Although the filing of claims was under the EU Insolvency Regulation governed by French law as the location of the proceedings, the question of whether the trust agent was the owner of the receivable was governed by New York law. Under the parallel debt structure, the issuer agreed to pay the bondholders and also the security agents on the basis that a payment to either the issuer or the agents discharged the other. The security secured the parallel debt. The court held that this did not lead to double

payment. It was comparable to a joint obligation. In fact at that time France had already introduced a *fiducie* into French law—in 2007.

A number of other countries recognise valid foreign trusts, eg Croatia and Romania. **13.82**

Conclusion

The commercial trust satisfies the eligibility tests of a key indicator, that is, it must be measurable, important economically, and reveal a clash or conflict between jurisdictions. It is considered that it also satisfies the test of being symbolic or representative of wider attitudes and hence useful as a more general indicator beyond the narrower confines of the specific indicator itself. In the case of the commercial trust there is clearly a divide between common law and civil code jurisdictions. However, instead of the Napoleonic jurisdictions being at the opposite pole to the common law jurisdictions, it is now generally Germany and some of the Roman-Germanic group which occupy this opposite pole as regards the commercial trust. **13.83**

The risk of no-recognition of a trust can often be mitigated by stating that the trust is governed by the law of a common law jurisdiction or sometimes by locating the trust in a common law country. **13.84**

14

CORPORATE LAW INDICATORS AND RISKS

Governing Law and Corporate Transactions

Shares compared to bonds

14.1 Why are corporate lawyers less interested in governing law than financial lawyers?

14.2 The main reason is that the centre of corporate law is the share, not a bond or a loan. Unlike a bond, a share in a company is governed by the law of the place of incorporation and cannot be governed by a law chosen by the company or the shareholder. Hence, a choice of governing law and courts to protect the shareholders' position as regards its shares and to manage the risks of a governing law is not available. With one swipe shares are thrown out of the governing law arena.

14.3 Shareholders are less interested in achieving the predictability of the terms of the share. These characteristics are contained in the constitution of the company and the terms of the share issue. But bondholders require the absolute predictability of the events of default and their ability to accelerate if there is an event of default. Bonds do not have votes for the management and they derive their 'vote' and their bargaining position from the covenants and events of default in the bond. For them, there must be certainty and predictability that they are entitled to that vote by virtue of their right to call a default. It is that right which gives the bondholder or lending bank a seat at the negotiating table. A shareholder on the other hand has a right to vote as the holder of the share and does not need covenants to control management actions since ultimately they can elect management. In any event, shareholders cannot normally cancel their shares and demand repayment because, unlike bonds and loans, their shares are usually permanent. It follows therefore that one of the main risks involved in the choice of governing law, ie whether the chosen governing law honours the need for predictability, is less relevant to shareholders, and hence to the centre of corporate transactions involving shares.

14.4 Shares are not as much involved with key indicators based on freedom of contract or business orientation, as is the case with financial contracts such as syndicated bank loans and international bond issues. There are many varieties of share and many varieties of protecting shareholders in corporate law, but shares are shares and you take what local corporate law gives.

14.5 The insulation of a contract, such as a syndicated bank loan, from foreign moratorium legislation and foreign exchange controls is highly significant and existential in some cases in financial transactions. See Chapter 6. You can achieve the maximum insulation by choice of governing law of a loan or bond. But you cannot change the governing law of a share to achieve insulation from similar interferences. The investor has to fall back on other protections, such as bilateral investment treaties or incorporating abroad.

14.6 You cannot move yourself as a shareholder up in the bankruptcy ladder priorities by a set-off or a security interest. Bankruptcy set-off is only available between debts, not shares. A company can secure a bond by a mortgage or charge, but a company cannot secure its liabilities under a share. Shareholders are therefore not in the least concerned with the bankruptcy ladder of priorities, which is a key concern to bank lenders and bondholders, as well as other financial creditors. Shareholders are at the bottom of the ladder of bankruptcy priorities. They are generally not able to prevent that subordination and therefore are the first to lose everything on the bankruptcy of the company.

14.7 In return for the inability to manage the risks concerned, shareholders generally profit more than creditors in terms of earnings and, unlike debts, the value of their shares can go leaping up if the company does well. One reason for this is that the company can leverage itself up by borrowing very large sums of money from banks rather than raising money from shareholders with the result that, after paying off the creditors, very large profits and increases in value go to the shareholders first. If they have a tiny stake in the overall capital, eg 2 per cent, and the other 98 per cent is borrowed money, then, if the profits are 105 per cent, 98 per cent plus 5 per cent for interest goes to the lenders, and the remaining 2 per cent goes to the shareholders. The lenders therefore make about 5 per cent, while the shareholders double their money—a 200 per cent return. That is called leverage and explains why there are so many private equity firms around buying companies where the acquisition is financed almost completely by bank money. Doubling your money each time is good business—if you can get it to work.

14.8 Perhaps another reason for this relative indifference to the management of risk by governing law in the case of corporates is that they are typically debtors to financial institutions and not creditors, so that, for example, the ordinary corporate might take the view that the predictability of events of default and terminations, for example is adverse to their interests. A corporation in financial difficulties may take the view that security interests or the inability of counterparties to terminate contracts on an insolvency of the corporation are inimical to their ability to be rescued, in which event they would prefer a debtor-friendly approach.

14.9 But this is not entirely open and shut. For example, set-off and netting encourage access to a much wider range of transactions by corporations with other counterparties. Solid security interests available to a bank to rescue the corporate in the case of financial difficulties make it more likely that lenders will continue with the rescue. Since many corporate transactions, such as takeovers, frequently depend upon the availability of finance, what is good for the financiers is also good for the corporate borrowers since the availability of finance is improved.

14.10 In any event, the protections against risk which can be achieved by a choice of governing law do not apply to shareholders, either at all or to a much lesser extent.

14.11 This is not to say that, apart from improving credit availability, governing law is irrelevant to corporate transactions. The main corporate transactions involve a large range of complex contracts. For example, most issues of shares involve subscription and underwriting agreements. Takeovers of public companies and agreements to buy non-public companies are just ordinary contracts of sale. This is also the case with a sale of a business. A joint venture agreement is a contract which is internationally mobile and usually long-term. Hence, virtually all of the key indicators about choice of governing law and choice of court can be relevant to some corporate contracts, apart from the actual transfer of shares, as they are to financial contracts. The parties will have some interest in the content of the governing law, for example, liability risks, predictability, issues which could arise on the insolvency of one of the parties, freedom of contract, business orientation, and the like.

14.12 Another significant difference is that the contracts involved in an issue of shares or a takeover or private sale of shares are short-term contracts which are closed within weeks or months, compared to the years of an outstanding bond issue. The period of exposure of corporate contracts is typically less than that of a bond issue or syndicated bank loan.

14.13 A final qualification is that corporate contracts, such as takeovers of public companies or sales of a private company shares, are not often between the same counterparties, and therefore there is no mutual build-up or clustering of criss-crossing obligations eligible for set-off and netting, as in the case of financial transactions (derivatives, loans, and deposits). The interdependence of parties is less than that found in, say, project finance.

14.14 This chapter covers the tenth letter in the sequence of the thirteen themes expressed in the mnemonic PIB—FEISST—CoRCO, standing for *p*redictability, *i*nsulation, *b*usiness orientation, *f*reedom of contract, *e*xclusion clauses, *i*nsolvency law, *s*et-off, *s*ecurity interests, *t*rusts, *c*orporate law, *r*egulatory law, *c*ourts, and *o*thers.

14.15 The key indicators discussed in this chapter in relation to corporate law are generally governed, not by a chosen governing law, but by the corporate law of the relevant jurisdiction. Hence, these indicators are significant in the sense that they evidence and support other trends in the families of jurisdictions.

Main corporate transactions

14.16 The main transactions which involve corporate law intensely are discussed in Chapter 3. They include (1) takeovers and leveraged buyouts of public companies, as well as the sale and purchase of private companies, (2) the raising of equity share capital and the reverse transactions buy-backs of shares, (3) sale or merger of a business, as opposed to the sale of shares, and (4) joint venture agreements. All of these transactions are internationally mobile in the sense that the parties could theoretically choose a governing law which is not the law of the place of incorporation of the company involved. In practice, there is likely to be a battle of the governing laws. The interest of the seller or issuer of shares is to reduce its disclosure obligations and its liability for disclosures, and to get paid either the price for the sale or the proceeds of an equity issue. The interest of a buyer or investor is to have as much disclosure as possible and to be able to reduce the price as much as possible. Who prevails depends on the bargaining strength of the parties and the market practice.

Structural methods of avoiding local corporate law

14.17 Where the rules of local company law are adverse to foreign investors, the risks concerned should be taken into account in the initial decision as to where to incorporate. These decisions are usually mainly based upon non-legal factors such as tax, government subsidies, employee availability and cost, the presence of a suitable markets and suitable skills, and so on. Sometimes, however, there may be significant corporate law factors which may deter incorporation in a country, such as harsh director liability, particularly director personal liability for deepening an insolvency, and aggressive litigation in relation to director liability for breach of their fiduciary duties, such as mis-selling or liability for an offering circular.

14.18 The most common structural methods of mitigating local corporate law is to form a shielding holding company in a convenient jurisdiction, or, what is often the same thing, to locate the local business in a local subsidiary so as to contain the local risk by the veil of incorporation. Most commercial jurisdictions scrupulously do not easily pierce the corporate veil so as to ignore the corporate protection and to render the holding company or the shareholders liable. It is not uncommon to pile a shell company on a shell company, like a tower of children's wooden bricks, so as to isolate the local risk as much as possible.

14.19 The alternative of migrating a company to another jurisdiction is not as feasible in most jurisdictions outside the US, although theoretically it can sometimes be done.

Conflict of laws in corporate transactions

14.20 The general rule in most commercial jurisdictions is that the law of the place of incorporation governs the internal workings of the company—such matters as the legal status of the company, its powers, the structure of corporate management, the split of powers between shareholders and directors, the personal liability of directors, the strength of the veil of incorporation, fusions of companies by universal merger, minority shareholder protections, and the like. See the books on conflict of laws.

14.21 For example, Rome I on contract applicable law, which applies in the UK and in EU Member States, excludes from its ambit questions governed by the law of companies and also the question of whether an agent, such as a director, is able to bind a principal, such as a corporation: see article 1(2).

14.22 Similarly, the EU Judgments Regulation provides in article 22(2) that in proceedings which have as their object the validity of the constitution or nullity of companies or the decisions of their organs, the courts of the Member State in which the company has its 'seat' have exclusive jurisdiction.

14.23 The overall effect is that the scope of a free choice of governing law is can be significantly limited by corporate law.

14.24 For example, in England the nature and extent of a director's liability to the *company* as director is governed by the law of the place of incorporation.

In *Konamaneni v Rolls-Royce Industrial Power (India) Ltd* (2002) 1 WLR 1269, shareholders in an Indian company sought to enforce a claim by the Indian company against an English company, it being alleged that the English company paid bribes to the managing director of the Indian company to secure a contract to construct and maintain a power station in India. *Held*: whether the shareholders could bring this claim—which was a derivative action—on behalf of the Indian company was an issue of substantive law, governed by Indian law as the law of the place of incorporation.

In *Base Metal Trading Ltd v Shamurin* (2004) EWCA Civ 1316; (2005) 1 WLR 1157, a director and employee of a company incorporated in Guernsey engaged in the purchase of metal originating in Russia which was then sold to foreign purchasers. To hedge the metal trading, a Russian director and employee of the Guernsey company traded futures on the London Metal Exchange. The company had no significant premises or activities in Guernsey or London, and all of the director's activities on the London Metal Exchange were conducted from Russia. The director's contract of employment with the company was governed by Russian law. The company brought proceedings against the director in England alleging that the director had engaged in speculative trades in breach of his duty to the company as a director. Under Russian law, the director was under no liability. *Held*: the nature and extent of the director's liability to the company as director were governed by the law of Guernsey as the law of the place of incorporation of the company.

14.25 However, this neat division between fettered corporate law and free governing law is not as clear-cut as that. This is mainly because of the clamouring demands of insolvency law and of the law at the location of the courts, both of which may insist on applying their own mandatory laws in this field if they determine that either corporate law or the governing law do not meet their standards.

Key Indicators of Corporate Law

Main and ancillary indicators

14.26 I choose two main key indicators relevant to corporate transactions. These are, first, giving financial assistance by a company for the purchase of its own shares and, secondly, director liability, especially for deepening an insolvency.

14.27 These two key indicators are considered to be reasonably measurable, to be economically important in transactions, to be symbolic or representative of the bias of jurisdictions, and to involve a clash or conflict of differing approaches.

14.28 I then list other possible indicators for potential inquiry, but without getting into any detail so as to keep the subject within bounds.

14.29 First, however, I mention some essential background on corporations in order to position the subject and the exploration of the key indicators.

Role of companies in modern societies

A company is a mark in a registrar's book. Yet this legal fiction, this creature of imagination, is one of the greatest inventions of the law, probably ranking only after the invention of money. In developed economies, often more than 90 per cent of business is carried out through a company which is therefore the dominant legal form for enterprise, production, and prosperity in most countries. They are available to everybody, whether individuals, families, or vast collections of people with millions of employees and shareholders. This is one reason that companies are at the centre of legal systems and why so much effort is expended on debating the most useful form of this legal creation, a debate which has being going on for nearly 200 years and which is fundamentally based on concepts of economic utility to enhance our survival and prosperity, mixed with a sense of justice, ethics, and morality. **14.30**

One result of this is that there is bound to be a conflict of moral policy, so much so that even in the US and the EU company law is not harmonized, although there are many common principles. **14.31**

The essential achievement of the idea is that shareholders delegate the management to the directors (which they would not be able to handle individually), but nevertheless share the profits, that the company is a separate legal owner of its own assets and liabilities which do not have to be invested in shareholders, that the shareholders do not bear the risk of the insolvency of the company, and the company does not bear the risk of the insolvency of the shareholders, that the company can raise large amounts of finance by share or debt issues which could not be carried out by individuals, and that the company has perpetual existence and is not susceptible to the thousand natural shocks that the flesh is heir to. **14.32**

The arrangement has disadvantages, especially that management may look after themselves rather than the shareholders. But the disadvantages are vastly outweighed by the advantages. This conflict is the main focus of corporate rules about disclosure and the loss of privacy, about corporate governance, director fiduciary duties to the company, and methods of reducing the adverse impact of the basic conflict of interests. Examples are the prohibition on transactions between the company and the directors or their families, or the taking by directors of opportunities which should have been retained by the company. **14.33**

There is no question that the effectiveness of the company could never be reproduced on such a large scale by individuals. History has also shown that for other reasons the function of companies could not be taken over by the state itself. **14.34**

Families of law and corporate law

There is often a strong link between the families of law and corporate law. For example, most corporate laws in the English-based group are based on the British Companies Act 1929 or 1948 or a predecessor. In some members of the mixed civil common law jurisdictions, corporate law may also come from a different family than the original family of the jurisdiction. For example, South Africa is a mixed jurisdiction originally based on Roman-Dutch law **14.35** from the Netherlands, but later it borrowed its corporate laws mainly from Britain, not the Netherlands. These corporate laws then spread to other jurisdictions in the South African cone, such as Botswana and Zimbabwe, but not over the Zambezi river into Zambia.

14.36 The corporate law of the leading corporate jurisdiction in the US, Delaware, is distinct from the other families of law. Corporate law in Germany is also distinct in some of its attributes, such as the highly articulated two-tier board, employee representation, and the compulsory subordination of loans in situations where the capital should have been provided by a share issue. In the EU some of the divergences have been partially ironed out by company directives, such as in relation to takeovers, but the differences between the families of law are still very perceptible.

Why corporate law differs from financial law: the straight line and the triangle

14.37 We have already discussed how an equity share as a form of capital differs from a bond as a form of capital. That distinction needs to be taken a stage further.

14.38 The major difference between the key indicators of corporate law and financial law is, on the one hand, that financial law commonly involves only two groups of interest, that is, debtors as opposed to creditors, so that in financial law one measures the policies of the group on a straight line spectrum from debtor to creditor. On the other hand, the measurement of corporate law involves three groups in a triangle—shareholders, creditors, and management—which complicates the policies. Thus, in corporate law England is protective of creditors and shareholders in various combinations, while Delaware is solidly protective of management. This is shown most dramatically in relation to takeover law but is found in other areas as well, such as the absence in Delaware of director liability for deepening the insolvency and the absence of prohibitions on a company providing financial assistance for the purchase of its own shares, both of which are found in English corporate law.

14.39 However, financial law and corporate law are profoundly affected by insolvency law, which is at the root of both financial law and corporate law. As mentioned above, one of the main purposes of the corporate form, apart from the mechanical convenience of vesting assets and the like, is to protect shareholders from the insolvency of the business and to protect the business from the insolvency of the shareholders. Most of the leading themes of corporate law, although influenced by the desire to enhance profits, are ultimately driven by the insolvency risk. Examples are minimum capital and maintenance of capital, the subordination of shareholders to creditors, director personal liability for deepening an insolvency, director liability for mis-management which leads to an insolvency, such as corporate governance principles (independent directors, tiered boards, audit committees), self-dealing by directors (since the syphoning away of assets can lead to the insolvency of the company), prospectus liability, piercing the veil of incorporation, accounting and disclosure, group theories, and the ultra vires rule, for example in relation to the giving of group guarantees.

14.40 Both classes of law share a specific feature that the law is layered between large and sophisticated participants on the one hand and smaller and less sophisticated participants on the other. This multi-layering is very perceptible in financial law, eg in relation to carve-outs for set-off and netting and security interests in financial markets, in relation to the regulation of offering circulars, and in relation to consumer credit law. Corporate law only has two main layers, the close, private, or family company which is not permitted to raise money from the public, compared to public listed companies with many shareholders who are allowed to raise money from the public and have to comply with special regulation. The policies for the layering in the corporate sphere are different from those for the layering in the financial sphere. The number of public companies tends to be small compared to private companies—in the UK in 2015 there were about 7,500 public companies out of a total of 3 million companies.

Objectives of corporate creditors, shareholders, and management generally

The purpose of summarising the main objectives of creditors, shareholders, and management, at the apex points in the triangle, is to illuminate how their interests conflict and also how they might unite. If they are united then the law is less likely to conflict, except to the extent that there are differing views about how to achieve that objective.

14.41

Objectives of creditors

The objectives of creditors such as banks and bondholders are primarily to ensure that they are paid and at the same time to make a profit on their provision of debt capital. In pursuit of this objective they support corporate laws which ensure the subordination of shareholders and which mitigate the risk of director mismanagement which leads to insolvency. They receive their protections partly via corporate law and partly by covenants by the borrower in credit agreements and bonds, eg to maintain financial ratios, not to grant a security interest to other creditors, and not to make substantial disposals of their assets. A change of control is often an event of default in bank loans or an event allowing creditors to call for a mandatory prepayment of the loan.

14.42

These covenants confer a 'vote' in the sense that, if they are not complied with, the creditors theoretically can accelerate the loan via events of default clause. Creditors therefore have a sanction for non-compliance. Unlike shareholders, creditors are not able to remove directors or vote on their capital formally. One significant impact of credit contracts is that shareholders are also shielded, that is, creditors protecting themselves from insolvency by loan covenants are also protecting shareholders from an insolvency. The capital providers are forced into a kind of cooperation. This helps to explain why a family of law which protects creditors can also protect shareholders since they are the same interest. If they are not the same interest, the jurisdiction protects creditors first before shareholders, as in the case of maintenance of capital and the prohibition on the giving a company financial assistance to buy its own shares, which effectively de-subordinates the shareholders who otherwise should be subordinated to creditors on insolvency. The latter prohibition is ferocious in traditional English-based jurisdictions outside England, but hardly known in traditional Napoleonic jurisdictions, at least outside the main developed countries in those groups. In

14.43

Objectives of shareholders

14.44 The objective of shareholders is to enjoy profits and hence the increase in value of their shares. Ideally they do this through the benefits of leverage, that is, the company borrows a large sum of money compared to its equity shares so that profits, after payment of interest on the loans, go to the equity shares first. Their basic objective is to ensure the company's solvency since in the ladder of priorities they are the first to lose if the company is bankrupt. Hence they have a deep interest in the company borrowing as much as possible, although not enough to threaten solvency. They have lesser interest in the maintenance of capital. They have a preoccupation with preventing a dilution of their voting power by the issue of shares to others, and, if they are a minority, they are interested in minority protections. They desire to control takeovers as much as possible, as in the UK, instead of control by the management of the target, as in Delaware. Promoters of Delaware would argue that control by the management of the target should increase the price paid to accepting shareholders.

Objectives of management

14.45 The objectives of the directors of the company are to be able to run the company with the minimum interference from the law, including rules imposing personal liability, to increase their personal wealth, and to maintain their position—which will usually be lost if the company is taken over or if the company becomes insolvent. That is why the dominant control of takeovers by the management of the target in Delaware suits them well. If the company is insolvent, their powers are either completely displaced or curtailed by an insolvency administrator.

Other constituencies

14.46 Other constituencies, such as the public generally and employees in particular, have an interest in the welfare of the company. These public interests include a wish not to see the collapse of the corporate sector which could reduce taxes, threaten the economy of the society, and lead to a depression. They also include specific interests such as orderly markets and the protection of the environment, both of which are achieved by special regulation mandatory in the jurisdiction and not subject to governing law freedom.

Financial Assistance to Buy Own Shares

What is financial assistance?

14.47 A principle of company law which is regarded as fundamental in most jurisdictions is that repayment of shareholders should be subordinate to the repayment of creditors in case insolvency intervenes, and that this principle should apply before insolvency in case insolvency occurs soon after the priority payment of share capital, perhaps as the result of the repayment of share capital, leaving the creditors stranded. This principle is called the maintenance of capital. The principle has, however, been eroded in many jurisdictions, very often by imposing duties on the directors to ensure that the company will remain solvent into the (short) foreseeable future.

One of the most important emanations of the maintenance of capital rule is the doctrine—largely (but not only) inspired by English company law and also by the German approach and then exported to all the EU via a company law directive—that a company may not give financial assistance for the purchase of its own shares or those of its holding company. The usual case is where a target group is required by a successful bidder to guarantee and secure bank loans made to the bidder to finance the takeover and is, therefore, highly relevant to the ability to finance a takeover. **14.48**

The commercial effect is not dissimilar to a repayment of share capital so that the acquiring shareholder receives financial benefit from the company ahead of the company's creditors. The payment of share capital is intended to be subordinated to the payment of creditors, in the bankruptcy ladder of priorities. **14.49**

The doctrine also catches loans by the company to the acquiring shareholder and extraordinary dividends or other transfers of assets by the company to the acquiring shareholder, also payment of debts, fees, and even prepayments. **14.50**

Often the transaction is void and a criminal offence. **14.51**

A twin objective in England was to prevent a bidder company, which proposes to pay for the target's shares in a takeover by an issue of its own shares, from ramping up the value of its own shares artificially. This could be achieved by secretly requesting a friendly third party to buy the bidder's shares (so as to drive up their value) on the basis that the bidder would indemnify the third party for any losses. This objective is met elsewhere by the criminal offence of market manipulation. **14.52**

Where the doctrine applies as a technique of maintaining capital, an initial question is whether it applies to private company subsidiaries. Sometimes it does, even in the case of EU countries where the relevant directive required its application only to public companies. **14.53**

Typically, it is a corporate doctrine applying only to corporations incorporated locally or having their seat locally. You cannot choose whether or not the prohibition applies by a choice of governing law. **14.54**

Where the doctrine applies only to public companies, the transaction can be achieved by converting the company into a private unlisted company and then sanctioning the financial assistance by shareholder resolutions or proof of solvency at the time of the transaction—commonly called a 'whitewash'. Where this route is not available, an alternative is for the target to merge into the acquiring parent after the acquisition, so that the security is given by the new company for its own obligations. A merger is complicated and expensive in many jurisdictions and often impracticable. In some countries, such as Belgium and France, the merger must have a sound economic rationale other than defeating the financial assistance prohibition. A reverse merger where the parent merges into the target is in most cases **14.55** unlikely to sidestep the prohibition because here it is the target's assets which are being used to pay for the share capital.

14.56 Direct loans to the target will normally escape the ban because the target is itself borrowing. However, upstreaming the proceeds from the target to the parent to pay back the parent acquisition borrowings from its banks will potentially be financial assistance and would have to be tested against the rules.

14.57 Even if there is no express ban, there may be an effective ban by reason of the duties of directors to act in the best interests of the company.

14.58 The severity of the doctrine is primarily influenced by the protection of creditors above shareholders, but this may be tempered by a strong policy in favour of facilitating a free market in the sale of companies, or alternatively by a hostility to public takeovers, a motive which may have partly influenced the strict provisions in France. A tough doctrine significantly weakens the ability of the bidder to finance a takeover for cash.

England

14.59 In England, the prohibition first emerged in a tough version in the Companies Act 1929, although it had been heralded by case law before then: see *Trevor v Whitworth* [1887] 12 App Cas 409. This was repeated in the Companies Act 1948, but mitigated in the Companies Act 1985 s 151, allowing a private company whitewash. The Companies Act 2006 ss 677–683 substituted a new financial assistance rule which applies only to public companies by reason of the EU Second Company Law Directive article 23.

14.60 In summary, where the shares in a public company are being acquired, neither the public company nor any subsidiary of the public company (this does not include foreign subsidiaries) can provide financial assistance for the purpose of the acquisition, either before or at the same time as or after the acquisition, subject to exceptions. But if the company whose shares have been acquired is later converted into a private company, the prohibition falls away: this is the usual procedure in a takeover. Where the shares being acquired are shares in a private company, no subsidiary of the private company that is a public company can provide financial assistance for the purpose of the acquisition, either before or at the same time as or after the acquisition. If the subsidiary that is a public company is to be converted to a private company, the prohibition falls away.

14.61 Traditional English jurisdictions based on the Companies Acts 1929 and 1948 usually have the tight prohibition, eg no assistance by abnormal dividends and no private company whitewash. Hong Kong has a whitewash. India has a tough version. In most of Canada, including Ontario, the test is tolerant if the corporation giving the assistance would remain solvent.

European Union

14.62 The EC Second Company Law Directive article 23 provides that, subject to certain exceptions, 'A company may not advance funds, nor make loans, nor provide security, with a view to the acquisition of its shares by a third party'. This article applies only to public companies (broadly)—a PLC, SA, AG, A/S, an NV, etc. Implementation differs in Member States. The prohibition is typically narrower than the 1985 English version, but a private company whitewash is unusual.

14.63 A 2006 directive amended the Second Company Law Directive by providing that Member States could permit public companies to grant financial assistance up to the limit of their distributable reserves subject to conditions, such as shareholder approval and a director's report.

France

14.64 French law is stringent on this matter. The Commercial Code article L 225 ff provides that a company may not provide financial assistance in the form of advances, loans, or security with a view to the subscription or purchase of its own shares by a third party. French law on the abuse of corporate assets by the directors (see articles 242–246) and the liability of directors under the bankruptcy law for defective management decisions (see articles 624–623) are so stringent that financial assistance by a target is not possible in the ordinary case. The French position has been exported to seventeen Ohada countries in Africa, that is sub-Saharan countries which have adopted an abbreviated but harmonised version of French business law.

Germany

14.65 The German prohibition is tough. Under section 71 of the Stock Corporation Act, an AG (public company) may not advance any funds, make any loans or provide security for the purposes of acquiring shares in the company or its parent.

14.66 Pursuant to section 30 GmbH-Act, the assets of a GmbH (private company) required for the maintenance of the registered share capital may not be paid out to the shareholders. Any distribution must exclusively be made out of the free assets, being the GmbH's assets less its liabilities (which includes liability reserves (*Rückstellungen*)) less the company's registered share capital.

14.67 These restrictions apply to payments and also to other benefits such as the granting of secured guarantees. An upstream security the enforcement of which would affect the registered share capital of the GmbH is not enforceable. Effecting the payment under the guarantee must be limited to distributable reserves. Any moneys paid out in excess of the registered share capital have to be paid back to the company (section 31 GmbH-Act). Under certain conditions, these rules apply to cross-stream security. It is common to include limits on the secured guarantee.

United States

14.68 Financial assistance is controlled by ordinary fraudulent preference law—if the assistance is granted in the suspect period before insolvency when the company is in fact insolvent and improves the position of shareholders who would otherwise be subordinated to creditors. However, few cases have succeeded and it is very unusual for financial assistance to be a problem in the US.

14.69 Leveraged buyout financings, whereby the buyer of a target company uses the assets of the target to finance the cost of the purchase, have been successfully attacked under state and bankruptcy fraudulent transfer rules when the financing rendered the target insolvent or (perhaps) significantly undercapitalised: see *US v Tabor Court Realty Corpn*, 803 F 2d 1288 (3d Cir 1986) —a particularly blatant case where the court could hardly have decided otherwise; compare *Credit Managers Association of Southern California v The Federal Company*, 629 F Supp 175 (CD Cal 1985).

Elsewhere

14.70 In China, financial assistance is prohibited and material transactions between the target and bidder must be disclosed.

14.71 An express prohibition does not apply in Japan, South Korea, Switzerland, and Turkey, but in each case the directors are likely to be fettered by fiduciary duties limiting their ability to consummate the transaction. Express prohibitions do not seem to be present in most of the South American Napoleonic republics.

Conclusion

14.72 The position in English common law jurisdictions is stringent in the traditional English-based countries where the law is based on the Companies Acts 1929 or 1948, but is ameliorated significantly in England itself and in other developed English common law countries, with the most tolerant being common law Canada. France and Germany take a strict view of the matter for both public and private companies. This seems to be less true in some traditional Napoleonic jurisdictions but this remains to be proved. In Delaware the doctrine is of little importance.

14.73 The patterns are complicated by the distorting triple tug of the three points of the triangle. One can speculate that a tolerant attitude in Delaware to financial assistance is pro-management and therefore broadly pro-debtor, a trend which is also in general exhibited by the pro-debtor approach of the US in the Bankruptcy Code of 1978 and the populist approach exhibited by US mass litigation. The severe emphasis on the prohibition in France seems to reveal a less sympathetic attitude to corporations, a policy approach which seems consistent, for example, with the largely pro-debtor interventionist approach in France to contract predictability and the dirigisme of the 1985 insolvency legislation in France.

14.74 England itself has moved away from the ferocious pro-creditor policy on this issue displayed in the Companies Act 1948. This shift may be caused by a persistent business orientation and a tendency towards freedom of contract. Both would tend to favour greater liberty for management.

Director Personal Liability

Introduction

14.75 The mainly mechanical and procedural provisions of board structure to improve corporate governance are totally overshadowed by director liability on insolvency which is when management failures are usually uncovered. Procedural problems, such as the English-based basic principle that only the company can sue the directors (not shareholders), except in the case of narrow derivative actions, are irrelevant in this context because it is the insolvency administrator who now brings the action, substantially on behalf of the company, now in substance managed indirectly by indignant creditors through their insolvency administrator.

Conflict of laws and director liability

14.76 Director liability in this context can be considered under a number of heads, but in almost all cases the liability is a matter for the law at the place of incorporation of the company and cannot be avoided by a choice of governing law. But there is a distinct trend in decisions in, for example, Germany to apply the law of the place where the insolvency proceedings are opened since some director duties, such as the duty to file for an insolvency proceeding when the company is actually insolvent, can also be considered as a matter for the protection of creditors decided by bankruptcy conflicts, instead of the law of the place of incorporation under the internal affairs doctrine. Again, the governing law is not a matter of choice.

Universal heads of liability

14.77 Directors will always be liable for contraventions of company law, such as failure to file financial statements or the payment of dividends out of capital, or for fraud, including fraudulent trading. Most developed jurisdictions also impose personal liability on directors for failure to account for taxes and social security payments deducted from the wages of employees.

Fraudulent trading

14.78 There are a few cases in Europe and elsewhere where a director has been held to be personally liable for incurring debts, such as by the purchase of supplies, when the director knew that the company was hopelessly insolvent and hence that it was likely that the company would be unable to pay its debts as they fell due. This is known in England as fraudulent trading where very few cases have succeeded because it has not been possible to prove that that directors genuinely believed that 'the clouds will roll away and the sunshine of prosperity will shine upon them again and disperse the fog of their depression', in the words of one English unreported case in 1960.

Wrongful or negligent trading

14.79 Wrongful trading is a different story. This is the incurring of debts which the director should reasonably have known that company would not be able to pay. The test is objective reasonableness. The personal liability is accompanied by the potential disqualification of the director as well. Some of the chief proponents of this approach are England, Ireland, Australia, Hong Kong, and New Zealand. But in Canada the liability is rare and is virtually unheard of in the US. The doctrine is known internationally as liability for deepening an insolvency, ie by failing to stop in time.

14.80 In England, the courts have applied the doctrine only in the case of gross irresponsibility and indeed in one case the court took the view that sometimes it is better to keep trading out of the difficulties. Cases in Belgium, the Netherlands, Germany, and Japan have arrived at similar results on the basis of tort liability for mismanagement and breach of directors' duties which are now owed to creditors as well as shareholders.

Duties to file on insolvency

14.81 The same motive to incentivise directors to stop early is shown by statutory duties on directors to petition for insolvency when the company is actually insolvent, and a duty on directors to call a shareholders meeting if there has been a serious loss of capital plus personal liability if the company fails to take adequate measures to deal with the problem. Neither of these duties exist in England and again are unheard of in the US, or at least in Delaware. One effect of the duty is that it can be very difficult for creditors to complete a work-out of an insolvent company since the directors must file and future trading out of the problem is not possible. An insolvency proceeding is almost always more prejudicial than a private work-out if the latter is possible.

14.82 In *France*, the debtor must file within forty-five days of the cessation of payments. The duty is absolute regardless of whether the date of cessation was difficult to determine and there was no deliberate omission (Cass Com, 14 January 1997—delay of several months), and regardless of whether there are recovery prospects: a work-out with creditors is discouraged by the courts since the aim is to restructure via a proceeding: see Cass Com, 8 October 1996.

14.83 In *Italy*, management is required to file for proceedings as soon as possible after becoming aware that the company is insolvent or its liabilities exceed its assets. If they fail to comply they may be personally liable for damages and also criminally liable.

14.84 In *Belgium*, the managers must file within thirty days of cessation (criminal liability as well). See BL, art 9. On the contrary, the directors must know of the insolvency, in which case they are liable for intent on the reasoning that creditors would not have suffered the loss they incurred if the company had declared bankruptcy.

14.85 In *Spain*, the directors are personally liable if they fail to file within two months after the date when they knew or should have known that the company was insolvent.

14.86 In *Germany*, whenever a situation of over-indebtedness or illiquidity (inability to pay debts as they fall due) has occurred, the director of a limited liability company (GmbH) must file for insolvency without undue delay and, at the latest, three weeks after the date when he knew of this situation. The same applies to board members of a public company (AG) and the directors of a general or limited partnership. See, for example, section 92 of the Companies Act (AG) and section 64 of the Limited Companies Act (GmbH). The duty is absolute.

14.87 In addition to criminal sanctions, the directors are personally liable to compensate the company and its creditors who suffer loss caused by the failure to file in due time.

14.88 The above duty is additional to the duty to convene a shareholders' meeting if an annual or interim balance sheet shows a loss of one-half the share capital. The directors are liable to pay compensation to the company for damages which could have been avoided by resolution or measures which would have been adopted by a shareholders' meeting if the meeting had been convened in due time.

14.89 Examples of jurisdictions where the directors have to call a shareholders' meeting and then take various measures to restore solvency in the case of a defined serious loss of capital include France, Luxembourg, Germany, Spain, and Switzerland. In the UK, the company must convene a shareholders' meeting but there is no civil liability for failure to take adequate steps.

Liability for negligent management

14.90 The 'business judgment rule' seeks to protect and promote the full and free exercise of the directors' managerial power by insulating all decisions from judicial review and shielding directors from liability for those decisions, even if they subsequently turn out to be mistaken and lead to insolvency. All that is required is that the directors acted honestly with a view to what they thought were the best interests of the company and with a minimum standard of competence. It seems that this general principle is espoused in many English-based jurisdictions, including Australia, by Canada, and emphatically by Delaware, by Finland, Norway, and Sweden, by Austria, Germany, the Netherlands, and Switzerland, and probably by Japan. The business judgment rule appears to give less protection to directors in Belgium, Luxembourg, and perhaps Spain, and very limited protection in France. In France, the insolvency of companies is frequently followed by the imposition of responsibility on directors and their personal bankruptcy to make up the shortfall of assets—*action en comblement de passif*. France had a long tradition of personal liability of directors for mismanagement dating back to 1935 and before. Under the 1967 insolvency legislation, directors were almost automatically personally bankrupted unless they could prove that they were not responsible for mismanagement, which typically was virtually impossible to prove. The onus of proof was changed in 1985. Case law shows that simple errors or negligence or imprudent acts are enough.

14.91 In jurisdictions which impose this stringent liability, business errors include borrowing beyond the capacity of the company to repay, committing the company to risky business ventures, irresponsibly continuing a loss-making business, inadequate budgeting, inadequate financial monitoring or supervision, inadequate insurance, unfunded capital investments, excessive dividends, or excessive executive remuneration having regard to the future financial needs of the company. Many of the cases render a director liable because the director failed to supervise a co-director or a manager.

14.92 It is probably true that director liability is most often found in relation to close or private companies but not large public companies, except in the case of banks, insurance companies, and the like where the public responsibility and the public indignation at insolvency are at their most intense. A further exception is the large public company dominated by a masterful but imprudent chief executive.

Conclusion

14.93 The patterns on whether this key indicator is symbolic or representative of wider policy approaches seems clearer in the case of the personal liability of directors for deepening an insolvency and for mismanagement leading to an insolvency.

14.94 Delaware is consistently protective of management. England is less protective but is still reluctant to impose liability on directors, probably because of the business orientation of protecting the corporate form. France appears to be the least protective of management and the least protective of the corporate form on this issue.

14.95 Again, it is insolvency which displays most clearly the policies of jurisdiction on these critical questions. It is insolvency which compels jurisdictions to choose their ideology.

Other Key Indicators of Corporate Law

Introduction

14.96 I set out below a number of other specific key indicators of the positioning of corporate law in relation to other jurisdictions. It will be recalled that, to be useful key indicators, these should be measurable, important in economic terms, symbolic, or representative of a general approach, and conflicting with other approaches elsewhere. Not all of these indicators satisfy these tests, but they are included in the list as matters for consideration. It is not feasible to conduct a detailed survey of each of these indicators across the leading jurisdictions.

Availability of the corporate form

14.97 Criteria include the cost and time taken to form a company; the ultra vires rule (vestigial in most countries); minimum capital, and minimum number of shareholders and officers; ease of transfer of private company shares; and the degree of relaxation of the normal public company rules for private companies, eg disclosure, subscription for capital in kind, and formalities. In commercial jurisdictions, companies can be bought off the shelf at minimal cost and there do not appear to be fundamental clashes of approach on the above matters. Hence these matters are not considered to be useful indicators. The cost and time to form companies in poor and destitute jurisdictions is a severe obstacle to enterprise and development.

Limited liability and the veil of incorporation generally

The issue of when the 'veil of incorporation' collapses or is pierced with the result that shareholders or lenders to the company become liable for the company's obligations—the shredding of the corporate fabric—is almost universally governed by the law of the place of incorporation. **14.98**

It would be possible, but difficult, to compare and measure comparative differences between the approach to the various situations in which the veil of incorporation may be pierced so that shareholders, especially group companies or in the case of one person companies, are liable for the debts of the company. **14.99**

As to the conclusivity of incorporation on formation of the company, on the whole the nullity of companies is relatively unusual in the main jurisdictions. In the UK the certificate of incorporation is conclusive and virtually unchallengeable. **14.100**

The piercing of the corporate veil tends to be limited to small family companies and but hardly ever in the case of public companies. The reasons for piercing are mainly undercapitalisation, disregard of corporate formalities, operating companies as a single group, comingling, and shareholder domination. **14.101**

In general, it is tentatively suggested that the piercing of the veil would be very unusual in commercial jurisdictions if the shareholders ensure that corporate formalities are observed, that assets are not commingled, and that the directors of the controlled corporation hold proper board meetings at which they take their own decisions in the interests of the company. It should not be relevant that the shareholders ultimately control policy of the company via their right to appoint the directors. Otherwise, the veil of incorporation would always be shattered. **14.102**

Single purpose companies

The firmness of the veil of incorporation is crucial in the case of single purpose companies, which are often 'brain-dead' in the sense that contracts with third parties completely control and restrict their freedom of action. These shell companies are widely used in securitisations, for acquisitions of companies, for holding a project (for a power station or a building or the pipeline), or a taxi cab (to shield the driver from liability), or a ship or aircraft, or as a depositary of investments in a jurisdiction which does not recognise the trust. In the latter case, it is crucial for that protection of the investments that the company does not incur other debts. **14.103**

14.104 Shell companies are frequently used in financing structures for takeovers of companies to achieve a 'structural subordination'. The bidding company Bidco is wholly owned by another company Midco, which in turn is wholly owned by Topco, which in turn is wholly owned by a private equity firm. The senior banks financing the bid lend to Bidco and the mezzanine or junior banks lend to Midco. If after the acquisition the target company runs into financial trouble, the banks as lenders to Bidco have recourse to the shares of the target pledged to them and the lenders to Midco get nothing if the shares are insufficient to repay the senior banks. In that way the structure of the deal makes sure that the junior lenders are subordinated to the senior creditors.

Central banks

14.105 Central banks are typically wholly owned by the sovereign state which appoints their directors and sometimes dictates monetary policy, such as interest rates. It is important for them that they should be treated as a separate legal entities, otherwise bondholders holding the bonds issued by the sovereign state could access the foreign reserves of the country held by the central bank if the sovereign state were to default. In fact, the English courts have been reluctant to pierce the veil of incorporation of a foreign central bank. If the banks wish to access the foreign reserves, they should have taken a guarantee from the central bank or lend direct to the central bank under the guarantee of the sovereign state. This is a good example of how predictability about the corporate veil or any other matter has to be consistent, notwithstanding that some creditors might complain that the result is adverse in their particular case.

Shareholders as de facto directors

14.106 Cases in England, Australia, Switzerland, Belgium, France, and the Netherlands have usually involved situations where the shareholder has effectively managed the company.

14.107 There are numerous cases around the world where lending banks have been held to be liable as de facto directors if they actively become involved in the management of an insolvent company and effectively take over the management of the company, eg in the US, Austria (the doctrine of abusive credit), France, and Switzerland.

Bankruptcy consolidation

14.108 Groups may everywhere be treated as a single entity for the purposes of financial statements, tax, and bank capital adequacy, but not consolidated so that their assets and liabilities are merged. On insolvency, each company in the group is generally treated as a separate entity, but there is quite some case law in the US on substantive consolidation. Consolidation on bankruptcy fusing the assets and liabilities of separate companies can be a disaster for external creditors. There are pooling provisions in New Zealand and some aggressive provisions in Italy, introduced in 2004. In Germany, a group may choose to be treated as a single company but very few companies have opted into this regime.

Subordination of shareholder loans

The *Deep Rock* doctrine in the US holds that shareholder claims against a debtor company, usually a subsidiary, can be subordinated to external claims if the shareholder, usually a parent, acted unconscionably in relation to the debtor company. This doctrine of equitable subordination has not been followed in Canada. **14.109**

Germany has a rather dangerous corporate law principle of the subordination of loans in a situation where the capital should have been provided by way of equity. Similar rules have been adopted in Austria, Greece, Portugal, Slovenia, and Spain. English-based jurisdictions subordinate a loan where the interest varies with the profits since this is deemed to be a feature of a partnership. This type of loan would not be normal market practice. **14.110**

Maintenance of capital

This group of criteria often goes under the name of maintenance of capital. The object is to ensure that creditors are paid before shareholders in the bankruptcy ladder of priorities. The criteria include a prohibition on the giving by a company all financial assistance to buy its own shares just discussed, the valuation of subscriptions for shares in kind, minimum capital, legal reserves, the prevention of dividends and distributions out of capital, the protection of a capital surplus, no par value shares, rules on share buy-backs, and the reissue of treasury shares. **14.111**

Shareholder equality and minority protections

Shareholder equality includes rules as to one-share one-vote (Germany, Japan, stock exchange rules) as opposed to the ability to divide shares into different classes with different rights (Anglo-American regimes), limits on preference shares (Latin American Napoleonic jurisdictions), pre-emption rights as opposed to selective issues to shareholders or to new diluting shareholders, and non-discriminatory buy-backs. **14.112**

Criteria relating to minority protections include the ability to requisition meetings, quorum and voting majorities, derivative suits, class actions, minority appraisal rights, and the right to apply to the court for redress in the case of oppressive conduct by the majority. These are all matters for the law of the place of incorporation. **14.113**

Corporate governance

This area receives a massive amount of attention in the literature. Mismanagement at the senior level prejudices both shareholders and creditors and in serious cases is usually a main cause of insolvency. **14.114**

The formal criteria include controls on self-dealing transactions and conflicts of interest, powers of shareholders to remove directors (robust in English-based jurisdictions, weakish **14.115** in Japan and Germany and very weak in the US) and to vote on director remuneration and compensation for loss of office, two tier boards, split of chief executive and chairman, independent directors, special audit, nomination and remuneration committees (the UK has a Corporate Governance Code dealing with most of these matters and applying only to major listed companies), allocation of powers between shareholders and management, and liability of the directors for financial statements and for prospectuses for securities offered to the public, and many others. The UK also has a Stewards Code which is a voluntary soft code applying to all institutional investors about the monitoring of companies whose shares they own.

Enforcement penalties

14.116 An important criterion is the extent to which fiduciary duties of directors are criminalised and the degree of punishment meted out for violations. In the US, convictions of erring directors have met with sentences of a length usually reserved for serial murderers. In 2005, Mr Ebbers, the chief executive of the American company WorldCom, whose bankruptcy was then the world's largest at the time (US$100 billion—subsequently succeeded by Lehman's in 2007, and then Greece in 2012, both over US$500 billion), was sentenced to gaol for twenty-five years for false financial statements in a prospectus.

Takeovers

14.117 One of the areas in which jurisdictions take sides relates to the takeover regime. There are two main issues. The first is whether the jurisdiction favours a relatively free market for public companies, or whether they are protectionist. Jurisdictions may be unsympathetic to what they regard as excesses of capitalism, for example, disapproval of the approach of private equity firms whose short-termism, they allege, destroys companies and jobs and prevents long-term planning.

14.118 The second issue is whether the jurisdiction protects management or shareholders or creditors most.

14.119 A good example of a takeover regime, which favours a relatively free market for public companies and at the same time protects both creditors and shareholders and subordinates the role of management to the right of shareholders, is the English takeover regime, which is codified by the Companies Act 2006 ss 942–992 and which is controlled by market participants, with little interference from the courts. This requires a mandatory bid for all voting shares once an offeror and its associates have obtained a specific threshold of voting control— 30 per cent—so that a bidder cannot obtain control on the cheap, thereby leaving a rump of shareholders who have to fall back on their legal protections as minority shareholders and who face a privatisation and delisting. The bidder has an obligation to treat all shareholders equally, such as a requirement that all shareholders receive the best price offered over a period of twelve months so that all shareholders share in the control premium. The bidder has an obligation to bid for legal voting control as opposed to less than 50 per cent. The regime makes provision for the compulsory acquisition of dissenting minorities, eg once the offeror has obtained over 90 per cent voting control (the 'squeeze-out'). There is a compulsory timetable. The offeror must be in a position to finance the offer ('certain funds'). The bid must not contain conditions outside the control of the offeror. Very importantly, the target may not take pre- or post-offer frustrating action ('poison pills'). There are stringent requirements as to the content of offering circulars by both offeror and target, including strict rules about forecasts.

14.120 The overall framework is reflected in other English-influenced states, such as Hong Kong, Singapore, and Australia, as well as India and South Africa and is more or less adopted by the EU Takeover Directive 2004 with significant deviations. The Directive also applies to the EEA states (Norway, Iceland, and Liechtenstein).

14.121 On the other hand, the regime in Delaware favours the management of the target who effectively can control the attitude to the bid: see *Unocal Corp v Mesa Petroleum Co*, 493 A 2d 946 (Delaware, 1985). Poison pills are allowed so as to frustrate the bid or to increase the price. The bidder is given much greater freedom of action.

14.122 Takeover regimes tend to regulate the interests of only management and shareholders (and sometimes employees), not creditors. Creditors have to fend for themselves.

Corporate guarantees

14.123 Guarantors are darlings of the law. That is because they usually did not receive the money but still have to pay it back. Hence. to the layman a guarantee is a baffling document bristling with curious legalese.

14.124 It is common for group subsidiaries to guarantee a bank loan or a bond issue, or for a sovereign state to guarantee a loan to its central bank, or for a finance subsidiary to be guaranteed by its parent. Many other commercial contracts, including leases of real property, are guaranteed, whether by ordinary guarantee or performance bonds or standby letters of credit.

14.125 The main problems with regard to guarantees are whether the guarantee is within the powers of the directors if their company does not receive substantial benefit from giving the guarantee, whether the guarantee constitutes prohibited financial assistance, whether the guarantee has a gift element which renders it voidable on insolvency if it is given when the company is actually insolvent, whether the guarantee constitutes a breach of financial ratio in a bank credit agreement, whether the guarantor is under a duty of disclosure, whether the terms of the guarantee are unreasonable contract terms, and in Europe whether the guarantee constitutes prohibited state aid. Guarantees by a company to benefit directors or members of their families in conflict of interest are probably doubtful in many jurisdictions.

14.126 Under both English and Delaware corporate law, the business judgment rule as regards guarantees by subsidiaries of their parents are usually liberal. In addition under English law a guarantees can generally cover an unlimited amount and there is virtually complete freedom to include clauses maintaining the guarantee notwithstanding variations of the guaranteed debt or security for the guaranteed debt, and clauses which prevent competition of claims between the guaranteed creditor and the guarantor in the insolvency of the common debtor. Immediate recourse to the guarantee without exhausting remedies against the borrower is allowed and the creditor can apply recoveries first to the unguaranteed debt, if so provided.

Conclusion

Economic and fairness justifications

14.127 One may conclude by considering the claims that each group at the points of the triangle have in favour of special protection.

14.128 The economic and fairness justifications in favour of protecting creditors is that banks and bondholders in particular provide the bulk of finance for business and prosperity and that this finance is ultimately derived from the money of the citizen. Creditors do not enjoy the profits which can be made out of equity shares, but the benefit of leveraging up on creditor money is a major source of profits going to shareholders.

14.129 The economic and fairness justifications in favour of protecting shareholders is that they also provide capital for business and prosperity and that they bear the greatest risks of enterprise.

14.130 The economic and fairness justifications in favour of protecting directors (management) is that, together with employees, it is their work, skills, and ingenuity which generate production and welfare. Because of the importance of the corporate form, it is disproportionate for them to bear personal liability, except in the most egregious cases of irresponsibility. The main issue for the law as regards management is that of what economists call the 'agency problem', that is, management are using other people's money and not their own. They might therefore be less prudent than they should be or pay themselves more than they are worth. But shareholders have the final word in that they can dismiss directors, although at a cost, which requires that institutional investors at least should be paying attention.

14.131 In addition it is considered that corporations, as a collectivity of people, should have regard to the betterment of society to the same extent expected of ordinary people.

14.132 It is in the light of these maxims, and others like them, that we should judge the legal policies of corporate law as regards supporting or not supporting the parties clustered at the three points of the triangle.

Comparative conclusions

14.133 US law (in substance Delaware, where most important US corporations are incorporated) has high protections and freedom for management and low creditor protections. For example, the maintenance of capital rules subordinating shareholders to creditors are relaxed, directors are rarely liable for deepening an insolvency, there is no material prohibition on a company giving financial assistance for the purchase of its own shares, and creditor legal controls on mergers are absent—banks must protect themselves by covenants in their credit agreements. Management has considerable freedom in relation to such matters as new share issues without mandatory pre-emption rights, selective buy-backs, and poison pills frustrating takeovers.

By contrast the company law of traditional English common law jurisdictions is protective of creditors, eg financial assistance and maintenance of capital. The English-based takeover regime, which is in in effect managed by market participants rather than the courts, shows business orientation and an absence of dirigisme. **14.134**

The rules in France on director liability seem to be the least sympathetic to business of all the major jurisdictions. **14.135**

These varying approaches in corporate law—at least on the key indicators discussed in more detail—might be more or less consistent with the approaches in financial law with English common law group on one side, the Napoleonic group on the other, and the Roman-Germanic group in the middle. Further comparative research would be required on the indicators briefly listed above, apart from the two main indicators of financial assistance and director personal liability, to authenticate this tentative conclusion. **14.136**

Delaware corporate law is distinctive in that, in the triangle of interests, the legal regime strongly favours management, which is not a stance taken by any of the other three large families in general. **14.137**

15
REGULATORY LAW INDICATORS AND RISKS

Introduction

Pervasiveness of regulation

15.1 Regulatory fields are now the leviathans of legal systems whose footprints are everywhere. There has always been state regulation but never on the scale ever dreamed of before the twentieth century.

15.2 I mention these fields only briefly because they override free transactions and free choice of governing law and courts and so cannot be significantly avoided except by refraining from doing business in the regulating territory and avoiding all contacts with a regulated territory. Since some of the regulatory rules have extraterritorial effect, even that can be difficult.

15.3 Most regulatory sets are necessary and desirable in the modern world. It is only where countries have legitimate policy differences on the extent of regulation or where the regulation or its enforcement are disproportionate that those doing business can properly seek to avoid adverse consequences. Regulation may be unjust, or excessive, or create unnecessary risks, or smother innovation and creativity, or impose unjustified costs, or sap enterprise. It may blot out the blue sky, when we should be at liberty.

15.4 This chapter covers the eleventh letter in the sequence of the thirteen themes expressed in the mnemonic PIB—FEISST—CoRCO, standing for *p*redictability, *i*nsulation, *b*usiness orientation, *f*reedom of contract, *e*xclusion clauses, *i*nsolvency law, *s*et-off, *s*ecurity interests, *t*rusts, *co*rporate law, *regulatory law*, *co*urts, and others.

Main fields of regulation

15.5 Everywhere in most developed countries there are regulations about health and safety, building regulations, about data protection, about transportation, about employees, about anti-trust and competition, about trades and professions, about the environment, about real estate development and zoning, about sanctions and embargoes, about money-laundering, about consumer credit, about food and drugs, about immigration, about corporate governance and listing, about financial reporting and disclosure, about landlord and tenant, about the disclosure of large shareholdings.

15.6 In emerging countries in particular there are regulations about foreign direct investment, about exchange controls, about subsidies and trade restrictions, and about the alien ownership of land. These are largely protectionist measures which are unsympathetic to the idea of a free and open economy.

15.7 In advanced societies there are probably about fifty or more regulatory regimes, each with its own big book and each with its own sub-specialities and sub-sub-specialities.

15.8 Although regulatory law has historical antecedents, it is almost entirely a twentieth-century invention. The concept of state interference through regulation paralleled political philosophies in the early twentieth century favouring absolutism. Many people thought that the state would rescue us from all problems.

15.9 Most of the regulatory regimes we have are necessary and useful in the core concept. For example, it is necessary in a market economy to have laws ensuring competition between corporations and ensuring that they do not engage in restrictive practices and do not achieve a monopoly position. We have to have building regulations, regulation on pharmaceuticals, on health and safety, on land development, and against pollution. But some of the regimes pose rule of law problems for the reasons given below.

Why regulation is different from the ordinary law

15.10 Regulatory law differs from ordinary law (such as contract law) for three main reasons:

- A *governmental regulator* which is an agent or arm of government is at the same time the legislator in the sense that it makes rules, the executive, in the sense that it monitors compliance with the rules, and is a judicial tribunal to punish offences. In other words, many regulatory bodies defy basic constitutional notions of the separation of powers and involve a concentration of power in a single governmental body.
- The law is *criminalised* in the sense that people can be disqualified from holding office in the case of violations and offending firms can be faced with substantial fines. The offending firm can be ruined or broken up. Notwithstanding the criminal nature of the sanctions, the subjects of the law often do not have the basic protections of the criminal law. Examples are the right to silence, proof beyond reasonable doubt, a right to trial by an independent tribunal, not a regulator which is both judge and prosecutor, open justice instead of secret settlements where nobody can tell whether the rule of law was observed or what the law is, proportionate penalty, fines calibrated to wealth, which is inconsistent with the criminal law rule that the convicted are treated equally, rich or poor, restraint from threatening behaviour, proof of dishonest intent, not just negligence, or some vague offence of lack of supervision without proof of complicity, the exclusion of evidence about previous 'convictions', and other rule of law principles. Regulation side-steps due process by relabelling the enforcement remedies as administrative penalties, but criminal they are beyond doubt.
- The rules are usually extremely *detailed*, prescriptive, intricate, and subject to rapid change. By virtue of the legislative power of many regulators, with or without central government control, they tend to use their rule-making powers to the full, so that many regulatory codes are enormous in size.

- The rules are sometimes *extraterritorial* so that they apply to everybody everywhere on the basis of slight contacts with the regulating jurisdiction. Accordingly, one state imposes its regulation and criminal penalties on residents of another state whose citizens are not represented in the legislature of the regulating state.

15.11 Financial regulation in the financialised world is necessary. The above comments show that what is required from regulators is restraint. The regulatory regime should also provide for proper checks on regulatory overreaching in the above areas. There are indeed some checks, and also some self-imposed restraints, depending on the jurisdiction.

Financial Regulation

Essentials of financial regulation

15.12 I take financial regulation as an example of an important regulatory field which also reveals differences of international approach.

15.13 Financial regulation began in the 1930s in the US. Before that it was more or less restricted to anti-gambling and usury statutes.

15.14 The basic principle is that anybody who by way of business sells or markets services involving financial assets within the jurisdiction must be authorised to do so by a regulator, including approval of their controllers and management.

15.15 Financial assets are mainly deposits, transferable financial instruments (such as shares, bonds, and units in collective investment schemes), and most derivatives.

15.16 The services in these financial assets which must be authorised are mainly:

- taking deposits from the public to on-lend (banking) or insurance
- dealing in, advising on, managing, safeguarding (custodianship), underwriting (or placing), or giving credit ratings, or providing data services with regard to, financial assets
- operating a collective investment scheme (mutual fund), a hedge fund, or a private equity fund, or an organised market or settlement system in relation to financial assets.

Financial regulators

15.17 Regulators are typically government-owned entities which have the power to make rules, to supervise regulated firms, and to impose administrative sanctions, such as fines and disqualification, subject to controls and appeals.

15.18 Regulatory rules are in addition to the normal law, eg about fiduciary duties, misrepresentation, and fraud. The regulators are charged with enforcing the regulations and investors may also have rights of civil action for damages.

Financial codes of conduct

Regulated firms in the financial field must: **15.19**

- have the prescribed capital and (especially in the case of banks) maintain the prescribed liquidity (ability to pay current debts out of cash or near-cash) and comply with other financial ratios
- comply with codes of conduct, such as managing conflicts of interest, safeguarding client assets, ensuring that financial products sold are suitable for the client, dealing fairly, remuneration, and making sure that promotions are fair. The rules are more relaxed in the case of professional or sophisticated investors
- in the case mainly of banks, not carry on non-financial businesses (or have a firewall between them), and sometimes only carry on derivatives businesses or speculative activities through an affiliate
- join a compensation fund which compensates individuals up to a limit on the insolvency of a bank or securities firm.

Prospectuses

Anybody who issues securities, such as bonds or shares, to the public must have the prospectus approved by the regulator. The prospectus must comply with rules as to its contents. Those involved, including the arrangers, have higher than normal liabilities for false or misleading statements. **15.20**

Frauds

It is a criminal offence, whether or not by a regulated firm, to commit a fraud, make false or misleading statements about financial assets, engage in market manipulation (such as misleading impressions and false rumours) about financial assets, or deal in financial assets on the basis of non-public price-sensitive information (insider dealing). Abusive market conduct may attract administrative sanctions. **15.21**

Managing regulatory risk

In general terms, the risk of financial regulation cannot be significantly controlled by a free choice of governing law or courts. Generally, a firm is caught by the regulatory net if regulated activities are carried out 'in' the territory of the regulated state. Regulation often also applies extraterritorially if the conduct is deemed to have an adverse effect in the regulated jurisdiction, such as a fraud. The question of what amounts to doing something within the regulated state, such as carrying on the business of taking deposits there or giving financial advice or selling securities, can depend on some very slight fine-trigger contacts. Thus, in the US, the federal securities legislation generally applies where there is a direct or indirect **15.22** use of the US mails or communication in interstate (and international) commerce, so that even sending an email into the US can be enough.

15.23 The EU and the EEA are largely free-trade areas for financial services. The scope of WTO liberalisation of cross-border services is limited. Regulators often agree to cooperate under memoranda of understanding. However, it is possible in many cases for regulated firms to deal with each other cross-border so long as they do not deal directly with ordinary local residents. This is less common in the case of taking deposits from the local public. A foreign firm can usually set up a local properly capitalised subsidiary to do business locally.

15.24 The whole world, or most of it, is virtually a free market in the case of prospectuses sent to sophisticated investors, as variously defined, in the case of the foreign exchange market, and in the sale of securities between regulated firms.

15.25 Apart from enforcement by a regulator, a risk for foreign firms is that of a private civil action brought by a claimant in the regulated state who claims, for example, fraud, negligent misrepresentation, or mis-selling. In this case the claimant will generally be suing in tort (delict), in which event different and more restrictive rules as to governing law and jurisdiction apply.

15.26 The main method of managing regulatory risk in the case of financial regulation is to establish a subsidiary in the jurisdiction concerned. A subsidiary will necessarily involve the costs of maintaining regulatory capital and local compliance staff.

15.27 A choice of governing law or courts which are those of a jurisdiction whose regulatory regime is considered disproportionate may inadvertently increase the slight business contacts which are sufficient to ground jurisdiction of regulators and private claimants in the adverse jurisdiction concerned.

Key Indicators of Financial Regulation

Key indicators generally

15.28 This section suggests four key indicators measuring financial regulation and also assessing the economic importance of all the indicators, whether they are symbolic of the jurisdiction's policies in other areas of law, and whether they exhibit a conflict or clash of contrasting policies.

15.29 It is not proposed to develop these key indicators to any great extent since they are not generally within the control of a choice of governing law and courts.

15.30 One may remark generally that the regulatory regime of a country in relation to financial services in particular is an indicator of wider attitudes towards crime and punishment, the rule of law, and freedom, as well as more specific attitudes towards business orientation which does not regard banks and financial firms as the enemy, predictability of the law, insulation of contracts from foreign interference, freedom of contract generally without dirigisme, the ability to control risks by exclusion clauses, creditor control of work-outs and of insolvency proceedings, free insolvency set-off and security interests, and proper safeguards for investments held in trust on a universal basis.

Differences in enforcement

One of the main differences between regulatory regimes is the zealotry of enforcement, especially criminalisation, overriding of criminal protections such as a presumption of innocence, the privilege against self-incrimination (as opposed to the duty to report non-compliance to the regulator), the need to prove dishonest criminal intent, proof beyond reasonable doubt, the exclusion of evidence of previous convictions, and the proportionality of punishment, such as fines. **15.31**

In the United States, there is strong financial encouragement of whistle-blowers secretly informing on internal non-compliance, including on matters which are administrative offences not characterised as criminal, and a requirement in settlements with banks for the appointment of an internal monitor who listens in to what is going on in the bank, in case management should be conspiring to do evil. **15.32**

It is probably true that the UK, Germany, and France are more moderate than the United States on these issues. **15.33**

A US example is the case of Mr Iguchi in 1995. Mr Iguchi was a trader at the New York office of the Japanese bank Daiwa, which was then the nineteenth largest bank in the world. He allegedly lost US$1.1 billion trading US Treasuries. When found out, management did not report the losses to the US regulators for two months. Daiwa said it had been advised by the Japanese regulators that disclosure would have an adverse effect on the Japanese banking system, which was then in trouble. The US regulators closed down Daiwa in the US. Daiwa settled for a fine of US$340,000,000. Mr Iguchi was jailed for four years and fined US$2.6 million. Later Japanese courts ordered executives and former executives of Daiwa personally to pay fines of US$775 million for the losses caused by the branch management in New York. See Hal Scott and Anna Gelpern, *International Finance: Law and Regulation* (3rd edn, Sweet & Maxwell 2012) 257–258. **15.34**

Differences in protectionism

The degree of xenophobia and protectionism are features which are difficult to measure. One measure is protectionist hurdles to authorisation and the rationing of licences, similar to restrictions on immigration of people. **15.35**

Another test is the openness or otherwise of the jurisdiction to offers of new securities and to the sale by foreigners to national residents of financial products, such as listed securities, custodianship, mutual funds, and financial management, that is, the degree of the paper wall as a barrier to foreign intrusion. **15.36**

15.37 In the advanced world there is almost completely a free market for secondary sales of listed bonds and equity shares but much less so for the taking of bank deposits, where protectionism is particularly noticeable.

Intensity of investor protection

15.38 The main indicator here is the extent to which consumer protection intrudes into the wholesale business market.

15.39 Consumers generally benefit from a kind of welfare state in relation to financial services, including deposit and investor compensation schemes, consumer ombudsman schemes, and the protection of investors by suitability rules. On the whole there is a reasonably clear divide between sophisticated investors and consumers.

Degree of freedom

15.40 A significant indicator is the degree of state intervention and control of financial services via the regulatory regime, just as the state may seek to regulate the economy via the insolvency regime. Prominent examples of the latter are bank resolution statutes installed throughout the Western world and elsewhere, which effectively nationalise the management of the bankruptcy of banks by vesting control in a state agency with no intervention by creditors and limited intervention by the courts.

15.41 Examples of departures from freedom include hurdles to authorisation, the degree of criminalisation, the degree to which regulatory complexity is a barrier to entry because of the need for the necessary resources to comply, micromanagement, costs on the industry to fund regulators and compensation schemes, bureaucracy, and the cost of compliance staff.

Conclusion

15.42 It would tentatively seem that the intensity of regulation in the EU, the UK and the US is approximately similar, but the intensity of enforcement would appear to be greater in the US, partly because of regulatory culture and partly because of the litigation factors discussed in the next chapter.

15.43 In the case of insolvency we have seen that a choice of governing law can play an important role in reducing business risks. This is not so in the case of financial regulation, or indeed most other fields of regulation. In this respect, regulation is an ally of the criminal law, but with only a modest genuflection in the direction of criminal protections of the accused.

16

COURTS, LITIGATION, AND ARBITRATION

Judiciary

Politicisation

16.1 It goes without saying that the judiciary of the chosen courts should possess impeccable integrity, should be independent. and should be impartial. All these qualities are considered to be undoubted in the case of the courts of England, France, Germany, and New York.

16.2 In some states in the US, including New York, judges (outside the Federal courts) are elected by popular vote so that the judiciary may be politicised. The members of the Supreme Court of the United States are often appointed by the government of the day according to their position on politicised matters, but this is not to say that New York or Supreme Court judges follow left wing or right wing of politics or that they do not carry out their higher duty to administer justice.

16.3 This chapter covers the twelfth letter in the sequence of the thirteen themes expressed in the mnemonic PIB—FEISST—CoRCO, standing for *p*redictability, *i*nsulation, *b*usiness orientation, *f*reedom of contract, *e*xclusion clauses, *i*nsolvency law, *s*et-off, *s*ecurity interests, *t*rusts, *co*rporate law, *r*egulatory law, *c*ourts, and *o*thers.

Business orientation

16.4 The key question is somewhat different from the question of integrity. This is whether the judiciary concerned with commercial cases have a business and commercial orientation. If they have little experience or knowledge of commercial transactions or are anti-business, then they might be inclined not to have a commercial orientation in their judgments, be inclined to support the consumer and the small business against large corporations, to be debtor-friendly as opposed to taking into account the interests of creditors as well, and to favour court intervention to protect the small against the big. An example of the latter would be creative use of the good faith doctrine in contract and the substitution of fairness in their eyes as opposed to strict predictability.

16.5 The approach of the judiciary in general may be influenced by their experience, or lack of it, in commercial affairs. In England, the judges of the senior courts are selected mainly from practising barristers who have practised before the courts and are therefore exposed to commercial issues, notably if they are members of the commercial courts. Commentators have often observed that in countries such as France and Germany where the judiciary is a career option from the time of completing student law studies, some members of the judiciary do not acquire significant practical experience of international markets. They may take with them the attitudes of their student days. In France, judges in the lower courts may be non-lawyers. In addition, in France and Germany, unlike England, it is not uncommon to recruit members of the judiciary from academia and even the civil service so that there is a danger of the law being professors' law, a frequent charge in Germany, or even civil servants' law, as opposed to practitioners' law. Sometimes' there is some centralisation of commercial matters in the courts of the commercial capital, as in the case of Paris and the federal courts in the Southern District of New York.

16.6 Nevertheless, one must be careful of possible stereotypes and of making over-simplistic judgments, which would require hard evidence to support them. Apart from the issue of the judiciary, it must make sense for academics and practitioners each to contribute their specific skills in order for a legal system to thrive and certainly not to shut themselves off from each other.

Judicial consensus building

16.7 The second key question is whether the courts can build a unified consensus about a legal approach which is not unsympathetic to business and enterprise. In England, the judges of the Commercial Court are concentrated in London and the number of judges is limited, so that a great deal of informal communication is possible. This factor may enhance predictability and a common line, in addition to the formal duty of courts to follow and adopt the judgments of higher courts—the doctrine of precedent.

16.8 It is hazardous to suggest that such matters as the non-politicisation, business orientation, or concentration of the judiciary and their background can be linked to trends in legal policy. Hence, criteria of this kind do not satisfy the test of measurability for a key indicator and so the above remarks must remain based on anecdotal evidence.

Choice of Courts and Risk Generally

Reasons for choice of courts and indicators

16.9 A choice of courts in order to back up the choice of governing law is crucial for the following reasons, amongst others:

- to benefit from the predictability approach in interpretation, which might otherwise be threatened by good faith and similar doctrines, as in France. See Chapter 5
- to avoid the invalidation of asymmetric clauses, again as in France. Asymmetric clauses are standard market practice in financial transactions. See paragraph 8.20
- to coincide the choice of courts with the governing law so that the court applies its own law accurately, rather than relying on expert evidence of that law in a foreign court
- to benefit from the commerciality, business orientation, and expertise of the chosen court. See Chapter 7
- to benefit from favourable conflict of laws rules. Courts apply their own conflicts of law principles, as opposed to those of the governing law. An example is the conflict of laws

rules applying the need for notice to the debtor of an assignment of a debt owed by the debtor in order to validate the assignment: see Chapter 7. Other examples potentially include the recognition of insolvency set-off, aspects of agreements for security interests, and commercial trusts: see Chapters 11, 12, and 13
- to protect the insulation from foreign laws achieved by the choice of an external governing law. See Chapter 6
- to avoid the mandatory rules of the forum.
- to avoid any rule that a bankruptcy court can override the jurisdiction clause in a contract or a clause prescribing that seat of an arbitration and claim that the action or arbitration can only be continued in the jurisdiction of the bankruptcy court.

16.10 In addition, there are other key indicators involved in the choice of courts which are discussed in this chapter in brief. They are:

- US litigation
- class actions
- discovery of documents

16.11 These are followed by a discussion of the following issues which are not considered to be significant litigation key indicators, mainly because of the absence of material clashes of policy, except at the fringes:

- pre-judgment freezes
- enforcement of foreign judgments
- sovereign immunity
- arbitration.

Role of the law of the courts

16.12 In general, most of the above seven matters are covered, not by the governing law of the contract but by the procedural law of courts in which the action is brought. It follows that the choice of courts involves significant risks and also enables parties to manage those risks by the choice of the most suitable court for the transaction concerned.

16.13 As to damages, according to article 12(1) of Rome I on contract applicable law in the European Union, 'within the limits of that powers conferred on a court by its procedural law, the consequences of a total or partial breach of obligations, including the assessment of damages in so far as it is governed by rules of law', are governed by the governing law of the contract. The US Conflicts Restatement, section 207 is to the same effect. Rome I continues to apply in the UK, notwithstanding Brexit. Hence, the governing law should cover the right to terminate, remoteness of damage, limits on damages, and the efficacy of a liquidated damages clause. That measure or quantification of damages remains to be decided by the law of the courts in England so as effectively to exclude the availability of punitive or treble damages on a contract governed by the law of a US jurisdiction.

16.14 Hence, if English governing law together with the English courts are chosen, then the issues discussed in this chapter should be governed by English law, unless an action is brought in a foreign court which will no doubt apply its own rules of damages and procedure, including class actions.

Trauma of litigation

16.15 The adjudication of disputes by the courts is almost always an ordeal which is both costly and time-consuming. Many attempts have been made to quantify the cost and time taken to resolve disputes in the courts of different countries but the comparisons are often doubtful because of the problems of comparing like with like and because blockages maybe ephemeral. It is probably the case that in some countries such as the United States, which is highly litigious society, more than 90 per cent of disputes are settled in advance of a court hearing. Hence, litigation and its burdens are merely used as a bargaining counter. The exchange of claims and defences plus the disclosure of relevant documents tends to sharpen the issues so as to facilitate a settlement.

16.16 One hesitates to suggest which of the courts of England, France, and Germany are quicker and less costly than the others with any degree of conviction.

Key Indicators of Litigation

US litigation

16.17 The status of litigation in the United States deserves a special comment because it is generally regarded as being an even worse ordeal than elsewhere amongst developed countries. This is because of a unique combination of factors which may be found individually in other jurisdictions but are rarely to be found all together in one country—an explosive cocktail. These characteristics of United States litigation, mainly tort litigation initiated by some members of the plaintiff bar, are mainly the following:

- Sometimes huge punitive damages for civil claims, typically treble the damages. Punishment is for the criminal law, subject to rule of law criminal protections of the accused, not the civil law. The civil law sanctions are compensation for loss, not a trebling of compensation. Criminal protections are side-stepped.
- Jury trials for civil trials, not merely criminal trials as in the English courts. Some US juries tend to favour the small against the big so that justice is not equal. They are not trained in the overall policies of the legal ideology and make their judgments on the merits of the case before them. The result is that the outcome of a case can be unpredictable and turn on the whims of juries rather than the law. In turn, the value of cases as a precedent for future decisions, and hence greater predictability, is weakened.
- No award of litigation costs against a losing plaintiff and contingent legal fees dependent on success. Hence, plaintiffs can sue without any risk of having to pay the costs of the other side or their own costs if they lose. Those who are attacked by litigation have to pay their own costs even if they win. Plaintiffs have nothing to lose and often their first move is to issue a writ before talking.

- Class actions. The essence of the class action by a representative claimant is numerosity of claimants and common issues. All members of the class are bound by the judgment or court-approved settlement, whether they have heard of the action or not. Members of the class do not have to opt in and are automatically included. This is good for the lawyers because it increases the size of the cake from which they can take a cut.
- An apparently unrestrained ability for plaintiffs to make any allegations that they like of fraud, dishonesty, and racketeering against a defendant, unsubstantiated by facts, in the hope that the defendant will be coerced into giving up and settling the case out of court. It is almost as if in some cases the plaintiff lawyers have a standard form. So long as it mentions fraud, aiding and abetting a crime, racketeering, conspiracy, theft, dishonesty, and the like several times on each page, they just send it out and fill in the facts later. The effect can be of abusive defamation and the menacing of defendants prior to trial under the cloak of judicial immunity. The hope of these lawyers is that, if they make sufficiently abusive allegations, however unfounded, which are lavishly reported in the media, they will be able to extort a settlement out of a firm just in order to get rid of the costs and harassment of litigation.
- An exorbitantly wide disclosure of documents worldwide, so that a plaintiff can conduct a fishing expedition to see if there is anything which looks bad and which might influence a jury, such as a silly email by an employee. Excessive disclosure can involve millions of documents, huge costs and time, and amount to a disproportionate persuasion under judicial authority.

16.18 In the US, the combination of the plaintiff-orientated litigation rules can lead to settlements favourable mainly to the lawyers—typically 33 per cent per cent of the award—while each claimant receives only a tiny amount.

16.19 The aim was to bring the court to the people but the system also succeeded in enriching lawyers. The costs to society of these activities include an increase in insurance premiums paid by the general population, absurd contortions by the people generally and their companies to exclude liability, and an atmosphere of hostility.

16.20 The conduct of those who habitually overreach in litigation is rendered even more questionable when they claim that they are doing this in the cause of morality, justice, and the small litigant. Even the luxurious mediaeval clergy did not take as big a cut as those more aggressive members of the plaintiff bar do under the banner of morality and charity. They bring the US legal system and lawyers into disrepute. As Geoffrey Chaucer remarked in the fourteenth century, 'If gold rusts, what will iron do?'

16.21 The lawyers concerned are not doing anything unlawful or improper under their bar rules or applicable law. They are doing their best for their clients.

16.22 An example of how litigation can involve unexpected risks in the US is the remarkable case of *Bondi v Citigroup* 423, NJ, Super, 32A 3d 1158 (App Div 2011) decided by the New Jersey Court of Appeal. Bondi was the insolvency administrator of a listed Italian milk company called Parmalat. Unknown to anybody outside, Parmalat was insolvent from 1990 to 2003 when it was revealed that a deposit of US$4 billion, entered in its financial statements as being held with the Cayman branch of an American bank, did not exist. The deposit was a straight forgery and a scam masterminded by two members of Parmalat's senior management. Bondi's claim against Citigroup was in substance that Citigroup knew of the fraudulent insolvency of Parmalat, but nevertheless continued to enter into financial transactions with Parmalat in order to earn fees. In other words, the fraudulent publicly listed company alleged that Citigroup was a fraudulent co-conspirator lending huge sums of money to known fraudsters over many years. The pleadings were well decorated with claims of dishonesty, fraud, and conspiracy, all done for greed. This time the jury got it right and the Bondi claim against Citigroup was dismissed. The New Jersey Court of Appeal also very properly dismissed the claim. So far, so good. What was wrong was that the initial claim that Citi knew all along about the fraud—which must have meant that a lot of people in the bank, including the credit committee at Citi, knew about it for all those years—was too incredible to be believed. Yet the trial judge let the case go ahead, which it did at enormous expense for a seventy-day trial. The English courts would never have let such a ridiculous case ever to go to trial and would never have permitted the allegations of fraud and dishonesty, which would have involved so many people at Citigroup, to appear in the pleadings without proper substantiation. Some of the other international banks involved with Parmalat settled. Perhaps they thought that the unjust reputational damage, costs, and unpredictability involved in that kind of litigation were too great, but we do not know.

Class actions

16.23 The purpose of a class action by a representative claimant is to deal with a situation where there are common issues but a large number of claimants. All members of the class are bound by a judgment or court-approved settlement. The court must certify the class in order to ensure that the procedure is just and fair.

16.24 The objects are to ensure that claimants have access to justice by pooling, that the defendant has to face only one action and can settle only once, judicial economy and the resulting decrease in costs, and the avoidance of inconsistent judgments. The main objection is that class actions encourage abusive litigation, especially in the US when combined with the other features of US litigation just listed. There are high incentives on the lawyers of the representative and defendants to settle. The representative usually settles so that it and its lawyers get a good chunk of money for a doubtful claim, and the defendants settle just to get rid of the hassle, however unmeritorious the claim. Hence, money changes hands secretly. In securities actions, abuse by US litigation was restricted by that Private Securities Litigation Reform Act 1995 and by the Securities Litigation Uniform Standards Act of 1998.

16.25 The key features of class litigation are whether potential claimants are automatically included and have to opt out, or whether claimants have to opt in, which is more difficult to arrange, especially if they are exposed to costs—which they are not in the US.

16.26 The US federal rules of Civil Procedure provide in rule 23 that a class action will only be permitted if '(1) The class is so numerous that joinder of all members is impracticable, (2) there are questions of law or fact common to the class, (3) that claims of the representative parties are typical of that claims of the class, and (4) that representative parties will fairly and adequately protect the interests of the class'.

16.27 Class actions of varying degrees of intensity are available in, for example, Ontario, Quebec, British Columbia, Australia in the federal court, the Netherlands (settlement agreements authorised under an act of 2013), Sweden, Taiwan, South Africa, and Italy. Sometimes, the class action is restricted to consumers, as in Italy and as in the UK since 2015 for collective proceedings for breaches of competition law. US class actions normally exclude foreign members because of foreign obstacles. The Dutch proceedings do not. The Dutch proceedings follow the US in automatically including claimants unless they opt out.

16.28 Apart from the UK class actions for breaches of competition law, the UK does not have US-style class actions, although there can be a group litigation order and a representative action. In the main, English law is hostile to mass tort litigation.

16.29 Class actions have been available in France since 2014 but limited to certain types of action such as health, environmental liability, discrimination, and personal data protection. Germany does not have a collective class action. Model case proceedings were introduced in 2018 but are highly limited and have nowhere near the intensity of the US class action.

Discovery of documents

16.30 In general. the English procedural rules do not allow the fishing expeditions permitted by US courts in relation to the disclosure or discovery of documents by each party relating to the case.

16.31 Document discovery is very restricted in France and Germany: generally in these jurisdictions the inquiring party has to specify the particular document they want and cannot call for all documents generically relating to the case.

Non-conflicting Indicators

Reason for exclusion

16.32 The four indicators briefly listed below are excluded from the range of key indicators because they do not satisfy the eligibility test that they demonstrate a material clash or conflict of policies. Although there are differences between jurisdictions on these matters, they are in most cases not sufficiently significant, subject here and there to qualifications.

Pre-judgment freezes

16.33 It seems that most leading states permit an application to the court by a creditor prior to the commencement of proceedings for an order prohibiting a potential debtor from removing assets from the jurisdiction prior to a judgment in order to evade enforcement. This is true of England and most, if not all, of the significant English-based jurisdictions (including Canada, Australia, Ireland, and New Zealand) and of France, Germany, the Netherlands, Italy, Greece, Denmark, Spain, and Portugal. In the US, pre-judgment attachment is mandated by the procedural rules of most US states. English law permits worldwide freezing orders but, of course, there may be local enforcement problems.

16.34 An EU Regulation of 2017 establishes a European account preservation order allowing a claimant to freeze moneys in a defendant's bank accounts across the EU. The UK and Denmark did not opt into this regulation.

Enforcement of foreign judgments

16.35 Almost all of the leading jurisdictions enforce final and conclusive money judgments of foreign states if the judgment debtor expressly submitted to the jurisdiction of the foreign court (and often in other cases as well) and do not examine the judgment on the merits, provided that the claim is not for taxes, fines or penalties. These procedures are subject to some quite basic conditions, such as a fair trial without fraud, due notice of the original proceedings to the debtor, and compliance with local public policy. Some jurisdictions (not England or New York) require reciprocity, which is usually easy to establish.

16.36 A treaty improves the position and also avoids delays. The UK has a large network of treaties. The EU Judgments Regulation of 2012 provides for the enforcement of all judgments rendered by EU courts by other Member States. The UK is no longer a member of this system but may in due course join the similar Lugano Convention. However, the judgments of English courts for money debts have widespread recognition around the world so the loss is mainly procedural in that a judgment creditor must obtain a local enforcement order, instead of a simple registration process under the EU Judgments Regulation. New York is not a member of the EU judgments system and that does not seem to bother anybody.

16.37 It is believed that the United States, Japan, and South Korea do not have any treaties. US judgments involving punitive damages have not been enforced in Japan, England, or Australia to the extent of the punitive element on grounds of public policy. US judgments based on jury awards are likely to receive greater scrutiny.

16.38 In the context of the transactions we are talking about in this work, the enforcement of judgments elsewhere is much less usual than would be expected. This is because if a defendant is solvent, then it can affect the reputation of a business to have an unsatisfied judgment hanging over it and in particular this could cause its credit to dry up. Most cases settle. If the defendant is insolvent, then in a large case the attempt by one creditor to win the race to the courthouse door and obtain priority will typically be prevented by other creditors, either by an agreed standstill or by a compulsory standstill imposed by an insolvency petition. It follows that the enforceability of a foreign judgment is not generally a significant issue in practice and they seem to be mainly confined to family or consumer matters.

16.39 They are more likely to be significant in relation to a judgments against foreign bankrupt sovereigns who decline to negotiate with their creditors in good faith. That situation arose in relation to Argentina in the years following its default in 2001 when, after obtaining a New York judgment for unpaid bonds, a hedge fund creditor NML launched a vast international enforcement campaign against Argentinian state assets abroad. One of their prizes was the attachment of an Argentinian military training ship located in Ghana—this was later set aside as being contrary to the law of the sea. Courts in France prevented attachments of bank accounts in France by the hedge fund because the moneys concerned were tax and social security claims and oil royalties. The court, somewhat unrealistically, held that, despite the waiver of immunity, assets of that kind had to be expressly mentioned specifically.

Sovereign immunity

16.40 The efficacy of waivers of sovereign immunity customarily found in loans, bonds, sales agreements, and other commercial contracts with sovereign states, central banks, and state entities, are generally upheld by the leading commercial states, except in relation to diplomatic bank accounts abroad. The US and the UK have legislation to that effect which also removes immunity from judgment and enforcement in cases of commercial transactions and commercial assets, except for central banks where a specific waiver is required. The UK State Immunity Act 1978 has been adopted in very similar terms in Singapore, South Africa, Canada, Pakistan, and Australia. In civil code countries, notably the Netherlands, France, Germany, Switzerland, Belgium, Italy, Japan, and others, de-immunisation has, ironically, been achieved by case law.

16.41 Hong Kong case law decides that sovereigns have absolute immunity in Hong Kong, but there was no waiver of sovereign immunity in that case. The 2011 case concerned also established that China accords absolute immunity to foreign states.

16.42 The fact that sovereign states are often requested to waive sovereign immunity in their commercial contracts does not change the reality that sovereign states are in a privileged position compared to ordinary corporations and individuals. It is believed that most sovereign states do not permit governmental assets within their territory to be attached by a creditor. As regards their external assets, these are often also protected because well-advised sovereign states locate their commercial assets in state entities, such as the central bank holding foreign reserves. The state entities are commonly treated in the leading jurisdictions as separate legal entities who are not responsible for creditors' claims against the sovereign state itself.

16.43 That situation helps explain why countries, such as the US and the UK have not been willing to pass legislation setting up a bankruptcy proceeding, such as a moratorium, for sovereign states. They are already above the law which applies to the rest of us.

Arbitration

Introduction

16.44 Arbitration instead of a submission to the courts of a named jurisdiction has historically been common in some commercial contracts, such as sale of goods contracts and construction contracts, but not financial contracts. I do not use arbitration as a key indicator because arbitration does not satisfy at least one of the eligibility tests for a key indicator, that is, material clash of policies between the main jurisdictions.

Advantages and disadvantages of arbitration

16.45 The main advantage of arbitration is that most countries are signatories of the New York Arbitration Convention of 1958 which requires contracting states to enforce arbitration awards.

16.46 It is sometimes maintained that an arbitral forum is neutral and that it avoids the risks of local courts. These advantages are also true in the case of a choice of external courts, such as the English or New York courts. Arbitration sometimes meets sovereign sensitivities to submitting to foreign courts.

16.47 Other advantages are that the parties can choose their own adjudicator, they can provide for the language of the arbitration, and the proceedings normally enjoy confidentiality. The parties can limit the scope of pre-trial disclosure or discovery of documents so that arbitration can be an escape from disproportionate American-style discovery. Arbitration is outside the European Union Judgments Regulation of 2012.

16.48 The disadvantages of arbitration which are often cited include that there is nothing to arbitrate (notably in financial contracts) and the arbitration is just an excuse to delay matters—it takes time to appoint the arbitrators and to arrange the proceedings. Also the arbitration forum is exclusive, although sometimes banks have required an optional arbitration clause. There may be jurisdiction disputes and often awards are final without appeal except on very limited grounds. It is generally not possible to obtain a summary or default judgment against a defendant who does not appear in the proceedings, but generally pre-award freezes are available through the courts to prevent the removal of assets from the jurisdiction to evade enforcement The procedures of the proceedings may be looser: it is arguable whether or not this leads to more delays if a defendant does not cooperate.

16.49 It is common for arbitration clauses to apply the rules of an arbitration institution, such as the international Chamber of Commerce, the London Court of International Arbitration, the American Arbitration Association, the Singapore International Arbitration Centre, the Hong Kong International Arbitration centre, the Swiss and Stockholm Chambers of Commerce, and PRIME Finance at the Hague.

16.50 The seat can be in a different jurisdiction from the country where any chosen arbitral institution is based. The choice of the seat is important because the local courts will have supervisory powers.

Use of arbitration in financial and corporate transactions

16.51 The following financial and corporate documents do not usually specify arbitration for dispute resolution if international, although there can be exceptional cases:

- syndicated bank credit agreements and loan transfer documents
- bond issue documents and their accompanying launch agreements (subscription agreements, paying agency agreements, trust deeds, and the like)
- derivatives agreements, usually based on the ISDA master agreement, foreign exchange contracts, and netting agreements

- securitisation documents, including transfers of the securitised receivables, servicing agreements, and liquidity agreements
- investment banking agreements, prime brokerage agreements, client agreements, corporate finance advisory mandates, investment advisory agreements, and dealing agreements
- asset management documents, such as fund and portfolio management agreements and custodian agreements
- specialised contracts relating to securities settlement systems, payment systems, and central counterparties
- agreements documenting security interests, repos, and financial leases
- in the corporate sphere, equity capital-raising documents, sale and purchase agreements for the sale of private companies, takeover offers, and joint venture agreements
- off-take contracts and other contracts involved in project finance
- insurance policies.

16.52 In the US, parties sometimes choose arbitration in non-credit contracts such as investment management contracts. The motive appears to be the avoidance of jury trials and adverse court litigation. ISDA has model clauses for arbitration in its master agreement but it is believed that the options are little used.

16.53 Arbitration seems to be very common in construction and other contracts employed in project finance. Many host government concessions for projects contain arbitration clauses.

16.54 Bilateral investment treaties, dealing for example with expropriations, are of much importance for projects in emerging countries. They typically give the private investor or lender direct rights to arbitrate disputes under the bilateral investment treaty, including disputes regarding expropriations.

Conclusions

16.55 The main conclusion in relation to the key indicators is that the English courts are reasonably safe on the matters listed in paragraph 16.9 and discussed in other chapters, such as predictability, commerciality, business orientation, insulation from foreign laws, favourable conflict of laws rules, and the like.

16.56 In relation to class actions, discovery of documents, and proportionality of damages, litigation in the US is in practice much more aggressive than is the case in England, France, or Germany, and is on its own. The US position is consistent with its fairly pro-debtor bankruptcy regime and even more so with the enthusiasm of US regulators as regards rigorous enforcement.

17
NON-LEGAL INDICATORS AND RISKS

Introduction

17.1 There are a number of significant factors which are not of a strictly legal nature but which often are important in the choice of law in courts and together sometimes overwhelming. This chapter covers the thirteenth and last letter in the sequence of the thirteen themes expressed in the mnemonic PIB–FEISST–CoRCO, standing for *p*redictability, *i*nsulation, *b*usiness orientation, *f*reedom of contract, *e*xclusion clauses, *i*nsolvency law, *s*et-off, *s*ecurity interests, *t*rusts, *co*rporate law, *r*egulatory law, *c*ourts, and *o*thers.

Familiarity of Governing Law

Brand recognition of a legal system

17.2 If a governing law and accompanying courts are widely selected for major contracts over a significant period time, then the market trusts the legal system simply because it has been used many times and because other people use it. The legal system is resorted to because it has become a brand with a glow of goodwill attached to it, a kind of halo. It is no longer necessary to investigate its tenets each time and, indeed, such an investigation would be enormously time-consuming and costly. In effect, the investigation would be impracticable since legal systems are vast and also because there are not that many lawyers who could make that kind of detailed comparison. Hence, transaction costs are greatly reduced and, where the use of a legal system has become a market practice, that choice ceases to be something which has to be negotiated each time. If it is challenged, then the response may well be that the deal will be prejudiced because the market or the parties are not familiar with a different law.

17.3 For example, if a commercial bank or investment bank is arranging a syndicated bank credit or an international bond issue and the borrower proposes an unfamiliar legal system instead of, say, English or New York law, then the arrangers may advise that that factor alone will make it unrealistic to sell the deal to international banks or bondholders. These factors give both English and New York law a strong advantage in the competition between legal systems by reason of their widespread use as international public utilities.

17.4 On the other hand, once a legal system acquires a material international visibility, then a major gaffe by the legal system can have adverse consequences. If the courts continue to adopt positions that do not accord with market expectations on a recurrent basis, then markets can rapidly lose confidence. They have a choice and it is right that they should have a choice.

Market reaction to legal gaffes

Some examples of this kind of reaction will suffice. **17.5**

In *Hazell v Hammerson and Fulham London Borough Council* [1992] 2 AC 1 (HL) the House of Lords in England decided that a London municipality, the Hammersmith and Fulham Borough Council, did not have the power to enter into interest rates derivatives so that the transactions were void. In fact, you would think that everybody would know that municipalities are not allowed to do anything other than collect rubbish and, indeed, there are many cases the world over where transactions with municipalities have been struck down as outside their powers. The decision caused consternation in the City of London. The Bank of England convened a committee to discuss the risks in English law and the committee's deliberations led to the establishment of the Financial Markets Law Committee composed of senior market participants and lawyers, chaired by a former member of the House of Lords, to consider 'uncertainties' in English law. **17.6**

During the consultations with the market at the time, the most frequent complaint, apart from the Hammersmith and Fulham situation and gripes about the regulatory burden, was a throw-away line by a judge in the English case of *Re Charge Card Services Ltd* [1986] 3 All ER 289 that it was 'conceptually impossible' for a debtor to create a charge over a debt back to its creditor. Such a transaction is not particularly common but it struck a chord and provoked indignation, because the court found it impossible to conceive of a transaction which the market could conceive of, because charge-backs where permissible under case law in England and in the other main jurisdictions, because at the time the new derivatives market presented very large risks, and because at the time the availability of close-out netting in England was doubted (wrongly) by some lawyers. This negation of charge-backs seemed vaguely to be an attack on netting. After that, market documents relying on set-off typically used what was called a 'triple cocktail', namely a flawed asset, a charge-back, and a contractual set-off, just to make sure. I do not need to explain the detail of flawed assets other than to say that both flawed assets and charge-backs were approved in *Re Bank of Credit and Commerce International SA (No 8)* [1998] AC 214 and all the fuss died down. What was remarkable about that situation was that a single remark by a court about an exotic transaction, which hardly anybody used or understood, could have raised such a furore as if some fundamental principle of civilisation had been denied. **17.7**

A third example of widespread dismay over an apparent technicality was a decision by a US Federal court in New York in 2012 which held that a standard clause in bonds and bank loan agreements that all of the borrower's obligations will rank pari passu with all its other unsecured liabilities meant that a borrower in financial difficulties had to pay all its obligations equally in fact. This upset the standard interpretation that the clause was just a harmless warranty that there was no mandatory law that discriminated between creditors by subordinating some of them to others, not that the borrower actually had to pay creditors equally. If correct, the interpretation of the court meant that hold-out creditors who did not agree a rescheduling approved by the majority of bondholders could force the sovereign debtor to pay them the full amount of their non-rescheduled amounts if the sovereign paid anything to the rescheduled bondholders. That would disrupt a rescheduling because then bondholders would have no incentive to agree a rescheduling since, if they had held out, **17.8** they would get paid in full anyway, or in any event they would have a disproportionately strong bargaining position. The case became a major concern, not only to bondholders and sovereign states who wanted to be able to restructure their debt if they were in potential difficulties, but also to the IMF, which saw this as a material threat to stability. The litigation rambled on for about five years until Argentina with great reluctance settled with the creditor NML. The same judge held in a later case that his original decision was a very special case on its facts because of the conduct of Argentina and was not to be taken as a precedent. So the bond market just shrugged it off and went on as before, all the more convinced that the world was full of legal pedants and metaphysicians.

Language

English as the language of international business

17.9 The language of many international business transactions is, as with aviation, conducted in English, especially financial transactions, and English is a *lingua franca* fluently spoken by a large number of business individuals.

17.10 If the governing law and courts chosen are those of a non-English jurisdiction, then it will likely be the case that court proceedings will be in the foreign language. Comparative law texts on the business transactions which are the subjects of this work are not in huge supply, and a full range of relevant statutes and especially case law are rarely published in translation. Major domestic commentaries on the crucial subjects are often too voluminous to be translated. The local law will tend to be more inaccessible to English-speaking parties except through the medium of lawyers in the country concerned.

17.11 Transaction documents, especially those involving the sale of or a security interest over a registered asset, may well have to be translated into the local language in order to be registered. The local language version will often be the governing version in terms of interpretation.

Reflections on English as a language

17.12 English is a problematic language mainly because of its non-rules about spelling and pronunciation. A frequently quoted example is the differing pronunciations of through, bough, thorough, and tough, even though the syllable -ough is spelt the same. Another reason is that the language often has two words with roughly the same meaning, but with a different nuance. This is because the language is really a mongrel language of two languages untidily bolted together, based on an Anglo-Saxon dialect (Germanic) of the invaders over the centuries from the 400s to the 900s AD after the Romans had left, and then Norman French (Romance) after the Norman invasion of 1066 led by William the Conqueror. The Norman French considered themselves superior to the local barbarians, and so there is both an Anglo-Saxon word and a Romance word for the same concept. Examples are love and desire, room and chamber, ways and means, goods and chattels, kingly and royal (and then later regal in the eighteenth century), duplicates or triplicates with shades of resonance so subtle as to be incomprehensible to a foreign speaker. Many of the important twins sprang from legal usage, in which the Normans excelled. On the other hand, English is ironically the most European of all languages.

Financial Centres

Attributes of a financial centre

17.13 Financial centres are like a much-used legal system in that they possess of networking advantages of clubs and a communal access to utilities.

17.14 The ideal financial centre has a diversity of financial businesses on its doorstep. A financial centre will include formal stock exchanges and off-exchange markets for securities and the listing of securities. The main advantages of organised markets are that clients can channel their orders via intermediaries in the market who deal with each other, that there are a large number of people available to do deals so that there is nearly always a counterparty willing to buy or sell (called liquidity), that the prices of deals are publicised so as to be transparent, that deals can be matched, that transactions can be settled via central counterparties discussed at paragraph 3.62, and that the markets are properly organised. Well-run markets have fit and proper persons as managers, have regulated members, have rules which provide for the suspension of dealings in the case of disorderly trading and for business continuity, ensure regulatory compliance and the absence of market manipulation and insider dealing, and promote fee competition. Listing enables an issuer to raise permanent capital from a large pool of investors and can enhance credibility. An issuer can use its shares to pay for takeovers.

17.15 A financial centre will also have other markets, such as an interbank deposit market, a foreign exchange market, a money market for short-term paper, and typically older markets for commodities and foodstuffs.

17.16 The centre should be well populated by commercial banks, investment banks who can arrange deals, and home mortgage banks, as well as specialist firms carrying out leasing and factoring. It will need a population of broker-dealers, and other institutions who deal in securities, such as pension funds, mutual funds, investment companies, hedge funds, private equity funds, insurance companies, and custodians or depositories of investments. It will need investment managers.

17.17 The above will come with a supporting cast of armies of data depositories, administrators of benchmarks (such as interest rates or the price of commodities), analysts, share registrars, bondholder trustee companies, professionals (such as accountants, lawyers, valuers, and notaries), transfer agents, information providers, and many others.

17.18 By many measures, London and New York are the largest financial centres in the world, although there are others. Some specialise in a segment, such as insurance (Bermuda) or mutual funds.

17.19 Strictly, nowadays financial centres could be virtual but in practice human beings are gregarious.

Financial centres and the legal system

17.20 The financial centre is underpinned generally by the local legal system and courts, which must be suited to this class of business. Financial firms prefer a regulatory set which maintains a high standard of conduct, but is neither disproportionate in its interventionism or in its penalties. They also prefer a high degree of predictability of contract, freedom and openness to business, and a legal culture which is not anti-business or disproportionately pro-debtor.

17.21 Financial transactions in these financial centres are typically internationally mobile in that transactions can be subject to other laws chosen by the parties if they wish. Some laws cannot be chosen by the parties, such as the regulatory regime, large parts of the bankruptcy regime, the listing rules for companies, and the like. It follows that these have to be suitable for the market.

17.22 It goes without saying that countries which have a financial centre benefit from additional taxes, employees, and exports, as well as the soft and hard power conferred by control of a financial centre.

Legal Infrastructure

Political and rule of law risks

17.23 Political risks, such as the risk of expropriation, the absence of the rule of law, a lack of personal security, corruption, arbitrary arrests, the abuse of power and the lack of any kind of legal efficiency or a proper court system can be deal-breakers and often are. Thus, the law in Belgium and the law in Congo Kinshasa may be very similar, but the legal infrastructure and the political risks are very different. In practice, it is often not possible to carry out, say, a project finance transaction in a country which is both destitute and has despotic leadership without the involvement of a multilateral development bank, such as the World Bank, or a political risk guarantee. A bilateral investment treaty between the host government and the countries of the main investors is helpful because case law has established for many years that private investors can arbitrate a claim under these treaties in an international arbitration forum. Regrettably, that still does not satisfy the ability to enforce an award against the sovereign state concerned.

17.24 In the case of France, Germany, the UK, and the US, these issues do not arise. As for other countries, mainly lesser developed countries, an assessment of the risks can be explored through the work of many institutions which rank countries according to political risk, corruption rule of law and legal infrastructure, such as Transparency International, the World Justice Project, the World Economic Forum and Heritage Foundation, plus many other official and private assessors.

Conclusion on legal infrastructure

17.25 If one tabulates the results of measuring institutions by a simple colour code of blue, green, yellow, and red, as against GDP per capita, it becomes dramatically apparent that there is a striking correlation between GDP per capita and the rule of law and similar legal infrastructure ranking. If the country is blue on legal infrastructure, it also usually has high GDP per capita and therefore greater wealth and prosperity. If the country is red on legal infrastructure, it is commonly a poor country with bad government. There are arguments about whether wealth produces rule of law or whether the rule of law produces wealth, but I suspect that they go hand in hand.

17.26 In any event, what the law says, that is, black letter law or law on the books, is different from legal infrastructure. They have yet to be kept separate in the measurement process. Otherwise, you just have noise and a blur from measuring too many things at once.

18
COMPARISON OF JURISDICTIONS OF THE WORLD

Identifying the Families of Jurisdictions

Importance of identifying families of jurisdictions

18.1 The foundation and the key to understanding world financial law is to identify all the jurisdictions of the world and to group them into families of law, families which derive from the same source. In fact, this is the only way in which comparative law can proceed in the field of private law, ie the fields we are concerned with in this book, such as contract, commercial law, financial law, corporate law, bankruptcy law, regulatory, and the like. If we could not deduce a method of grouping legal systems and their policy outcomes, then comparative lawyers and practitioners would be faced with just a disorganised hubbub of noise and confusion, rather than an ordered and comprehensible musical harmony.

Themes and key indicators

18.2 In this chapter, I identify and define the main families of law and place them into groups and sub-groups. I also explain how I arrived at a methodology to identify the jurisdictions by reference to certain key indicators. As so often mentioned, legal indicators must be measurable, economically important, symbolic, and clashing.

18.3 You can build the house of comparative law by tracing the history of legal systems since almost all jurisdictions have borrowed their laws from somebody else, either by emulation and imitation or by virtue of past imperialism. The history and sources will get you some of the way, but, for the identification to be sharp and accurate, we need legal indicators which precisely fix the jurisprudence of a territory. We need clear beacons or landmarks which are determinative of the content of the law, rather than just stereotyped cultural speculations or indicators which do not satisfy the four tests I mentioned above and which are therefore weak.

18.4 If we can do that with convincing and credible results, and if we can discover why the disarray has happened, then we are a long, long way down the road to solving comparative law, which at the moment is often looking the wrong way and fragmented. Comparative law requires a proper foundation across all the main areas of private law, if it is not to be in disarray and splintered into separate sects who never talk to each other.

18.5 One of the questions is whether there is a consistency or pattern of legal policies as regards the main themes. I have reasonable universal data for most of the 320 jurisdictions on the topics of insolvency set-off, security interests, trusts, and a variety of other bankruptcy indicators—which are considered to be the most powerful—but the scope of the data for such matters as predictability in contract and indicators used for business orientation, freedom of contract, exclusion clauses, corporate law, regulation, and litigation does not extend to all 320 territories. Nevertheless, if a significant number of jurisdictions in a family group have the same view on an aspect of law within the scope of this book, it seems probable that the law on that same aspect in the rest of the group would be similar, at least as regards law on the books, as opposed of course to legal infrastructure.

The triple polarisation of law

18.6 Just as the world is dominated by three universal religions—Christianity, Islam, and Buddhism (the latter is a distant third behind the two mega-religions)—so it is with families of law. The object of this chapter is to identify the members of the three major families of law in the world—the common law jurisdictions developed mainly by England and the US, the Napoleonic jurisdictions developed mainly by France, and the Roman-Germanic jurisdictions mainly by Germany with others, such as the Dutch.

18.7 Just as religions split into sects, so also with the families of law. As discussed in Chapter 1, we end up with about eight groups, composed in turn of sub-divisions, and sub-divisions of sub-divisions—just as you would find in any taxonomy of plants or birds or mammals or galaxies or religions or philosophies. The degree of fineness of the layers depends on how much you want to be a lumper or a splitter. If you are a lumper, then you lump things together for the convenience of overall comprehension, the motorways but not every street, lane, byway, or path, whereas when you are actually on your walk, you may well need to be a splitter.

18.8 To summarise, the eight families of law are:

- American common law
- English common law
- Napoleonic
- Roman-Germanic
- mixed civil/common law
- Islamic
- new or transition
- unallocated.

18.9 The mnemonic for these is big four plus MINU.

18.10 The groups are completely dominated by the three major groups so that if you understand the fundamental approaches of these three major groups, then you discover the formula, the key, the code, the secret to understanding all of them. If we were to take a much broader brush and blur some of the lines between some jurisdictions and amalgamate others, then in very crude terms a division of the world into 40 per cent English-American common law, 30 per cent Napoleonic, 20 per cent Roman-Germanic, and 10 per cent the rest would not be too far out.

Development of Legal Indicators for Comparative Law

Herstatt 1974

18.11 This section explains how I developed the methodology displayed in this book and how I arrived at the result by a circuitous and unexpected route.

18.12 In 1974, German bank Herstatt was closed by the German authorities in the middle of the afternoon by reason of insolvency. The losses suffered by other banks internationally were enormous because these bank counterparties had foreign exchange contracts with Herstatt and had paid their leg of foreign currency, especially in Japanese yen when Tokyo was open much earlier, but had not been paid the US dollar leg by Herstatt because New York had not opened at the time of the closure of Herstatt. This was the first warning clang of the bell.

British Eagle 1975

18.13 In 1975, a decision of the highest court in England, the House of Lords, held that a clearing system operated by airlines was ineffective on the bankruptcy of one of the participants which was the upstart airline British Eagle. The airlines were netting off reciprocal airline ticket payments and the like, first between bilateral pairs and then multilaterally. The effect of the multilateral set-off meant that a debt owed to British Eagle got taken away from the liquidation estate of British Eagle to set off against another airline's debt: the claims were not mutual. The invalidity was perfectly correct because when a company becomes bankrupt, a creditor cannot just walk in and collect the sofa and the television to cover the creditor's claims. Assets of a bankrupt are frozen for division of the proceeds amongst creditors. The case was *British Eagle v Air France* [1975] 2 All ER 390. Nothing wrong with that. Except that payment clearing systems in the US for dollars, the similar system for sterling in the UK, and other major payment systems in the world all operated on exactly the same principle of multilateral set-offs. If a participating bank became insolvent, the losses could be so enormous that other clearing banks might collapse, taking the banking system with them. That was the second clang of the bell.

Iran 1979

18.14 In 1979, when the Iranian revolution installed an Islamic Ayatollah in place of the Shah, the central bank of Iran, Bank Markazi, required large American banks in London to repay their deposits on Monday morning. The State of Iran and large number of state entities, such as the oil company, owed substantial loans to American and other banks. The American banks organised a vote of all of the syndicates of banks, which included Japanese, Canadian, and European banks, and on the basis of that vote (or lack of it) called in their loans. They then sent a telex to Bank Markazi in English and Farsi saying that the banks were setting off the loans against the deposits. They did not get a reply and nor did Bank Markazi get back its deposits. This time the bell only rang out a faint ting because the event showed what could be done with set-off. It prevented huge losses since the Iranians had repudiated the loans so they would have got their deposits back but not paid their loans. Ironically the set-off was legally dubious, because, as in the *British Eagle* case, the criss-crossing claims were not mutual. That is because the banks owed the deposits to Bank Markazi but the loans were owed by different legal entities. In the clamour of the day, those arguments were dismissed on the basis that Iran and all its entities were fused. So the bell should have rung an alarm. The matter was settled in the Algerian Accords brokered by President Carter.

Sovereign bankruptcies in the 1980s

During the 1980s, more than 40 per cent of the sovereign states in the world—mainly emerging countries—became bankrupt and thereby put the solvency of major international banks at risk. If a little bank like Herstatt could cause such mayhem and loss, what would happen if a major bank failed? **18.15**

At the same time, there were two other developments which gave central banks nightmares. The first was that the foreign exchange market was now huge, a many times multiple of world GDP, as a result of the freeing of exchange rates by President Nixon when the US came off the gold standard after the Vietnam War and the general increase in financial flows from rising prosperity. The second was that derivatives had appeared in markets to deal with the volatility of interest rates and the value of foreign currencies. Derivatives are in substance a way by which market participants could take out insurance against these risks. Just as you could insure your house against a fire or your car against a crash, you could also insure risks of the crash of your currency or a fire in your interest rates. In 1987, the International Swaps and Derivatives Association published its master agreement which made it feasible to manage risks on the enormous volume of derivatives which now ran to many trillions of dollars. **18.16**

It was calculated at the time that on any particular day one bank could have an exposure of more than 20 per cent of the foreign exchange market and that, if that bank failed, again the banking system could receive a mortal blow which would send it flying. It was also calculated that it might be possible to reduce exposures of these other banks on their transactions with a bankrupt bank by more than 90 per cent on a good day. Therefore, you had a 90 per cent better chance of staying alive if you could terminate the contracts and set off the losses and gains between the parties. **18.17**

The conundrum of insolvency set-off

In 1989, I published a book on English and international set-off with 1,246 pages of text. In the closing stages of writing this text, I wrote to lawyers in sixty-nine countries asking them for their laws on set-off to enable me to explore the 'international' part of the work. The replies posed an impenetrable puzzle. This was that in England set-off between parties who were both solvent was difficult and restricted. But if one party was insolvent, the set-off was mandatory and had to take place. But in France, just twenty-two miles across the Channel, with a similar European culture and state of development, set-off between solvent parties was very easy and sometimes automatic when the debts matured; however, if one party was **18.18** insolvent, the set-off was prohibited. So what could possibly be the explanation of this complete reversal of policies? Hidden in this seemingly arcane, abstruse, and scholastic point in a little-known subject called set-off—a small singer in the chorus of law—was a secret of some magnitude. It was of some magnitude because of the huge risks in markets which could be miraculously reduced by set-off.

18.19 The solution to the puzzle which I arrived at was that England was protecting creditors, such as banks, sellers, and shipowners, but France was protecting debtors.

18.20 If both parties were solvent, then English law wanted the creditor to be paid—pay now, litigate later. So the debtor had to pay the creditor—the bank, the seller, the shipowner—without delay so that the creditor got paid immediately. This was important for cash-flow—protection of the creditor.

18.21 But if the debtor was insolvent, the creditor got paid by the set-off. This was the only way the creditor could get paid—protection of the creditor again.

18.22 France, however, gave parties the right to set off if both parties were solvent so as to protect debtors and thereby interrupting payment in cash—protection of the debtor but not the creditor. But if the debtor was insolvent, the French prohibition on set-off enlarged the debtor's estate because the creditor had to pay in full but did not get paid by the insolvent—protection of the debtor again.

18.23 Not at all obvious at first, but obvious once you saw it.

18.24 After that, everything fell into place. England had very wide security interests, but France did not. France protected debtors against loan terminations and the like via the good faith doctrine in contracts, but England favoured predictability, which is what creditors want, and therefore did not intervene to override express termination rights.

18.25 Other conundrums also unravelled, for example the absence of the trust in civil code jurisdictions, the problems about having to give the debtor on a debt notice of the sale, which inhibited security interests over receivables and securitisations, and the presence in English-based jurisdictions of tracing embezzled money through mixed bank accounts, not available in civil law countries. These five legal indicators were astonishingly accurate in defining the legal approach of a jurisdiction in its private law, when taken together. All the indicators satisfied the four tests, ie that they were measurable, symbolic of wider attitudes to risk, that (except for tracing) they involved enormous amounts, and that they revealed intensely conflicting policies. For example, both set-off and security interests defy the equality of creditors on bankruptcy because a creditor with a set-off and a creditor with collateral get paid out of the assets of the bankrupt in priority to other creditors, who may not get paid anything at all, except a derisory dividend.

18.26 The picture which I developed on the basis of these indicators was that France was red on all of my tests, Germany was red on half of them and blue on half of them, and that England was blue on all of them. You therefore had a perfectly symmetrical chart, all red on one side, all blue on the other, and the piece in the middle being half red and half blue. Since the law of around 85 per cent of the world jurisdictions is roughly based on the law of one of these countries, in one stroke we had a revolutionary method of piercing the darkness of law, we could open the door to let the light shine in. That heraldic tableau, that flag of the world, with its three panels of audacious simplicity, represented—at least up to around the year 2000—the three spectacular ideologies in a single dramatic vision. To me, this was like the slime in the petri dish, something which only happens once in a lifetime and only accidentally.

The discovery was made in 1988. Apart from articles, the results were published in my books on international finance in 1995. I produced privately circulated coloured maps in 1995, 1997, 2003, and 2005 (two editions). A set of maps was published in 2008, and the theory expanded in later editions of my financial law books in 2007 and 2019. **18.27**

This was by no means the first time that lawyers had suggested families of law. I believe it was the first time that families of law were defined accurately by a set of indicators which worked, rather than vague references to culture or to weak indicators, like codification or the doctrine of precedent. **18.28**

General Features of the Families of Law

Export of legal systems

The universal religions were exported by a mixture of coercion—as where rulers decreed a state religion (Darius of Persia, Ashoka of India, and Theodosius of Rome)—and voluntary conversion. So it was with legal systems. Both religions and legal systems had bouts of imperialism. Christianity, Islam, and Buddhism were all imperial exports on a grand scale. Incredibly, Christianity started in Jerusalem and Islam in one small city in the Arabian Peninsula, Mecca. **18.29**

Western Europe was economically the most dominant region in the world in the period around the 1830s, a period described by economists as the Great Divide when Western European economies pulled away from the rest. The Western European nations concerned exported their legal systems by imperialism, emulation, or significant influence. About half of the world's legal systems adopted a Western legal system voluntarily. Those who did took the latest model, eg most of Latin America after independence from France, partly via Spain in the nineteenth century, post-Meiji Japan from Germany in the early twentieth century, and post-revolutionary Turkey from Switzerland in the 1920s. Following the collapse of the USSR in 1991, the new Russian civil code was influenced by the Dutch new civil code which happened to be the latest in the early 1990s. People buy the latest car. The result is that now out of the 320 or so jurisdictions, more than 85 per cent draw their inspiration from three fundamental approaches developed originally by three jurisdictions—England, France, and Germany (with others). **18.30**

This is what I call the "triple polarisation" of law, when the jurisdictions of the world consolidated into the three basic approaches introduced by imperialism and emulation of the West. These ideologies are now represented in more than 85 per cent of the world's territory, holding more than 95 per cent of the world's population and producing more than 90 per cent of world GDP. **18.31**

18.32 History has seen many empires—Egyptian, Assyrian, Chinese, Greek, Persian, Macedonian, Mauryan, Gupta, Roman, Parthian, Sasanian, Arab, Ottoman, Mongol, Russian, Aztec, Inca, Spanish, African, British, French, and a multitude of others—all vanished, crumbled into dust. Some of these empires were extremely long-lived. The Byzantine Empire lasted more than 1,000 years, from circa 300 to 1453. Others lasted more than 500 years—the Roman Empire, the Arab Empire of the initial caliphates after Muhammad's death followed by the Ummayad and Abbasid dynasties (632–1258), the Khmer Empire, the Ottoman Empire, and the British and French Empires. The longest of all is the Chinese Empire, from about 200 BC to the present, with interruptions.

18.33 The advanced legal systems had been in the works for hundreds of years. Like science and medicine, they were useful. Like religions, they were ideologies, a set of beliefs.

Limited overlap between families of religion and law

18.34 There is little overlap between the families of religion and the families of law. This is because the Europeans disseminated three main families of law, but only one religion—Christianity. In some Islamic countries, there continues to be a battle for superiority between the received modern Western legal regime and ancient sharia law.

Diversity of cultures within the legal families

18.35 History has thrown up some extraordinary alliances in the spread of religions. Thus, the United States, Russia, and Malawi are in the same Christian family of religion. Similarly, in the case of the families of law the historical accident of the reception of legal systems resulted in some quite unexpected line-ups. The main legal groups include countries which are poor and rich, democratic and despotic, as with the religious groups. There are some other oddities. For example, why is China now so different from Russia? Both emerged from communist economies and reformed their private law at about the same time. Russia has a complex amalgam, but China determined to adopt a system of business law which is uncannily like English law of the nineteenth century, ie exceptionally pro-business, at least on paper. The initial surprise vanishes when one appreciates that China is a developing country now and so it is not strange that it should adopt business laws which are similar to the business laws of a major developing country in nineteenth-century Britain.

Rejection of a foreign ideology?

18.36 Some countries did not react well to a foreign religion. Buddhism was eventually seen as an interloper in both China and Japan. Christianity was a reject in most of Asia. However, the families of law met with very little rejection after independence of the countries concerned, mostly more than fifty years ago, and these rejections were not mainly to do with the content of the law but with a political philosophy—socialism. For example, in the decades after independence, Indian and Pakistan introduced laws that more or less savaged the liberal English model which they had received, but Hong Kong and Singapore did exactly the opposite and welcomed English law with great enthusiasm. One can see the difference in economic performance, which one must admit did not result only from the legal system. India and Pakistan adopted socialism, which was anti-business. Hong Kong and Singapore supported business enterprise.

Use of world maps

Elsewhere, I have produced some maps which exhibit the groups of jurisdictions and the position on various legal issues. In teaching comparative law, I used to get the students early on to colour in a large version of these maps according to whether they thought the country was basically English, Napoleonic, Roman-Germanic, or a mixture. The students generally had very little difficulty in identifying the right legal system, except that they almost always got Israel and Malta wrong. **18.37**

What is a jurisdiction?

Legal provinces or jurisdictions range from enormous jurisdictions, both in terms of population and geographic size, like China and Brazil, to tiny micro-states like Niue in the Pacific. **18.38**

A legal jurisdiction is different from a nation state—there are currently just under 200 sovereign states. The latest sovereign states to be formed and recognised are South Sudan, Kosovo, East Timor, and Montenegro. There are others waiting in the wings. Many nation states have a large number of internal jurisdictions. Thus, the United States has fifty-one (if we include the District of Columbia) and the British Isles has seven. The question of legal distinctness has nothing to do with who has overall sovereignty. The criterion as to whether a territory is a separate jurisdiction is whether the law is sufficiently different to merit separate investigation. **18.39**

A legal jurisdiction must have land, people who live there and are not just visitors like scientists, a de facto government, and laws which are different from the laws of other territories. There is no legal definition of a jurisdiction, but this definition tracks the conventional definition of a sovereign state under public international law, except that jurisdictions have to have a different legal system. You cannot have a territorial realm without law. **18.40**

Bouvet Island is not a jurisdiction, despite its territory of 4.9 square kilometres poking menacingly out of the South Atlantic, the remotest island in the world. Nobody lives on Bouvet Island and, indeed, nobody would want to live on Bouvet Island. Pitcairn Island just makes it with a population of only fifty-seven—the descendants of the mutineers of HMS Bounty in 1767. **18.41**

The government does not have to be recognised by other sovereign states. The Turkish Republic of North Cyprus, proclaimed in November 1983, is not recognised by anybody except Turkey but is a jurisdiction. I do not include two break-away territories from Georgia in the Caucasus namely, Abkhazia and South Ossetia—they do not have a sufficiently **18.42** settled system of private law to qualify. The same applies to western Morocco. Questions remain over Puntland, Somaliland, and South-Western Somalia, which are all breakaways from Somalia. Somaliland has a defiant Companies Act of 2004 based on a British model.

18.43 The smallest jurisdiction is the Vatican—0.17 square kilometres. The Vatican is also the smallest sovereign state. Its laws emanate from some higher authority. Russia is by far the world's largest legal jurisdiction with 17,100,000 square kilometres, almost twice as large as its nearest rival (Canada). Some jurisdictions punch well above their physical size. Both New York State and England, which together provide the governing law of a large portion of international wholesale contracts, are about the same (rather small) size. New York State has 122,000 square kilometres and England 130,000 square kilometres.

18.44 For those interested, the correct answer to the seven jurisdictions in the British Isles is England, Scotland, Northern Ireland, Isle of Man, Jersey, Guernsey, and Alderney and Sark, although knowledgeable lawyers in the Channel Islands may well dispute the last three. Scotland is basically a Roman jurisdiction with a direct view back to Roman law as codified by Justinian's lawyers in the 530s. The Channel Islands are as a matter of strict constitution not part of the United Kingdom but were islands belonging to the Duchy of Normandy before the Norman conquest of Britain in 1066 and therefore belong to the British Crown. Their law is largely based on pre-Napoleonic Norman law, although now much anglicised.

Which laws are family of law and which laws are not?

18.45 Some classes of law are determined wholly by the family of law; others not at all.

18.46 The family of law is an excellent indicator of *commercial*, *financial*, and *corporate law*, such as contract, the sale of goods, insurance, intellectual property, real property, litigation, and bankruptcy, and also torts or delicts (that is, civil wrongs and injuries such as motoring negligence or defamation). These are all mainly the province of private law.

18.47 It is generally true that in modern states the *criminal* law and the laws relating to the *family*, sex, and inheritance are determined by the family of law. But this fit is weak in the case of divorce and in the case of legal approaches to sex, such as gender discrimination, abortion, homosexuality, premarital sex, and adultery. In these cases, the international scene is complex, a violent confrontation. *Regulatory* law sits uneasily between private law and the criminal law, not quite knowing where it belongs.

18.48 Adherence to the *rule of law* tends to be determined by the degree of economic development of the country, not family of law. Rich countries generally exhibit a sound adherence to the rule of law, such as the independence of the judiciary, and the absence of corruption and of expropriations without compensation. The observance by poor countries of the rule of law is generally not good.

18.49 The *constitutional* law of a country—whether a country is a theocracy or autocratic or a democracy—is nothing to do with family of law. All the families of law contain countries which are variously autocratic or democratic.

18.50 At one time, comparative lawyers thought that the main differences between jurisdictions was the degree of codification and the adherence to the doctrine that lower courts should follow the decisions of higher courts so as to increase predictability. For various reasons, these formal traits are no longer considered to be major distinguishing characteristics and there are other much more important distinctions between the content of the law.

Main competing legal systems

A competing legal system is one which publicly discloses intentions to serve, or to continue to serve, as the governing law for internationally mobile transactions. That definition substantially narrows the field down to about fourteen or fifteen. It is suggested that they are: **18.51**

- common law: England, New York, Singapore, Hong Kong, Ireland
- Napoleonic: France, Belgium, Luxembourg
- Roman-Germanic: Germany, the Netherlands, Sweden, Switzerland
- mixed: China, Japan.

It is considered that there are strong similarities between the members of each group. For example, the law in Singapore and Ireland on the criteria discussed in this work is considered to be very similar, although there are a large number of detailed differences. It is thought that Singapore and Ireland do not have their own case law on article VIII 2b of the IMF Agreement, discussed in Chapter 6, although it is fair to say they are unlikely to take a different view from England. Smaller jurisdictions, such as Luxembourg, are less likely to have the richness of case law of the main jurisdiction in their group. Disputes in Sweden often go to arbitration so that the case law may be thinner. Sweden and Switzerland are steady business-orientated jurisdictions and may well be more conservative and commercial than Germany on the unpredictability of the good faith doctrine in contract, but it can be difficult to be precise about trends. **18.52**

Apart from England and New York, if any of the other jurisdictions has serious intent to offer itself as an international governing law on a world scale—as most of those jurisdictions do in different degrees of intensity—those jurisdictions would have to accept what would be involved in performing this role. **18.53**

Countries such as Italy, Spain, Austria, and Norway do not appear to be interested. Some jurisdictions have prominence in, or have ambitions in the direction of, niche areas, such as insurance (Bermuda), securitisations and private equity or hedge fund limited partnerships (Cayman), and Mauritius (investment funds and offshore holding companies). There is a vacuum for regional financial centres, such as in sub-Saharan Africa and in South America. **18.54**

We can now proceed to describe briefly the main family groups and indicate broadly who their members are. **18.55**

American Common Law Jurisdictions

Members of the group

The group is comprised mainly of the fifty states of the United States of America, plus the District of Columbia, plus an additional ten jurisdictions. They are the Pacific islands of **18.56**

American Samoa, Guam, Marshall Islands, Micronesia, Northern Marianas, Palau (Belau), Wake Island, the West African territory Liberia and the Caribbean islands of Puerto Rico and the Virgin Islands (US). Although originally Napoleonic, for most purposes Louisiana is now common law: bankruptcy law in the US is federal and all states have adopted the Uniform Commercial Code.

Historical background

18.57 The US inherited its legal system from England and is a common law jurisdiction. American common law jurisdictions took over and developed the English legal system from 1776 onwards before the great English legal inventions of the nineteenth century, such as the universal English fixed and floating charge and the English form of corporation with its own distinctive characteristics. Academic scholarship systematically codified commercial law in the semi-official 'Restatements' by the American Law Institute, in a series of Uniform Acts, and in the Uniform Commercial Code, which was a model for adoption by the individual states. The country is a legal laboratory and a legal factory.

Legal culture and key indicators

18.58 US law differs from English law partly because of a more pronounced populist streak in US culture. Historically, this may have originated in American individualism or the Puritan spirit of equality or from the suspicion, particularly felt by agricultural migrants, of authority, money, wealth, and power. This inclination meant that their bankruptcy law is more protective of debtor corporations (and individuals) than English law—which traditionally protects creditors. It meant that they developed a system of litigation which is highly protective of plaintiffs (typically identified with individuals fighting big corporations): the country is extremely litigious. It meant that even civil trials still require a jury, not just criminal trials as in England, with a result that the outcome of civil litigation often depends upon the unpredictable views of a lay jury. It meant that they were the first nation to introduce anti-trust (competition) laws to break up the dominant position of large corporations, and the first nation—largely as a result of the Great Depression of 1929—to impose intense intrusive regulation of securities and banking, including the nationalisation of bank insolvency law. Regulation dominates the legal system and its enforcement can be aggressive. The result is that the legal system is not the free intensely pro-business legal system you would expect. That crown is taken by traditional English-based legal systems.

18.59 As regards the key indicators, in general, on the evidence of the specific key indicators chosen, the continental American common law legal systems espouse such values as contract predictability, business orientation, freedom of contract, and the triple super-priority claimants on insolvency—creditors with a set-off, secured creditors, and commercial trusts. As regards technical nuancing indicators, they do not require notice of the assignment of a receivable to be given to the debtor for the validity of the assignment on the bankruptcy of the seller, and they allow the tracing of embezzlement proceeds through mixed bank accounts. The corporate law, if based on Delaware, strongly favours management in the triangle of creditors, shareholders, and management. As mentioned above, the regulatory system is intense and aggressively enforced. The litigation system is the wild west compared to the other leading jurisdictions. Apart from the triple super-priority claimants, the other bankruptcy indicators tend to be pro-debtor.

Conclusion

18.60 If one averages out the above key indicators, the conclusion seems to be that, in the combined ranking of these key indicators, the American common law jurisdictions are ranked as three in the full rankings of 1357, or green in the broader bands of blue, green, yellow, and red. This is considered to be so at least in the case of the comparison of American common law jurisdictions as against English common law, France, and Germany, and probably across their respective groups as well. Subject to qualifications, there appears to be a reasonable degree of consistency in this pattern and in the ranking on most of the issues.

English Common Law Jurisdictions

Members of the group

18.61 This group comprises about eighty-five jurisdictions, or sixty-six if one treats Australia and common law Canada as substantially each a unified bloc. The jurisdictions are:

> Akrotiri and Dhekelia, Anguilla, Antigua and Barbuda, *Australia* (eight jurisdictions—Australian Capital Territory, New South Wales, Northern Territory, Queensland, South Australia, Tasmania, Victoria, and Western Australia), Bahamas. Bangladesh, Barbados, Belize, *Bermuda*, Bhutan. British Virgin Islands, Brunei Darrusalam, *Canada*, excluding Quebec (ten jurisdictions—Alberta, British Columbia, Manitoba, New Brunswick, Newfoundland, Northwest Territories, Nova Scotia, Ontario, Prince Edward Island, and Saskatchewan but not including the territories of Nunavut and Yukon), *Cayman Islands*, Cocos (Keeling) Island (Australia), Cyprus, Dominica, *England*, Falkland Islands, Fiji, Gambia, Ghana, Gibraltar, Grenada, Guyana. *Hong Kong*, *India*, *Ireland*, Isle of Man, *Israel*, Jamaica, Kenya, Kiribati, Malawi, *Malaysia*, *Mauritius*, Montserrat, Myanmar, Nepal, *New Zealand* (plus the Cook Islands, Pitcairn, Tokelau), *Nigeria*, Niue, Norfolk Island (Australia), *Northern Ireland*, *Pakistan*, Papua New Guinea, St Helena, St Kitts and Nevis, St Lucia, St Vincent and the Grenadines, Samoa, Seychelles, Sierra Leone, *Singapore*, Solomon Islands, Sri Lanka, South Sudan, Sudan, Tonga, Trinidad and Tobago, Turkish Republic of North Cyprus, Turks and Caicos Islands, Tuvalu, Uganda, Vanuatu, Zambia.

18.62 It is likely that all the jurisdictions will be influenced by English case law, but this may not always be the case.

18.63 The law may be overlaid by strict Sharia law in Sudan and partially so in Pakistan.

18.64 The Dubai International Financial Centre, the Abu Dhabi Global Market and the Qatar Financial Centre have each adopted a version of modern English law, particularly insolvency law.

18.65 A large and important group have been attracted to English common law indicators—either the trust or insolvency set-off, or both. They have become anglicised. These jurisdictions include China, Japan, and Taiwan. They are currently located in the mixed civil/common law group.

18.66 The following are or were hybrid French-English systems: Mauritius, St Lucia, Seychelles, and Vanuatu. Mauritius and Seychelles have adopted versions of English insolvency law, together with insolvency set-off, the universal corporate charge, and the trust.

18.67 British Indian Ocean Territory, which is a defence base, and South Georgia and Sandwich Islands, both of which have no permanent population, are not counted.

18.68 Sri Lanka was originally Roman-Dutch and there may be some differences, notably in relation to land law, but not on the triple priority claimants.

Historical background

18.69 The group is based on the former British Empire. Normally, the British introduced their own legal system, especially in the fields of contract, company, and bankruptcy law. On independence, mainly between 1947 and 1970, the newly independent countries adopted English law, subject to local statutes.

18.70 England did not codify its legal system comprehensively and so did not have a marketable legal system in the eyes of jurisdictions wishing to reform their law. By contrast, the main continental Europeans outside Scandinavia had a codified package which they could deliver neatly.

18.71 India, Pakistan, and Bangladesh were formerly parts of British India until 1947, when the country broke up into two and later into three with the split off of Bangladesh in the east from Pakistan in the west. Pakistan has still not resolved the clash between English law and the Muslim sharia law, while Malaysia took this in its stride.

18.72 Britain had a mandate over Palestine between the wars: on independence Israel chose to adopt English law but Jordan chose to follow Napoleonic law, popularised in Egypt and more debtor-oriented than English law. Other escapees included the Southern African countries, Quebec, the Channel Islands and, not to be forgotten, Scotland—all in the mixed common/civil law group.

18.73 Some of the very small jurisdictions in the group are important in financial and corporate law, eg Singapore and Hong Kong, as well as the Cayman Islands.

Legal culture and key indicators

18.74 In the nineteenth century, Britain was the leading economy in the world and England had a precocious commercial and financial law attuned to a liberal market economy—well-suited to developing countries. The enthusiasm for enterprise was not held up by any religious antipathy to money or the aggrandisement of wealth: the legal approach was secular.

18.75 This secular view is shown by the fact that the private legal system was dramatically friendly to capital provided by bondholders and banks. They were seen as in substance the holders of the savings of the people who were therefore the real creditor. The overriding desire was to use capital to bring prosperity—which is what they succeeded in doing. At the same time the private ordinary law was free, without bureaucratic restrictions, and backed by a judiciary which valued the freedom of capital but yet espoused austere Victorian views about morality in business conduct, an unbeatable combination. It is no surprise therefore that English law became an international standard, an international public utility for large financial and commercial contracts, and one of the most important exports of the English. English law as an export ranks in world importance only second after their largest export, the English language.

18.76 English law is positive on most of the key indicators—that is, those relating to predictability, business orientation, freedom of contract, exclusion clauses, insolvency, and corporate law. The litigation system allows greater discovery of documents than is common in France and Germany, but less than in the United States. The regulatory system and its enforcement appear average for developed countries.

18.77 The group is positive on the triple super-priority claimants of insolvency set-off, security interests and the commercial trust, virtually without exception. However, some members of the group have adopted versions of article 9 of the American Uniform Commercial Code. These include common law Canada, Australia, New Zealand, Kenya, Nigeria, Pakistan, Zambia, and a few others.

18.78 The technical nuancing indicators of the absence of compulsory notice to debtors of assignments of receivables and the ability to trace embezzled money through mixed bank accounts are positive, but the compulsory notice may still be necessary in the case of assignments of debts by individuals because of 'reputed ownership' provisions in traditional English individual bankruptcy legislation. These reputed ownership provisions never applied to corporates and were abolished in England for individuals in 1986.

18.79 The degree of acceptance in the group as a whole of English notions in relation to the key indicators of predictability of contract, business orientation, freedom of contract, and exclusion clauses is convincing in Singapore, Australia, New Zealand, Ireland, and common law Canada, and possibly elsewhere too. It is thought that English decisions have persuasive influence in the main members of the group, and especially in traditional countries. India, Pakistan, and Bangladesh may be outliers. The tenets of English law may be qualified in Islamicised countries and in countries which are autarchies, such as Myanmar.

18.80 The company law in most of these countries is recognisably based on English company law as it was at the time of independence, although some of the jurisdictions have been

282 COMPARISON OF JURISDICTIONS OF THE WORLD

influenced by Canadian company law (Barbados), or Australian or New Zealand company law for Pacific territories. Corporate bankruptcies and insolvency rescue laws are also recognisably based on English precedents, especially in the inner group of England, Ireland, Singapore, Australia, and New Zealand, but not Canada (insolvency law is federal in Canada). Note that South Africa is in the mixed group.

18.81 Regulatory regimes differ, generally according to the degree of development of the country concerned. It has not been possible to measure procedural rules such as class actions outside England.

Conclusion

18.82 The evaluation of the chosen key indicators would seem on the whole to justify a ranking of English law as one in the 1357 ranking, including the main competing jurisdictions of Singapore, Ireland, and Hong Kong. The Australian jurisdictions and New Zealand would be contenders if they wished to assume the burdens. There may be significant qualifications to this in many members of the group because of political risk and a limited legal infrastructure, but probably not as regards black letter law on the books.

Napoleonic Jurisdictions

Members of the group

18.83 This group comprises about eighty-six jurisdictions. The jurisdictions are:

Abu Dhabi, Adjaman, Algeria, Andorra, Angola, *Argentina*, *Belgium*, Benin, Bolivia, *Brazil*, Bulgaria, Burkina Faso, Burundi, Cameroon, Cape Verde, Central African Republic, Chad, Chile, Colombia, Comoros, Congo (Brazzaville), Congo (Kinshasa—formerly Zaire), Costa Rica, Dubai, Djibouti, Ecuador, *Egypt*, El Salvador, Equatorial Guinea, Eritrea, Ethiopia, *France*, French Guiana, French Polynesia, French Southern and Antarctic Territories, Fujairah, Gabon, *Greece*, Guadeloupe, Guatemala, Guinea, Guinea-Bissau, Haiti, Honduras, *Iran*, Iraq, *Italy*, Ivory Coast, Jordan, Lebanon, *Luxembourg*, Macau, Madagascar, Mali, Martinique, Mauritania, Mayotte, *Mexico*, Monaco, Morocco, Mozambique, New Caledonia, Nicaragua, Niger, Paraguay, Peru, Philippines, *Portugal*, Réunion, Romania, Ras Al-Khaima, Rwanda, St Barthélemy, St Martin, St Pierre and Miquelon, San Marino, São Tomé and Príncipe, Senegal, *Spain*, Syria, Togo, Tunisia, Umm al Quwain, Uruguay, Venezuela, Wallis and Futuna Islands, Bankruptcy law in the United Arab Emirates (here represented by each emirate) is federal and UAE is part of this group.

18.84 The foundation civil code is that of 1804 in France. The foundation bankruptcy codes are those of France 1807 and 1838.

Napoleonic sub-groups

18.85 As to European Napoleonic jurisdictions, Belgium, France, Luxembourg, and Monaco had identical codes. Those of Italy, Greece Portugal, Spain, Bulgaria, and Romania are Napoleonic in inspiration. San Marino (Italy) and Andorra (between France and Spain) are pre-Napoleonic and may be in a special group of their own.

18.86 Domestic French law is often extended to dependencies—about ten of them, such as French Guiana, French Polynesia, Wallis and Futuna, and New Caledonia.

18.87 Traditional Napoleonic jurisdictions include such territories as Eritrea and Ethiopia (via Italy); Burundi, Congo (Zaire), and Rwanda (via Belgium); Angola and Mozambique (via Portugal); and Egypt, Lebanon, Mauritania, Morocco, and Tunisia (via France).

18.88 Ohada Napoleonic are seventeen African jurisdictions which have adopted uniform acts based on French law: Benin, Burkina Faso, Cameroon, Central African Republic, Chad, Comoros, Congo (Brazzaville), Congo (Kinshasa—the Democratic Republic of the Congo), Ivory Coast, Gabon, Guinea, Guinea-Bissau, Equatorial Guinea, Mali, Niger, Senegal, Togo, all originally Napoleonic via France except Equatorial Guinea (Spain), and Guinea-Bissau (Portugal). Ohada is the Organisation for the Harmonisation of Business Law in Africa established by treaty in 1993. General uniform acts have been adopted. Ultimate appeals from member states on the treaty and the uniform acts can be made to a supranational court of appeal, the Common Court of Justice and Arbitration in Abidjan.

18.89 In Sharia Napoleonic jurisdictions, Napoleonic commercial law is or may be in abeyance in varying degrees and overridden by strict Islamic Sharia law: Algeria, Djibouti, Iran, Iraq, Jordan, Mauritania, and Syria. All received Napoleonic law via France (sometimes with Egypt as intermediary).

18.90 The following Middle East jurisdictions are to a greater or lesser extent influenced by or have installed codes based on the Napoleonic model, originally via Egypt; Bahrain; Kuwait; Oman; Qatar; and the United Arab Emirates. They are classified as Islamic jurisdictions, but the UAE emirates are tentatively classified as Napoleonic.

18.91 Some members of this group could equally be classified as Napoleonic or Islamic: thus Jordan is treated as just in the Napoleonic group, and Kuwait as just outside. The enclave financial centres in Abu Dhabi, Dubai and Qatar are based on English law.

18.92 Latin American Napoleonic and the Philippines comprise about 18 jurisdictions: Argentina, Bolivia, Brazil, Chile, Colombia, Costa Rica, Ecuador, El Salvador, Guatemala, Honduras, Mexico, Nicaragua, Paraguay, Peru, Philippines, Uruguay, and Venezuela. The Philippines is arguably more properly a member of the mixed civil/common law group: it has the trust via California and insolvency set-off via its adoption of the US Bankruptcy Act of 1898, but its civil and commercial codes, including provisions on security interests, are understood to be Napoleonic in inspiration, via Spain.

18.93 The Dominican Republic has joined the mixed group on the main triple super-priority indicators, as from 2015.

18.94 Panama is treated as mixed civil/common law—it has insolvency set-off and the universal trust by statute.

18.95 Some originally Napoleonic jurisdictions are classified in other groups. Quebec was originally Napoleonic but in functional terms is almost wholly Anglo-American common law on the main financial criteria. This is because bankruptcy law in Canada is federal, because Quebec has adopted laws regarding security interests which are functionally very similar to the rest of common law Canada, and because Quebec has the universal trust by statute. Hence, Quebec is classified as a member of the mixed civil/common law group. Louisiana is treated as now belonging to the American common law group. As in Canada, US federal bankruptcy legislation applies, and Louisiana has the UCC, including article 9 on security interests.

18.96 Malta is Napoleonic-based but has insolvency set-off by contract and the universal trust for movables. It is classified as a member of the mixed civil/common law group.

18.97 East Timor was originally a Portuguese colony but its constitution provides that Indonesian law applies—basically Dutch law. It is therefore recorded as being a member of the Roman-Germanic group.

Historical background

18.98 When the French codes were written down, they were a masterpiece of legal style. The story is often told that the Civil Code was initially prepared by the Duc de Cambacérès and that, on the instructions of the revolutionary National Assembly in 1793, he produced the first draft in six weeks, with a verve aided no doubt by the proximity of a fully operative guillotine. The Assembly, with typical client unreality, wanted it in a month. It was many years before it was finally settled. Portalis was a leading influence but Napoleon himself attended many drafting meetings. The Civil Code came into force in 1804, and the Commercial Code was completed in 1807. In the much-quoted remark, Napoleon could truly say when he was in exile on St Helena: 'It is not in winning 40 battles that my real glory lies, for all those victories will be eclipsed by Waterloo. But my Code civil will not be forgotten, it will live forever." It is equally often mentioned that the nineteenth-century French novelist Stendhal is said to have read part of the Civil Code every day to refine his feelings for the language.

18.99 Because they were such charismatic legal codes, they were attractive to other countries, which rapidly imported them as the most civilised model that one of the most civilised nations in the world could provide. They were a neat package, ready to be used.

Legal culture and key indicators

18.100 France is opposite to England on most of the key indicators, such as predictability, business orientation, freedom of contract, insulation against article VIII 2b of the IMF Agreement, exclusion clauses, and in particular on insolvency set-off and security interests. However there has been some convergence as regards insolvency set-off in France and the institution of the trust, adopted by France in 2007. Insolvency set-off is still a long way from the bullet-proof English version, and netting is prejudiced by preventing parties from terminating contracts on the insolvency of the counterparty. But the leading countries do have financial markets carve-outs. The convergence is more noticeable in Belgium and Luxembourg. Italy has had the German version of insolvency set-off since 1942. Litigation is proportionate compared to the United States, and the enforcement of financial regulation appears moderate.

Luxembourg and possibly Belgium may be more reluctant to override the express terms of a contract by reason of the good faith doctrine than France, and for various reasons Belgium in particular has a strong business orientation on some of the indicators. It has not been possible to check the position in all of the other Napoleonic jurisdictions on the key indicators for predictability, freedom of contract, and the like, but it is suggested that the general direction is likely to be common to the group as a whole. However, as regards the commercial trust, many jurisdictions in the Napoleonic group have installed various restricted versions, particularly in Latin America, and it may well be that the group as a whole will be inclined to recognise foreign commercial trusts, as in the case of France, Luxembourg, and Italy. **18.101**

Outside carve-outs, security interests in most of the group do not match the English or American versions in terms of scope, although Belgium again has made great strides in that direction. **18.102**

The risks of personal director liability in the case of insolvency seems unusually high. The insolvency regime generally in France is debtor-protective and is much less sympathetic to private work-outs than in England. This is consistent with the debtor-protective interventionism of the courts in other areas. **18.103**

As regards the technical nuancing indicators, traditional members probably still retain the need for notice to the debtor of assignments of a debt (the original French CC, article 1690) although that this may not be true in Latin American countries. It seems doubtful whether any of them allow tracing of embezzled proceeds through mixed bank accounts. **18.104**

Conclusion

On balance, it seems appropriate to allocate seven to France in the ranking of 1357. **18.105**

The tenets of the family group will appeal to many people and there is no doubt that they are held with great conviction in France and elsewhere. The international business community therefore have a choice, which is as it should be. **18.106**

France is a key country for the development of law in the future on account of the sheer size of the Napoleonic group and the fact that many of the jurisdictions in the group will look to France for the leadership which it clearly inspires. The country, with its jurisprudence and commitment to the development of the law, is one of the world's most dedicated and proven leaders in law and has been for more than two centuries. **18.107**

Roman-Germanic Jurisdictions

Members of the group

18.108 There are about thirty-four jurisdictions in this group. See Map: Roman-Germanic jurisdictions. Plate 6. The jurisdictions are: Åland Islands, Aruba, *Austria*, Bonaire, Bosnia, Croatia, *Czech Republic, Denmark*, East Timor, Estonia, Faeroe Islands, *Finland, Germany*, Greenland, Hungary, Iceland, Indonesia, Kosovo, Latvia, Lithuania, Montenegro, *the Netherlands, Poland*, Saba, Serbia, Sint Eustatius, Slovakia, Slovenia, *South Korea*, Suriname, *Sweden, Switzerland*, Thailand (doubtfully), Turkey.

18.109 The following eleven jurisdictions are treated as part of the mixed civil/common law group, but the underlying inspiration is Roman-Germanic, usually Roman law, sometimes via either Germany or the Netherlands: Botswana, *China, Japan*, Lesotho, Liechtenstein, Namibia, *Scotland, South Africa*, Swaziland, *Taiwan*, and Zimbabwe.

18.110 The inclusion of these mixed jurisdictions would enlarge this group to forty-three jurisdictions, including the world's most populous country and the world's second, third, and fourth largest economies after the US. Nevertheless, they have been partially anglicised.

Sub-groups of Roman-Germanic jurisdictions

18.111 The jurisdictions in this group fall into several sub-groups, apart from Germany itself. These sub-groups include the Dutch group (the Netherlands, Indonesia, and others), the Scandinavian group, and the Austro-Swiss group comprising Austria, Switzerland, Turkey, and the former Yugoslav territories, and former transition countries (Poland, Czech Republic, Slovakia, Hungary, and the Baltics).

18.112 South Korea is a member of this group, but the eclectic Thailand only marginally.

Historical background

18.113 The German civil code, the impressive BGB (*Bürgerliches Gesetzbuch*) was put together after the industrial revolution in Germany as a result of 13 years' work ending in the mid-1890s and came into force on 1 January 1900. The German Commercial Code (the HGB) stemmed from 1861 and the final version also came into force in 1900. The precocious German Bankruptcy Act was enacted in 1877 and not replaced until the 1990s, which shows what an enduring law it was.

18.114 German ideas had advanced some way beyond the Napoleonic view in terms of economic development and prosperity. On the other hand, the codes were strongly influenced by jurists who were steeped in Roman law, who brought the juristic archaeology of the Roman remains to a new intensity and, who, being academics, may not have had a high esteem for merchants and money. This helps to explain why the German view was mid-way between the Napoleonic and English view. It has been called professors' law.

18.115 The group is predominantly a northern hemisphere ideology with substantial representation in north-western Europe, Scandinavia, the Baltics, Central Europe and the Balkans, spreading through to Russia and Turkey. There is a gap in the Middle East, but substantial representation in East Asia including South Korea and Indonesia. China, Japan, and Taiwan, although classified as mixed civil/common law, were strongly influenced by German law.

18.116 Apart from the Southern African group of five jurisdictions south of the Zambezi river and stopping at the English jurisdiction of Zambia (the five are all treated as mixed civil/common law), there is virtually no representation in the southern hemisphere, with only Aruba and the former Netherlands Antilles in the Caribbean and with Suriname the sole representative in South America. There is no representation in North Africa.

18.117 The German ideology was transmitted primarily by the strength of the codes which have been in the works for most of the nineteenth century. These codes formed the basis for the legal system in Japan some thirty years after the Meiji restoration in 1867. The codes then found their way to Korea by virtue of Japanese colonialism (1905) and then into China, largely by the reason of the influence of Japanese jurists in China in the 1930s and subsequently during the Second World War. It was this system which found its way to Taiwan, then called Formosa, partly by reason of Japanese conquests (1895) and bolstered on the ejection from mainland China in 1949 of Chiang Kai Shek and the Kuomintang by communist forces led by Mao Tse Tung.

18.118 The Netherlands' contribution is also notable. The Netherlands was colonised by France in Napoleonic times but subsequently returned to its commercialised Roman roots reflecting Dutch mercantile and financial supremacy in Europe in the seventeenth century and after. It was this system which was transmitted by Dutch settlers to the Cape of Good Hope and was in turn carried upwards to the rest of Southern Africa. The Russian Civil Code is influenced by the Dutch Civil Code—the latest model in the early 1990s.

Legal culture and the key indicators

18.119 On almost all of the key indicators, Germany occupies a roughly middle position between England on one side and France on the other. The adoption of contract good faith in Germany, the Netherlands and especially Switzerland and Sweden is not as intrusive as in France on our indicators of contract predictability. The hostility to exclusion clauses seems greater than under English law in wholesale transactions. There is adverse case law in Germany on insulation against foreign exchange controls under article VIII 2b of the IMF Agreement.

18.120 As regards the triple super-priority bankruptcy indicators, insolvency set-off is medium in the jurisdictions which have it (not Slovakia, for example), and security interests are medium, that is, not as wide as those of the American and English-based jurisdictions, but wider than the Napoleonic jurisdictions. There are profound objections to the commercial trust, much more so than in the Napoleonic jurisdictions. The corporate doctrine of maintenance of capital is severe.

Conclusion

18.121 The above summary would seem to justify the placing of most of the Roman-Germanic jurisdictions at the five mark in the sequence of 1357. Germany's argument would be that it is perfectly reasonable to be middle of the road between extremes, to be the golden mean.

Mixed Civil/Common Law Jurisdictions

Members of the group

18.122 There are about eighteen jurisdictions in this group. They are: Alderney and Sark, Botswana, *China*, Dominican Republic, Guernsey, *Japan*, Jersey, Lesotho, Liechtenstein, Malta, Namibia, Panama, *Quebec*, *Scotland*, *South Africa*, Swaziland, *Taiwan*, and Zimbabwe.

18.123 All these jurisdictions have continental European roots but they have the common law institution of the trust plus one or more of the key indicators associated with the common law systems, either insolvency set-off or a wide security interest. Quebec and Scotland have both. In other words, they all exhibit a drift towards the ideology of the English common law approach.

18.124 There are four sub-groups.

18.125 The Channel Islands group comprise Alderney and Sark, Guernsey, and Jersey—small island possessions of the UK Crown located in the English Channel a few miles off the coast of France. The legal systems were originally based on pre-Napoleonic French law. Alderney and Sark are strictly separate jurisdictions. They were anglicised through proximity and being part of the British Isles.

18.126 The East Asian sub-group comprises China, Japan, and Taiwan. The underlying influence is Roman-Germanic via Germany, but they all have the trust by statute. Both Japan and Taiwan were influenced by the US. These jurisdictions all have insolvency set-off. However, in all of them, security interests are not as wide as in the English-based jurisdictions.

18.127 The remarkable feature of China is that its laws in this area seem like a codification of English law, especially the trust. No doubt Singapore and Hong Kong were influential, but the driving force may have been that they adopted the trends of a nineteenth century rapidly developing jurisdiction (England) because they are now a rapidly developing country. Contrast Russia, which started out at about the same time on market laws, but did not adopt insolvency set-off and has a very lukewarm trust. Unlike China, in the formative 1990s, Russia did not appear to have a strong commercial culture.

18.128 The southern African sub-group are all in the southern cone of Africa and comprise Botswana, Lesotho, Namibia, South Africa, Swaziland, and Zimbabwe. Their underlying legal systems came from pre-Napoleonic Holland in the seventeenth century when Holland was the financial centre of Europe employing a commercialised Roman law which the subsequent British settlers did not see fit to change, except at the margins. All have the trust.

These jurisdictions also have a quite wide universal security interest. They do not have insolvency set-off, subject to a South African financial markets carve-out.

18.129 As to the others in the group, Liechtenstein has the trust by statute, and also insolvency set-off. Security interests are on the Swiss-Austrian model and are more limited than in Germany and the Netherlands. Malta allows insolvency set-off by contract (since 2003) and has the universal trust by statute (except land). Quebec is functionally similar to common law Canada on the main criteria, but Quebec requires mandatory notice to the debtor of assignments and tracing has not been checked. Bankruptcy law in Canada is federal and there is a degree of consensus on other financial law matters among the provinces. Panama was originally Napoleonic, but has insolvency set-off and the trust by statute. It is only marginally part of this group. Scotland has the trust, a universal floating charge by statute and insolvency set-off, but notice to the debtor of an assignment is mandatory. Whether the Dominican Republic intended to introduce the trust by article 64 of Law 141-15 should be investigated.

18.130 Even in this group, the trust may not be universal—thus the Jersey trust does not extend to land. In Japan, practitioners are adverse to using the trust and regard it with suspicion. There may be other limitations in the group.

18.131 It is part of the ironic wit of history that this group should include countries as various as Swaziland, Zimbabwe, Panama, Scotland, and Jersey. The fact that it also includes both China and Japan means that it is an important group. The historical origins are in fact easily explicable if one follows colonial and economic history.

18.132 Japan's codes were originally German. The common law aspect resulted from US occupation after the Second World War.

Conclusion

18.133 The jurisdictions in this group which are based on the Roman-Germanic family have a pronounced drift towards the English common law group. This is also true of those based on the Napoleonic family, but the drift is less because of the Napoleonic pull. It is tentatively suggested that the approach as regards contract matters, such as predictability, business orientation and freedom of contract, especially in the case of South Africa and the Channel Islands, and especially Scotland, is significantly influenced by the English common law group.

Islamic Jurisdictions

Members of the group

18.134 A list of about eleven jurisdictions is: Afghanistan, Bahrain, Kuwait, Libya, Maldives, Palestinian Administered Territories, Oman, Qatar, Saudi Arabia, Somalia and Yemen.

18.135 These jurisdictions are treated as Islamic on the ground that religious objections to a central tenet of the modern credit economy—an interest-bearing loan or deposit—either prevents debt contracts with interest or has inhibited the installation of bankruptcy laws, or both. Strict Sharia law also objects to insurance and the assignment of debt claims.

18.136 Bahrain, Kuwait, Oman, Qatar, and the Yemen have a Napoleonic colouring, but are treated as hybrid Islamic-Napoleonic and allocated to this group. Some have Napoleonic civil and commercial codes, eg Oman's Commercial Code 1990, the Civil Code of 1985, and the Commercial Code of 1993 in the UAE, and Yemen's Commercial Law of 1991.

18.137 Jordan and the UAE are classified as Napoleonic: both are borderline in that group. The financial centre enclaves in Abu Dhabi, Dubai, and Qatar are based on English insolvency law.

18.138 Djibouti, Iran, Iraq, and Syria are classified as Napoleonic because of the underlying codes. They could be equally convincingly be classified as Islamic.

18.139 Apart from original Napoleonic influences via Egypt, Somalia is probably now de facto Islamic.

18.140 In Saudi Arabia, Sharia law prohibits interest and any offending transactions will be unenforceable. In Bahrain, Kuwait, Qatar, Yemen, and probably Oman, it may be that interest is permitted under the civil code (or equivalent) and is enforceable, at least in commercial transactions not involving individuals. The position in Afghanistan seems uncertain.

18.141 Bankruptcy laws of a sort are present in some of these jurisdictions, but in most cases are inchoate and extremely slim. Resort to formal bankruptcies appears to be rare. It is not easy to ascertain what their view is about such issues as set-off and the trust, or such matters as director liability and the treatment of contracts on insolvency. In particular, it is often hard to ascertain whether the courts will adhere to Sharia law in the commercial context.

18.142 There is a proto-trust—the waqf.

18.143 Islamic loans and security interests adopt one or other form of title finance as a security substitute, such as a conditional sale or a lease. The various methods of coping with the ban on interest were practised in Europe until the Renaissance and after.

18.144 Effectively, there is a war of religious law versus secular law going on in these countries and, as mentioned, in many Napoleonic countries in the Middle East as to whether Sharia law or a modern western legal system dominates. The state of the conflict differs according to the country.

Conclusion

18.145 The Fertile Crescent was a leader in law and in civilisation during the ancient days of Mesopotamia. There was a similar renaissance of law in the ninth century in the region. Sharia law is not attuned to modern finance and commerce and it may be some time before the gap is bridged and there is a new renaissance.

New or Transition Jurisdictions

Members of the group

18.146 There are approximately eighteen jurisdictions in the category of new jurisdictions as follows: Albania, Armenia, Azerbaijan, *Belarus*, Cambodia, *Georgia*, *Kazakhstan*, Kyrgystan, Laos, North Macedonia, Moldova, Mongolia, *Russia*, Tajikistan, Turkmenistan, *Ukraine*, Uzbekistan, and Vietnam.

18.147 These jurisdictions have sometimes been called transition or emerging jurisdictions. They were formerly communist countries which subsequently adopted programmes of law reform re-establishing private property and reflecting market economic principles as opposed to corporatist economies controlled by the state. Most have enacted civil codes, bankruptcy laws (including reorganisations with creditor voting), and laws governing security interests. On the whole, the laws in the 'stan' countries are basic, apart perhaps from Kazakhstan.

18.148 Albania was originally Napoleonic via Italy: another borderline jurisdiction. It has insolvency set-off, but not the trust—echoing Italy. Moldova also has insolvency set-off and in addition a universal interest.

18.149 Cambodia has an Insolvency Law 2008. Laos has a brief framework Law on the Bankruptcy of Enterprises 1999. Mongolia has a Bankruptcy Law 1997, and Vietnam a Bankruptcy Law 2014.

18.150 By way of summary, apart from former communist countries in Eastern Europe, and subject to a few exceptions, almost all of the jurisdictions in this group do not have insolvency set-off, have weak security interests, and do not have a commercial trust. On these fundamental issues the jurisdictions are similar to unreformed members of the Napoleonic group. It is probably the case that it would be difficult to determine judicial trends on contract predictability, freedom of contract, exclusion clauses, and the like. No candidate for a regional governing law for international transactions has yet emerged.

Conclusion

18.151 It is probably difficult for these jurisdictions to make up their minds on the basic issues, when advisers from Western Europe themselves differ fundamentally on those issues.

Unallocated Jurisdictions

Members of the group

18.152 Six jurisdictions are, for one reason or another, not allocated. They are: Antarctica, Cuba, North Korea, Paracel Islands, Spratly Islands, and the Vatican.

High seas and space

18.153 In addition, the high seas and space are governed by a body of laws, but they are not separate territorial jurisdictions. They are the commons.

Statistics on the Families of Law

18.154 Table 18.1 shows some rough statistics in percentages on the families of law and the 320 jurisdictions as at around 2019:

Table 18.1 Statistics in percentages on the families of law

Group of jurisdictions	No	Population %	Area %	GDP %
Am CL	19	4.5	8	25.5
Eng CL	27	31.6	23	13.2
Napol	27	22.5	29	17
Rom-Ger	10.5	10	8	15
Mixed	5.6	22	10	24.4
Islamic	3.4	1.9	4	1.5
New	5.6	7	17	3.2
Other	1.8	0.5	1	0.2

The figures are order of magnitude only to give an impression of relative size in relation to other groups. The calculations are my own calculations based on the classification of jurisdictions set out in this chapter. The underlying statistics for population, area, and GDP of each country, which I adjusted and used for the calculations, were based on *The Economist Pocket World in Figures* (2022 edn).

18.155 The big four (American and English common law, Napoleonic, and Roman-Germanic) and the mixed jurisdictions together account for nearly 90 per cent of the number of jurisdictions, nearly 90 per cent of the population of the world, around 80 per cent of the land area of the world, and about 95 per cent of its GDP.

18.156 The mixed group includes China, Japan, Quebec, and the Southern African cone countries and so one would have to apportion the contributions of the group of the big four families to assess their overall individual contributions to world law. There are arguments in favour of apportioning most or some of the New group to the big four since many aspects of their private law were transplants from the West. Some of the Islamic jurisdictions have also borrowed for the West. If that is the case, then almost all of world law was borrowed from or influenced by a Western model.

Conclusion on the Families of Law

18.157 Whenever in history an empire collapsed, there often followed a period of disruption, as when the Romans withdraw from Britain in the fourth century. The break-up of the

European empires began in the early nineteenth century with Haiti and the South American republics. It gathered speed in the twentieth century, ending with the decolonisation of the Russian Empire in the 1990s.

If there was no modern legal system already in place in the former colonies, as in the case of Latin America and the USSR, the desire of the former colonists to install one was one of their first priorities, however difficult and time-consuming the work. Law was an urgent objective. **18.158**

The export of law in the last 300 years or so was a major event in history. The rule of law and the laws embodied in legal systems are now the single most significant ideologies in the world and the most important in terms of our survival. **18.159**

The purpose of comparative studies like this, however imperfect, is to assist societies to comprehend how they stand in relation to everyone else so that they may better decide whether to stay or change. **18.160**

19
PROTECTING A GOVERNING LAW

The Need for Protection

Responsibility

19.1 A legal system is a fundamental national asset which requires constant upkeep and maintenance. The maintenance is required not only to keep up with changing circumstances but most of all to protect the legal system from the government of the day which may sometimes have crowd-pleasing policies, and from special interests who are unable to take a larger view of the role of the law. As said, the law expresses the credentials of a civilisation and its set of ethics and principles of conduct. The statute book is not the place where a society expresses its rage or desire for revenge. It is not a place where opportunists seize the chance to get through convictions which are not held by the majority of the population, or where the law is used for an improper purpose. Where a legal system is used internationally, there is no room for narrow provincialism, nor some selfish interest or self-regarding insularity, nor is there room for xenophobia.

19.2 In democracies, the law is made by a representative assembly. Some of the law is judge-made law by virtue of the decision-making power of the judiciary in those jurisdictions where the rulings of higher courts bind the lower courts.

19.3 Much law in modern societies may not be well understood by the general population, which is the reason that they elect representatives to achieve that for them. The representatives rely on civil servants to bring forward the relevant policies. Typically, a government will consult widely on new legislative proposals outside such areas as taxation. The risk is that the civil service seeks to please the incumbent government by vote-catching legislation which plays to the gallery or is a short-term fix or does not take into account the bigger picture or the role of the ideology.

19.4 That leads to the conclusion that a legal system, such as English law, which is of worldwide importance, requires a specialised and independent body to scrutinise relevant legislation. Recently, there have been too many cases of close shaves where civil servants and interest groups nearly got through damaging legislation which was moderated at the last moment. An example in England was the UK Corporate Governance and Insolvency Act 2020 rushed through in a few days under the cover of Covid-19, while everybody was looking the other way. This almost brought into question the netting of contracts, but for a robust last minute intervention.

19.5 One of the main obstacles is that governments often resent having some independent body which might interfere with their policies. However, the record shows a necessity for such bodies in modern democracies. Examples are central bank control of monetary policy, such as interest rates and inflation which, in the absence of independent and expert control can easily be manipulated by politicians. Other examples are governmental bodies concerned with budget responsibility and with economic statistics. Clearly, an independent body can only comment on but not vote on or delay legislation.

Going back further in history, one may cite the role of the Royal Society in the promotion of science and innovation in England. **19.6**

International examples of law monitoring bodies

It is worth examining national and international bodies tasked with this duty of surveillance. **19.7**

The American Law Institute was founded in 1923 to deal with uncertainties and complexities in the law. It has about 3,000 elected members who are judges, academics, and practitioners. Probably, its two greatest achievements are the Restatements of the Law—which are essentially codifications,—and the model law, the Uniform Commercial Code, undertaken jointly with the National Conference of Commissioners on Uniform State Laws and adopted in all states. **19.8**

There is also a European Law Institute. **19.9**

The equivalent in England is the Law Commission, which is often tasked with special projects which require expert review and whose activities are not politicised. Another significant law reform body in England is the Financial Markets Law Committee, which was set up by the Bank of England in the early 1990s to deal with 'uncertainties' in financial law and which has had an excellent record. **19.10**

There are also a number of significant international institutions which play a major role in the development of legal instruments. **19.11**

UNIDROIT is the common name for the International Institute for the Unification of Private Law. It was established in 1926 as part of the League of Nations and re-established in 1940. As at 2019, it had sixty-three member states including Australia, Belgium, Canada, China, France, Germany, Greece, India, Ireland, Italy, Japan, Luxembourg, Netherlands, South Korea, Russia, South Africa, Spain, Sweden, Switzerland, and Turkey. It prepares conventions, model laws, and guides. Its greatest achievement is probably the Cape Town Aircraft Convention and protocols, but it has had others. Some of its other works, such as financial leasing and factoring, have not achieved wide acceptance. It is based in Rome. **19.12**

UNCITRAL—the UN Commission on Trade Law—combined with INSOL International to produce a Model Law on Cross-Border Insolvency in 1997 which has been successful although limited in scope compared, for example, to the EU Insolvency Regulation of 2015. The other success of UNCITRAL was the Convention on the International Sale of Goods. **19.13**

19.14 Other main institutions at the international level concerned with law projects include the multilateral development banks such as the World Bank, the Asian Development Bank, the European Bank for Reconstruction and Development, the Inter-American Development Bank, and the African Development Bank. The World Bank, for example used to conduct a doing business survey which ranked countries according to the quality of their laws and business practices, now abandoned.

19.15 Other official and semi-official institutions who take an active interest in legal systems include central banks, the Basel Banking Supervision Committee, which is a committee of the Bank for International Settlements set up in 1974 and whose main achievements have been in the field of standards for the capital adequacy of banks, the International Organisation of Securities Commissions set up in 1974 and based in Madrid, the Financial Stability Board set up in 1999 by the G7, the Financial Action Task Force set up in 1989 to deal with money laundering, and the International Association of Deposit Insurers.

19.16 The two main accounting bodies are the International Accounting Standards Board which publishes what are now called International Financial Reporting Standards, and the US Financial Accounting Standards Board established in 1973. US accounting rules are drawn up almost entirely by the profession and its statements, interpretations, and the like form a body of accounting principles known as Generally Accepted Accounting Principles.

19.17 In addition, there are bar associations, of which the two largest are the International Bar Association and the American Bar Association.

19.18 In the important countries there are a large number of other people interested in the law and participating in its formation—bank associations, insurance associations, derivatives dealers, associations of insolvency practitioners, societies, councils, forums, institutes, groups, conferences—a mass of organised lobbies. Let us not forget the International Swaps and Derivatives Association, Inc, the Institute of International Finance in Washington, and the Loan Market Association in London.

19.19 Everybody has a club. They produce a manifold of international standards, codes, guidelines, statements of practice, and recommendations.

Achievements and weaknesses

19.20 What are the main lessons we learn from of the public or official bodies as opposed to private associations?

19.21 The first is that the progress of the work and the productivity of some of these bodies can sometimes be glacial. This is perhaps because they do not have a permanent leadership or secretariat or because the members are just too international and diverse so there is never a consensus. Sometimes, law reform projects end up simply as a battle of legal nationalisms.

19.22 The second is that it is typical of a few international bodies to confine themselves to generalised vagaries which are the minimum which everybody can agree and are of little value. The law must confront difficult policy conflicts which often require the meticulous weighing up of conflicting alternatives. Ultimately, the law has to decide one way or the other.

19.23 A third problem is that it is often the case that those responsible for maintaining the legal system or transforming it do not know what the ideological options are and are not aware of the sharpness and urgency of the conflicting policies and how important it is to be able to work them out and to make a decision. The book of the laws requires clarity and certainty of direction, a sound philosophical foundation.

A body to protect English law

19.24 English law is an international ideology and an international public utility which is of great importance for the benefit of nations and which is valuable as a national asset. It would seem remiss if England did not go to special lengths to protect and maintain its legal system as regards the type of areas we are covering.

19.25 A body set up for this purpose should have a mandate which is clear in its objectives, and which is generic enough to cover a wide class of situations in order to avoid internal constitutional objections to its work. It could be tasked to protect, promote, and enhance English commercial, financial, and corporate law and regulation, with special regard to both its domestic and international use. The scope would be wide enough to allow, for example, the undertaking of codifications, commentary on significant legislation being brought forward by Parliament, and commentary on judicial trends.

19.26 The form of the association should be one which does not attract administrative bureaucracy or formality of governance. It should have an elected board, a chief executive, and a secretariat.

19.27 The permanent members should be appointed by the board on meritocratic principles. Special members should be appointed for particular tasks whose size or area of expertise requires this.

19.28 It is useful to ensure that the participants include members of the senior judiciary (often retired), legal practitioners who are more likely to know how the law works in practice, academics who are more likely to have kept up with the detail of the law, and market participants who are sufficiently well-informed about the law to understand the issues.

19.29 The group should be an elite of exceptionally talented, diligent, and intellectual people, not amateurs or dilettantes. It should be a privilege to belong to the group and the group should feel high esprit and esteem.

19.30 The members should be familiar with statistical and economic analysis. The members should have a business orientation and be internationally minded.

19.31 The majority of the funding should be provided by large law firms. A degree of state funding could be considered that should not be sufficient to prejudice the independence of the body from government influence.

19.32 The body could be called the Royal Society of Law, if it achieves the necessary patronage, otherwise the Institute of English Law.

Conclusions

19.33 Legal systems which are widely used as the governing law of international business contracts have a special duty to their users to ensure that they stand above domestic concerns and exercise a special discipline in the interest of the wider society of nations and in the interests of their prosperity and safety.

20
HISTORY AND THE FUTURE

A Reconsideration of Legal History

Different timing of the Industrial Revolution

Why was it that the three Western European philosophies, which covered almost the entire world, were so different in their outcome in business law? **20.1**

Although there were many cultural influences and counter-influences, one major reason for the difference between the three great groups based on England, France, and Germany could be a much simpler historical circumstance. **20.2**

This was the timing of the impact of the Industrial Revolution in relation to the timing of the crystallisation of the three great legal traditions. **20.3**

The Industrial Revolution was first felt in England after about 1750. This happened at a time when the economic philosophy was one of *laissez-faire*, as pronounced in Adam Smith's *Wealth of Nations* published in 1776. This propounded the theory of the invisible hand of the market. By the early nineteenth century, when Britain had more or less been through the first stages of its Industrial Revolution, the ideas of total market liberalism were the prevailing mainstream consensus. The attitude was 'capital is king', and 'the railways must be built'. **20.4**

Hence, if the banks wanted all of the corporate assets as security for a loan, they got it. If the banks then wanted to be able to enforce their monopolistic security in one hour after a default by the debtor by appointing a friendly accountant as a receiver, do go ahead. If the receiver fired all the directors and took complete charge of the company without any reference to the courts, please be my guest. These eighteenth and nineteenth-century lawyers had got it into their minds that it made no sense to switch off a power station on an enforcement and that the real creditors who were being protected were the depositors with banks, so that protecting banks was in effect protecting the savings of the people. **20.5**

However, security interests under the French system were hugely different. It was not possible to cover all the assets and enforcement was difficult, involving applications to the court and long delays. There was no concept whereby a creditor could take over the management of the business through a receiver on enforcement. One may infer that when the Napoleonic codes were crystallised, which was in the last decade of the eighteenth century, the Industrial Revolution had not really hit France to any great degree. The people who were drafting the code were still living in the earlier agricultural world, where money-lenders were an irritant and where trade and finance were somewhat contemptible. It did not occur to them that banks needed security interests to secure loans for railways or power stations or steel mills or factories; nor did it occur to them that one needed some way of netting off exposures **20.6** between banks in payment systems or between counterparties in markets to reduce exposures. Why would they? There were no big power stations requiring huge amounts of finance to be secured and there were no such thing as large amount payment systems. Trade could get along quite well enough without these things.

20.7 This understandable lack of awareness of the commands of the future was more especially so in light of the fact that the French Civil Code was based on work which had taken place in the eighteenth century, especially books by Robert Pothier (1699–1772), well before the onset of major industrialisation in France. His *Treatise on Obligations* was published in 1760. The ground-breaking work of Jean Domat in systematising the customary law of Paris went back to 1694.

20.8 The fact that France was aiming for codifications, such as in relation to security interests, probably prevented the development of the universal security interests for corporations—the famous fixed and floating charge—which was entirely the product of case law and practice in England during the nineteenth century.

20.9 When we came to the Roman-Germanic system, the Industrial Revolution had certainly swept through Germany—the codes were in the works from about 1850 onwards, although only promulgated in 1900. However, the really important law—the bankruptcy law—was enacted in Germany in 1877, at the height of the Industrial Revolution in Germany and following the Commercial Code of 1861. It was no surprise, therefore, that the Roman-Germanic system, as evidenced in the great codes and in the bankruptcy legislation, had a distinct creditor bias in order to encourage capital. On the other hand the codes were drafted by conservative academics immersed in Roman law and it may well have been the influence of this academic approach, with its somewhat aristocratic disdain for trade, finance, and the money-grubbing customs of merchants, which resulted in the Roman-Germanic system being somewhere in between the Napoleonic and the common law view on pro-creditor and pro-debtor attitudes.

20.10 One of the leading German thinkers of the nineteenth century was Friedrich Carl von Savigny. In his book *The Law of Possession* of 1803, he took the Roman idea of possession and presented it as an organising principle. He was therefore one of the chief promoters of the doctrine of false wealth, which has done so much harm to legal systems. He advised against immediate codification and wanted Germany first to find out its national spirit. Other German jurists involved in the Civil Code project included Windsheid, whose first draft in 1887 was rejected as being too technical and unreadable, with innumerable cross-references harassing the reader, like the busy footnote. Another expert was Rudolph Sohm (1841–1917), an expert in the history of ecclesiastical (canon) law. In any event, the final version was completed in 1896 and the BGB entered into force on 1 January 1900.

20.11 It seems unlikely that religion was a major factor in the different approaches in England, Germany and France, ie because the northern countries were Protestant and France was Roman Catholic. It is certainly true that Catholicism was more conservative on commercial matters and especially usury, but usury was abolished at the time of the French Revolution when the codes were being drafted. The explanation advanced by Max Weber that it was the Protestant ethic of hard work and thrift which led to economic advance seems doubtful as the main force underlying legal developments. Religion was not a significant political influence on most secular law by this time. Law was promulgated by secular authorities, not by priests.

Indelibility of existing law

20.12 Why then did these nineteenth century views cling on for so long—for nearly 200 years now? For example, the 2016 reforms of the good faith doctrine in French law moved very little towards greater predictability, notwithstanding how much finance and commerce have changed since 1804.

20.13 One reason for the inertia seems to be that all three of the philosophies were extremely successful. A successful legal regime is almost as indelible in its basic propositions as a successful religion. Once the ideology takes hold, and especially if it originally had compelling content at its core, it becomes resistant to change, even if the case for change resulting from changed circumstances is overpowering. A detailed comparison of the three great camps shows an adherence to a historical tradition which cannot be explained by real differences in current need, or current economic circumstances, or current culture.

20.14 In any event, the differences between the originating countries—England, France, and Germany—have now narrowed somewhat, probably as a result of increasing financialisation and hence the size of risks. This is clearly shown by a degree of rapprochement by France, Belgium and Luxembourg towards the adoption of the three super-priority insolvency claimants. The gulf between the ideologies is more perceptible in the case of emerging countries which received one of the legal systems and left it as it was. National competition has also been a factor in legal change.

Cultural Revolution of 1968

20.15 1968 was the year marking major cultural and political shifts in the West which had been building up for some time. The hierarchies of society were challenged and the authority of elders debunked. There were protests about the Vietnam War and the nuclear build-up, protests in which students played a major part. In France, the philosophies of Michel Foucault, Jacques Derrida, Jacques Lacan, and Jean-Francois Lyotard denounced everything that the eighteenth century Enlightenment stood for and all its values were mocked by them as having no value. This deconstructivism swept through universities in the 1980s. Politics changed from the steady conservatism of the early 1960s to a militant left-wing activism in the 1970s, both in the UK and in continental Europe. In parts of Europe, such as France and Italy a sizable proportion of the population supported a philosophy which was not sympathetic to banks, corporations, and business and which ultimately lost ground only when the more extreme form of the philosophy crumbled into dust when the Berlin Wall crumbled into dust. The ideas of this anti-capitalist movement reappeared later in the anti-Wall Street movement in the United States and later in various other similarly motivated cultural movements elsewhere to the present day.

20.16 To return to the 1970s, in the United States Ralph Nader led a consumer revolution. In Britain, Parliament passed the Consumer Credit Act in 1974 and the Unfair Contract Terms Act 1977. In 1979, the English law professor Patrick Atiyah wrote a book on the rise and fall of freedom of contract.

20.17 A revealing way of following cultural trends in the law is to track the progress of insolvency rescue statutes. As discussed in chapter 10 on insolvency law indicators generally, insolvency arouses such passions that insolvency laws and particularly corporate rescue statutes are a kind of barometer of a jurisdiction's overall attitudes on such matters as intrusion on transactions and predictability generally in the interests of protecting the debtor and the political demands of protecting jobs. Chapter 10 shows that one can measure a number of indicators which capture the pro-creditor or pro-debtor credentials of a jurisdiction with reasonable conviction.

20.18 Apart from various rudimentary compositions in earlier centuries, one of the first corporate rescues with voting on a plan was the English corporate scheme of arrangement introduced in 1870 without any stays on creditor actions and hence highly protective of creditors. This preceded the first permanent US Bankruptcy Act of 1898, which had a modest composition procedure to deal with the widespread failure of all railroads in the last quarter of the nineteenth century. This was revised somewhat in 1938. The US Congress passed the Bankruptcy Code of 1978, containing the famous reorganisation in Chapter 11. This was pro-debtor, but in that respect it was far exceeded by the French *redressement judiciaire* of 1985 where, amongst other things, the court controlled the plan, not the creditors. In the UK, the Insolvency Act 1986 introduced a rescue procedure which was mild compared to the dirigisme of the French rescue statute, where major decisions were taken by the court, not by creditor voting. In 1979, Italy brought in an extraordinary administration for large enterprises which dispensed with the courts and put the politicians in charge. In Spain, a Decree-Law of 1969, following the *Matesa* case, contemplated that the administration of a company could be granted to employees as well as creditors. The legislation was subsequently extended to allow the seizure of companies providing public services. One of the most remarkable of these statist insolvency statutes of the era was the 'sick companies' legislation in India. Once the government put a company on the sick companies list, creditors were effectively expropriated. This legislation was abolished only in 2018.

20.19 But by then, as a result of the global financial crisis starting in 2007, most governments in developed countries had nationalised the bankruptcy law of banks, basing themselves on a 1933 US statute plus the compulsory conversion of debt to equity ('bail-in'), and had also introduced draconian regulatory control of the financial sector, such as the leviathan Dodd-Frank Act of 2010 in the US and a string of at least twenty major financial regulations in Europe. European financial regulation hardly existed before the mid-1980s so the process from freedom to control took just over twenty years, virtually all of it a direct or indirect reaction to the threat of the insolvency of banking systems. In other words the regulatory outburst and statism were driven by bankruptcy.

20.20 From the mid-1990s onwards and particularly after 2000 the number of countries which introduced major changes to their bankruptcy legislation multiplied, including both developed and emerging countries, together with continuing insolvency reforms in transition countries emerging from communism.

20.21 What this short historical survey shows is that the development of the law is directly influenced by two important factors, one of which is changes in political culture between the polar opposites of left and right, and the other of which is economic crises which have an immediate impact on law-making by legislators.

20.22 If we take this medium-term historical view, it seems possible that radical trends commencing in the symbolic marker year of 1968 could have penetrated through to the judiciary in, say, Italy and France in the 1980s. For example, much of the activity in the courts in France on the contract doctrine of good faith was from the 1980s onwards when student class of the 1968 culture was maturing into seniority. Some of the judges at the time appear to have taken less account of the needs of the business community for predictability, business orientation and the defence of creditors against bankruptcies. This view seems to have prevailed in France in the 2016 reforms to the Civil Code as regards contract, notwithstanding major and forward-looking reforms to French financial law after 2003. However, our areas of law seemed to have been unshaken by the 1968 factor in, for example, Germany and Switzerland.

20.23 Meanwhile, in England the concentration of the senior judiciary in London, plus an inherited embedded pro-business orientation, plus the arrival of the euromarkets in the late 1960s, propelling London into its role as the world's largest financial centre, all acted as a brake on legal radicalism. For example, the potential of the Unfair Contract Terms Act 1977 to disrupt contract predictability was neutered by the emphasis of the courts on freedom of contract, and the validity of exclusion clauses in wholesale markets was neutered by the courts, just as they more or less neutered the statutory imposition of personal liability of directors for deepening an insolvency, known as wrongful trading, except in manifestly irresponsible cases. The courts encouraged freedom of contract and business orientation, trends which are dramatically heightened by recent decisions of the UK Supreme Court about penalty causes and other matters. London was just too important as an international financial centre, and the role of English law as a governing law for international business contracts was too significant, to allow onslaughts on the main tenets of the ideology.

20.24 If the above two propositions—the impact of the Industrial Revolution in relation to the timing of the crystallisation of commercial laws, and the medium-term impact of the 1968 revolution on legal policies—bear some relation to the truth, then we have an additional explanation of the divides between the three great European legal systems.

20.25 It is inescapable that the law is influenced by the politics of the day. The ideal is that the law should stay above the daily clamour and turbulence of politics and should not bend with every passing gale or storm. The law should move with measured step.

Brexit

20.26 It is considered that Brexit did not have a material adverse effect on the classes of law discussed in this book. But it did have an impact on the financial economy of the City of London by reason of the loss of the passport for financial services into Europe in some areas of finance The impact of Brexit was mainly constitutional in such matters as sovereignty, but not contract.

20.27 The UK retained the core of Rome I and Rome II, although these were largely in effect codifications of existing English private international law. The UK enacted into domestic law, with necessary consequential changes, virtually the whole of the European financial regulatory regime. The UK lost the benefits (and disadvantages) of the EU Judgments Regulation 2012 on the recognition and enforcement of Member State judgments, but English judgments already have one of the best foreign enforcement records in the world. In addition the EU Insolvency Regulation 2015 fell away, but again England has adopted the UNCITRAL Model Law on Cross-border Insolvency and has a sophisticated set of conflicts of laws rules in any event.

20.28 One effect of Brexit is that the UK will not have to adopt future European Union measures which could be harmful to the English legal ideology in the business sphere, such as proposals for a European contract law, proposals which at present would not conform with such concepts as predictability and freedom of contract in England. The UK would also escape European measures on insolvency, which might intrude even further into the moderate English regime.

20.29 A disadvantage perhaps is that the UK will not be formally present in negotiations towards further conformity of private law in Europe and therefore less able to influence how all the European legal systems should take the law forward in the world generally, not only for themselves, but also as an illustration for legal directions in the rest of the world.

Roman law and the present

20.30 Both France and Germany claim that their codifications are the true inheritors of Roman law. The Dutch also claim this. Scotland and South Africa have a direct view back to Rome, more or less unencumbered by contemporary codifications. Meanwhile, the English customarily assert that their legal system owes nothing to Rome and they did it all themselves as an expression of their doughty freedoms. They make this claim notwithstanding that the faculties of law at Oxford and Cambridge taught Roman law for centuries. Although the reception of Roman law in England was a fraction of that in continental Europe, it is suggested that the Roman contribution was more than is commonly believed in England.

20.31 In one way or another, it is suggested that all the present day great families of law based on continental Europe, and perhaps some features of the common law families too, owe their basic ideas to Roman law, notwithstanding that Roman law did not contemplate the huge changes in commercial and financial law which have taken place over the last century. The result is that the legal contribution of Rome is probably the greatest contribution to civilisation through laws of any sovereign state ever.

20.32 After the final fall of Rome in 476, its laws became detached from its territory of Italy. They were compiled into a quasi-codification in Constantinople in the 530s. That compilation floated around as a ghostly ideology in the ether for many centuries until its reappearance in Italy in the 1100s. That ideology permeates the basics of much world law now. Nothing demonstrates more potently the dramatic conclusion that a legal system, like a philosophy or a religion, can become detached from the territory which originally created it, a territory which no longer itself owns the ideology.

The future

20.33 The three great issues for the future are, first, whether the law will continue to expand at the present rate and become even more unmanageable, even with the aid of artificial intelligence; secondly, whether the existing families of law will remain as they are with roughly the same members; and, thirdly, whether the dominance of English and New York law will continue as a duopoly or whether other contenders will successfully challenge their dominance. One of the most intriguing questions is what emerging countries will do with the legal systems they inherited from the past. The law is moving everywhere in unpredictable directions. Everywhere it is in motion. It seems likely that the law generally in the world will not stay still and that the situation in fifty years from now will be entirely different from the present. If past history is anything to go by, the content of the law of the future will be very unexpected.

20.34 Everybody has a chance.

21

CONCLUSION

Weighting of the Main Themes

Methods of weighting

21.1 This book chose thirteen themes to be measured by a much larger number of key indicators. The themes were, in relation to contract, predictability, insulation, business orientation, freedom, exclusion clauses, and, generally, insolvency, insolvency set-off, security interests, commercial trusts, corporate law, regulation, courts, and non-legal matters. These themes were measured by the use of major key indicators in terms of symbolic importance, together numbering nearly thirty areas, and a large number of other key indicators which were not examined in detail, bringing the total up to around seventy areas.

21.2 Lawyers advising on business transactions are entitled to inquire which of the key indicators or themes are the most important.

21.3 The answer is that there is no fixed answer. It depends on the detailed facts and circumstances of each transaction. At a minimum level, insolvency set-off may not be top of the agenda in the case of a borrower which is rated AAA by all the main credit rating agencies. It would, however, increase in importance if the debtor has a low credit rating so that insolvency is a real issue. In the foreign exchange market, the availability of set-off and netting is crucial, even though the transactions themselves may be contracts for only two days. It is the sheer colossal numbers which makes set-off and netting so important. A company which is making issue of share capital is not likely to regard insulation by governing law of the transaction against foreign exchange controls as being of the slightest importance, but a syndicate of banks financing a project in a country suffering high political risk would be very interested in that insulation. Credit rating agencies generally recognise the importance of the actual transaction when they rate particular bond issues, rather than the issuer generally.

21.4 The answer also depends on such factors as whether the party concerned is a debtor or a creditor and also on the customary practices of a market, adherence to which are likely to facilitate a deal, regardless of whether this suits the party as debtor or creditor.

21.5 For example, corporations as borrowers of bank loans or issuers of bonds may prefer the more relaxed attitude to debtors shown by the main Napoleonic jurisdictions. But this may not be acceptable to the financial market concerned and so might inhibit the financing of the deal. On the other hand, corporations in their capacity as sellers may prefer a regime which gives them greater freedom to exclude liability, a greater business orientation, greater freedom of contract, and strict predictability of contract terms, without court intervention.

21.6 The real question is how many of the important risks can be managed by choice of governing law and how many are outside management by this method, especially insolvency risks and regulatory risks. The answer to that question resolves into an issue of how much freedom we actually have under our legal systems comparatively.

The Nature of Freedom

21.7 Earlier in this book, I drew attention to the 1830 painting by Delacroix hanging in the Louvre in Paris and titled *Liberty Leading the People*. The whole of society, as it then was, is represented in this painting—youth, merchants, peasants, soldiers, and others. They were all armed to fight for liberty. I mentioned then that the law is the opposite of liberty because the law restricts us, ties us down, fetters, and manacles us. The question therefore is, was she right? The answer I gave is that the law should restrict us only so as to liberate us, in order that we may survive, as the Chilean miners did, but not most of those on the raft of the *Medusa*.

21.8 Yet it will be apparent to the reader of this book that, wherever we look in the modern world, we see ourselves surrounded by the ironclad battalions of the law, advancing on us, more ferociously armed than Liberty herself and her companions, even more determined to get their way.

21.9 We did not have had the mnemonic of legal controls 6C–TRITO a century ago, but we have it now.

21.10 People who live in free democracies have no idea how awful it is, and terrifying too, to live in a tyrannical country run by predatory despots. They have no idea on how hard you have to work, how stern are the disciplines you have to observe, how patient you have to be, to preserve the freedoms that you have, and how courageously you have to fight against those who would deprive you and oppress you if they had the chance. It only takes a few years of negligence and carelessness, even a few months, to lose it all if the people are looking the wrong way, if they are heedlessly not watching what is happening to them.

21.11 Many of the matters we have been discussing in this book are not of the order just mentioned. However, the law is all around us and the classes of law discussed in this book permeate our societies. The dedication needed to maintain the values of a legal system are as strong as those needed to maintain political freedoms. The law in our societies is the central ideology of how we live and the law is constantly in danger from those who see the law as an instrument mainly to capture and manacle us, put the bird in a cage. There is no question how disciplined we have to be to ensure that that does not happen and that our scriptures are a source of freedom, that they are our servant, not our master.

Choices of Governing Law

21.12 This book has shown some of the characteristics of four of the leading legal systems and therefore of many of the adherents in the same families of law. The four representative jurisdictions I have chosen have each made a remarkable contribution to civilisation and to the scriptures of societies, and each of those four has achieved great prosperity in material welfare, as well as in the advancement of science and thinking. The law is our means of survival so that we on the planet may survive long enough to discover what the universe means and hence master our destiny. It is therefore to be expected that, in this major common endeavour, we will experiment with many different solutions about the direction of our laws.

21.13 Some would say that the law should be harmonised the world over and that we should all be subject to the same laws. Even if that could be achieved, it is doubtful that that would necessarily be a desired objective. The peoples in the world may in various basic ways be very similar and have similar needs and desires. On the other hand, people have many opinions and societies should be able to reflect those opinions in areas where uniformity is not essential. One result is that there is competition between legal systems, and a sharpened wish to improve on what has gone before. That is as it should be.

SOURCES AND REFERENCES

Introduction

This discussion of sources and references is intended to be a more meaningful (and hopefully more useful) review of sources and references than the blankness of footnotes and bibliographies.

Abbreviations of Works Cited

Set out below are abbreviations for works cited several times in this review:

Dicey: L Collins and others (eds), *Dicey, Morris and Collins on the Conflict of Laws* (15th edn, Sweet & Maxwell 2012). This massive work is the leading authority in England.

IECL: Konrad Zweigert and Ulrich Drobnig (eds), *International Encyclopaedia of Comparative Law* (JCB Mohr 1971–).

Wood on Finance: a series of nine volumes in the series *The Law and Practice of International Finance* (all published by Sweet & Maxwell 2019) by Philip Wood, as follows:

1. *Principles of International Insolvency* (3rd edn)
2. *International Insolvency: Jurisdictions of the World* (1st edn)
3. *Comparative Law of Security Interests and Title Finance* (1st edn)
4. *Security Interests and Title Finance: Jurisdictions of the World* (3rd edn)
5. *International Loans, Bonds, Guarantees, Legal Opinions* (3rd edn)
6. *Set-off and Netting, Derivatives, Clearing Systems* (3rd edn)
7. *Project Finance, Securitisations, Subordinated Debt* (3rd edn)
8. *Conflict of Laws and International Finance* (2nd edn)
9. *Regulation of International Finance* (2nd edn)

Wood, *Priests and Lawyers*: Philip Wood, *The Fall of the Priest and the Rise of the Lawyers* (Hart Publishing 2016)

Wood's Maps: Philip Wood, *Maps of World Financial Law* (Sweet & Maxwell 2008)

Zweigert and Kotz: K Zweigert and H Kötz, *An Introduction to Comparative Law* (Tony Weir tr, 3rd edn, OUP 1998)

Discussion of Sources

Practice and case law, not books

Perhaps unusually for a law writer, from the early days in the 1970s, my work in this area originated almost wholly in my practice and from my own primary research, rather than from the books or the early comparative literature. The working out of the comparative law framework and the identification of the principal key indicators was derived mainly from my investigation of case law, statutes, and consultations with foreign lawyers, beginning in the 1970s. I established my methodology by 1988. At that time, there was virtually no other literature on the law of international finance, so far as I was aware.

The literature began to appear in the 1990s, first as a trickle and then expanding somewhat in the early 2000s. Even now, the comparative literature on the main transactions discussed in this work and written by practitioners who have actually done the deals, is quite thin, apart from essays in edited books, rather than a single comparative work by a single author who could work out the links and the connections. The result is that I had to work out just about everything by myself.

In carrying out that task, I had three great advantages. The first was that I had an international practice which meant that I was in virtually daily contact with a large number of senior law firms all over the world, totalling several hundred in all. That meant that I was able to discuss the law in a huge number of jurisdictions in great detail with exceptional experts, especially in cases where they had to deliver legal opinions on transactions. The second advantage was that I worked in a large international law firm which had many overseas offices and therefore I came to acquire an intimate knowledge of how legal systems worked in practice and of what was really going on in the law internationally. The third advantage was that, for a couple of years, I was in charge of the know-how in my firm, and then, after retirement as a partner, for ten years I headed a think-tank in the firm called the Allen & Overy Global Law Intelligence Unit. This meant that one of my activities was to conduct very large international surveys of areas of law relevant to the work of the firm and to help build databases.

The effect of this is that most of my original sources were primary materials in the form of statutes and case law around the world, plus detailed memoranda and legal opinions from foreign law firms. These sources far exceeded the sources which I cite in the next section.

These sources enabled me to write a series of works on the law and practice of international finance, beginning with a single textbook in 1980 and culminating (after a couple of intervening editions) in a series of nine volumes totalling 3,000,000 words in 2019 and previously including a university textbook and a book of stylised maps on world financial law published in 2008. These works have been highly influential in the formation of this book. Effectively, I had covered all the jurisdictions in the world on some subjects. As a result, in those books I was able to work out a classification of jurisdictions which is substantially adopted in this book, although comparativists have been proposing other detailed classifications for at least half a century. The most formative work in terms of thinking and the working out of a framework was, for the unexpected and fortuitous reasons given in Chapter 8, my *English and International Set-off* published in 1989. This little subject seemed to sing no arias but remained humbly in the chorus, for me to find out that the topic went through legal systems like a harsh laser, telling us who won and who lost, what was debt, what was property, what was a legal entity, what this or that jurisdiction thought about debtors and creditors. It turned out that the topic was absolutely crucial to the world's biggest financial markets and also to the basic infrastructure of international finance. It was the key to unlocking the door.

Almost all of my works were published by Sweet & Maxwell, except that my book *The Fall of the Priests and the Rise of the Lawyers*, published in 2016 by Hart Publishing, encapsulated my then thinking that legal systems embodied the main features of the morality and sense of justice around the world. No doubt other jurisprudential philosophers have pronounced similar theories in history, but I have not heard of anyone doing so in the terms that I do and I arrived at my propositions independently of their works. On the whole (through no fault of the authors), I did not find those works to be of great relevance to what I was actually doing in practice.

This note is effectively the main footnote to this work.

Discussion of References by Chapter

Introduction

The references below are mainly restricted to comparative law works, not those on domestic law. This is not a bibliography, but rather a list of suggestions which the interested reader may wish to follow up.

Chapter 1 What this book is about

The felicitous phrase 'internationally mobile transactions' comes from a report by Oxera, *Economic Value of English Law* (October 2021).

There are many works on legal risk for the purposes of financial regulation, which do not, however, generally deal with governing law risk. See, however, Roger McCormick, *Legal Risk in the Financial Markets* (2nd edn, OUP 2010).

The ranking of jurisdictions by a colour code of blue, green, yellow, and red originated in my maps of world financial law in the mid-1990s, which were ultimately published in *Wood's Maps* in 2008. On the whole, these maps from their earliest appearance tended to support the 1357 ranking on most measures, with the result that this approach is not new but has been available in the maps and my books for around twenty-five years.

Chapter 2 Role of law

I first developed the idea of law as the essential survival ideology comprehensively in Wood, *Priests and Lawyers*, although it had been heralded in certain of my earlier works. I used the idea of English and New York law as 'international public utilities' in papers many years previously.

Chapter 3 Scope of contracts

On the scope of contracts, I would refer the reader to the standard works on banking and on old economy subjects, such as sale of goods, intellectual property, insurance, and other commercial topics.

As to syndicated credit agreements and international bond issues, see P Cresswell W Blair, G Hill, and P Wood, *Encyclopaedia of Banking Law* (Butterworths, Loose-leaf 1982–); and G Delaume, *Legal Aspects of International Lending and Economic Development Financing* (Oceana 1967), a historical gem which was written by a former member of the legal team at the World Bank, copiously documented by reference to former transactions, and which presaged many of the problems which came to the fore in the early days of the Euromarkets in London. A leading text on international bond issues is by my former colleague, the late G Fuller, *The Law and Practice of International Capital Markets* (3rd edn, LexisNexis Butterworths 2012). Amongst many other excellent works on these subjects, I would mention F Graaf, *Euromarket Finance: Issues of Euromarket Securities and Syndicated Eurocurrency Loans* (Kluwer 1991), H Scott and A Gelpern, *International Finance: Law and Regulation* (3rd edn, Sweet & Maxwell 2012); R Tennekoon, *The Law and Regulation of International Finance* (Butterworths 1991); R Wight and others, *The LSTA's Complete Credit Agreement Guide* (McGraw-Hill 2009); S Paterson and R Zakrzewski (eds), *McKnight, Paterson and Zakrzewski on the Law of International Finance* (2nd edn, OUP 2017), and books on international finance by C Bamford and others (eds), Volume 5 of my own work, *Wood on Finance*, also deals with these subjects and provides many snapshots of the actual documents so that the reader can follow what they say. The Loan Market Association in London has published many books on their standard agreements for syndicated credits, forms which are dominant for English law agreements.

As to the classification of assets in Chapter 3, there is another classification in *Wood on Finance*, vol 3, in the context of security interests, which also contains a commentary on the usual terms of security interests.

As to derivatives, see especially S Firth, *Derivatives Law and Practice* (Sweet & Maxwell 2003–), SK Henderson, *Henderson on Derivatives* (LexisNexis 2003); J Castagnino, *Derivatives* (3rd edn, OUP 2009); and *Wood on Finance*, vol 5, again accompanied by snapshots.

As to project finance, see a notable work, also by former colleagues: G Vinter, G Price, and D Lee, *Project Finance: A Legal Guide* (4th edn, Sweet & Maxwell 2013). See also J Dewar (ed), *International Project Finance* (2nd edn, OUP 2015); *Wood on Finance*, vol 7.

As to securitisations and the sale of receivables, see J Deacon, *Global Securitisation and CDOs* (Wiley 2004); D Munoz, *The Law on Transnational* (OUP 2010); *Wood on Finance*, vol 7.

As to central counterparties, see *Wood on Finance*, vol 6, ch 25.

As to mutual funds, see *Wood on Finance*, vol 9.

As to private investment funds, see P Athanassiou, *Research Handbook on Hedge Funds, Private Equity and Alternative Investments* (Edward Elgar Publishing 2012); T Spangler, *The Law of Private Investment Funds* (2nd edn, OUP 2012); M Hudson, *Funds* (Wiley 2014).

As to corporate transactions, see under ch 14 below.

As to commercial transactions, see the scholarly work by J Dalhuisen, *Dalhuisen on International, Commercial, Financial and Trade Law*, vol 6 (Hart Publishing 2022). For a collection of materials, see R Goode, E McKendrick, and J Wool, *Transnational Commercial Law* (OUP 2004). For construction law, see J Uff, *Construction Law* (13th edn, Sweet &Maxwell 2021).

As to consumer credit, see the interesting work by R Gelpi and F Julien-Labruyère, *The History of Consumer Credit* (Liam Gavin tr, Macmillan, 2000).

Chapter 4 Governing law and choice of courts

A well-trodden subject. See Dicey for England and, amongst numerous other outstanding works, C Proctor (ed), *Mann and Proctor on the Law of Money* (8th edn, OUP 2022); R Fentiman, *International Commercial Litigation* (OUP 2010). See also the precocious piece by O Lando, 'Private International Law: Contracts' (1977) in *IECL*, vol III, C. See *Wood on Finance*, vol 8, which in chs 3–25 contains an international study of choice of law and courts and the position in the absence of choice.

Chapter 5 Predictability

Chapters 5, 7, 8, and 9 are in one way or another concerned with the ordinary law of contract, a subject on which there is an abundance of standard works in all the leading jurisdictions. They are all dealt with together here.

On contracts generally and in particular the topics covered in the above chapters, see *Wood on Finance*, vol 5 and, for the history from Roman times, the monumental work by R Zimmermann, *The Law of Obligations* (Juta 1990). See also *IECL*, vol 8.

As to the good faith doctrine in contract in ch 5 and exclusion clauses in ch 9 (not including offering circulars and the like), see O Lando and H Beale, *Principles of European Contract Law* (Kluwer 2000); J Baaij and others (eds), *Interpretation of Commercial Contracts in European Private Law* (Intersentia 2020); J Beatson and D Friedman (eds), *Good Faith and Fault in Contract Law* (OUP 1995); J Cartwright and S Whittaker, *The Code Napoleon Rewritten: French Contract Law after the 2016 Reforms* (Hart Publishing 2017); J Cartwright and M Hesselink (eds), *Precontractual Liability in European Private Law* (CUP 2008); L DiMatteo and M Hogg (eds), *Comparative Contract Law: British and American Perspectives* (OUP 2015); N Jansen and R Zimmerman, *European Contract Law* (OUP 2018); Hein Kotz, *European Contract Law* (2nd edn, OUP 2017); B Markesinis and others, *The German Law of Contract: A Comparative Treatise* (Bloomsbury 2006); E Steiner, *French Law: A Comparative Approach* (2nd edn, OUP 2018); R Zimmerman and S Whittaker (eds), *Good Faith in European Contract Law* (CUP 2000); M Reiman and R Zimmerman (eds), *The Oxford Handbook of Comparative Law* (OUP 2006); *IECL*, vol 7.

For analyses of French contract law, see S Rowan, *Remedies for Breach of Contract: Comparative Analysis of the Protection of Performance* (OUP 2012); S Rowan, *The New French Law of Contract* (OUP 2022); R Youngs, *English, French and German Comparative Law* (3rd edn, Routledge 2014). For English law on these topics, see E Peel, *Treitel: The Law of Contract* (15th edn, Sweet & Maxwell 2020). For US law, see A Farnsworth, *Contracts* (4th edn, Aspen 2004); G Banks, *New York's Contract Law* (New York State Bar Association 2015); R Lord, *Williston on Contracts* (31 vols, 4th edn, Thomson Reuters 2021). See also J Cartwright, *Contract Law: An Introduction to the English Law of Contract for the Civil Lawyer* (3rd edn, Hart Publishing 2016).

Most books on insolvency will discuss the anti-deprivation rule used as a key indicator in ch 7. There is an expanded treatment of the subject in *Wood on Finance*, vol 1, ch 23.

For further discussion of the comparative law on the nullification of non-assignment clauses, see *Wood on Finance*, vol 3, ch 17.

As to liability for offering circulars in ch 9, see D Busch and others (eds), *Prospectus Regulation and Prospectus Liability* (OUP 2020); P Conac and M Gelter, *Global Securities Litigation and Enforcement* (CUP 2019). *Wood on Finance*, vol 9, ch 35 contains a detailed study of prospectus liability which is considered to support the conclusions in ch 9 of this book on the international liability for offering circulars and the like.

Chapter 6 Insulation of contract from foreign laws

For insulation, see the works cited under ch 4. See also C Proctor (ed), *Mann and Proctor on the Law of Money* (8th edn, OUP 2022).for article VIII 2b of the IMF Agreement, and *Wood on Finance*, vol 8, ch 9. Sir Joseph Gold, former general counsel of the IMF, wrote a series of papers discussing article VIII 2b of the IMF Agreement.

Chapter 7 Business orientation

See under ch 5.

Chapter 8 Freedom of contract

See under ch 5.

Chapter 9 Exclusion clauses

See under ch 5.

Chapter 10 Insolvency law indicators and risks

A vast field nowadays, regarded as niche well into the 1970s, although clearly one of the most important of all private law disciplines in terms of impact on the law. J Dalhuisen, *International Insolvency and Bankruptcy* (Mathew Bender 1982) was an early classic and still valuable for its perceptiveness and historical material. M Broude and others (eds), *Collier International Business Insolvency Guide* (Lexis, 2003–) has a good spread of jurisdictions. Collier is a leading name in commentaries on US bankruptcy law. J Marshall (ed), *European Cross-Border Insolvency* (Allen & Overy LLP, Sweet & Maxwell, Loose-leaf 2004–2016), now regrettably discontinued, covered the ground superbly in the EU. See also I Fletcher, *Insolvency in Private International Law* (3rd edn, OUP 2007). INSOL International published multi-jurisdictional studies on insolvency topics, including on directors in the twilight zone, cross-border insolvency, and the avoidance of antecedent transactions. T Jackson, *The Logic and Limits of Bankruptcy Law* (Harvard UP 1986) is a classic for explaining what bankruptcy is for. See also B McBryde, A Flessner, and S Kortmann (eds), *Principles of European Insolvency Law* (Kluwer 2003); S Gleeson and R Guynn, *Bank Resolution and Crisis Management* (OUP 2016); R Lastra (ed), *Cross-Border Bank Insolvency* (OUP 2011); D Faber and others (eds), *Ranking and Priority of Creditors* (OUP 2016); C Mallon and S Waisman, *The Law and Practice of Restructuring in the UK and US* (OUP 2011). For the European Insolvency Regulation, see G Moss,

I Fletcher, and S Isaacs, *The EU Regulation on Insolvency Proceedings* (3rd edn, OUP 2016). D Skeel's essay 'An Evolutionary Theory of Corporate Law and Corporate Bankruptcy' (1998) 51(5) V and L Rev 1325 is a succinct study. *Wood on Finance*, vol 1 covers the main topics comparatively over sixty-seven chapters and nearly 900 pages. *Wood on Finance*, vol 2 contains summaries of insolvency law in all of the world's jurisdictions.

Chapter 11 Insolvency set-off

This was the topic which unexpectedly helped me the most personally in working out what was going on in private comparative law. See my *English and International Set-off* (Sweet & Maxwell 1989), which was based on a direct reading of the case law. See also an excellent work by R Derham, *The Law of Set-off* (3rd edn, OUP 2003). Other specific works in English on set-off include W Johnston, T Werlen, and F Link (eds), *Set-off Law and Practice* (OUP 2018), which is a jurisdiction-by-jurisdiction survey of thirty jurisdictions; R Palmer, *The Law of Set-off in Canada* (Aurora 1993); S McCracken, *The Banker's Remedy of Set-off* (3rd edn, Bloomsbury 2010); Francis Neate (ed), *Using Set-off as Security* (Graham & Trotman 1990)—also a jurisdiction survey; and P Pichonnaz and L Gullifer, *Set-off in Arbitration and Commercial Transactions* (OUP 2014). *Wood on Finance*, vol 6 has a world survey of set-off and netting and of carve-out statutes. Works on insolvency law, including the many international surveys, usually also deal with set-off.

Chapter 12 Security interests

My main source was experience, the original statutes, and foreign lawyers, supplemented by jurisdiction surveys. See M Bridge and G Stevens, *Cross-border Security and Insolvency* (OUP 2001); W Johnston (ed), *Security over Receivables* (OUP 2008); G McCormack, *Secured Credit under English and American Law* (CUP 2004); F Dahan (ed), *Secured Financing in Commercial Transactions* (Edward Elgar Publishing 2015); K Potok, *Cross-border Collateral: Legal Risk and the Conflict of Laws* (Butterworths 2002); G Yeowart and R Parsons, *The Law of Financial Collateral* (Edward Elgar Publishing 2016); W Jon, *Cross-Border Transfer and Collateralisation of Receivables* (Hart Publishing 2018). There are many commentaries on article 9 of the Uniform Commercial Code. The authentic work about how article 9 came to exist was by its main drafter, G Gilmore, *Security Interests in Personal Property* (Little Brown 1965). Works on security interests and related subjects by, or edited by, L Gullifer are particularly valuable. See also *Wood on Finance*, vols 3 and 4. Vol 4 contains summaries of the law on security interests in all of the jurisdictions of the world.

Chapter 13 Commercial trusts

Apart from standard works on trusts in the various common law jurisdictions, some useful references are the classic article by V Bolgar, 'Why No Trusts in the Civil Law?' (1953) 2 Am J Comp L 204; W Diamond, *International Trust Laws and Analysis* (Blackwell's, Loose-leaf 1995–); W Fratcher (ed), *International Encyclopaedia of Comparative Law*, vol VI (JCB Mohr 1971–) ch 11; J Glasson and A Gore (eds), *International Trust Laws* (Chancery Law Publishing Loose-leaf 1992–); M Graziadei, U Mattei, and L Smith (eds), *Commercial Trusts in European Private Law* (CUP 2005); D Hayton (ed), *Modern International Developments in Trust Law* (Kluwer 1999); D Hayton, S Kortmann, and H Verhagen (eds), *Principles of European Trust Law* (Kluwer 1999); M Lupoi, *Trusts* (Simon Dix tr, CUP 1997); M Lupoi (ed), *Trust Laws of the World: A Collection of Original Texts* (ETI Editore 1996); B McCutcheon and P Soares, *Euro-trusts: The New European Dimension for Trusts* (Legal Studies Publishing 1993); Lionel Smith (ed), *The Worlds of the Trust* (CUP 2013); A Thiele, *Collective Security Arrangements: A Comparative Study of Dutch, English and German Law* (Kluwer

2003); D Waters, 'The Institution of the Trust in Civil and Common Law' 252 *Recueil des Cours*, Collected Courses of the Hague Academy of International Law (Martinus Nijhoff 1995); W Wilson (ed), *Trusts and Trust-like Devices*; C de Wulf, *The Trust and Corresponding Institutions in the Civil Law* (1965); *IECL*, vol 6.

As to custodianship, see A Austen-Peters, *Custody of Investments: Law and Practice* (OUP 2000); J Benjamin, *Interests in Securities* (OUP 2002); M Yates and G Montagu, *The Law of Global Custody* (2nd edn, Bloomsbury Publishing 2013); P Wood, 'Commercial Trusts in an International Context' (2013) 29(384) Trusts and Trustees 267; *Wood on Finance*, vol 1, chs 13–17.

Chapter 14 Corporate law indicators and risks

See R Kraakman and others, *The Anatomy of Corporate Law* (OUP 2004); J Maitland-Walker, *Guide to European Company Laws* (Sweet & Maxwell 1997); M Andenas and F Wooldridge, *European Comparative Company Law* (CUP 2009); A Dorresteijn and others, *European Corporate Law* (3rd edn, Wolters Kluwer 2017); A Cahn and D Donald, *Comparative Company Law* (2nd edn, CUP 2018); G Griffiths (ed), *International Acquisition Finance* (2nd edn, OUP 2010); D Cooke and J Dow, *Private Equity: Law and Practice* (2nd edn, Sweet & Maxwell 2004); L Gullifer and J Payne, *Corporate Finance Law* (2nd edn, Hart Publishing 2015); E Ferran and L Ho, *Principles of Corporate Finance Law* (2nd edn, OUP 2016); S Singleton, *Joint Ventures and Shareholders' Agreements* (6th edn, Bloomsbury 2021); *IECL*, vol 13; *Wood's Maps*.

Chapter 15 Regulatory law indicators and risks

There is a huge literature on all aspects. Oxford University Press is a major publisher in this field. See eg N Moloney, *EU Securities and Financial Markets Regulation* (3rd edn, OUP 2014); N Moloney and others (eds), *The Oxford Handbook of Financial Regulation* (OUP 2015). See also K Alexander, *Principles of Banking Regulation* (CUP 2019).

As to international monetary stability, see eg R Lastra, *International Financial and Monetary Law* (2nd edn, OUP 2015). See also *Wood on Finance*, vol 9, which at a mere 991 pages is a succinct text on the regulation of international finance.

Chapter 16 Courts, litigation, and arbitration

R Mulheron, *The Class Action* (Hart Publishing 2004).

For surveys of the enforcement of foreign judgments, see C Platto (ed), *Enforcement of Foreign Judgments Worldwide* (Kluwer 1989), which contains country and regional reports prepared by members of the International Bar Association; L Garb and J Lew (eds), *Enforcement of Foreign Judgments* (Kluwer, Loose-leaf 1995) and D Campbell (ed), *International Execution Against Judgment Debtors* (Oceana, Loose-leaf 1998). The detail may be out-of-date but it is thought that the general position described remains broadly true.

For arbitration, see J Golden and C Lamm (eds), *International Financial Disputes: Arbitration and Mediation* (OUP 2015); P Friedland, *Arbitration Clauses for International Contracts* (2nd edn, JurisNet 2007). See also generally *Wood on Finance*, vol 8.

Chapter 17 Non-legal indicators and risks

On financial centres, see R Laulajainen, *Financial Geography: A Banker's View* (Routledge 2003); *Wood on Finance*, vol 9. Many institutions in Britain and elsewhere maintain comparative data.

Chapter 18 Comparison of jurisdictions of the world

The following works remind us of the state of the art in past times: R David and J Brierley, *Major Legal Systems in the World Today* (3rd edn, Stevens 1985); H Gutteridge, *Comparative Law: An Introduction to the Comparative Method of Legal Study & Research* (2nd edn, CUP 1949); F Lawson, *A Common Lawyer Looks at the Civil Law* (University of Michigan Law School 1953); A von Mehren, *The Civil Law: Cases and Materials for the Comparative Study of Law* (2nd edn, Prentice-Hall 1977); E Rabel, *The Conflicts of Laws: A Comparative Study* (University of Michigan 1958–1964).

See generally A Watson, *Legal Transplants: An Approach to Comparative Law* (University Press of Virginia 1974); *IECL*, vol 2; *Wood on Finance*, vols 1–9; *Wood's Maps*.

Chapter 19 Protecting a governing law

I owe the suggestion of a kind of Royal Society for the law to G Beringer, CBE, KC Hon.

Chapter 20 History and the future

The theories of the impact of the Industrial Revolution and the impact of the cultural movements after 1968 are my suggestions, independent of the books. For books on the history of law, see eg the classic *Zweigert and Kotz on Comparative Law*; O Robinson, T Fergus, and W Gordon, *European Legal History* (3rd edn, Butterworths 2000); P Stein, *Roman Law in European History* (CUP 1999); J Baker, *An Introduction to English Legal History* (4th edn, LexisNexis 2002,). For a succinct introduction, see B Wauters and M de Benito, *The History of Law in Europe* (Edward Elgar Publishing 2017). Chapter 3 of Wood, *Priests and Lawyers* contains a fuller history of law, especially after 1830, and the reasons for its growth, including statistics.

There is a brief history of insolvency law in ch 4 of *Wood on Finance*, vol 1.

Chapter 21 Conclusion

No citation relevant.

INDEX

1357 ranking 1.72–1.80, 5.12, 18.60, 18.82, 18.104, 18.120

absolutism 15.8
Abu Dhabi Global Market 18.64
abuse of dominant position 2.54–2.58
abusive credit 10.89, 14.107
act of state doctrine 6.20–6.22
Afghanistan 12.47
African Development Bank 19.14
agency agreements 3.86
aircraft
  security interests 12.67
Albania 18.147
Algerian Accords 18.14
American Arbitration Association 16.49
American Bar Association 19.17
American common law jurisdictions, *see* families of jurisdictions, New York law
American Law Institute 19.8
Arab Empire 18.32
arbitration 1.62, 4.81–4.83
  advantages of 16.45–16.47
  conclusions 16.55–16.56
  definition 4.81
  disadvantages 16.48–16.50
  financial and corporate documents 16.51–16.54
  history of 16.44
  insolvency override of 4.84–4.85
  see also choice of courts
Argentina 1.58, 7.21, 17.8
  foreign judgments 16.39
Ashoka of India 18.29
Asian Development Bank 19.14
assets
  contracts 3.1–3.15
    asset-related contracts 3.2–3.4
    classes of asset 3.5–3.6
    goods 3.10–3.12
    intangible assets 3.7–3.9
    land 3.13–3.15
  definition 3.5
  see also property
Atiyah, Patrick 20.15
Australia 12.47, 13.60, 13.75
  insolvency set-off 11.54, 11.56, 11.59
  wrongful trading 14.79
Austria 4.61, 13.35

Bangladesh 13.32
Bank of England 17.6

bankruptcy *see* insolvency law
banks
  arranging banks
    liabilities of 9.37–9.42
    offering memorandum 9.37
  central 14.105
  contracts 3.92–3.96
  insolvency law 10.56–10.61
  law and 2.78–2.82
  syndicated bank credits 9.29
Basel Banking Supervision Committee 19.15
Belgium 2.77, 4.61, 6.34, 6.6, 7.36, 8.48, 10.66, 13.75, 17.23
  good faith doctrine 18.100
  insolvency 20.13
    duties to file on 14.84
    set-off 11.24–11.25, 11.61, 11.85, 18.99
  security interests 12.47, 18.101
  underwriter liability 9.55
  wrongful trading 14.80
Bell, John 5.78
Bermuda 13.60, 18.54
best public title
  definition 3.122
  for receivables 3.123–3.124
  see also contracts
big pocket liability
  arrangers and underwriters 9.35
bilateral investment treaties (BITs) 6.24, 12.91, 14.5, 16.54, 17.23
Bolgár, Vera 13.51
bondholder democracies 8.60–8.78
  English law 8.64–8.68
  collective action 8.60–8.63
  international use 8.73–8.75
  key indicator, relevance of 8.76–8.78
  voting 8.60–8.63
  US law 8.69–8.72
  see also freedom of contract
bondholders 3.92–3.96
bonds
  international bond issues 9.30
  shares *vs.* 14.1–14.15
  unregulated bond prospectuses 9.45
Botswana 14.35
Boyron, Sophie 5.78
Brexit 2.59, 4.36, 11.23, 16.13, 20.25–20.28
British Virgin Islands 13.60
broker agreements 3.86
Buddhism 18.36

Burundi 2.77
business judgement rule 14.90
business orientation 1.62
  bankrupt corporations
    deprivation of assets of 7.32–7.38
    'flip clauses' as a deprivation 7.34–7.35
    joint ventures 7.32–7.33
    post-commencement proceeds of
      security 7.37–7.38
    turnover subordinations 7.36
  compulsory notice of the assignment of
    receivables 7.14–7.31
    conflict of laws on compulsory notice of debt
      assignments 7.26–7.31
    criticism of compulsory notice of debt
      assignments 7.24–7.25
    international position on compulsory notice of
      debt assignments 7.20–7.23
    notice of assignment, reasons for 7.14–7.19
  economic development 7.1–7.6
  history of 7.10–7.13
  indicators of 7.39–7.41
  judiciary 16.4–16.6
  measurement of 7.7–7.9
business transactions 1.38–1.42
Byzantine Empire 18.32

Cambodia 2.77, 18.148
Canada 5.70, 12.47, 13.60, 18.128
  bankruptcy law 18.94
  insolvency set-off 11.57, 11.62
  reasonable contract performance 5.46
capital maintenance 14.111
Carter, Jimmy 18.14
carve-out statutes 11.16
  jurisdictions 11.17–11.18
  see also insolvency: set-off
cause, concept of 9.27
  see also exclusion clauses
caveat emptor rule (beware the buyer) 5.107
Cayman Islands 12.16, 12.91, 18.54
central counterparties 3.58–3.66
centre of main interests (COMI) 10.16, 10.33–10.34,
  10.37, 10.44, 10.53, 11.24, 12.10, 12.78, 12.89,
  13.69, 13.72
Chad 2.77
charge, definition 12.1
charter agreements 3.86
chattels 3.10, 3.12
Chaucer, Geoffrey 16.20
Chiang Kai Shek 18.116
China 5.42, 12.40, 13.33, 13.36, 13.54, 13.61, 13.62,
  18.116, 18.35, 18.36
  Chinese Empire 18.32
  financial assistance 14.70
  insolvency set-off 11.68
choice of courts
  arbitration 4.81–4.83
    insolvency override of 4.84–4.85

corporate law 4.17–4.18
EU Judgments Regulation 4.66–4.74
factors influencing 4.45–4.55
freedom of choice and 8.12–8.19, 8.31–8.32
  court intervention 8.7–8.8
Hague Convention in Choice of Court Agreements
  (2005) 4.80
jurisdiction clauses 4.56–4.59
  insolvency override of 4.84–4.85
jurisdiction over torts 4.75–4.79
long-arm jurisdiction 4.60–4.65
risk and 16.9–16.16
  law of the courts, role of 16.12–16.14
  litigation, trauma of 16.15–16.16
  reasons for choice of courts 16.9–16.11
see also governing law, jurisdiction
  citation 1.60–1.61
class actions see litigation
clearing houses 3.47, 3.130, 11.20
Clearstream 2.46
CLS Bank 2.46, 2.53, 2.55, 3.56
codification 5.16–5.20
  see also predictability
collateral, definition 12.1
colonialism 18.116
  see also imperialism
COMI see centre of main interests
commercial agreements
  contracts 3.86–3.88
commercial law 2.60, 10.9, 18.1, 18.46, 18.57, 18.89,
  18.135, 20.23
commercial transactions
  contracts 3.100–3.101
communism 2.42, 20.19
common law see families of jurisdictions
companies see corporations
competitor imitation 2.59–2.61
compulsory notice of the assignment of receivables
  see business orientation
conflict of laws
  corporate transactions 14.20–14.25
  director personal liability 14.76
Congo Kinshasa 17.23
consents 5.111–5.113
  see also good faith doctrine
constitutional law 18.49
consumer law 4.29
  choice of courts 4.20
contract law
  choice of courts 4.22
  methodological focus on 1.47–1.51
  freedom of choice 1.4–1.6
  see also contracts
choice, freedom of see freedom of choice
commercial trusts 13.1–13.84
  conclusions 13.83–13.84
  definition of trust 13.5–13.11
  international survey of trust recognition 13.32–13.38
    civil law trust statutes 13.33

INDEX 319

family groups 13.35–13.38
Napoleonic group 13.34
key indicators 13.31
non-recognition as unjust enrichment 13.1–13.4
objections to the trust 13.39–13.55
   background 13.39–13.40
   false wealth 13.41
   illegal proceeds, impact on tracing of 13.48
   legal systems globally, impact on 13.52–13.55
   priority risks 13.42
   rejection of the trust, history of 13.49–13.51
   specificity, doctrine of 13.47
risk mitigation 13.56–13.82
trust recognition 13.56–13.82
   domicile of trustee 13.77–13.80
   EU Insolvency Regulation 13.68–13.76
   foreign governing law 13.81–13.82
   governing law of trust contract 13.58–13.68
   Hague Trusts Convention 1985 13.59–13.68
   objectives 13.56–13.57
   trust assets, location of 13.68–13.80
use of trusts 13.12–13.30
consensus building 16.7–16.8
see also judiciary
contracts
assets, based on 3.1–3.15
   asset-related contracts 3.2–3.4
   classes of asset 3.5–3.6
   goods 3.10–3.12
   intangible assets 3.7–3.9
   land 3.13–3.15
banks 3.92–3.96
best public title:
   definition 3.122
   for receivables 3.123–3.124
bondholders 3.92–3.96
central counterparties 3.58–3.66
chains of contracts for predictability, significance of 3.102–3.107
changes of:
   unilateral 6.1–6.4
commercial agreements 3.86–3.88
commercial transactions 3.100–3.101
construction/building 3.86, 13.27
corporate management 3.92–3.96
corporate shares, sale of 3.75–3.77
corporate transactions 3.73–3.74
corporations 3.96
cryptocurrencies 3.138–3.141
decentralised finance 3.138–3.141
derivatives 3.41–3.47
digital contracts 3.138–3.141
equity capital, raising of 3.78–3.79
exchanges 3.58–3.66, 6.25
false wealth, doctrine of 3.119–3.121
   comparative survey for sales 3.129–3.133
   conclusions 3.137
   objections to 3.125–3.128
financial contracts 3.71–3.72, 3.99
financial transactions 3.20–3.21
foreign exchange contracts 3.56–3.57
freedom of *see* freedom of contract
functional classification of 3.16–3.19
funds 3.67–3.70
green contracts 3.142–3.143
grouping of 3.1
guarantees 3.30
insulation *see* insulation of contract
interdependence of 3.108–3.110
joint venture agreements 3.83–3.85
law of 4.29
lenders 3.97–3.98
loan transactions 3.22–3.29
manufacturing 3.86
matching 3.108
multiple mutual contracts 3.111–3.113
netting of 8.40–8.43
pre-contract disclosure 5.103–5.110
   background 5.103–5.106
   English law 5.107
   French law 5.108
   international law 5.109–5.110
priorities 3.134–3.136
property and 3.116–3.118
receivables transfers 3.48–3.55
real property agreements 3.89–3.90
reasonable performance 5.46
restructuring agreements 3.31–3.33
risk factors 3.91
sale or merger of business 3.80–3.82
securitisations 3.48–3.55
security interests 3.134–3.136
set-off 8.40–8.43
shareholders 3.97–3.98
smart contracts 3.138–3.141
standard forms 3.114–3.115
terminations 5.53–5.88
   English examples 5.69–5.76
   French law 5.77–5.80
   French legal interventionism 5.80–5.85
   German law 5.86–5.87
   insolvency 5.88, 10.85–10.87
   policies of upholding 5.61–5.68
   The Laconia case 5.60
   typical termination clauses 5.53–5.59
title finance 3.34–3.40
types of 3.86
universal basic standards 5.49–5.52
see also contract law
conventions 4.21, 4.29
cooperate, duties to 5.115
see also good faith doctrine
corporations
as black bags 9.36
contracts 3.96
   management 3.92–3.96
   shares, sale of 3.75–3.77
   transactions 3.73–3.74

corporations (*cont.*)
  corporate structures
    risk, minimisation of 12.91
    insolvency law 10.56–10.61
    role in modern societies 14.30–14.34
    single purpose 14.103–14.104
    small and medium-sized 12.18
    special purpose 12.14–12.17
  see also corporate law
corporate law 2.78–2.82, 4.29, 14.1–14.137, 18.46
  avoiding local corporate law, structural methods of 14.17–14.19
  companies, role in modern societies 14.30–14.34
  conclusions 14.72–14.74, 14.93–14.95
  corporate transactions 14.1–14.25
    conflict of laws 14.20–14.25
  choice of court 4.17–4.18
  creditors, objectives of 14.41–14.43
  director personal liability 14.75–14.95
    conflict of laws and 14.76
    background 14.75
    fraudulent trading 14.78
    insolvency, duties to file on 14.81–14.89
    negligent management, liability for 14.90–14.92
    negligent trading 14.79–14.80
    universal heads of liability 14.77
    wrongful trading 14.79–14.80
  families of law and 14.35–14.36
  financial assistance to buy own shares 14.47–14.71
    English law 14.59–14.61
    EU 14.62–14.63
    financial assistance, definition of 14.47–14.58
    France 14.64
    Germany 14.65–14.67
    international approaches 14.70–14.71
    US law 14.68–14.68
  financial law *vs.* 14.37–14.40
  governing law 14.1–14.25
  indicators and risks 1.62
  key indicators 14.26–14.29, 14.96–14.137
    background 14.96
    bankruptcy consolidation 14.108
    capital, maintenance of 14.111
    central banks 14.105
    comparative conclusions 14.133–14.137
    corporate form, availability of 14.97
    corporate guarantees 14.123–14.126
    corporate governance 14.114–14.115
    economic and fairness justifications 14.127–14.132
    enforcement penalties 14.116
    limited liability 14.98–14.102
    main and ancillary 14.26–14.29
    minority protections 14.112–14.113
    shareholder equality 14.112–14.113
    shareholder loans, subordination of 14.109–14.110
    shareholders as de facto directors 14.106–14.107
    single purpose companies 14.103–14.104

    takeovers 14.117–14.122
    veil of incorporation 14.98–14.102
    management, objectives of 14.45
    other constituencies 14.46
    shareholders, objectives of 14.41, 14.44
    shares compared to bonds 14.1–14.15
  see also companies; corporations; Delaware law
Costa Rica 6.21
courts 1.62
  court law 4.29
  freedom of choice 1.4–1.6
  risks of 1.10–1.13
  see also arbitration; choice of courts; judiciary; litigation
COVID-19 pandemic 10.86, 19.4
credit default swaps (CDSs) 3.30, 3.41, 9.79
credit rating agencies (CRAs) 1.10, 21.3
creditors
  objectives of 14.41–14.43
criminal law 4.29, 18.47
  choice of court 4.16
Croatia 13.82
cryptocurrencies
  contracts 3.138–3.141
***culpa in contrahendo* (fault in contracting)** 5.98–5.99
cultural diversity 18.35
Cultural Revolution (1968) 20.14–20.24
currencies 3.56
Cyprus 4.58

Darius of Persia 18.29
debt assignments
  compulsory notice of 7.14–7.31
    conflict of laws 7.26–7.31
    criticism of 7.24–7.25
    international position 7.20–7.23
    reasons for 7.14–7.19
  see also business orientation
decentralised finance
  contracts 3.138–3.141
deconstructivism 20.14
Delacroix, Eugène 2.25, 8.6, 21.7
Delaware law 2.46, 2.51, 14.36, 14.38, 14.44, 14.45, 14.72
delict 1.49, 4.27, 4.34, 4.69, 4.75, 5.17, 5.94, 5.99, 9.78, 15.25, 18.46
democracy 2.58
  see also bondholder democracies
Denmark 4.61, 5.40, 9.77
depositary receipts 13.18
Depository Trust Company (DTC) 2.46, 13.13
derivative liability 9.79–9.96
  disclaimer, typical forms of 9.79–9.82
  German law 9.93–9.96
  UK law 9.83–9.90
  US law 9.91–9.92
  see also exclusion clauses
derivatives 3.41–3.47
  definition 18.16

Derrida, Jacques 20.14
digital contracts 3.138–3.141
  see also contracts; cryptocurrencies
director personal liability 14.75–14.95
  conflict of laws and 14.76
  background 14.75
  fraudulent trading 14.78
  insolvency, duties to file on 14.81–14.89
  negligent management, liability for 14.90–14.92
  negligent trading 14.79–14.80
  universal heads of liability 14.77
  wrongful trading 14.79–14.80
disclaimer
  typical forms of 9.79–9.82
  see also derivative liability
discretions 5.111–5.113
  see also good faith doctrine
dishonest conduct 5.49
documents
  corporate 16.51–16.54
  discovery of 16.30–16.31
  drafting 1.59
  financial 16.51–16.54
  unregulated *see* unregulated offering documents
Domat, Jean 20.6
dominant position
  abuse of *see* abuse of dominant position
  advantages of 2.51–2.52
Douglas, William O. 8.70
Dubai International Financial Centre 18.64
due diligence 1.10, 5.107, 9.9–9.10, 9.33, 9.4, 9.55, 9.57, 9.63, 9.68, 9.75, 12.11
duties to cooperate 5.115
  see also good faith doctrine

East Timor 18.96
economic value of law *see* law: economic value of
Egypt 4.65, 13.34
embezzlement 4.35, 10.88, 18.25, 18.103
empires *see* colonialism; imperialism
enforcement remedies 12.87
English common law jurisdictions *see* families of jurisdictions
English language *see* language
English law 1.14–1.16
  asymmetric jurisdiction clauses 8.30
  bondholder collective action 8.64–8.68
  British Eagle 18.13
  British Empire 18.32
  class actions 16.28
  Clearing House Automated Payments System (CHAPS) 3.47
  contract terminations 5.69–5.76
  Corporate Governance Code 14.115
  derivative liability 9.83–9.90
  English common law group 1.17
  EU, departure from *see* Brexit
  exchange contracts 6.32
  exclusion clauses 9.9–9.19

  families of jurisdictions/law in English common law 18.61–18.82
    conclusions 18.82
    historical background 18.69–18.73
    key indicators 18.74–18.81
    legal culture 18.74–18.81
    members of the group 18.61–18.68
  financial assistance to buy own shares 14.59–14.61
  freezing orders 16.33
  good faith doctrine 5.32–5.33
    English right to voluntarily choose 5.47–5.48
  insolvency law
    contracts, protection of 6.53–6.54
    regulation 4.84–4.85
    set-off 11.52–11.59, 11.71, 11.82–11.83
  insulation of contract 6.12–6.17
  jurisdiction of 18.44
  Law Commission 19.10
    'Smart Legal Contracts' report (2021) 3.141
  legal uncertainty 17.6
  London, importance as a financial centre 20.22
  long-arm jurisdiction 4.61
  pre-contract disclosure 5.107
  pro-creditor policy 14.74
  protection of governing law 19.24–19.32
  restrictions on assignments 8.44–8.45
  Scotland and Roman law, influence of 18.44, 20.29
  security interests 12.49–12.62, 18.24
  shareholders' meetings 14.89
  sovereign immunity 16.40, 16.43
  Stewards Code 14.115
  treaties, network of 16.36
  underwriter liability:
    regulated prospectuses 9.71
  wrongful trading 14.79–14.80
Enlightenment era 20.14
environmental liability 4.34
equity capital
  raising of 3.78–3.79
Euro Medium Term Note Programme 9.47
Euroclear 13.6, 13.13
European Bank for Reconstruction and Development 19.14
European Court of Justice (ECJ) 4.76
European Economic Area (EEA) 11.31, 14.120, 15.23
European Law Institute 19.9
European Stability Mechanism (ESM) 6.11
European Union (EU)
  choice of courts 4.66–4.74
  Commission 2.59, 6.11
  financial assistance to buy own shares 14.62–14.63
  freezing orders 16.34
  insolvency law 10.29–10.38
    commercial trusts 13.68–13.76
    set-off 11.27–11.33, 11.43
  security interests 12.87
  UK departure from *see* Brexit
exchange contracts 6.31–6.36
  see also insulation of contract

exchange control
  global financial crisis 4.58
  regulations 6.25, 6.37
  subsequent 6.30
  see also insulation of contract
exclusion clauses 1.62, 9.1–9.98
  civil code countries 9.20–9.22
  derivative liability and *see* derivative liability
  documents *see* unregulated offering documents
  English law 9.9–9.19
  France 9.23–9.28
  in general 9.1–9.5
  key indicators, summary of 9.6–9.8
  unregulated documents *see* unregulated offering documents; underwriter liability
  US law
    arranging banks, liability of 9.43–9.44
    fraud, universal liability for 9.50–9.54
    unregulated disclosure documents 9.31
  see also underwriter liability
extraterritoriality 4.24, 15.10

factoring of receivables 3.34, 3.55, 12.29–12.30
fair trial 16.35
fairness, duty of 5.29, 5.50
  justice and 2.9–2.10, 2.81
  justifications 14.127–14.132
false wealth doctrine 3.119–3.121
  comparative survey for sales 3.129–3.133
  compulsory notice 7.24, 7.30
  conclusions 3.137
  objections to 3.125–3.128
  see also contracts
families of jurisdictions 1.17–1.25, 12.39–12.48, 18.1–18.159
  American common law jurisdictions 18.56–18.60
    conclusions 18.60
    historical background 18.57
    key indicators 18.58–18.59
    legal culture 18.58–18.59
    members of the group 18.56
  comparative law 18.11–18.28
    British Eagle 18.13
    Herstatt 18.11–18.12
    insolvency set-off 18.18–18.28
    Iran 18.14
    sovereign bankruptcies 18.15–18.17
  conclusions 18.156–18.159
  corporate law and 14.35–14.36
  English common law jurisdictions 18.61–18.82
    conclusions 18.82
    historical background 18.69–18.73
    key indicators 18.74–18.81
    legal culture 18.74–18.81
    members of the group 18.61–18.68
  general features 18.29–18.55
    competing legal systems 18.51–18.55
    definition of jurisdiction 18.38–18.44
    diversity of cultures 18.35
    foreign ideology, rejection of 18.36
    identifying families of law 18.45–18.50
    legal systems, export of 18.29–18.33
    limited overlap between families 18.34
    maps, use of 18.37
  identifying 18.1–18.10
    importance 18.1
    key indicators 18.2–18.5
    themes 18.2–18.5
    triple polarisation of law 18.6–18.10
  Islamic jurisdictions 18.133–18.144
    conclusions 18.144
    members of the group 18.133–18.143
  jurisdictions specially covered 1.22–1.25
  mixed civil/common law jurisdictions 1.18, 12.9, 18.121–18.132
    conclusions 18.132
    members of the group 18.121–18.131
  Napoleonic jurisdictions 18.83–18.106
    conclusions 18.104–18.106
    historical background 18.97–18.98
    key indicators 18.99–18.103
    legal culture 18.99–18.103
    members of the group 18.83–18.84
    sub-groups 18.85–18.96
  new or transition jurisdictions 18.145–18.150
    conclusions 18.150
    members of the group 18.145–18.149
  Roman-Germanic jurisdictions 18.107–18.120
    conclusions 18.120
    historical background 18.112–18.117
    key indicators 18.118–18.119
    legal culture 18.118–18.119
    members of the group 18.107–18.109
    sub-groups 18.110–18.111
  statistics 18.153–18.155
  summaries of 1.17–1.21
  unallocated jurisdictions 18.151–18.152
    high seas and space 18.152
    members of the group 18.151
  see also families of law
family law 18.47
fiduciary relationships 5.107, 9.86, 9.92
Financial Action Task Force (FATF) 19.15
financial assistance to buy own shares 14.47–14.71
  definition of 14.47–14.58
  English law 14.59–14.61 EU 14.62–14.63
  France 14.64
  Germany 14.65–14.67
  international approaches 14.70–14.71
  US law 14.68–14.68
  see also corporate law
financial centres 17.13–17.22
  attributes 17.13–17.19
  legal system and 17.20–17.22
financial contracts 3.71–3.72, 3.99
  see also contracts
financial law 18.46
  corporate law *vs.* 14.37–14.40

financial markets 12.25–12.28
Financial Markets Law Committee 17.6, 19.10
financial regulation
  enforcement, differences in 15.31–15.34
  essentials 15.12–15.16
  financial assets:
    definition 15.15
    services 15.16
  financial codes of conduct 15.19
  financial regulators 15.17–15.18
  frauds 15.21
  freedom, degree of 15.40–15.41
  key indicators 15.28–15.41
  investor protection, intensity of 15.38–15.39
  prospectuses 15.20
  protectionism, differences in 15.35–15.37
  regulatory risk management 15.22–15.27
  see also regulation
Financial Stability Board (FSB) 19.15
financial transactions 3.20–3.21
flip clauses *see* business orientation
floating charges 18.128
foreign exchange contracts 3.56–3.57
  see also contracts
foreign judgments
  enforcement of 16.35–16.39
forum shopping 4.48
Foucault, Michel 20.14
France 5.10, 5.17, 5.19, 13.33, 13.55
  action en comblement de passif 14.90
  asymmetric jurisdiction clauses 8.28, 8.32
  bondholder collective action clauses 8.73
  civil codes 20.6, 20.21
  class actions 16.29
  commercial trusts 13.81
  contract terminations 5.77–5.80
  debtor interventionist approach 14.73
  directors' personal liability 14.90, 14.135
  documents, discovery of 16.31
  Empire 18.32
  exclusion clauses 9.23–9.28
  exchange contracts 6.36
  financial assistance to buy own shares 14.58, 14.64
  foreign judgments 16.39
  foundation civil codes 18.84, 18.97
  freedom of contract 8.8
  French Revolution 8.34, 13.55, 20.10
  good faith doctrine 5.34, 5.47, 5.100–5.102, 5.119, 18.100, 20.11
  insolvency law 10.92, 14.73, 20.13
    duties to file on 14.82
    set-off 11.26, 11.60, 11.85, 18.22, 18.24, 18.99
  judicial profession 16.5
  jurisdictional family 18.104–18.106
  legal interventionism 5.80–5.85
  non-assignment clauses 8.55
  notice of debt assignments 7.22, 7.30
  pre-contract disclosure 5.108
  redressement judiciaire 5.82, 0.17

security interests 12.47, 18.24, 20.5–20.7
  see also families of jurisdictions; Napoleonic jurisdictions
fraud 9.19, 13.43
  financial regulation 15.21
  fraudulent information 5.49
  fraudulent trading 14.78
  no exclusion for 9.33
freedom of choice
  of contract law 1.4–1.6
  of courts 1.4–1.6
  financial regulation 15.40–15.41
  nature of freedom 21.7–21.11
freedom of contract 1.62, 8.3, 9.17, 20.15
  assignment of receivables, prohibitions on clauses restricting 8.33–8.45
    bans on assignments, restrictions of 8.33
    English law 8.44–8.45
    marketability of property 8.34–8.36
    marketability of receivables 8.37–8.39
    set-off and netting of contracts 8.40–8.43
  bondholder collective action *see* bondholder democracies
  free choice of governing law 8.12–8.19, 8.31–8.32
    insolvency set-off 11.22–11.26
  freedom as a value 8.1–8.11
    court intervention 8.7–8.8
    in general 8.1–8.5
    liberty *vs.* restriction 8.6
    predictability 8.7–8.8
  key indicators 8.9–8.11
  non-assignment clauses *see* non-assignment clauses
  non-symmetrical jurisdiction clauses 8.20–8.30
funds
  contracts 3.67–3.70

GDP (gross domestic product) 1.53, 2.37, 2.39, 2.64, 2.70, 2.74, 7.1, 1.55, 10.67, 13.13, 17.25, 18.16, 18.154
Gelpern, Anna 15.34
gender 18.47
Generally Accepted Accounting Principles 19.16
gentlemen's agreements 5.93
Germany 5.10, 5.25, 5.39, 6.11, 13.35, 13.75, 20.21
  bankruptcy consolidation 14.108
  Berlin Wall, fall of 20.14
  bondholder collective action clauses 8.74
  civil and commercial codes 18.112, 20.9
  contract terminations 5.86–5.87
  derivative liability 9.93–9.96
  documents, discovery of 16.31
  exchange contracts 6.36
  financial assistance to buy own shares 14.65–14.67
  foreign exchange controls 18.118
  good faith doctrine 5.47
  Herstatt 18.12
  industrial revolution 20.8
  insolvency law 10.93
    duties to file on insolvency 14.86
    set-off 11.24, 18.99

Germany (cont.)
  judicial profession 16.5
  jurisdictional families 18.118, 18.120
  non-assignment clauses 8.56
  over-collateralisation 12.46, 12.77
  professors' law 18.113
  Roman law, influence of 13.40
  Stock Exchange Law 9.76
  subordination of loans 14.110
  trusts 13.16
  wrongful trading 14.80
  see also families of jurisdictions; Roman-Germanic jurisdictions
Gibraltar 13.60
Gilmore, Grant 12.56
global financial crisis (GFC) 3.82, 3.93, 4.58, 20.18
global jurisdictions 1.7–1.9
good faith doctrine 4.22, 4.75, 5.29–5.48, 8.8, 8.19, 8.32, 9.22, 16.4, 16.9, 16.39, 18.52, 18.100, 20.11, 20.21
  agreements to negotiate in good faith 5.114
  consents 5.111–5.113
  discretions 5.111–5.113
  duties to cooperate 5.115
  England 5.32–5.33
  English right to voluntarily choose 5.47–5.48
  France 5.34
  in general 5.29–5.31
  hardship clauses 5.116–5.119
  legal examples 5.35–5.42
  other cases 5.120
  US law 5.43–5.46
  see also predictability
goods
  contracts 3.10–3.12
governing law 4.1–4.44
  choice of law clause 4.32
  choices of 21.12–21.13
  commercial trusts 13.58–13.68
    foreign governing law 13.81–13.82
  consumer law 4.20
  contract law 4.22
  corporate law 4.17–4.18, 14.1–14.25
  court procedure 4.19
  criminal law 4.16
  economic value 2.36
    of physical clustering 2.63–2.64
  express choice, in absence of 4.12
  familiarity of 17.2–17.8
  free choice of 4.4–4.11, 4.40–4.42, 8.12–8.19, 8.31–8.32
  insolvency law 4.25, 4.26
  insolvency set-off 11.22–11.33
  international conventions 4.21
  international principles 4.3
  less freedom than contracts 4.33
  matters decided by 4.13
  matters not decided by 4.14–4.32
  monopoly, as a 2.46–2.68

    abuse of dominant position 2.54–2.58
    competitor imitation 2.59–2.61
    dominant positions to users, advantages of 2.51–2.52
    hard and soft power 2.46–2.49, 2.65–2.66
    multiplier effects 2.53
    protection of value, importance of 2.62
    soft power 2.46–2.49, 2.67–2.68
    vital need, fulfilment of 2.50
  narrowing scope of 4.14–4.15
  non-contractual claims 4.33–4.44
  non-contractual liabilities 4.34–4.39
  overriding laws, mnemonic for 4.29–4.31
  property transfers 4.23
  protection of 19.1–19.33
    achievements 19.20–19.23
    conclusions 19.33
    English law 19.24–19.32
    law monitoring bodies 19.7–19.19
    need for 19.1–19.32
    responsibility 19.1–19.6
    weaknesses of 19.20–19.23
  regulatory law 4.24
  risks of 1.10–1.13
    main areas, outline of 1.62
    main issues, mnemonic of 1.63–1.64
    measurement 1.65–1.68
  role of 2.19–2.26
  scope of 4.43–4.44
  security interests 12.69–12.82
    collateral, scope of 12.78–12.82
    publicity, scope of 12.78–12.82
    role of 12.69–12.70
    security agreement 12.71–12.75
  scope, narrowing of 1.69–1.71
  tort law 4.27–4.28
  ubiquity of 1.2–1.3
Great Divide 18.30
Greece
  bankruptcy 6.10–6.11, 10.55, 14.116
green contracts 3.142–3.143
  see also contracts
guarantees
  contracts 3.30
Guernsey 13.36, 13.61, 13.62
Gulf countries 2.60

hard power 2.46–2.49
  English law 2.66
  US dollar 2.65
hardship clauses 5.116–5.119
  see also good faith doctrine
Hayton, David 13.12
Henry VIII, king of England 13.41, 13.43
Heritage Foundation 2.39, 17.24
hire purchase 3.34
history of law 20.1–20.33
  Brexit 20.25–20.28
  Cultural Revolution (1968) 20.14–20.24

future prospects 20.32–20.33
indelibility of existing law 20.11–20.13
Industrial Revolution 20.1–20.10
reconsiderations 20.1–20.33
Roman law 20.29–20.31
home loans 12.13
Hong Kong 5.76, 13.32, 13.60, 18.36
insolvency set-off 11.54, 11.56
sovereign immunity 16.41
wrongful trading 14.79
Hong Kong International Arbitration Centre 16.49
human rights 5.49

Iceland 4.58
ideology
foreign, rejection of 18.36
as law 2.1–2.3
religious 2.58
imperialism 18.29–18.30, 18.32
incorporation *see* **corporate law**
India 5.18, 13.54, 18.36
insolvency set-off 11.54
'sick companies' legislation 20.17
Industrial Revolution 20.1–20.10, 20.23
inflation 2.79, 19.5
insider dealing 2.65, 2.77, 4.16, 15.21, 17.14
insolvency law 1.62, 4.25–4.26, 4.29, 10.1–10.95
ability to trace money 10.88
anti-deprivation rule, scope of 10.88
Bank of Credit and Commerce International 10.55
bankruptcy and:
essential elements of 10.11–10.12
ladder of priorities 10.81–10.84
legal systems, impact on 10.13–10.15
banks 10.56–10.61
conclusions 10.90–10.95
contract and lease terminations 10.85–10.87
contract terminations 5.88
corporations 10.56–10.61
corporate law and:
consolidation 14.108
creditor control 10.88
debt-equity conversions 10.88
deprivation of assets of 7.32–7.38
'flip clauses' 7.34–7.35
joint ventures 7.32–7.33
post-commencement proceeds of
security 7.37–7.38
turnover subordinations 7.36
detrimental acts 10.38
director personal liability 10.88, 14.81–14.89
entry criteria for rescue proceedings 10.88
equity shares 10.83
essential elements of 10.11–10.12
EU Insolvency Regulation 10.29–10.38
commercial trusts 13.68–13.76
excluded claims 10.83
financial assistance 10.88
Gibbs principle 6.54

Greek 6.10–6.11
handling insolvencies, methods of 10.17–10.23
harmonisation 10.29–10.61
importance of 10.1–10.5
insulation of contract 6.42–6.46
international diversity 10.27–10.28
judicial rescue plans 10.24–10.25
creditors 10.26
key indicators of 10.62–10.89, 10.88–10.89
ladder of priorities 10.81–10.84
legal systems, impact on 10.13–10.15
Lehmans 10.55, 11.46, 14.116
lender liability 10.88
mandatory rules 10.6–10.10
negative pledges 10.16
netting:
carve-out statutes 11.16
excessive intricacy of 11.19–11.21
jurisdictions 11.17–11.18
definition 11.7–11.9
importance of 21.3
key indicator, as a 11.1–11.4
policies 11.11–11.15
two-way payments 11.10
opening state applicable law, exceptions
to 10.39–10.42
outside the treaties 10.53–10.55
override:
arbitration 4.84–4.85
jurisdiction clauses 4.84–4.85
pari passu creditors 10.83
preferences, avoidance of 10.88
priority claimants 10.83
relevance of 10.1–10.10
reorganisation plans, approval of 10.88
risk mitigation, methods of 10.16
sale of contracts and receivables, invalidity of 10.88
security interests 12.6, 12.88–12.90
set-off 1.62, 11.1–11.84
armour-plated protections 11.34–11.42
assignees 11.79–11.84
build-ups, avoidance of 11.78
carve-out statutes 11.16
jurisdictions 11.17–11.18
comparative survey 11.34–11.84
conclusions 11.85–11.86
definition 11.5–11.6
English common law jurisdictions 11.52–11.59
EU protections 11.18, 11.22–11.24, 11.27–
11.33, 11.43
families of jurisdictions 18.18–18.28
free contract choice 11.22–11.26
key indicator, as a 11.1–11.4
importance of 21.3
intervenors 11.79–11.84
mixed civil/common law
jurisdictions 11.67–11.73
mutuality 11.74–11.77
Napoleonic jurisdictions 11.60–11.64

insolvency law (cont.)
  policies 11.11–11.15
    protection by governing law 11.22–11.33
    Roman-Germanic jurisdictions 11.65–11.66
    two-way payments 11.10
    US law 11.44–11.51
    walk-away clauses 11.10
  sharia law and 18.140
  sovereign bankruptcies (1980s) 18.15–18.17
  sovereign states 10.56–10.61
  subordinated creditors 10.83
  super-priority claimants 10.83
  triple super-priority insolvency claims 10.62–10.65
    central counterparties 10.74–10.80
    contract governing law, role of 10.72–10.73
    eligibility tests 10.67–10.71
    legal families, attitude of 10.66
  UNCITRAL Model Law 10.29–10.31, 10.43–10.52
  work-outs 10.24–10.25
    creditors 10.26
    rescue statutes vs. 10.16, 10.18–10.23
    support of 10.88
  see also business orientation; corporate law; debt assignments
Institute of International Finance 19.18
insulation of contract 1.62
  destabilising laws, background history of 6.8
  English law 6.12–6.17
    insolvency contracts, protection of 6.53–6.54
  exchange contracts 6.31–6.36
  exchange control regulations 6.37
  Greek bankruptcy 6.10–6.11
  illegality at place of performance 6.47–6.52
  IMF agreement 6.5–6.6, 6.25–6.41
  key indicator 6.7
  Latin American republics 6.9
  local insolvency proceedings 6.42–6.46
  no external assets 6.42–6.46
  stabilisation clauses 6.24
  subsequent exchange controls 6.30
  unilateral changes of contract 6.1–6.4
  US law 6.18–6.23
insurance 2.4, 2.37, 3.44, 3.75, 3.86, 3.103, 3.105, 4.12, 7.29, 9.2, 9.13–9.14, 9.79, 11.23, 12.7, 14.91–14.92, 18.16
Inter-American Development Bank 19.14
interest rate swaps 3.42, 9.89
interest rates 3.109
International Accounting Standards Board (IASB) 19.16
International Association of Deposit Insurers (IADI) 19.15
International Bar Association (IBA) 19.17
International Chamber of Commerce (ICC) 16.49
international conventions see conventions
International Financial Reporting Standards (IFRS) 19.16
International Monetary Fund (IMF) 1.62, 4.21, 6.5–6.6, 6.11, 6.17, 6.25–6.41, 17.8, 18.52, 18.99, 18.118

International Organisation of Securities Commissions (IOSC) 19.15
international principles 4.3
International Swaps and Derivatives Association (ISDA) 2.46, 2.50, 2.51, 2.53, 2.57, 3.42–3.43, 3.114, 5.48, 5.56, 5.116–5.117, 7.10, 8.13–8.19, 8.27, 9.21, 9.25, 9.82, 9.89–9.90, 11.84, 16.51–16.52, 18.16, 19.18
internationally mobile transactions 1.35–1.37, 3.85
investor protection 15.38–15.39
investor presentation roadshow 9.47
invisible hand of the market, theory of 20.3
Iran 4.65, 18.14
Ireland 6.6
  insolvency set-off 11.54, 11.56
  wrongful trading 14.79
Islamic jurisdictions 1.18, 12.9, 18.133–18.144
  conclusions 18.144
  members of the group 18.133–18.143
  see also sharia law
Isle of Man 13.60
Israel 18.37
  insolvency set-off 11.54
issuer liability 9.32
Italy 7.21, 13.61, 18.147, 20.17
  bankruptcy consolidation 14.108
  insolvency law:
    duties to file on insolvency 14.83
  set-off 18.99

Japan 4.7, 4.61, 5.42, 7.21, 7.30, 33, 13.54, 18.30, 18.36, 18.116, 18.129, 18.131
  bondholder collective action clauses 8.75
  express prohibitions 14.71
  insolvency set-off 11.68
  non-assignment clauses 8.56
  security interests 12.46
  wrongful trading 14.80
Jersey 13.36, 13.61, 13.62
  insolvency set-off 11.67
joint ventures
  agreements
    contracts 3.83–3.85
  bankruptcy 7.32–7.33
  business orientation 7.32–7.33
judicial precedent
  doctrine of 5.21–5.26, 18.28
  see also predictability
judicial rescue 10.24–10.25
  creditors 10.26
  see also insolvency law
judiciary
  business orientation 16.4–16.6
  judicial consensus building 16.7–16.8
  politicisation 16.1–16.3
  see also arbitration; courts; litigation
jurisdiction
  clauses 4.56–4.59
    insolvency override of 4.84–4.85

non-symmetrical 8.20–8.30
scope of coverage 4.57
definition 18.38–18.44
exclusive vs non-exclusive 4.59
families of *see* families of jurisdiction
long-arm 4.60–4.65
nation states compared 18.39
new/transition 1.18
over torts 4.75–4.79
unallocated 1.18
see also choice of courts
justice 1.43–1.46

Keynes, John Maynard 6.26
Khmer Empire 18.32
Korea *see* North Korea; South Korea
Kuwait 4.65
Kyrgyzstan 2.77, 4.65

Lacan, Jacques 20.14
land contracts 3.13–3.15
see also property
language
English as a *lingua franca* 17.9–17.11, 18.75
reflections 17.12
Laos 4.8, 4.65, 18.148
Latin America 4.7, 18.30
insulation of contract 6.9
law 2.1–2.83
economic value of 2.36–2.45
costs of law 2.42–2.45
governing law 2.36
valuation methods 2.37–2.41
governing *see* governing law
growth of law:
banks 2.78–2.82
corporations 2.78–2.82
developments since 1830 2.69–2.73
impact of 2.69–2.82
money and law 2.78–2.82
reasons for 2.74–2.77
history of *see* history of law
ideology, as 2.1–2.3
indelibility of 20.11–20.13
means of survival, as a 2.13–2.18
monitoring bodies 19.7–19.19
moral basis of 2.8–2.10
religion and 2.31–2.35
role of 2.1–2.19
limits 2.27–2.31
societies without 2.4–2.7
sources of 9.34
stability of 5.27–5.28
triple polarisation of 18.6–18.10
utility, as a 2.11–2.12
League of Nations 19.12
lease agreements 3.86
Lebanon 13.34
legal gaffes 17.5–17.8

legal history *see* history of law
legal infrastructure 17.23–17.26
conclusions 17.25–17.26
political risks 17.23–17.24
rule of law risks 17.23–17.24
legal policies
morality and justice of 1.43–1.46
legal system
brand recognition 17.2–17.4
see also families of jurisdiction
lenders
contracts 3.97–3.98
liability 10.88
Lepaulle, Pierre 13.12
liability *see* banks; big pocket liability; derivative
liability; director personal liability; exclusion
clauses; issuer liability; lenders; limited
liability; underwriter liability
liberalism 20.3
licence agreements 3.86
Liechtenstein 13.61, 13.62, 18.128
limited liability 14.98–14.102
litigation 1.61
key indicators 16.17–16.43
class actions 16.23–16.29
documents, discovery of 16.30–16.31
foreign judgments, enforcement of 16.35–16.39
non-conflicting 16.32–16.43
pre-judgment freezes 16.33–16.34
reason for exclusion 16.32
sovereign immunity 16.40–16.43
US litigation 16.17–16.22
trauma of 16.15–16.16
see also arbitration; courts; judiciary
Loan Market Association (LMA) 3.24, 3.114, 8.27, 9.21, 19.18
loan transactions
contracts 3.22–3.29
see also securitisations
London Court of International Arbitration (LCIA) 16.49
long-arm jurisdiction *see* jurisdiction
Luxembourg 6.11, 7.22, 13.61
asymmetric jurisdiction clauses 8.29
exchange contracts 6.36
insolvency 20.13
set-off 11.24–11.25, 11.61–11.63, 11.85, 18.99
security interests 12.47
Lyotard, Jean-Francois 20.14

maintenance of capital principle 14.47, 18.119
Malta 13.61, 13.62, 18.37, 18.95, 18.128
management *see* corporate law
mandates and heads of terms 5.89–5.102
international summary 5.94–5.102
market practice 5.89–5.93
see also predictability
Mao Tse Tung 18.116
maps 7.20, 18.37

328 INDEX

market abuse 2.65
marketability
  property 8.34–8.36
  receivables 8.37–8.39
Mauritius 18.54
  insolvency set-off 11.58
measurable, important, symbolic (or representative) (MISC) tests 1.33, 5.14, 5.28, 6.7, 7.7, 8.4, 11.1, 12.92
methodology and scope 1.26–1.61
  amounts involved 1.52–1.58
  business transactions 1.38–1.42
  citation 1.60–1.61
  contracts, focus on 1.47–1.51
  drafting documents, assumptions as to 1.59
  key indicators 1.26–1.33
    number of 1.34
  internationally mobile transactions 1.35–1.37
  legal policies, morality and justice of 1.43–1.46
Mexico 12.47
minority protections
  corporate law 14.112–14.113
MINU (Mixed, Islamic, New, Unallocated) 1.21
MISC tests *see* measurable, important, symbolic (or representative)
mistake, doctrine of 5.110
mnemonics
  6C-Trito 1.70–1.71, 1.78, 4.29–4.30, 6.45, 8.6, 8.11, 12.69, 21.9
  PIB—FEISST—CoRCO 5.7, 6.4, 7.6, 8.5, 9.8, 11.4, 12.4, 13.4, 14.14, 15.3, 16.3, 17.1
mobile transactions *see* internationally mobile transactions
Moldova 12.9, 18.147
money
  laundering 2.65, 19.15
  law and 2.78–2.82
Mongolia 18.148
monitoring bodies 19.7–19.19
morality
  law and 2.8–2.10
  legal policies 1.43–1.46
Multi-Currency Cross Border form 8.17
multilateral development banks 17.23
mutuality *see* insolvency: set-off

Nader, Ralph 20.15
Napoleon Bonaparte 18.97
Napoleonic codes 13.49, 20.5
Napoleonic jurisdictions 1.17, 7.22, 7.30
  codification 5.16
  commercial trusts 13.34
  false wealth, doctrine of 3.129, 3.131
  families of law 18.83–18.106
    conclusions 18.104–18.106
    historical background 18.97–18.98
    key indicators 18.99–18.103
    legal culture 18.99–18.103
    members of the group 18.83–18.84
    sub-groups 18.85–18.96
  insolvency set-off 11.60–11.64
nationality 4.61
negligence
  negligent management, liability for 14.90–14.92
  negligent trading 14.79–14.80
Netherlands 5.40, 8.49, 9.75, 13.33, 13.61, 14.35
  abusive security, principle of 12.76
  colonialism 18.117
  insolvency set-off 11.66
  security interests 13.41
  trusts 13.16
  wrongful trading 14.80
netting *see* contracts; insolvency law: netting
New York law
  American common law group 1.17
  anti-Wall Street movement 20.14
  Bankruptcy Court 7.35
  bankruptcy law 10.91
  bondholder collective action 8.69–8.72
  class actions 16.17, 16.23–16.27
  Clearing House Interbank Payments System (CHIPS) 2.65, 3.47, 11.76
  Deep Rock doctrine 14.109
  derivative liability 9.91–9.92
  documents, discovery of 16.30
  dollar currency 2.46, 2.59, 3.45
  exchange contracts 6.33
  families of jurisdictions/law 18.56–18.60
    conclusions 18.60
    historical background 18.57
    key indicators 18.58–18.59
    legal culture 18.58–18.59
    members of the group 18.56
  Federal Deposit Insurance Corporation 3.82
  Financial Accounting Standards Board 19.16
  financial assistance to buy own shares 14.68–14.68
  fraud, liability for 9.50–9.54
  good faith doctrine 5.43–5.46, 5.97, 5.100
  Great Depression 3.82
  insolvency set-off 11.44–11.51
    adequate protection 11.49
  insulation of contract 6.18–6.23
  litigation 16.17–16.22
    burden of 16.15
    mass litigation and populism 14.73
  minimum contacts 4.61
  New York law generally 1.14–1.16
  pre-judgment attachment 16.33
  Restatement of Conflicts of Law 4.12, 4.19, 4.36, 4.39, 5.17, 6.48, 16.13, 18.57
  Securities and Exchange Commission 8.70
  security interests 12.49–12.62
  sovereign immunity 16.40, 16.43
  tort law 4.42
  treaties 16.37
  underwriter liability
    regulated prospectuses 9.60–9.70

unregulated prospectuses 9.48–9.49
  arranging banks, liability of 9.43–9.44
  fraud, universal liability for 9.50–9.54
  unregulated disclosure documents 9.31
New Zealand 12.47
  bankruptcy consolidation 14.108
  corporate set-off 11.55
  wrongful trading 14.79
Nigeria 12.47
Nixon, Richard 18.16
non assignment clauses
  bans on 8.59
  jurisdictions permitting 8.46–8.49
  nullification of 8.55–8.58
  prohibition of 8.50–8.54
non-contractual
  claims 4.33–4.44
  liabilities 4.34–4.39
non-legal features 1.62
North Korea 2.77

Oman 4.8
Ottoman Empire 18.32

pactum de non cedendo 8.47
Pakistan 13.32, 18.36
pandemic *see* COVID-19 pandemic
pension trusts 13.17
personal liability *see* director personal liability
physical clustering 2.63–2.64
place of the relevant intermediary approach 12.78
Poland 5.42
Portalis, J. E. M. 18.97
Portugal 11.61
possession, concept of 20.9
Pothier, Robert 20.6
power *see* hard power; soft power
pre-contract disclosure *see* contracts
predictability 1.62, 3.92
  codification 5.16–5.20
  contract terminations 5.53–5.88
    English examples 5.69–5.76
    French law 5.77–5.80
    French legal interventionism 5.80–5.85
    German law 5.86–5.87
    insolvency 5.88
    policies of upholding 5.61–5.68
    The Laconia case 5.60
    typical termination clauses 5.53–5.59
  freedom of choice 8.7–8.8
  good faith doctrine *see* good faith doctrine
  judicial precedent, doctrine of 5.21–5.26
  key indicators 5.8–5.15
  legal value, as a 5.1–5.7
  mandates and heads of terms 5.89–5.102
    international summary 5.94–5.102
    market practice 5.89–5.93
  pre-contract disclosure 5.103–5.110
    background 5.103–5.106

English law 5.107
French law 5.108
international law 5.109–5.110
stability of the law 5.27–5.28
universal basic contract standards 5.49–5.52
PRIME Finance 16.49
Principles of European Contract Law
  (PECL) 5.38, 5.40
property
  contracts and 3.116–3.118
  marketability of
    history 8.34–8.36
  real property agreements 3.89–3.90
  transfers 4.23, 4.29
  see also assets; land contracts
proprietary restitution 13.48
protectionism 15.35–15.37
  see also financial regulation
publicly listed companies 12.19–12.22
Putin, Vladimir 6.38

Qatar Financial Centre 18.64
Quebec 6.9, 12.40, 18.128

real time gross settlement 11.76
reasonableness test 9.18, 9.19, 14.79
receivables transfers
  contracts 3.48–3.55
regulated prospectuses *see* underwriter liability
regulation 1.62, 4.29, 15.1–15.43, 18.47
  conclusions 15.42–15.43
  criminalisation of law 15.10
  detailed rules 15.10
  extraterritorial rules 15.10
  fields of 15.5–15.9
  financial *see* financial regulation
  governmental regulators 15.10
  ordinary law *vs.* 15.10–15.11
  pervasiveness of 15.1–15.3
regulatory law *see* regulation
religion 18.29, 18.35, 20.10
  ideologies 2.58
  law and 2.31–2.35
repos (sale and repurchase) 3.34–3.37, 3.114, 4.81,
  9.21, 10.83, 11.28, 12.2, 12.25, 12.29, 12.63,
  12.83, 16.51
reputed ownership provisions 18.78
restructuring agreements
  contracts 3.31–3.33
risk mitigation *see* choice of courts: risk and;
  commercial trusts; financial regulation;
  insolvency law
risks of governing law *see* governing law: risks of
Roman Empire 1.16, 18.32
Roman-Germanic jurisdictions 1.17
  codification 5.16
  false wealth, doctrine of 3.129, 3.131
  families of law 18.107–18.120
    conclusions 18.120

330 INDEX

Roman-Germanic jurisdictions (*cont.*)
   historical background 18.112–18.117
   key indicators 18.118–18.119
   legal culture 18.118–18.119
   members of the group 18.107–18.109
   sub-groups 18.110–18.111
  insolvency set-off 11.65–11.66
  security interests 3.136
Roman law 1.16, 2.12, 2.72–2.73, 13.40, 18.44, 18.113, 18.127, 20.8–20.9, 20.29–20.31
Romania 13.82
Rowan, Solene 5.24
rule of law 2.6, 2.23, 2.35, 2.39, 4.9, 6.39, 8.19, 15.9, 15.10, 15.30, 16.17, 17.25, 18.48, 18.158
  risks 1.62, 17.23–17.24
Russia 13.37, 14.24, 18.30, 18.35, 18.43, 18.157
  civil code 18.117
  Ukraine, war against 6.38

sale of goods agreements 3.85
sale and leaseback 3.34, 12.2, 12.29, 12.58
San Marino 13.61
Saudi Arabia 4.8, 4.65
Scott, Hal 15.34
secured debt *see* security interests
securitisations 3.116, 4.81
  contracts 3.48–3.55
security interests 1.62, 12.1–12.92
  aircraft 12.67
  bankruptcy 12.88–12.90
   enforcement 12.7
  comparative law of 12.34–12.68
  conclusions 12.32–12.33, 12.92
  contracts 3.134–3.136
  corporate structures
   risk, minimisation of 12.91
  definition 12.1–12.5
  enforcement remedies 12.87
  English law 12.49–12.62
  EU Directives 12.28, 12.63–12.66
  families of jurisdictions 12.39–12.48
  financial markets 12.25–12.28
  floating charges 12.42, 12.44
  governing law and 12.10, 12.69–12.82
   collateral, scope of 12.78–12.82
   publicity, scope of 12.78–12.82
   role of 12.69–12.70
   security agreement 12.71–12.75
  home loans 12.13
  importance of 12.12–12.31
  insolvency, protection against 12.6
  international summary 12.9–12.11
  key indicators of 12.7–12.8
   importance test 12.12
  location of court 12.10
  priority hierarchy 12.8
  pros and cons of 12.34–12.38
  publicity 12.7
  publicly listed companies 12.19–12.22
  registration requirements 12.10
  scope of 12.7, 12.76–12.77
  secured debt 12.7
   permissible 12.85
   transfers of 12.86
  ships 12.68
  small and medium-sized companies 12.18
  sovereign states 12.23
  special purpose companies 12.14–12.17
  takeover bids 12.8
  title finance 12.29–12.31
   recharacterization of 12.83
  trade finance 12.24
  trustees of security 12.8, 12.84
  unsecured creditors, priority over 12.7
  US law 12.49–12.62
  use of 12.12–12.31
  voidable preferences 12.8
set-off *see* contracts; insolvency law: set-offs
sex *see* family law; gender
shareholders
  contracts 3.97–3.98
  de facto directors, as 14.106–14.107
  equality 14.112–14.113
  loans, subordination of 14.109–14.110
  objectives of 14.41, 14.44
  see also corporate law
shares
  bonds *vs.* 14.1–14.15
  see also corporate law; financial assistance to buy own shares
sharia law 18.34, 18.89, 18.139
ships 12.68
shorting 3.34
Singapore 6.6, 13.32, 18.36
  insolvency set-off 11.56
Singapore International Arbitration Centre (SIAC) 16.49
smart contracts
  contracts 3.138–3.141
Smith, Adam 20.3
socialism 18.36
soft power 2.46–2.49
  hard economic value and 2.67–2.68
software systems 9.28
Sohm, Rudolph 20.9
sources of law 9.34
South Africa 4.61, 14.35, 20.29
  insolvency set-off 11.70
South Korea 5.42, 18.116
  express prohibitions 14.71
  security interests 12.46
sovereign debt 6.10–6.11, 10.58, 17.8
sovereign immunity 16.40–16.43
sovereign states 12.23
Spain 8.47, 13.33, 13.75, 18.30, 20.17
  duties to file on insolvency 14.85
  insolvency set-off 11.26, 11.61, 11.64
specificity, doctrine of 13.47
  see also commercial trusts

INDEX 331

standard forms
  contracts 3.114–3.115
stabilisation clauses 6.24
  see also insulation of contract
state interference, concept of 15.8
Stendhal (French writer) 18.97
stock exchanges 7.10–7.11
Stockholm Chamber of
    Commerce 16.49
structural subordination 14.104
Sweden 4.61, 5.42, 18.52
  insolvency set-off 11.66
SWIFT messaging system 2.46, 2.53, 2.55
Swiss Chamber of Commerce 16.49
Switzerland 5.42, 9.78, 13.35, 18.52, 20.21
  bondholder collective action clauses 8.73
  express prohibitions 14.71
  insolvency set-off 11.66
syndicated bank credits 1.14, 1.42, 1.57, 1.57,
    3.22–3.29, 3.92, 3.114, 4.41, 4.81, 5.56,
    5.89, 5.91, 5.116, 6.9, 8.61, 9.29, 11.84,
    16.51, 17.3

takeovers 14.117–14.122
tangible movables 3.10
Thailand 4.65
Theodosius of Rome 18.29
title finance
  contracts 3.34–3.40
  security interests 12.29–12.31
    recharacterization 12.83
tort law 4.27–4.29
  jurisdiction over torts 4.75–4.79
tracing illegal proceeds 13.48
trade finance 12.24
Transparency International 2.39, 17.24
Triple Polarisation 12.39, 13.53, 18.31
trusts 1.62, 12.84
  see also commercial trusts
Turkey 6.9, 18.30, 18.42
  express prohibitions 14.71
Turkmenistan 4.8
Turks and Caicos Islands 13.60

Ukraine 4.58
  Russian war against 6.38
UNCITRAL Model Law
  insolvency law 10.29–10.31,
    10.43–10.52
underwriter liability
  international law 9.55, 9.72–9.78
    liability, intensification of 9.56–9.57
    US law 9.60–9.70
    see also exclusion clauses
  regulated prospectuses 9.56–9.78
    English law 9.71
  unregulated prospectuses
    English law 9.46–9.47
undue influence 8.21

UNIDROIT (International Institute for the
    Unification of Private Law) 5.38, 8.50, 19.12
Uniform Customs and Practice (UCP) 2.50, 2.51,
    2.53, 2.57, 3.114
Uniform Customs and Practices for Documentary
    Credits 2.46
United Kingdom (UK) *see* English law
United Nations Commission on International Trade
    Law (UNCITRAL) 8.41, 8.50–8.51, 10.29–
    10.30, 10.43–10.53, 11.40, 19.13, 20.26
United Nations Convention on Contracts for the
    International Sale of Goods (CISG) 4.21
United States (US) *see* New York law
unjust enrichment 3.127, 4.35, 4.38, 5.97, 7.17, 10.88,
    13.7, 13.48
  non-recognition as 13.1–13.4
  see also commercial trusts
unregulated offering documents 9.29–9.78
  arranging banks, liability of 9.37
  big pocket liability:
    arrangers and underwriters 9.35
  corporations as 'black bags' 9.36
  English law:
    arranging banks, liabilities of 9.38–9.42
  fraud, no exclusion for 9.33
  international bond issues 9.30
  issuer liability 9.32
  offering memorandum 9.37
  sources of law 9.34
  syndicated bank credits 9.29
  see also exclusion clauses
unregulated prospectuses *see* exclusion clauses;
    underwriter liability
use agreements 3.86
USSR (Union of Soviet Socialist
    Republics) 18.30, 18.157

Vatican City 18.43
veil of incorporation 14.98–14.102
  central banks 14.105
Venezuela 6.3, 6.9
Vietnam 4.8, 18.148
Vietnam War 18.16, 20.14
von Gierke, Otto Friedrich 13.50
von Jhering, Rudolf 5.98
von Savigny, Carl 20.9
voting *see* bondholder democracies

waiver of immunity 16.39
Weber, Max 20.10
weighting methods 21.1–21.6
White, Harry Dexter 6.26
'whitewashing' 14.55
Whittaker, Simon 5.78
William the Conqueror, king of
    England 17.12
Windscheid, Bernhard 20.9
work-outs 10.24–10.25
  creditors 10.26

World Bank 4.10, 17.23, 19.14
  Doing Business Survey 2.39
World Economic Forum 2.39, 17.24
World Justice Project 2.39, 17.24
World Trade Organization
      (WTO) 15.23

World War II 6.15, 13.131, 18.116
WorldCom 1.58, 9.58, 14.116
wrongful trading 14.79–14.80, 20.22

Zambia 12.84, 13.32, 14.35
Zimbabwe 14.35